Anti-Submarine Warfare i
World War I

This study investigates the employment of British aircraft against German submarines during the final years of the First World War. This book also places the air anti-submarine campaign in the wider history of the First World War.

The Royal Naval Air Service invested heavily in aircraft of all types – aeroplanes, seaplanes, airships, and kite balloons – in order to counter the German U-boats. Under the Royal Air Force, the air campaign against U-boats continued uninterrupted. Aircraft bombed German U-boat bases in Flanders, conducted area and 'hunting' patrols around the coasts of Britain, and escorted merchant convoys to safety. Despite the fact that aircraft acting alone destroyed only one U-boat during the war, the overall contribution of naval aviation to foiling U-boat attacks was significant. Only five merchant vessels succumbed to submarine attack when convoyed by a combined air and surface escort during World War I.

This book examines aircraft and weapons technology, aircrew training, and the aircraft production issues that shaped this campaign. Then, a close examination of anti-submarine operations – bombing, patrols, and escort – yields a significantly different judgment from existing interpretations of these operations. This study is the first to take an objective look at the writing and publication of the naval and air official histories as they told the story of naval aviation during the Great War. The author also examines the German view of aircraft effectiveness, through German actions, prisoner interrogations, official histories, and memoirs, to provide a comparative judgment. The conclusion closes with a brief narrative of post-war air anti-submarine developments and a summary of findings.

Overall, the author concludes that despite the challenges of organisation, training, and production the employment of aircraft against U-boats was largely successful during the Great War.

This book will be of interest to historians of naval and air power history, as well as students of World War I and military history in general.

John J. Abbatiello is a serving officer in the US Air Force. He has a Ph.D. in War Studies from King's College London.

Cass Series: Naval policy and history

Series Editor: Geoffrey Till

This series consists primarily of original manuscripts by research scholars in the general area of naval policy and history, without national or chronological limitations. It will from time to time also include collections of important articles as well as reprints of classic works.

Anti-Submarine Warfare in World War I

British naval aviation and the defeat of the U-Boats

John J. Abbatiello

LONDON AND NEW YORK

First published 2006
by Routledge
2 Park Square, Milton Park, Abingdon, Oxon, OX14 4RN

Simultaneously published in the USA and Canada
by Routledge
711 Third Avenue, New York, NY 10017

Routledge is an imprint of the Taylor & Francis Group

First issued in paperback 2011

© 2006 John J. Abbatiello

Typeset in Garamond by
RefineCatch Ltd, Bungay, Suffolk

British Library Cataloguing in Publication Data
A catalogue record for this book is available from the British Library

Library of Congress Cataloging in Publication Data
A catalog record for this book has been requested

ISBN13: 978-0-415-76383-7 (hbk)
ISBN13: 978-0-415-51273-2 (pbk)

In Memory of Elaine Abbatiello, 1939–2005

Contents

Tables and maps

Abbreviations

AD	Air Division Memo Number
ACNS	Assistant Chief of the Naval Staff
Adm	Admiral (see Appendix 2 for this and other officer rank equivalents)
ADM	Admiralty Papers, Public Record Office
AHB	Air Historical Branch
AIR	Air Ministry Papers, Public Record Office
AOC	Air Officer Commanding
ASD	Anti-Submarine Division
ASR	*Anti-Submarine Report*
ASW	Anti-Submarine Warfare
BdU	*Befehlshaber der Unterseeboote* [U-Boat Flotilla Leader]
BEF	British Expeditionary Force
BIR	Board of Invention and Research
Capt	Captain
CAB	Cabinet Papers, Public Record Office
CB	Admiralty Confidential Reference Books
CCA	Churchill College Archives, Cambridge
Cdr	Commander, RN
C-in-C	Commander-in-Chief
Col	Colonel
DAD	Director, Air Department, *or* Director, Air Division
DAS	Director, Air Services
DASD	Director, Anti-Submarine Division
DF	Direction Finding
DNI	Director, Naval Intelligence
Doc. No.	Document Number
DOD	Director, Operations Division
FAAM	Fleet Air Arm Museum, Yeovilton
FB	Flying Boat
FdL	*Führer der Marineluftschiffe* [Commander of Airships]
FdU	*Führer der Unterseeboote* [Commander of U-boats]
Flt Cdr	Flight Commander, RNAS

Flt Lt	Flight Lieutenant, RNAS *or* RAF
FSL	Flight Sub-Lieutenant, RNAS
GHQ	General Headquarters
GM	General Memorandum
GOC	General Officer Commanding
GRT	Gross Registered Tons
HP	Horsepower
HS/CID	Historical Section of the Committee of Imperial Defence
IWM/SA	Imperial War Museum, Sound Archive, Lambeth
IWM/DD	Imperial War Museum, Department of Documents, Lambeth
JRUSI	*Journal of the Royal United Services Institute*
KTB	*Kriegstagebuch* [War Diary]
LHCMA	Liddell Hart Centre for Military Archives, King's College London
Lt	Lieutenant, RN *or* RAF
MUN	Ministry of Munitions Papers, Public Record Office
NAO	*Naval Air Operations Report*
nd	no date provided
NHB	Naval Historical Branch, MoD, Whitehall
NID	Naval Intelligence Division *or* Department
NMM(CL)	National Maritime Museum, Caird Library, Greenwich
OC	Officer Commanding
OUP	Oxford University Press
PRO	Public Record Office, National Archives, Kew
R-Adm	Rear-Admiral
RAECE	Rear-Admiral, East Coast of England
RAF	Royal Air Force
RAFM(H)	RAF Museum, Hendon
RFC	Royal Flying Corps
RN	Royal Navy
RNAS	Royal Naval Air Service
RNASS	RN Airship Station
RUSI	Royal United Services Institute
SO	Senior Officer
SOO	Secret Operations Order
Sqn Cdr	Squadron Commander, RNAS
Sqn Ldr	Squadron Leader, RAF
SS	Sea Scout Airship
TH	Technical History
TLS	*The Times Literary Supplement*
US	United States
USN	US Navy
USNAS	USN Air Service
USNIP	*US Naval Institute Proceedings*
V-Adm	Vice-Admiral

VADP	Vice-Admiral, Dover Patrol
VAECE	Vice-Admiral, East Coast of England
VA2BS	Vice-Admiral, Second Battle Squadron, Grand Fleet
Wg	Wing
Wg Capt	Wing Captain, RNAS
Wg Cdr	Wing Commander, RNAS *or* RAF
WO	War Office Papers, Public Record Office
W/T	Wireless Telegraph

Acknowledgements

Whether intentionally or not, historians are the products of their own times; each brings his or her own circumstances into their writing. Although I am not a naval aviator, I must confess that I am a US Air Force pilot and therefore bring a unique perspective to the subject of World War I naval aviation. This monograph started as a doctoral dissertation; I must thank the US Air Force in general, and the Air Force Academy's Department of History in particular, for providing me the opportunity to study my two historical loves: air power history and the history of the Royal Navy in the Great War. I extend my heartfelt thanks to my Department Head, Colonel Mark Wells, USAF, who has been a respected teacher, mentor, and colleague since we first met over 20 years ago. I also thank his predecessor, Brig-Gen Carl W. Reddel, USAF (Ret.), for his help and encouragement. The Air Force Institute of Technology supported my studies financially and administratively.

To my King's College London supervisor, Professor Andrew Lambert, and his colleagues at the Department of War Studies – especially Dr Joe Maiolo and Dr Christina Goulter – I express my sincere gratitude for their expert guidance. Also, I am indebted to the archivists, librarians, and historians at the many collections I've visited. These terrific folks made my research a joy, especially: Malcolm Llewellyn-Jones, Kate Tildesley, Jennie Wraight, Ian Mackenzie, and the rest of Chris Page's staff at the Naval Historical Branch; Seb Cox and his archivists at the Air Historical Branch; Jan Keohane and her colleagues at the Fleet Air Arm Museum; Peter Hart of the Imperial War Museum's Sound Archive; Anne Hassinger of the Naval Institute; Tom McCulloch of the OUP Archives; and the staffs of the Public Record Office, National Maritime Museum, Imperial War Museum, Liddell Hart Centre, Churchill College Archives, RAF Museum, Hendon, and the KCL, RUSI, University of London, IHR, and British Libraries. I acknowledge the kind permission of these archives, especially the Trustees of the Liddell Hart Centre and Imperial War Museum to quote from their collections. My neighbour in Northwood, Alexander Spears, provided translation help with Michelsen's *Der U-Bootskrieg*, a particularly difficult text, while Roma Beaumont of the Geography Department at King's provided the background image for my maps.

To my fellow students at King's, especially Malcolm Llewellyn-Jones, Peter Nash, Nick Black, Warwick Brown, and the rest of the 'Ole Codgers', I must say 'thank you' for sharing your experiences and ideas with me. Also, I extend my gratitude to Col Phil Meilinger, USAF (Ret.), and Lt Col Roy Houchin, USAF, for reading some of my earlier chapter drafts and sharing their expertise in air power history. I must mention my fellow officers, professors, students, and friends for their help and encouragement during my studies, especially Derek Varble, Mike Neiberg, Dennis Showalter, and John Grenier.

Finally, I'd like to thank my wife and my two sons for their patience and understanding during my three years as a research student and 18 years as a serving officer. Without my fabulous family, all of this would have little meaning.

Monument, Colorado
4 May 2005

Introduction: British naval aviation and the U-boat menace

On the morning of 22 September 1917, a Royal Naval Air Service (RNAS) Large America flying boat sighted a small U-boat near the Dutch coast. The submarine was on the surface and steering north-east away from the East Hinder Bank. Flight Sub-Lieutenants N. A. Magor and C. E. S. Lusk piloted Curtiss H-12 No. 8695, the only Large America stationed at the Dunkirk Seaplane Station. Due to the patrol's planned proximity to German seaplane bases in Flanders, two Sopwith Pups from Dunkirk's Seaplane Defence Flight escorted the patrol mission. Upon sighting *UB32*, one of the *UBII*-class of coastal submarines operating with the Flanders *U-Flotilla*, Magor and Lusk immediately initiated a high-speed descent from their cruising altitude of 4,100 feet. The target was seven miles to the south-west of their position.[1]

Shortly thereafter *Kapitänleutnant* Hans von Ditfurth of *UB32* realised his submarine was under attack and ordered an emergency dive. A strong wind blowing from the west may have hindered the U-boat crewmembers watching the horizon towards the direction of the attack, thus delaying the crew's reaction. When Magor and Lusk reached their target, *UB32*'s conning tower was still visible above the surface. Two well placed 230-lb bombs struck the submarine just aft of the conning tower and exploded. As the H-12 climbed away, the flight engineer, Leading Mechanic R. A. Lucas, observed a 'large bubble and wreckage and large quantities of oil'.[2] The escorting fighters verified these hits along with a substantial amount of wreckage on the surface.[3] Lusk later noted in his logbook that 'oil and debris [were] flung up and [a] big piece of wreckage' resulted from the explosions.[4]

UB32, which had departed from Zeebrugge on 10 September, failed to return to port and later was assumed lost with no survivors.[5] Large America No. 8695, on the other hand, was grounded for an entire week after the attack due to hull deterioration. It had arrived at Dunkirk only in July 1917 and would be withdrawn before the end of the year. This single aircraft accounted for five U-boat sightings and two attacks during only 16 patrol flights flown between July and October 1917.[6]

The engagement of 22 September 1917 – one of over 200 air attacks against German submarines in Home Waters – was the *only confirmed case* of a British aircraft destroying a U-boat without the aid of surface vessels during

the First World War. There were five probable successes where aircraft working with destroyers or patrol vessels sank U-boats.[7] During the closing years
of the First World War, aircraft increasingly contributed to the Royal Navy's
anti-submarine effort – a struggle in which an overall failure would have
meant disaster for Britain and the Allies and victory for Germany. For a
number of reasons the sinking of *UB32*, with the events preceding and
following the action, represents a microcosm of the story of aircraft versus
U-boats during the Great War.

No. 8695's attack took place during a period of rapid expansion of RNAS
anti-submarine forces, growth initiated late in 1916 but not bearing fruit
until the summer of 1917 and beyond. The Large America, one of many new
aircraft designs that provided substantial increases in endurance and bomb
load relative to other fixed-wing aircraft, was likewise beginning to arrive in
greater but still limited numbers. Although their superior performance
offered clear operational advantages, these flying boats were plagued by
maintenance, production, and training difficulties. The British attempted to
alleviate shortages through two methods: replacing seaplanes with land-
based aeroplanes (for example, DH-4 aircraft assumed the anti-submarine
patrol mission at Dunkirk in January 1918) and with the assistance of American naval aviation, which took over the Dunkirk seaplane station on 1
February 1918.[8] These two trends – aeroplane substitution for seaplanes and
American promises of help – were even more important throughout the
British Isles later in 1918. The 22 September 1917 engagement also took
place during an area patrol and was unrelated to convoy escort operations.
This fact highlights the historical debate over the apparently misguided
policy of 'U-boat hunting' operations, which will be addressed later in this
study.

Finally, as in many of the crucial issues concerning the use of aircraft
against U-boats during the Great War, most historians narrated this incident
inaccurately. In 1934, the British official air historian incorrectly wrote
that on 22 September 1917 *UC72* was destroyed by a Large America escorted
by Sopwith *Camels*.[9] The official naval historian reported that No. 8695
destroyed *UC72* in the southern North Sea.[10] Robert Grant, expert on Great
War U-boat losses, told most of the story correctly except for the course of
the U-boat.[11] Popular historian John Terraine wrote that the attack occurred
inside the 'Spider Web', a patrol system based around the North Hinder Light
Vessel and flown exclusively by Large Americas stationed at Felixstowe.[12]
Although these inaccuracies may seem trivial, they represent a general trend
of inaccuracy and misunderstanding in the literature of Great War naval
aviation in Britain.

Purpose and methodology

This monograph examines the role of British aircraft in defeating Germany's Unrestricted Submarine Campaign of 1917 and 1918. Despite air power's limited achievement in destroying U-boats outright, aircraft made an important contribution to deterring U-boat commanders from operating in the vicinity of merchant vessels. This air effort absorbed a great deal of attention and resources from the British war machine, and the British developed this innovative role for air power without the benefit of historical experience to guide operations. Both aircraft and submarines were new weapon systems in 1914 and as a result the Great War witnessed naval combat in three dimensions on a significant scale for the first time. This inquiry will therefore investigate this intersection of air and U-boat warfare in order to uncover the difficulties of employing new technologies (aircraft) to defeat new threats (submarines) that employed an ancient strategy (commerce warfare).

Superimposed on this question is another important issue: the historiography of this air effort. Although the literature of this campaign comprises an extensive collection of official histories, secondary works, and memoirs, no single volume deals exclusively with air anti-submarine warfare in World War I. With the exception of the British and Canadian official air histories, pertinent details of the campaign are widely scattered across a range of texts. A key difficulty is the fact that this subject does not fit neatly into popular history because it crosses the boundaries of air power and sea power studies. Air and naval histories of the Great War see the campaign as only a minor issue in a greater conflict and offer only a few paragraphs or at best a chapter to explain it.[13] Likewise, the numerous extant surveys of naval aviation tend to view the RNAS's air campaign against U-boats simply as a forerunner to operations in World War II. These brief treatments do not adequately explain this campaign and oversimplify the key issues, especially the magnitude of the air effort, the revolutionary development of infrastructure, and the evolution of employment techniques.

A focused study – one that examines technology, tactics, operations, policy, training, and production – is therefore necessary to make sense of this campaign. If Michael Howard's assertion that 'the historian cannot escape from the present' is correct, then the opinions of past historians must be analysed.[14] This study will re-examine the subject from new perspectives, relying largely on the primary evidence to assess the veracity and integrity of the secondary literature. Close scrutiny of the pertinent documents reveals a more complete understanding of the employment and effectiveness of aircraft against U-boats during the Great War.

The Public Record Office's Air Ministry collection in the AIR 1 series forms the bulk of available documents on this subject. The Air Historical Branch collected these documents from RNAS, Royal Flying Corps, Royal Air Force, Admiralty, and Air Ministry sources in order to prepare the official air history series of the Great War, and many historians have since used this collection.[15] Some portions of this series, however, have not been sufficiently scrutinised. Large volumes concerning naval aviation in the PRO's Admiralty documents (in ADM 1, 116, 137, and 186, for example) unfortunately have remained relatively untouched despite their value to gaining a deeper understanding of RNAS operations. PRO records from the Cabinet (CAB), War Office (WO), and Munitions (MUN) series further highlight aspects of this air campaign.

Other collections, many of them previously untapped in academic writing, also help to illuminate the topic. Logbooks, diaries, personal correspondence, and other pertinent material from the Fleet Air Arm Museum, Imperial War Museum, RAF Museum, and other repositories provide unique personal views of air anti-submarine warfare. Finally, a superb collection of Admiralty documents and papers of naval historians at the Naval Historical Branch (MoD) prove especially useful to understanding the Admiralty's staff study process.

Scope and organisation

Although Britain worked with allies towards defeating Germany's U-boats, this monograph focuses on the British experience of using aircraft as anti-submarine weapons. Also, this study only addresses the employment of aircraft in Home Waters, arguably the most important naval theatre of the war.[16] British naval air operations in the Mediterranean and the air anti-submarine efforts of the Entente Allies will only be mentioned to provide context. American naval air operations – closely linked to the British effort in Home Waters – deserve slightly more attention but remain a secondary focus. An investigation of a single, national effort facilitates both a thematic approach to the subject and an examination of the workings of defence establishments in employing new technology for which there was no precedent.

Many types of aircraft participated in air anti-submarine work. Fixed-wing aircraft – aeroplanes, seaplanes, and flying boats – made the numerically largest contribution to these operations. Non-rigid airships and kite balloons (which were towed by warships) also proved useful in hindering the U-boat campaign. The advantages and drawbacks of each of these weapons systems in anti-submarine operations, along with a discussion of technological problems and efforts to solve them, will be approached in Chapter 1. Chapter 2 follows with an examination of training and aircraft production as applied to air anti-submarine work. These chapters set the stage for the three chapters covering the actual development of air anti-submarine operations.

The employment of aircraft against U-boats fell into three broad areas. First, bomber aircraft attacked U-boat bases, attempting to damage or destroy supporting facilities and undermine U-boat crew morale. The ebb and flow of these efforts will be addressed in Chapter 3. Second, patrol systems, whereby aircraft conducted area patrols over fixed sectors or 'hunted' U-boats known to be in certain locations, occupied the attention of naval air units around the coasts of Britain and will be covered in Chapter 4. Chapter 5 closes the operational discussion with a view of aircraft in the escort role, operations that proved extremely useful in hindering U-boat attacks against convoys. These three roles for aircraft in anti-submarine warfare were complementary and reflected the Admiralty's greater strategy of attacking U-boats incessantly, wherever they could be found.

Although commentary regarding the secondary literature will run throughout the investigation, the next two chapters assess a specific set of sources dealing with the effectiveness of aircraft against U-boats. Chapter 6 will analyse British staff studies and official histories, which formed the basis for the majority of the other forms of secondary literature concerning maritime air operations in World War I, and will address key issues regarding their purposes and conclusions. To corroborate an accurate comparison with the British opinion, the German view of aircraft as anti-submarine weapon systems appears in Chapter 7. Finally, Chapter 8 concludes with a brief discussion of Interwar and World War II developments and achievements in air ASW, for comparative purposes, and closes with a summary of findings.

Although this subject could have been approached in a chronological fashion, the thematic method lends itself to a better understanding of the interrelationship among the use of aircraft against U-boats and other crucial wartime issues. This approach also appreciates emerging thought processes in each area and highlights how most senior and mid-level Admiralty leaders evaluated naval air power realistically, far from the supposed 'mental rigidity' of senior British naval officers expressed by some historians.[17] Moreover, the evolution of organisation and supervision of naval aviation explains the changes in production and employment priorities that affected the development of maritime air doctrine.

Organising naval air assets

One of the most important issues regarding the employment of aircraft against U-boats during the First World War centred on British organisation and administration of naval and air forces. Changes at the highest levels of Admiralty leadership caused an almost constant reorganising of naval air supervision and policy; such inconsistent senior supervision meant that the anti-submarine role for aircraft did not mature steadily. In order to provide an organisational and therefore political context for this study, a brief overview of naval air supervision is necessary.

The proliferation of civilian and military aviation following the Wright Brothers' 1903 success eventually led to an Advisory Committee for Aeronautics of 1909 and the Haldane Committee of 1911–1912. Established by the Cabinet in order to investigate the future of military and naval aviation, these bodies closely followed worldwide air developments.[18] In early 1912 Haldane recommended the formation of a Royal Flying Corps, with separate military and naval wings as well as a Central Flying School and a general reserve. From July 1912, an Air Committee of naval and military representatives served as a forum to exchange views but wielded no executive power – the individual services controlled their new air assets directly. This committee met until the start of the Great War, when it dissolved.[19] Thus, from the start of military and naval aviation in Britain, the Admiralty and War Office controlled their own air policies with little Cabinet level interference or supervision.

Lord Derby's Joint War Air Committee (February to April 1916) and Lord Curzon's First Air Board (May to December 1916) tried to resolve differences between the RFC and RNAS regarding increasingly competitive aircraft production policies, but both failed since the respective ministries retained executive power and naturally saw their own interests as paramount. When David Lloyd George became Prime Minister in December 1916, he established Lord Cowdray's Second Air Board, a committee allowed to control aircraft and engine design and production policy, absorbing the respective support branches from the RFC and RNAS, but still wielding no power over operational policy. German daylight Gotha raids against London led to the Smuts Committee of July 1917, and this investigation concluded that Britain needed a separate air service. Further committees, such as the short-lived Air Organisation and Air Operations Committees, preceded the establishment of an independent Air Council in January 1918. Three months later, the Royal Air Force became operational, absorbing the former RNAS and RFC into a single air service.[20]

Thus at the highest political level, the Admiralty retained the control of operational naval aviation policy until the transition to Air Ministry supervision began in January 1918. Unfortunately, the senior leadership of the Admiralty almost continually changed during the war years, leading to inconsistencies in aviation priorities. Winston Churchill held the First Lord post at the start of the war, with Prince Louis of Battenberg as his First Sea Lord colleague. Prince Louis left the Admiralty in October 1914, being replaced by the colourful Sir John Fisher – his second tenure as First Sea Lord. The Churchill/Fisher administration, which was very supportive of an aggressive naval air arm, lasted until May 1915, when Fisher resigned over the Dardanelles campaign and Churchill was ousted as part of a shake-up in Asquith's government.[21] A. J. Balfour, a former Conservative Prime Minister (1902–5), then assumed the First Lord portfolio, and Sir Henry Jackson, a wireless specialist, took the top uniformed post. This team, 'two philosophical scientists' as Robin Higham puts it, supported a renewed rigid airship programme, one that had been suspended since Britain's first zeppelin, the *Mayfly*, broke up on a breezy day in September 1911.[22]

Another government change in December 1916 brought a new Prime Minister, David Lloyd George, and in turn the Cabinet appointed Sir Edward Carson and Sir John Jellicoe to replace Balfour and Jackson. Carson left in July 1917, probably because he had not done enough to counter the U-boat menace, and Sir Eric Geddes assumed his portfolio. Lloyd George then dismissed Jellicoe in December 1917 and appointed Sir Rosslyn Wemyss in his place. As Higham argues, these changes in senior leadership meant inconsistency in policy and a 'spasmodic' supervision of Admiralty programmes.[23]

Finally, within this environment, changes in the direct supervision of naval aviation followed each change in the Admiralty's higher leadership. The first step in providing supervision for naval aviation, resulting from Haldane's recommended RFC of naval and military flying units, was the Admiralty's decision in May 1912 to establish an Air Department under Captain Murray Sueter. A hard-charging innovator who participated in the introduction of both submarines and airships into the Royal Navy, Sueter supervised the gradual growth of 'the Naval Wing of the Royal Flying Corps' from the Central Air Office at Sheerness.[24] Ultimately, he reported to the Commander-in-Chief The Nore for the administration and discipline of the RNAS, which assumed that title officially in July 1914.

RNAS growth caused by the start of the Great War proved too much for the C-in-C of a single naval district to supervise. In February 1915, the Admiralty placed all of the RNAS – including stations, seaplane carriers, aircraft and personnel – directly under Sueter for both operational and administrative purposes.[25] As a result, Sueter rapidly gathered and dispatched air contingents for both Flanders and the Dardanelles in early 1915. Unfortunately, Sueter lost the blessings of ministerial support when Churchill and Fisher left office. In July 1915 Balfour and Jackson, anxious to secure control of what they considered an overly autonomous organisation, rescinded the Air Department's newfound independence and put all air stations – over 50 in total – under the direct operational command of the regional naval district in which they resided.[26] The Calshot Seaplane Base would serve the C-in-C Portsmouth, the naval air stations in the vicinity of Dunkirk would fall under the Vice-Admiral Dover Patrol, and so on. Just as any other specialised forces in the Royal Navy such as destroyer or submarine flotillas, air stations now fell under local, regional command.[27]

In September 1915, Balfour and Jackson relieved Sueter and appointed Rear-Admiral Sir Charles L. Vaughan-Lee as the new 'Director of Air Services'. Sueter then assumed the title of 'Superintendent of Aircraft Construction', a position limited to supervising the design and supply of naval aircraft.[28] Vaughan-Lee had no experience in aviation matters, but was committed to returning the RNAS to its support role within the Admiralty.[29] While at least one historian saw this shuffle as a positive change, with the RNAS becoming more 'naval' in character, most considered it a step backward.[30] Nevertheless, Vaughan-Lee did little to focus the growth of the RNAS towards naval cooperation. His March 1916 mission statement for the RNAS reflected the need to defend naval aviation against Royal Flying Corps competition for resources. The 'Policy of the RNAS' reiterated the requirement for naval flyers, familiar with naval operations, to carry out the following duties: long-range bombing attacks on enemy fleets and bases (listed first); patrol of the coasts of Britain to seek out enemy vessels, submarines, aircraft, and mines; assistance to the fleet with reconnaissance and gunnery spotting; and, finally, offering help to the Army 'whenever and wherever required'.[31] Such a statement of diverse tasks demonstrated the Air Department's reluctance to focus on any one sphere of naval aviation.

Vaughan-Lee's responsibilities ended in December 1916 with the reorganisation of the Admiralty after Jellicoe's arrival. As a result of the experience of the first two air boards, which clearly demonstrated the need for an 'air voice' on the Admiralty Board, Carson and Jellicoe established the position of Fifth Sea Lord to oversee all naval aviation activities. Commodore Godfrey Paine, first commandant of the Central Flying School and later Commodore of the RNAS Training Establishment at Cranwell, took up the position in January 1917.[32] As a lieutenant, Paine had served aboard HMS *Ramillies* with Jellicoe, when the latter was second-in-command.[33] During Paine's tenure, Lloyd George forced design and production cooperation upon the RNAS and RFC through the Cowdray Air Board, yet operational control of naval air assets remained with commanders of naval districts.[34] Paine oversaw the substantial proliferation of naval air stations along the coast of Britain as a result of the increasingly dangerous submarine menace. Stephen Roskill states that Paine, a man of sound judgment 'but lacking in imagination and inspiration', sympathised with efforts to centralise the air effort under joint air boards.[35] As Fifth Sea Lord, he sat on the Cowdray Air Board as a full member. Paine became one of the most senior naval officers to join the RAF and assumed the titles of Master-General of Personnel on the First Air Council (January–April 1918) and Inspector-General of the RAF (from April 1918), retiring from the junior service in 1920.

The final wartime iteration of naval air supervision came about after the approval of plans to form an independent Air Ministry and Royal Air Force. In December 1917 Admiral Wemyss, who was at the time the Deputy First Sea Lord, proposed the establishment of an office within the Admiralty staff that would liaise with the Air Ministry. When he replaced Jellicoe as the First Sea Lord in January, Wemyss established this new office, the Air Division, under Wing Captain F. R. Scarlett. The Air Division was staffed by RAF officers, most of whom were former RNAS members, and charged to keep a close watch on the RAF's maritime air units.[36] Scarlett had wide experience in naval aviation, serving in RNAS staff and field appointments since he learned to fly in 1913. In August 1918, Wemyss replaced him with Colonel R. M. Groves, also an experienced former RNAS station commander, wing commander, and staff member.[37] Both Scarlett and Groves were progressive thinkers but held a position designed to offer advice and not to command. It is also interesting to note that the Air Division staff numbered only 13 officers and nine civilians, a drastic reduction from the approximately 250 officers and warrant officers and over 100 civil staff working directly for the Fifth Sea Lord in December 1917.[38] The RAF itself did not form a maritime air organisation above the group level; each principal naval district commander had an RAF air group directly under his operational command.[39]

Thus each change in senior leadership within the Admiralty drove a corresponding change in the way naval air assets were controlled and organised. Except for a brief period in 1915, there was no organisation that exercised operational control of the Admiralty's maritime air power as a whole. Each naval district commander employed his air assets as he saw fit, and this arrangement remained in force after the RAF's formation.

Aircraft and anti-submarine warfare

Within this evolving supervisory environment the RNAS and later RAF developed the anti-submarine role for aircraft. It is important to note here that such operations did not commence at the start of the Unrestricted Submarine Campaign in February 1917, but at the start of the war. Also, this role for aircraft did not suddenly appear in August 1914 but had been initially addressed before the war began.

Although the Admiralty dismissed French experiments involving the use of captive balloons to spot primitive submarines in 1899, Royal Navy trials in 1905 identified the height advantage of a balloon's basket in searching for mines and possibly submarines.[40] The advent of powered flight led to further experiments, accelerated in part by a forward looking paper by Lieutenant H. A. Williamson, RN, investigating the use of seaplanes to spot submerged submarines in 1912.[41] Williamson had the unique qualification of being both a submarine officer and a pilot, earning his pilot certificate at his own expense in 1911. The paper proposed using aeroplanes for submarine patrols because of their advantage of extended visibility at heights well above those available to a ship's lookout. Eventually making its way to the Admiralty, the paper earned Williamson a letter of appreciation from the senior officers of the Royal Navy, but more importantly led to a series of experiments on the viability of his proposal.[42]

Conducted under the supervision of Acting Commander C. R. Samson, commander of the naval flying school at Eastchurch Air Station, and representatives of HMS *Acteon* (the RN Torpedo School), the October 1912 trials in the Firth of Forth demonstrated that seaplanes could usually see a periscope above the surface in clear weather and sometimes distinguish the outline of 'the hull below the surface'. Additionally, the slow diving speeds (taking up to five minutes) of early British submarines meant that 'except in very clear weather' seaplanes could arrive over the submarine in order to drop a bomb before it could spot the aircraft and dive for safety.[43]

Knowledge of the usefulness of aircraft in anti-submarine warfare began to proliferate. In May 1913, Lieutenant C. D. Burney published an article in *Naval Review* that proposed the use of seaplanes to scout ahead of the fleet in search of enemy submarines and to attack them if discovered.[44] The Admiralty's Submarine Committee had made the same suggestion in 1912.[45] Also, pre-war submarine visibility exercises continued at the Calshot Seaplane Station under Lieutenant Arthur Longmore in early 1914.[46]

The potential of aircraft thus was immense. Anti-submarine patrol, however, was only one of many future roles the Admiralty considered for aeroplanes, seaplanes, airships, and kite balloons. During the war, the RNAS employed aircraft for long-range bombing, reconnaissance, gunnery and artillery spotting, aerial photography, air defence and interception, and even torpedo attack. RNAS units supported Royal Navy commanders not only in Home Waters, but also in East Africa, the Dardanelles, and throughout the Mediterranean theatre. Yet of these various roles and missions, naval aviation made the most important contribution in anti-submarine warfare in Home Waters, where by the Armistice a force of over 600 aircraft flew in support of commerce protection – the 'centre of gravity of the naval war', according to historian Paul Halpern.[47] Before embarking upon a study of these operations and the post-war histories that described them, it is first necessary to examine the technological issues surrounding this novel role for aircraft.

1 Technology

Aircraft and U-boats

The First World War witnessed tremendous advances in a variety of military technologies: explosives, propulsion, communication, and transportation, just to name a few general areas.[1] For the first time field units 'pulled' technology from science and industry; naval airmen wrote requirements papers spelling out exactly what kinds of performance characteristics they desired in future aircraft.[2] The Admiralty's Board of Invention and Research liaised with the scientific community in order to help solve a wide array of naval technological problems.

Technological innovation is an important facet of this study; technology determined capability and capability drove operations. Although technological solutions were only one part of the anti-submarine equation, a close analysis of the capabilities of World War I aircraft and submarines is an essential first step in this examination of Britain's use of aircraft in the anti-submarine campaign. Much has been written about the individual weapon systems of naval air power during the Great War, but the literature fails to place the technology within the context of anti-submarine warfare.[3] Understanding the capabilities and limitations of fixed-wing airplanes, airships, and kite balloons *relative to each other* will set the stage for this study's later examination of operations. Additionally, this chapter will investigate the technological problems of early air anti-submarine warfare – problems posed by the environment, the available equipment, and the U-boats themselves.

Capabilities and limitations

Combat between aircraft and submarines during the Great War represented an intersection of two new technologies. While mankind had been fascinated by the potential of both flying and underwater travel for hundreds of years beforehand, there were further remarkable similarities between early aircraft and submarines. These weapon systems were new to warfare in 1914, being developed as operationally effective models only within the preceding half-decade.[4] Both aircraft and submarines were first envisioned simply as reconnaissance platforms, yet later emerged as tools of total war. Both relied on a vast array of sub-technologies, including petrol or diesel engines and electric generators, wireless telegraphy, weaponry of various sorts, and the related sciences of aerodynamics and fluid dynamics in their designs. All of these sub-systems and associated fields of study developed rapidly between 1914 and 1918 and pulled the capabilities of the aircraft and submarines to higher and higher levels of performance, while constituting a larger, three-dimensional revolution in military affairs begun during the First World War and completed during World War II.[5]

In combat both aircraft and submarines could absorb a great deal of punishment from the enemy and still operate effectively. Machine gun bullets passing through an airplane's canvas skin hardly made a difference to its flying characteristics while U-boats were known to withstand attacks of dozens of depth charges and still continue on a mission.[6] On the other hand, both systems had a number of Achilles' heels – such as broken petrol pipes in airplanes or oil leaks in submarines – that could render the weapon system useless until repaired. Most importantly, aircraft and submarines pushed naval warfare into three dimensions, adding height and depth to the two-dimensional naval engagements of the past.

Each weapon system had its distinct advantages relative to the other. Submarines had poor visibility, lying low on the water, but enjoyed the advantages of stealth and escaping counterattack by diving. However, 'para-doxically', as Norman Friedman states, 'the submarine commander must shed his cloak in order to perform most of his missions' – especially when attacking a ship.[7] Aircraft possessed speed and height as assets but had poor endurance and weapon loads in comparison with naval vessels. The height advantage was an essential aid to visibility, physically restricted by the curva-ture of the earth. While the crow's nest on a battleship, perhaps 75 feet above the waterline, might provide visibility to ten nautical miles in clear weather, an observer in an aircraft flying at 1,000 feet would be able to see objects as far as 36 nautical miles.[8] According to historian Lee Kennet, at 3,000 feet the 'horizon retreated to something like 60 miles'.[9] The bridge of an anti-submarine P-boat, one of the workhorses of the coastal convoy system, had only a five-mile effective radius of vision.[10]

Fixed-wing aircraft technology progressed by leaps and bounds during the Great War. One need only consider a comparison between the Wright Flyer of 1903, barely able to lift off the ground, and the Handley Page O/400 bomber of 1918, capable of carrying almost a ton of bombs over hundreds of miles by day or night, to realise the scope of technological accomplishment. Indeed, aeroplanes of 1918 had more in common with aeroplanes of 1939 than with those of 1914. Airships – a less-glamorous yet important partner in naval aviation – did not make as many technological leaps as airplanes, but their efficiency and performance advanced significantly during the war.

Heavier-than-air craft

The fixed-wing maritime aircraft employed against submarines fell into three general categories: aeroplanes, float seaplanes, and flying boats. Since technology was advancing so rapidly, the RNAS and RAF employed scores of different aircraft designs. Only the most important models, in terms of numbers employed and effectiveness, will be discussed in the survey below.

The term *aeroplane* was an early twentieth-century word for a fixed-wing aircraft 'fitted with wheels and designed to land on solid ground'. Seaplanes differed from aeroplanes in that the wheels were replaced with floats in order to operate from the surface of the water. The flying boat, also able to land and takeoff from the water, was a separate category of seaplane because the fuselage was a buoyant hull like that of a boat; in other words, it was more like a boat with wings than an aeroplane that could float.[11]

A survey of the main types of maritime aircraft used against submarines demonstrates the rapid advances in performance during the war years, primarily resulting from the availability of more powerful and efficient engines.[12] At the start of the war, the RNAS employed a variety of multi-purpose aircraft; at this time there was no distinction between fighter, bomber, or reconnaissance types. Early Sopwith, Farman, Avro, Short and similar designs populated RNAS land-based squadrons, while the first float seaplanes were simple adaptations of aeroplane models. The last of this first generation of aeroplanes was the Sopwith 1½ Strutter of 1916, which saw service in northern France as both a fighter and bomber attacking German U-boat facilities in Flanders and conducting coastal anti-submarine patrols in south-western England.

While Short and Caudron bombers added greater carrying capacity to the Dunkirk bomber force in late 1916, the year 1917 witnessed the introduction of the DH-4 and the Handley Page O/100; both employed the latest Rolls-Royce Eagle engine and were used as bombing and reconnaissance platforms. The DH-9 and Handley Page O/400 were 1918 derivatives of these earlier designs. The DH-6, a training aircraft, saw service at home in the anti-submarine patrol role, but only as a stopgap measure until more suitable aeroplanes could be produced. The only purpose-built, anti-submarine aeroplane to see service, the Blackburn Kangaroo, well suited to its role with long endurance and a respectable bomb load, was built too late to have a major impact on the war effort as only 11 of these twin-engine machines saw action by the Armistice.[13] Table 1.1 illustrates the increasing capabilities for aeroplanes associated with the anti-submarine campaign during the war years.

Seaplanes also made important advances in performance during the Great War. By the middle years of the war, float seaplane development had evolved two basic types, the single-seat light reconnaissance seaplane and a longer-range two-seat version. The smaller design, typified by the Sopwith Schneider and the various derivatives of the 'Baby', saw service in many roles from both shore stations and seaplane carriers. Used variably as anti-zeppelin fighters,

Table 1.1 RNAS aeroplane performance

Name	Typical engine	Crew	Endurance & max speed	Typical bomb load	In use
Avro 504A	80 HP Gnôme	1	4.5 hrs 82 mph	4 × 20-lb	1914–15
BE2c	70 HP Renault	2	3.25 72	4 × 25-lb	1914–16
Farman Variants	80 HP Gnôme	2	3 60–66	Total of 100-lb	1914–16
Sopwith 1½ Strutter	130 HP Clerget	1	4.5 102	4 × 65-lb	1916–17
Short Bomber	250 HP RR Eagle	2	6 77	4 × 230-lb or 8 × 112-lb	1916–17
DH-4	250 HP RR Eagle	2	3.5 119	2 × 230-lb or 4 × 112-lb	1917–18
Handley Page O/100	2 × 266 HP RR Eagle	3–4	7.5 85	14 × 112-lb or equivalent total	1917–18
DH-9	230 HP BHP	2	4.5 111	460-lb total	1918
DH-6	90 HP RAF	1	2.5 75	100-lb total	1918
Blackburn Kangaroo	2 × 250 HP RR Falcon	3	8 98	1 × 520-lb or 4 × 230-lb	1918

Sources: Thetford (1991), *Jane's*, and Tables, AIR 1/2423/305/18/45.

light bombers, and reconnaissance aircraft, the end of the war saw their final use in south-east England air units as anti-submarine patrol aircraft. Their relatively good manoeuvrability meant that they at least had a chance of surviving an engagement with an enemy seaplane. The larger Short two-seat seaplanes, along with the Fairey Campania and similar designs, were also employed as shipboard reconnaissance aircraft but more importantly saw extensive service in most anti-submarine air groups, which benefited from their respectable bomb load and range.[14]

Although there were a number of smaller flying boat designs by Curtiss, Norman Thompson, and Franco-British Aviation,[15] the Curtiss Large America – and the family of related models – stood out as the leading flying boat of the anti-submarine air campaign. This class originated from Glenn Curtiss's desire to win Lord Northcliffe's 1913 prize, a sum of £10,000 to the first person to fly across the Atlantic in 72 hours. The start of the Great War brought continued development that eventually produced the H-12, the first Large America design.[16] The RNAS purchased these models for war use, the first service flights being flown in early 1917.

Wing Commander J. C. Porte, who worked with Curtiss before the war and commanded the RNAS base at Felixstowe, improved the H-12, which suffered from a weak hull and insufficient armament for self-defence. The primary design limitation of early flying boats was the need for hydroplaning efficiency in order to takeoff with the limited engine power available. A hydroplaning hull, with its relatively flat bottom, did not provide a strong structure for landing or seaworthiness. Experimenting first with smaller Curtiss designs and later with Large Americas, Porte steepened the 'vee' of the hull to provide a sturdy landing platform and better sea keeping qualities. Employing new and more powerful Rolls-Royce engines and bristling with six Lewis guns for self-defence, Porte's F2a and subsequent derivatives proved to be formidable anti-submarine weapon systems, combining long range with a powerful bomb load and defensive capability.[17]

RNAS and later RAF flying squadrons had to contend with a number of disadvantages in early fixed-wing aircraft, but these were offset by the specific capabilities of each weapon system. Aeroplanes, flying from aerodromes along the coast of Britain, possessed a number of important advantages over other types of aircraft. First, they did not rely on the state of the sea to takeoff, a limitation for seaplanes and flying boats. Also, a typical grass field would allow takeoffs and landings into the wind regardless of direction or strength, strong winds being a limitation to airship operations. Aeroplanes had fewer maintenance requirements and had a shorter launching routine

Table 1.2 Float seaplane and flying boat performance

Name	Typical engine	Crew	Endurance & max speed	Typical bomb load	In use
Sopwith Schneider	100 HP Gnôme	1	2 hours 87 mph	1 × 65-lb	1915–16
Short 184	260 HP Sunbeam	2	2.75 88	520-lb total	1915–18
Short 320	320 HP Sunbeam	2	3 72	2 × 230-lb	1917–18
Hamble/ Sopwith Baby	110 or 130 HP Clerget	1	2 90–100	2 × 65-lb	1915–18
Curtiss H-12	2 × 275 HP RR Eagle	4	6 85	4 × 100-lb or 2 × 230-lb	1917–18
Curtiss H-16	2 × 375 HP RR Eagle	4	6 98	4 × 230-lb	1918
Felixstowe F2a	2 × 345 HP RR Eagle	4	6 95	2 × 230-lb	1917–18
Felixstowe F3	2 × 345 HP RR Eagle	4	9 91	4 × 230-lb	1918

Sources: Thetford (1991) and *Jane's*.

than other aircraft. For a given engine horsepower, aeroplanes were faster, could carry more bombs, and were more manoeuvrable than their seaplane cousins. If the opportunity presented itself, these advantages enabled aeroplanes to attack submarines more quickly and with a greater punch than any other type of aircraft. They could cover a larger patrol area in a given time due to their typically faster speed. Additionally, they could usually defend themselves better than any other type except the Large America flying boat.[18] Finally, for performance reasons a sustained bombing campaign against the U-boat bases of Belgium could realistically only be carried out by land-based bombers.

The primary technological handicap of using aeroplanes to fight the antisubmarine campaign, compounded by the disadvantages of limited numbers of suitable types and the need for new coastal aerodromes, appeared in the problem of flying over water. Aeroplane engines performed better than those installed in seaplanes simply because they were not exposed to the salt water and severe strain associated with taking off from the surface of the sea, an activity that required extended periods of maximum power.[19] Nevertheless, there was the fear of having to ditch in the sea if operating beyond gliding distance of land, a necessity in submarine hunting. To offset this disadvantage, one senior RNAS officer proposed fitting out aeroplanes with air bags, capable of keeping a ditched aeroplane afloat long enough to allow the rescue of the crew. Also, employing pilots with seaplane flying experience would help to overcome the anxiety of flying aeroplanes offshore. In December 1917 Wing Captain C. L. Lambe, commanding the naval air units of the Dover Patrol, went as far as to request the replacement of his Dunkirk seaplanes with DH-4 aeroplanes for the reasons explained above; the Admiralty approved his request and by March 1918 No. 17 Squadron (RNAS) was operating DH-4 bombers, equipped with special 375 HP Rolls-Royce engines and inflatable air bags under the wings, to conduct anti-submarine patrols above the Dover Straits.[20] After the formation of the RAF in April 1918, aeroplanes such as the DH-4, DH-6, and DH-9 significantly reinforced the air patrol effort in Home Waters.

The original purpose of the seaplane, on the other hand, was to enable fixed-wing aircraft to operate with the fleet wherever it chose to go.[21] One of the chief advantages of float seaplanes in the anti-submarine war was that they operated from bases on the coast of Britain, within immediate striking distance of their patrol areas above the shipping lanes. The ability to alight on the water was useful for saving the crew in the event of engine failure and subsequent ditching. The floats often saved the aircraft itself; veteran G. E. Livock recalls how floatplanes 'that managed to get into the air frequently arrived back hours later in tow of a minesweeper or minelayer'.[22]

The chief limitations of the float seaplane resulted from the use of wood-sheathed floats. Usually situated in parallel pairs below the wings and engine, with a smaller float under the tail, the floats lacked the strength required to operate in rough seas. Thus, the floatplanes usually had to launch and alight on lakes or enclosed harbours in order to increase their chances of completing a successful takeoff or landing. The sea conditions along the northern coast of Cornwall prevented the operation of seaplanes for the duration of the war.[23] Totally calm seas, on the other hand, were a hindrance since a headwind was necessary to gain the all-important wing lift for takeoff. The floats themselves added a large amount of weight to the basic airframe, especially when they leaked and took on extra water, requiring larger engines than similarly sized aeroplanes.[24]

A further limitation specific to the anti-submarine campaign was the fact that the RNAS operated only single-engine float seaplanes. The combination of a large engine and the preference for placing it in front of the cockpit (tractor) as opposed to behind (pusher) meant that forward visibility for the pilot and observer was severely restricted. Although the tractor design of these aircraft may have helped their aerodynamic properties, it certainly left much to be desired as a reconnaissance platform. This limitation was also evident in single-engine aeroplanes, but to a lesser extent due to their better manoeuvrability compared with float seaplanes.

Flying boats demonstrated a marked improvement over the floatplane designs. Wing Captain Lambe neatly summed up the advantages of the Large America flying boat in a letter to Vice-Admiral Sir Reginald Bacon:

> i. Large radius of action, enabling six hour patrols to be carried out. ii. Larger capacity for carrying bombs. iii. Ability to fly for some distance on a single engine. iv. Ability to land on the water in calm weather in the event of engine failure.[25]

Both the Admiralty's Operations Division and Air Department found Large Americas especially desirable anti-submarine aircraft due to their superb bombing accuracy. The twin-engine configuration of the Large America gave the observer an unhindered forward view to search the horizon and to aim his bombs. This aircraft also employed the larger 230-lb bomb found to be extremely useful when attacking U-boats.[26] The ability to carry a larger crew (at least four but sometimes more) was a further advantage providing more sets of eyes for spotting periscopes and more defensive gun positions manned.

Nevertheless, the advantages of flying boats were offset by a few serious difficulties. First, their large size meant that the pilot's controls were heavy and proved exhausting, especially on lengthy missions in bad weather. The Large Americas required expensive hangars and ramps to support their operations; if left out in the open, the hulls of these aircraft deteriorated rapidly.[27] Finally, it must be remembered that the Large Americas were basically large wooden boats with wings. They had to be carefully designed and built – employing contractors with boat-building experience – and meticulously maintained.[28] 'In commission' rates therefore suffered accordingly and will be examined later in this chapter.

The great majority of fixed-wing anti-submarine aircraft were improve-ments on earlier designs, which did not necessarily have U-boat patrols in mind as a potential role. The RNAS and RAF therefore had many limita-tions in performance to overcome, which they accomplished admirably through adaptation and innovation. Another area of technological adap-tation, crucial to the air anti-submarine effort, was the use of airships in the anti-submarine role.

Airships and kite balloons

Lighter-than-air craft, generally known by the term *airships*, played a critical role in the British air campaign against U-boats. There were three general categories of airships in existence during the Great War. Common to all rigid, non-rigid, and semi-rigid designs was the ability to use hydrogen gas for lift, rudders and elevators for turning and pitch control, and the use of one or more engines to drive attached propellers for propulsion.

Rigid airships were the largest of the lighter-than-air craft and derived their shape from a light, metal framework that contained a series of airbags. Since large ship volumes meant more hydrogen-producing lift, rigids enjoyed the highest potential for lifting weight. Rigid airships, varying in design from ship to ship, normally had multiple engines, large space for crew accommodation, and were well armed. While the German Zeppelin pro-gramme met with success, the British rigid programme suffered from design and production difficulties, exacerbated by an inconsistent development policy over years of regime change at the Admiralty.[29]

Rigid airships, as a distinct class of aircraft, actually contributed very little to the anti-submarine campaign with only nine being completed during the war and few of those seeing operational service. One rigid, *R-29*, actually stood out as an exception during its five-month wartime career. This aircraft, its massive 539-foot length and almost one million cubic feet of volume driven by four 300 HP Rolls-Royce engines, participated in three attacks against U-boats (one of them successful after receiving reinforcement from several British destroyers and trawlers).[30] The operations of smaller lighter-than-air craft outpaced those of the larger rigids by a wide margin, however.

The second category, the non-rigid airship, was the most numerous type in British service. Here a single bullet shaped gasbag, typically made from layers of cotton fabric and rubber, supported a car which carried one or more engines and the crew. A variety of designs emanated from Admiralty work-shops and varied tremendously in size from the early Sea Scout designs to the larger North Sea class. From the start, however, these aircraft were designed specifically with anti-submarine warfare in mind and took advantage of their capabilities to carry out such patrols.[31]

The Admiralty's own airship factory at Kingsnorth designed and built the Sea Scout airship, the first and smallest of the mass-produced non-rigids. In March 1915, at the instigation of First Sea Lord Fisher, RNAS airship pilots and mechanics attached a wingless BE2 airplane fuselage to a pre-war spare envelope to create the first prototype of the class, designed to search narrow waters such as the Straits of Dover and the Irish Sea for U-boats.[32] Easy to produce and simple to fly, the SS proved an effective patrol aircraft and began to populate new airship stations during the spring and summer of 1915. This airship led the way to further non-rigid designs.

The first Coastal airship, with designers now attaching two Avro fuselages (with the engines at each end of this longer car) to a larger tri-lobe envelope, made its maiden flight in May 1915. The larger size of the envelope gave greater lifting capability to support a crew of five, a respectable bomb load and larger fuel tanks for increased endurance. The modified Coastal Star class employed a wooden car and other modifications for crew comfort. Meant to work with the fleet until rigids became available, the North Sea non-rigids were first flown in early 1917 and were even larger than Coastals, but initially suffered from fuel line and drive shaft problems. The novelty of this type was a fully enclosed cabin slung below the envelope holding a crew of ten, five men in two watches for extended flights. Airship authority Ces Mowthorpe calls the North Sea's final production run 'perhaps the finest non-rigids in the world'; they saw extensive service in 1918 at airship bases in Scotland.[33]

The true airship workhorse of the anti-submarine campaign, however, was the small SS Zero (SSZ) non-rigid, an improvement upon the original SS design. The crew benefited from a watertight, streamlined wood cabin, which housed a single Rolls-Royce Hawk engine. Situated at the rear of the car in the pusher configuration and producing 75 HP, the Hawk was purpose-built for airship work with excellent low-power qualities and tremendous endurance. Airship veterans lauded the SSZ's reliability and 'handiness'.[34] Two final versions of the basic SS design – the SS Experimental and the SS Twin, both with two reliable engines and a slightly larger envelope – did not enter service until the closing months of the war and therefore only saw limited use at airship stations.[35]

Table 1.3 Non-rigid airship classes

Class {No. fielded in British Wartime Service}	No. of engines	Crew	Envelope size	Length	Endurance at cruise speed	Max bomb load
Sea Scout (SS) [36]	1	2	60–70,000 cf	143 ft	8 hrs	160-lb
Coastal (C) [31]	2	4 or 5	170,000 cf	195 ft	14 hrs	450-lb
Coastal Star (C*) [22]	2	5	210,000 cf	207–218 ft	24 hrs	600-lb
SS Zero (SSZ) [66]	1	3	70,000 cf	143 ft	12 hrs	350-lb
North Sea (NS) [12]	2	10	360,000 cf	262 ft	20+ hrs	700-lb

Sources: Thetford (1991); Mowthorpe (1998), *Battlebags*; and DAD Memo, AIR 1/208/15/226/194, AD3252.

The final category of airship, the semi-rigid, was employed in Britain only in limited numbers. The semi-rigid airship differed from the non-rigid only by the use of a metal or wood keel that ran along the bottom of the ship, offering additional support to the shape of the gasbag. A pre-war Parseval semi-rigid, named *Naval Airship No. 4*, was used in early reconnaissance patrols, later joined by three more of the same type, but all were soon restricted to the training role.[36]

The two principal advantages of airships over fixed-wing aircraft in the anti-submarine campaign were better endurance, which increased the time available for patrol and convoy escort, and the ability to fly in low clouds and fog.[37] One North Sea airship flew a 55-hour mission in April 1918.[38] Indeed, airships generally made superb platforms for navigation since they turned without the compass-upsetting bank angle inherent to aeroplanes and seaplanes.[39] The commander at Capel Airship Station (near Dover) outlined the advantages of later airship models in the anti-submarine war in January 1918. According to Squadron Commander R. Coke, airships performed anti-submarine patrols better than fixed-wing aircraft because their endurance was greater; they could 'slow down and hover' to make a thorough search; they could communicate and navigate better; they could outclimb and dive any seaplane or aeroplane; and cockpit tasks were fewer, giving the crew more time to search for submarines. The SSZ type of airship, Coke continued, had an especially superb view of the sea, and with no wings to obstruct observation as heavier-than-air craft had. The disadvantages, of course, were admittedly the reliance upon relatively calm winds, the threat of enemy aircraft, and the need for hangars to properly service the airships.[40] Two further advantages of airships, mentioned in an RAF Staff College lecture, included the fact that 'sea-sickness is unknown' and engine failures did not force the pilot to land. In the event of an engine malfunction, the airship became a free balloon while the crew's engineer worked on repairing the engine.[41] These capabilities and limitations were generally common to all non-rigid airships classes.

A further disadvantage of airships was that they required a large ground crew to recover the aircraft; the small SS type, for example, required 25 men to secure the airship after landing on calm days and over 40 men in rough weather.[42] Additionally, the infrastructure required by airships, including hydrogen production facilities, large hangars, and an army of maintenance specialists, posed a considerable drain on RNAS resources. The hydrogen content of the envelope posed a significant risk from enemy fire and lightning; sparks from a ship's funnels destroyed at least one non-rigid by igniting the hydrogen gas.[43] Finally, airships were relatively slow with a top speed of 40 to 55 miles per hour in calm wind for most classes. This meant that they were handicapped in attacking U-boats, especially when facing a strong headwind.[44]

There is one final category of lighter-than-air craft that the Admiralty and RAF employed with some success during the Great War: the kite balloon. Kite balloons were akin to small airships in shape but were not self-powered and were towed by naval vessels ranging in size from large gunboats to dreadnoughts. The capability of kite balloons, evolving from the experience gained in France and the Dardanelles in artillery spotting, was finally adapted to moving vessels in 1916 after a number of Admiralty trials. The 'M' type kite balloon, with stabilising fins and a two-man basket, became the preferred design for naval use.[45] By the end of the war, 247 vessels of all types were fitted out for kite balloon towing, including 108 vessels detailed for anti-submarine operations in Home Waters.[46]

The advantage of the kite balloon was superb visibility, as in all aircraft. An observer, situated in a car suspended from a standard Royal Navy kite balloon, was reportedly able to spot a surfaced submarine at 12 miles in normal visibility and up to 28 miles in clear weather.[47] Added to this the two-man crew enjoyed direct communications with their towing vessel via voice telephone, offering escort captains almost immediate warning of sighted torpedo tracks, U-boat periscopes, or distant conning towers.[48] Finally, kite balloons depended only on the weather, the stamina of the crew, and the condition of the envelope in order to stay aloft. Thus the amount of time flown above a vessel could be extensive, with patrols lasting for days and including over 24 hours of observation time, day or night. The balloon was normally brought down only to change observers (a pair typically flying in four hour shifts) or to replenish the balloon's hydrogen level.[49] This weapon system could operate when other types of aircraft could not and was only limited by severe winds, lightning, and the need for resting the observers. On the other hand, kite balloons required maintenance bases ashore, with a support infrastructure comparable to that of the non-rigid airships. Additionally, strong or gusty winds in rough weather caused a 'jerky' ride for the observers, at times hindering effective observation.[50]

Although the official historian of the RAF claimed that the investment of resources to airship development retarded the growth of the fixed-wing arm of the RNAS, airships provided an important capability, supplementing fixed-wing aircraft in the anti-submarine campaign.[51] When fixed-wing aircraft could not fly due to low clouds or fog, airships typically could. When fixed-wing aircraft had to return to base in order to refuel, airships remained at the scene of a U-boat sighting for hours. Finally, when powered aircraft could not reach the distant U-boat danger zones, kite balloons flown from warships could give escort forces the ability to observe from above. As anti-submarine systems, the capabilities of the different types of aircraft complemented each other in the air campaign against Germany's U-boats. There were, however, a number of technological challenges that required solutions in order to make aircraft effective in this endeavour.

Anti-submarine technological challenges

Flying in conjunction with naval operations was and is a vastly different activity compared with army support aviation. The hazards of early flying, especially from mechanical problems and weather, applied to all spheres of aviation but naval flyers faced a more difficult challenge because they flew over water, characterised by few landmarks and rapidly changing climatic conditions.[52] Subsequently, aeroplanes required a vast supporting infrastructure of technological development – of navigational instruments, communication gear, and weaponry;[53] airships would add a reliance on hydrogen production. During World War I, the British tended to rely on technology – both new weapons and improvements on 'traditional' ones – to solve many of the tactical problems they faced.[54] Although the attrition battles of the Western Front represented an exception to his theory, David Edgerton's interpretation of British thinking – 'the basic strategy of the English state as one of relying on technology as a substitute for manpower' – is an accurate reflection for the nineteenth and twentieth centuries.[55] In World War I aviation, they looked to more powerful and more efficient engines to carry larger loads over longer distances and to develop useful equipment for navigation, communication, and ordnance delivery.[56] A survey of how the Admiralty and Air Ministry attempted to solve these problems sheds light not only on the great strides made in aviation technology during the war years, but also reveals a high level of commitment – evident in both the RNAS and the RAF – to use technology to defeat German unrestricted submarine warfare.

Performance and reliability are fundamental factors to the success of any weapon system and these basic elements were especially critical to the use of aircraft in the anti-submarine campaign. The determining component of aircraft performance during the First World War, at least in the British view, was the source of power – the engine.[57] The Admiralty recognised this in 1914 (when the few British aero engine firms relied almost exclusively on French engine designs) and cultivated relationships with private engine firms, seeking to stimulate competition in order to advance designs of high-powered engines required for seaplanes. Instead of designing the engines themselves, as the RFC's Royal Aircraft Factory did, the Admiralty's Air Department installed engineering officers with the major engine designers – such as Rolls-Royce, Sunbeam, and Clerget – to communicate requirements and negotiate contracts for the RNAS. This led to a competitive, market environment whereby manufacturers were able to design engines of increasing performance, such as the successful Rolls-Royce 250 HP Eagle.[58]

Larger engines meant less risky takeoffs for seaplanes and increased endurance and bomb-carrying capacity for all fixed-wing aircraft. By spring 1917 RNAS aircraft enjoyed the use of high-powered Rolls-Royce, Renault, and Sunbeam engines extensively. Although the light Baby seaplanes required only the smaller Clerget and Gnôme fighter engines, the DH-4, Handley Page O/100, Large America series, and Fairy Campania all used Rolls-Royce Eagle engines of 250 HP or more. Short floatplanes employed 240 HP Renaults or high-powered Sunbeams.[59] Thus by early 1917 engine designers had essentially solved the issue of aircraft power for aeroplanes and seaplanes.

Engine reliability was an entirely different matter, however. New engine designs could take months to resolve mechanical problems; the Rolls-Royce Eagle first ran on the test bench in March 1915, was first delivered in October 1915, but was not serving in combat units until early 1917.[60] Maintaining engines in war conditions required dependable sub-systems. For example, early British engines relied on stocks of German-built magnetos, a device that provided electricity for continuous ignition in the engine. Once the war started, British manufacturers had to develop a magneto industry from scratch, and the earlier, home-built types failed consistently in the field until they matured later in the war.[61]

Similarly, engine failures during patrols afflicted the float seaplane arm especially. One veteran recalled that seaplanes at Portland suffered engine failure 'once in three patrols'.[62] The experiences of two pilots, J. H. Bentham and C. S. Mossop, further illustrate the impact of engine reliability upon operations. During the month of December 1917, Bentham flew eleven patrol missions from Newlyn Seaplane Station in western Cornwall. Seven of these sorties, flown in Short 240 seaplanes, resulted in curtailments – four for engine or engine-related reasons and three for strong winds or bad weather. Two of the mechanical curtailments ended in forced landings after which Bentham had to be towed back to the station.[63] Likewise between 9 July and 12 August 1918 Mossop, flying mostly Wight floatplanes from Calshot Air Station near Portsmouth, flew 24 missions of which 16 were submarine hunting patrols. Two of these patrol missions ended early because of weather, six were curtailed for engine trouble, and his last mission ended when part of his seaplane's tail fell off in the air, leading to a fatal crash.[64] Thus one-quarter of his sorties had to be terminated early – sometimes only minutes after takeoff – during a two-month period due to engine malfunctions.

Improvements in maintenance practices may have caused a decline in engine failures in 1918. If Handley Page maintenance procedures were typical of most other naval aircraft, the adoption of a daily engine inspection regime by well-trained specialists following strict guidelines may explain increased engine reliability.[65] From January 1918 to the Armistice, Large Americas at Yarmouth flew 64,000 patrol miles and only experienced three forced landings due to engine trouble.[66] During the last six months of the submarine campaign, approximately 8 per cent of seaplane and flying boat anti-submarine patrol missions and 4 per cent of aeroplane patrols were curtailed because of engine problems.[67]

Engines were not the only source of problems in maritime aircraft. Flying boats were especially difficult to maintain due to their large hulls, which tended to leak, especially those not housed in hangars.[68] Wing Captain Lambe, writing from Dunkirk, reported that his seaplane squadron possessed a single Large America for 96 days. No. 8695, mentioned above as the only aircraft to sink a U-boat unaided, flew only 16 patrols in three months. Weather hindered operations on 32 of those days, but a leaking hull and engine problems grounded the aircraft on 48 days.[69] T. C. Gordon, a flying boat pilot based at Houton in the Orkneys late in the war, recorded in his diary that only three of 18 flying boats and seaplanes were fit for patrols on 15 July 1918; two months later only one out of 25 flying boats was in commission. The primary problem here was a lack of carpenters for hull maintenance.[70]

The performance and reliability of airships presented an entirely different kind of problem. Lifting capacity, which would provide for more bombs and more fuel for endurance, had little to do with engines in airships. Lifting power was simply a matter of the volume of hydrogen held in the envelope, hence the increase in envelope sizes of non-rigid designs as the war progressed. Early airships normally employed light aeroplane engines for propulsion; since envelope noses blew in during high speed flight, endurance characteristics were much more important than power in an airship engine. The significant difficulty with adapting these low-power engines for airship use was the need for reliability over long periods of time at slow speeds. Slow speeds meant that airflow over the engine was not high enough to keep the engine properly cooled. Aeroplane engines were designed for short flights at high power, not lengthy airship flights at low power. Thus the early SS non-rigids, using 70 HP Renault and other similar aeroplane engines, tended to overheat often. Commanders of Coastal airships at Longside (near Aberdeen) complained that they could not carry out assigned missions with their unreliable engines.[71] Also, the need to start an engine by turning the propeller or hand cranking a starting handle meant that in-flight restarts, if required, created a hazard for flight engineers.[72]

Rolls-Royce once again produced a solution to Admiralty requirements in the form of the Hawk engine. Producing only 75 to 100 HP, the Hawk was specifically designed for non-rigid airship operations. The keys to this engine's success were its superb performance under extended periods and the ability to restart easily in the air.[73] By the last six months of the war, airships of all types were suffering approximately 3 per cent mission curtailments due to engine problems, a low figure largely influenced by the excellent reliability of the Hawk engine and the advantage of twin-engine airships being able to continue flight with one engine inoperative.[74]

Although naval air power did not completely overcome its engine and flying boat hull reliability issues, engine power had developed sufficiently to provide aircraft with respectable bomb loads and endurance, both requirements of an effective anti-submarine patrol force. The environment in which they worked, however, would provide another challenge to maritime aviators during the Great War.

During the Great War flying conditions often dictated the pace of operations, since many types of aircraft lacked the ability to operate during high winds, calm or rough seas, poor visibility, or low clouds. If one considers the additional challenge of flying over the vast emptiness of the seas, it becomes apparent that naval aviators fought their air war not only against German submarines but also against their hazardous flying environment. As the official air historian noted, 'the sailor is always at war with the sea as the airman is at war with the air, but the naval airman has to reckon with both'.[75]

As the first half of this chapter demonstrated, different aircraft types had different capabilities and limitations regarding their ability to operate in poor weather. Analysis of a three-month period in 1918 illustrates how the weather could affect flying operations in different coastal areas (see Table 1.4). Thus during this period of consistently good weather, airships in two air groups only flew two-thirds of the time while those based in Yorkshire only flew approximately one day out of three. Although commanders tended to be more conservative regarding the use of airships in questionable weather conditions, Table 1.4 does indeed illustrate their limitations.

Greater numbers and a variety of aircraft types helped to minimise the effects of weather by offering alternatives to air commanders; when one type of aircraft could not fly, another type could usually be found to carry out the required anti-submarine patrols or convoy escorts. The abundance of coastal air stations in 1918 meant that if the coastal weather – which could vary tremendously from one area to the next even if only a few miles away – grounded a portion of an air group, it was likely that the weather at one or more of the remaining bases would allow the launch of patrols to cover most of the group's flying responsibilities.[76]

Flying over the water provided another challenge. Seaplanes and flying boats were designed with this in mind and later maritime aeroplanes normally came equipped with flotation gear for ditching at sea. Seaplanes and flying boats required an infrastructure of ramps for launching and hangars for protection. Similarly, the relatively delicate non-rigid airship force required extremely large hangars and when these were not available relied on mooring stations surrounded by trees, which offered at least some protection from the wind.

Navigation over the water was yet another problem; maintaining awareness of one's position was difficult in the absence of ground references. When out of sight of the coastline, maritime aircraft relied on three tools. The first, if available, was the system of light vessels established in coastal areas for maritime navigation.[77] Large Americas from Felixstowe, for example, used the North Hinder Light vessel, 52 miles off the coast, as a navigational reference along with the many others that populated coastal shipping routes.[78] British direction finding stations provided a second navigational tool. These stations, originally built to pinpoint U-boat positions by tracking their wireless

Table 1.4 Number of flying days available, 1 July–30 September 1918

Aircraft type	South-west England	Channel coast	North-east England
Seaplanes	84	87	90
Aeroplanes	89	87	91
Airships	67	65	35

Source: *WIA*, Appendices: XVIII.

transmissions, were especially useful to airships. Their slower speeds made them more susceptible to the effects of wind drift and hence navigational errors.[79] The final and most important method of navigation over water was dead reckoning. Aviators simply kept track of their course, airspeed, and time in order to estimate their position on the navigational chart. Two key measurements were required for accurate dead reckoning navigation: the aircraft's course and ground speed, both affected by the wind.

Aircraft heading and airspeed could be measured fairly accurately by the aircraft's own instruments.[80] Large America flying boats, for example, used a vertical compass graduated every two degrees, and all of the principal performance instruments were located on a single instrument panel in front of the pilot.[81] Applying the wind's effects to the known heading and airspeed would result in the aircraft's course and speed over the sea. Winds could be estimated from meteorological officers at the home station, but once out to sea winds could easily change in both speed and direction. Observing the effects of the wind on the sea offered one way of estimating the course and strength of the wind. Advanced models of bombsights were also used for determining wind drift.[82] On larger aircraft, two crew members could usually devote much of their time to navigation – the two pilots on Large Americas or the pilot and observer on two-seat aeroplanes, float seaplanes, and airships.[83]

Although challenging, flying over water presented problems existing technology could solve. Many of these solutions also applied to cloud flying, though flying into clouds made scouting for U-boats impossible and therefore not worth the risks. Night flying was yet another area of innovation, since U-boats operated in the darkness, and the potential of operating aircraft at night was too tempting to ignore.

Although the RNAS had experimented with night flying in June 1914, German night Zeppelin attacks against London in January 1915 forced the RNAS to consider a night flying capability.[84] These German attacks not only generated the necessity to intercept enemy aircraft at night, but may also have provoked the British into trying their own night bombing raids against facilities in occupied Belgium and elsewhere. Later in the war, the RNAS and RAF developed night flying operations to an advanced degree. Although bombing Flanders U-boat bases was the primary arena for employing night aviation to counter Germany's submarine campaign, naval aviators discovered a measured benefit from night convoy escort missions. Specifically, flying at night became important for the anti-submarine campaign as some of the German U-boat commanders switched to night surface attacks against shipping. During February and March of 1917 approximately one-quarter of all Home Waters attacks on British vessels were at night. A year later, the proportion was one-half.[85]

To accomplish this task, two sets of technological problems needed to be addressed. First, the ability to operate the aircraft at night was a basic prerequisite for effectiveness. Could the pilot take off, navigate, and return to his base safely in the darkness? The second set of problems concerned weapons employment and hunting operations; if the crew could fly at night to the target or patrol area, would they be able to spot a conning tower or drop bombs accurately?

By the start of the unrestricted submarine campaign, the British had for the most part solved the basic problems of operating aeroplanes at night. RNAS units in south-east England had by early 1916 developed techniques for taking off and landing at night, using rows of burning petrol cans to illuminate the landing ground and the direction of the wind. Flares and flashing lights became the primary means of communication between aircraft and their aerodromes.[86] By 1918 the system had evolved into an electric lighting apparatus, laid out in the shape of the letter 'T', for takeoff and landing, with an elaborate system of communication by coloured flares and Aldis lamp light signals. Navigation to and from the target area relied on dead reckoning with star and moon observations as a backup. The RNAS required its compasses to be readable 'by day or night', and usually employed radium paint or small lights for illumination of the compass card.[87] Additionally, a system of lighthouses, spaced apart at ten-mile intervals behind friendly lines, helped the aircrew navigate back to the home aerodrome if conditions allowed them to be seen. By 1918, pilots and observers had grown accustomed to the local landmarks in northern Belgium and could easily navigate at night regardless of the moon's illumination.[88] For landing, the Air Ministry developed a night altitude indicator to help the pilot judge his height during the final 500 feet of his approach. Even crash sights and bomb craters on the home aerodrome would be marked with red lights to help pilots avoid unexpected obstructions upon landing.[89]

The major problem associated with seaplane and flying boat missions at night, which remained unresolved during World War I, was the ability to land on the surface of the water with limited illumination and no ground references to aid the pilot. The Cooper Night Landing Stick, seeing trials on Large Americas in August and September 1918, was simply a long pole mechanically attached to the elevator. Extending 14 feet below the hull, it would touch the water before the hull did as the flying boat landed, causing the elevator to deflect automatically in order to raise the nose to the landing attitude. Fears over the device's strength prevented its adoption for general service.[90] The RNAS also experimented with float-mounted flares as an aid to water landings.[91]

Airships used similar basic techniques; however, they benefited tremendously from the ability to climb and descend almost vertically and to proceed at extremely slow speeds in order to avoid running into trees and other obstacles at night. Being stationed near the coast enabled them to make use of local lighthouses for navigation when necessary.[92] Otherwise, navigation at night over water used the same techniques mentioned above. With the ability to navigate between their bases and their operating areas, all aircraft would then have to face the challenges of conducting their war tasks, either bombing or visually searching, at night.

Although the first RFC night bombing unit was not established until February 1917, RNAS bombers had learned of its benefits in early 1915 during night raids against naval objectives in Flanders.[93] By 1916 RNAS Sopwith 1½ Strutters and Short Bombers regularly attacked at night, taking off a few hours before dawn in order to be able to land in daylight.[94] These night bombing operations continued in 1917 and 1918 using Handley Page heavy bombers.

As the RNAS commander at Dunkirk reported, the advantages of night bombing were immense. Night flying made the bombers almost impervious to German anti-aircraft fire, which enabled them to bomb from lower altitudes thus increasing their accuracy. The local weather pattern, where calm winds and good visibility predominated during the hours of darkness, was another advantage. Finally the Handley Page, carrying more bombs than six DH-4s and using half the fuel, required no air escort at night, since the Germans had not yet developed an effective night interceptor capability.[95] By 1918, a typical Handley Page night bomber crew approached the target silently, in a power-off glide, to avoid detection from the sound of the engines before dropping their bomb load at low altitude. If caught in German search-lights, the pilot would put the aircraft into violent jinking manoeuvres to escape observation.[96]

Patrolling the sea-lanes and escorting convoys proved more problematic at night. Opinions were mixed during the war as to the utility of night airship patrols. Vice-Admiral Bacon supported the idea of night airship patrols for the Dover Straits in May 1915, where the U-boats were supposedly crossing the area on the surface at night, but fire from friendly anti-aircraft guns was a genuine concern.[97] Admiral Sir F. T. Hamilton, commanding in Scotland, ruled out airship night flying in 1916 and only grudgingly allowed them to fly at night in 1917.[98] By 1917 Scottish airship stations regularly launched Coastal airships before sunrise in order to have them in position above the sea-lanes by dawn, while at least one Longside airship pilot flew four night patrols during the course of a single week in June.[99]

By 1917 the Dover command considered night flying a promising tool, especially in order to put the airship above its patrol area before daybreak, a time regarded as likely to be fruitful in spotting a surfaced U-boat.[100] The airship station at Polegate and its substations, responsible for the eastern English Channel, flew over 1,000 hours of night flying between May 1918 and the Armistice.[101] This no doubt was part of Vice-Admiral Sir Roger Keyes's renewed efforts to completely block the Dover Straits as a U-boat transit area – efforts that finally sealed this chokepoint in mid-1918.[102]

Escorting convoys provided another opportunity for night flying. In April 1918 a 55-hour patrol of *NS-3* met with little difficulty in maintaining contact with a convoy it was escorting during periods of moonlight illumination. When the moon was obscured, however, the airship could only keep sight of the convoy by flying astern of it and maintaining position by referencing the stern lights of the ships.[103] Again, the value of night escorts was not in spotting a U-boat at night, but in being with the convoy at dawn in order to maximise the useful daylight in searching for U-boats in the vicinity.

In July 1918 the Admiralty's Anti-Submarine and Air Divisions considered the employment of searchlights from airships. They concluded that the benefit of limited illumination would be outweighed by the disadvantage of the airship giving up its position to a surfaced submarine, which could then fire on the airship.[104] During the following month the Air Division recommended that airships flying convoy escorts at night be limited to using light signals only for recognition, emergencies, or as specifically ordered by the local Senior Naval Officer.[105] Parallel evaluations for fixed-wing aircraft discovered that much of the limited bomb-carrying capacity would have to be sacrificed in order to carry the heavy searchlight systems. Parachute flares promised better illumination possibilities, but the position of the U-boat would have to be known beforehand to avoid a massive expenditure of these devices, which weighed 80 pounds each.[106]

Unfortunately, night patrol work was typically not very useful even for airships since the ability to spot anything on the water at night was minimal. On bright moonlight nights, however, patrols near areas of known U-boat mine-laying activity were considered 'worth the risk' of being attacked by a submarine on the surface. The primary benefit for airship night flying was found in the ability to launch before dawn and be 'on their beats during the whole of the hours of twilight and daylight'.[107]

In April 1918, seaplanes from Fishguard experimented with four night patrols by moonlight and found that ships and objects were 'fairly easily discernible, and with the help of an Aldis lamp, unmistakeable'.[108] Nevertheless, the inability of seaplanes and flying boats to find U-boats at night combined with the risk of night landings meant that they were largely limited to day operations.

The RNAS had considered the use of aircraft to bomb submarines as early as 1912, and the Navy's technical orientation served it well in developing weapons and delivery systems.[109] In dealing with the U-boat threat during the Great War aircraft required effective bombs and means of delivering them accurately in order to destroy, damage, or at least threaten U-boats. Although a 1916 RNAS Gunnery Memorandum suggested that a 16-lb bomb landing directly on a submarine would be sufficient to destroy it, the first few years of the war demonstrated that bombs of 100-lbs or less were of little use against submarines.[110] Additionally early bombsights did not account for wind and often required the use of printed charts and tables in flight. Starting from the middle years of the war, however, the RNAS made tremendous leaps in bomb sizes, largely as a result of performance increases of the aircraft that carried them, and in sighting apparatus.

Aircraft theoretically did not need to make a direct bomb hit in order to sink a submarine. Just as with depth charges, an explosion close to the U-boat's hull should have been sufficient to destroy or seriously damage it. The questions of course were how large the bomb had to be and how close to the

U-boat it needed to explode. Trials at HMS *Vernon* demonstrated that a bomb containing a 40-lb explosive charge needed to discharge within 10 feet of a submarine to 'destroy or severely damage a submarine'; for 120-lbs of explosive the distance was 35 feet.[111] The adoption of the 230-lb bomb, containing 140-lbs of amatol in a 90-lb sheet steel case, soon followed and was first used against a U-boat in June 1917. Fortunately, this programme coincided with the fielding of aircraft capable of carrying such bombs on anti-submarine patrols, such as the larger two-seat float seaplanes and the Large Americas. The December 1917 *RNAS Anti-Submarine Report* recommended that field units carry a new light-case 520-lb bomb 'whenever possible'. Even though the larger bomb would reduce the aircraft's patrol time due to the extra weight, air commanders continued to press for more destructive 520-lb bombs for their units in 1918.[112] By April 1918 these large bombs were still in the developmental stage and few 520-lb bombs are mentioned in submarine attacks; only the later Large America flying boats and the Blackburn Kangaroo were capable of carrying it.[113] Thus the 230-lb bomb became the primary anti-submarine weapon of larger aircraft, including airships, while smaller patrol aircraft still relied on the lighter 100-lb and 65-lb bombs. One tactic adopted by the RAF in 1918 called for dropping a pair of 230-lb bombs as a salvo, each one projecting a 40 foot destructive radius for a respectable kill zone, to enhance the chances of a kill.[114]

Fusing these anti-submarine bombs properly created another challenge. The 230-lb bomb was originally developed as a light-case, high explosive bomb used for destroying buildings; the idea was for the bomb to penetrate the roof before exploding inside the structure. It therefore did not use a nose impact fuse, but instead relied on a delay fuse in the tail that could be set to use a 0.05-, 2.5-, or 15-second delayed internal detonator; the delay length had to be set before flight. For anti-submarine use, the 2.5-second delay was used and typically caused the bomb to explode 80 feet below the surface. The problem with this configuration, realised but not solved during the war, was that a submarine on the surface or deep in the water was almost immune from damage from these bombs.[115] A technical conference in June 1918 recommended that aircraft employ a mix of 230-lb 'depth' bombs and 100-lb 'contact' bombs to provide flexibility in submarine attacks. Some units chose to provide differing weapons loads in a formation of patrol aircraft for the same reason. Although it was technically feasible, variable fusing, where the depth could be set in flight, did not gain support from RAF technical officers and was not attempted.[116]

There were, however, a few air-delivered alternatives to bombs as anti-submarine weapons. Historian Dwight Messimer mentions the production of two small aerial depth charges. The Type C, with a 35-lb charge, detonated through the extension of a lanyard attached to a float, while the Type C*, of 65-lb, used a hydrostatic pistol set to fire at a depth of 50 feet.[117] These aerial depth charges were actually Hale's Bombs adapted with special fusing gear, but their limited explosive power made them useless.[118] Technical experts assumed that depth bombs were just as good if not better than any conventional depth charge designs.[119] Maritime aviators also considered aerial mines; a scheme to develop and field such weapons for mining the Bruges-Zeebrugge Canal never progressed beyond the experimental stage due to damage from impact, water leaks, and the infeasibility of dropping mines in daylight from low altitude (required for accuracy) in a highly defended area.[120] Finally, technical experts pushed for the use of a 1½-pounder or 37mm gun mounting for aircraft to shoot at U-boats, potentially holing the double hull in order to prevent the submarine from diving.[121] Although airborne trials with a recoil-less 2-pounder Davis gun had been conducted in 1916, the use of small calibre artillery on British maritime aircraft appears never to have progressed beyond the experimental stage.[122]

The question of bomb aiming absorbed a great deal of developmental energy during the war years as well. The pre-1916 bombsights, the Nail, Lever, and Central Flying School (or CFS) sights, all had serious deficiencies regarding accuracy and ease of use. The primary problem was in measuring and accounting for the effect of the wind on the flight path of the bomb. A bomb fell at the same rate in all conditions from a given height but acquired the ground speed of the aircraft, minus a correction for bomb drag, as soon as it was released. Calculating the angle of release therefore required an accurate ground speed relative to the target.

Ground speed could be calculated in flight by either recording the time required to pass two points on the ground or by measuring the wind at altitude and adjusting the indicated airspeed, as taken from the cockpit indicator. The Equal Distance Sight, developed by Warrant Officer Scarff of the RNAS, made use of the first method of ground speed calculation; a fixed sight and a reversible stopwatch (adjusted for the aircraft's height) made operation simple. Unfortunately it proved difficult to work the stopwatch while under anti-aircraft fire, and altitude and airspeed had to be held steady throughout the bomb run. Attacks had to be conducted either directly upwind or downwind to minimise lateral errors. The sight was suitable for attacks against submarines but required manoeuvring into the wind before making the bomb run, adding precious seconds to the attack sequence as the U-boat dove for safety. Six hundred of these sights were produced in 1916 and 1917.[123]

The Drift bombsight series, invented by Lieutenant Commander H. E. Wimperis, used the second method of wind compensation. Known winds could be ascertained before the bomb run by flying at right angles to the wind direction and lining up a drift bar with the actual path over the ground. This automatically adjusted the sight for wind, negating the need for a stopwatch; the observer then dialled in the planned altitude and indicated airspeed for the attack. The sight was now set for use. Again, the actual bomb run had to be made either directly into or directly away from the wind, although one version of the instruction manual offered techniques for attacks across the known wind.[124] Winds could also be forecast at the home station through observing anti-aircraft artillery bursts and measuring their course and speed through a mirror system. This method gave bomber aircrews the ability to plan their approach to the target before taking off on a mission. Airships could obtain the exact wind speed by flying into the wind, throttling back, and bringing the airship to a hover with the engines running slowly.[125] The airship's indicated airspeed equalled the wind speed in these circumstances. The Drift bombsight appeared in high altitude, low altitude, and airship versions and was the most widely used British naval bombsight of World War I.[126]

'The most important bomb sight of the war', in Christina Goulter's opinion, was the Wimperis Course Setting bombsight. Setting the standard for bombsights until World War II, this sight incorporated a working compass with the basic concepts of the Drift bombsight.[127] The new sight, first tested in December 1917 on flying boats, allowed the aircrew to attack a target, including a moving submarine, from any direction with superb accuracy. Trials in Large Americas and Handley Page night bombers demonstrated that the Course Setting sight was 'extremely simple to operate', but required close cooperation between the observer, who worked the sight, and the pilot, who steered the aircraft by his partner's commands. RNAS and RAF contractors produced approximately 720 of these by the end of 1918.[128]

Thus by the last two years of the war, naval aviators possessed powerful bombs (230-lb and 520-lb) and accurate sights (Drift and Course Setting) capable of inflicting damage on U-boats. Although a post-war staff study claimed that aircraft destroyed ten U-boats and 'probably seriously damaged' a further 22 submarines during the entire course of the war, historians today agree that the most probable result of these aircraft attacks was only one U-boat destroyed by an aircraft acting alone and five others sunk by air patrols assisted by surface vessels.[129] Nevertheless, the fact that U-boats submerged to escape during most aircraft attacks leads to the conclusion that the Germans respected the potential damage of a well-aimed salvo of aircraft bombs.[130] Many attacks therefore had to be carried out just as the submarine submerged or seconds after it left the field of view; the aim point for dropping bombs at this point depended on educated guesses based on known U-boat diving rates, turning radii, and submerged speeds.[131] The odds favoured the U-boat, as the results confirmed.

One of the principal advantages of aircraft in the anti-submarine campaign was the ability to communicate. Their relatively small bomb load meant that communicating with surface vessels would offer a better chance of bringing more munitions to bear on a U-boat. Communications gave aircrew the opportunity to warn merchant vessels of submarine threats or mines. Within most coastal commands, aviators soon grew dependent on effective communications in order to provide air reinforcement to suspected U-boat sightings. Thus, communicating was not only a benefit but became a necessity in the anti-submarine campaign.

Communications could be accomplished through a number of different means. When in sight of another aircraft or a surface vessel, most naval aircraft used Aldis lamps for Morse code signalling. Employing a 12-volt electric lamp within a 4-inch mirror, this device had a pistol grip, trigger, and telescopic sight for ease of flashing a light signal at a ship or another aircraft. Although there were complaints concerning the use of this lamp onboard small anti-submarine vessels of the Auxiliary Patrol, Aldis signalling remained an effective means of immediate communication, with a reliable range of 4 to 5 miles and a maximum range of 17 miles.[132]

Flares could also be used in pre-arranged numbers and colours for communication. Observers on airships and seaplanes had the additional capability of using 24-inch naval signalling flags, and the semaphore system of waving two flags could be accomplished from airships.[133] If for some reason these systems did not prove convenient, airship captains always had the option of descending, shutting off the motor, and shouting to a surface vessel to pass information.[134]

The wireless telegraph (W/T), however, bore the essential task of *long-range* communication for aircraft. Early spark W/T sets were extremely heavy; the set procured for the rigid airship *Mayfly* of 1911 weighed 500 pounds.[135] Decreasing sizes and increasing performance of W/T sets made them standard equipment on non-rigid airships and most seaplanes during the war years.[136] The Type 53 spark transmitter of the Coastal airship class, for example, weighed just over 100 pounds and had a range of 100 to 120 miles. Since these devices were usually powered by electricity from the engine, a larger engine meant more power and range for the signal. The Fairey Campania large floatplane, introduced in July 1917, used a main, engine-driven transmitter of 250 to 300 miles range and a battery-powered backup transmitter providing a range of 150 miles. Wireless receivers were typically much smaller and lighter, the common Type Tb receiver weighing only 6 pounds and able to receive signals from 150 miles away. The introduction of continuous wave transmitters further reduced weight and increased range; the Type 57 transmitter weighed only 40 pounds with all of its associated gear and batteries and possessed a 250 to 350 mile effective range when installed in a Short floatplane.[137] Continuous wave W/T, introduced to field units in the spring of 1918, was considered more reliable and experienced less interference than the earlier spark transmitters.[138]

The use of W/T from aircraft added a number of capabilities to aircraft. In two-seat aircraft the observer worked the wireless, while in aircraft with larger crews a W/T operator was typically a designated crewmember, acting as an additional Lewis gunner when necessary. Although not all merchant vessels were equipped with wireless, all convoy commodores were and thus a reliable means of communication existed with the formations aircraft were detailed to protect.[139] Naval vessels maintained a listening watch on aircraft frequencies whilst on patrol, and aviation Morse signals were shortened and simplified in order to make transmissions more efficient and timely. Using wireless, patrol aircraft could communicate with their home stations in order to report U-boat sightings, call in reinforcements, or request assistance in case of emergencies.[140]

Direction finding (DF) was an additional tool for aircraft. Although all anti-submarine forces potentially benefited from the U-boat intercept information calculated by DF stations around the coasts, aircraft could verify their own positions by sending wireless signals to these stations. Air headquarters could also track their own aircraft and move them to positions of known U-boat intercepts or sightings. Aircraft on patrol were even known to pick up German U-boat transmissions on their own receivers and could approximate the distance by the strength of the signal.[141]

Although the use of W/T required well-trained operators and was 'complicated by engine and air noise, splashes of engine oil and the risk of fire', wireless communication systems were force multipliers for maritime air units.[142] Wireless telephone, using voice communication in place of Morse keying, would have been an even greater advantage had it been fielded in time.[143] Nevertheless, the communications capabilities of 1918 – taken for granted today – represented a technological leap of immense proportions and greatly enhanced the effectiveness of aircraft in the anti-submarine campaign.

One of the primary difficulties in anti-submarine warfare during the Great War was detecting the location of the submarine. As mentioned at the beginning of this chapter, aircraft had the advantage of height in trying to spot a submarine's periscope or conning tower visually. Altitude not only extended the visual horizon but also freed the aircraft crewmember's line of sight from some of the effects of air density and mist.[144] Coloured goggles met with some success in filtering the light in order to aid in visually detecting a U-boat's conning tower or periscope.[145]

Nevertheless, trying to sight a periscope or conning tower from the air was still a difficult proposition, especially in the choppy seas and misty air prevalent around Britain. Detecting a *submerged* submarine from the air presented a far greater challenge, especially in the murky waters surrounding the British Isles. Although clear water enabled aircraft to sight submarines below the surface of the water to a limited depth (sometimes as deep as five fathoms),[146] as soon as the U-boat dove deep it was relatively safe from detection.

Development of the hydrophone in Britain, for use from shore stations as well as from vessels, attempted to deal with this detection problem. The hydrophone was an advanced underwater microphone used to detect the sounds of a U-boat's machinery. The Board of Invention and Research and the Admiralty's experimental establishments had invested a great deal of time and resources into underwater acoustics and hydrophone technology during the war.[147] Various iterations of this device evolved for use with warships. Specifically, the Admiralty fielded the Portable General Service hydrophone – a very basic, non-directional listening device – in late 1915 for use in small vessels. Towed and directional models followed and saw service with hydrophone hunting flotillas as early as summer 1917.[148]

One of the primary difficulties associated with using hydrophones with surface vessels was the simple fact that a hunted U-boat could hear the approach of the vessel well before the ship's hydrophone operator could identify the presence of the U-boat. The U-boat commander could rest on the bottom or use a slow, silent speed in order to remain undetected. Mating the hydrophone with seaplanes or flying boats offered a potential solution to this problem, however. Seaplane engines transmitted only a slight amount of noise to the water and could thus employ hydrophones after landing without giving away their position to the U-boat.[149]

RNAS units in the Mediterranean were the first to experiment with hydrophones from seaplanes during the spring of 1917. The first trial in Home Waters took place in July 1917 where a float seaplane from Dundee Air Station was able to detect electric motor noises at four miles distance.[150] The RNAS conducted further trials at Westgate Air Station in early 1918. Three problems became evident. The non-directional hydrophone available for the trials was not very useful in pinpointing the location of the U-boat. Also, float seaplanes had poor sea keeping properties and could not operate in this listening role unless seas were relatively calm. Finally, if the engine was shut off in order to save fuel and ease the observer's task of listening to the hydrophone headset, restarting the engine proved to be a challenge. Some floatplane models had a single air bottle, or only one chance, to start the engine. Others required the observer to stand precariously on the float while he operated a hand crank to initiate an engine start. Even if the engine started, a floatplane with a war load of bombs, wireless, two crewmembers, and other equipment experienced difficulty taking off in the open ocean.[151]

Employing flying boats with a bi-directional hydrophone showed more promise, however, in minimising the drawbacks of previous floatplane trials. Experiments in May 1918 demonstrated that the Large America flying boat, equipped with a retractable pole that housed a bi-directional hydrophone, needed only a modified sea anchor (to prevent excessive drifting of the aircraft while resting on the surface) to operate effectively.[152] This led to the Anti-Submarine Division ordering 35 sets of this hydrophone gear for flying boat units in Britain with 15 more for units in the Mediterranean.[153] Tactics called for the aircraft to alight on the water to listen, then take off to attack the target if located with the hydrophone set. With multiple aircraft, one or more could remain airborne to drop bombs on the U-boat while the listening aircraft directed the attack.[154] According to the Anti-Submarine Division's technical history, poor weather during the autumn of 1918 (combined with a scarcity of Large Americas) meant that little use was actually made of this new technology.[155]

In the meantime, airship units pressed ahead with similar trials. In December 1917, a BIR scientist suggested using hydrophones from airships because they could tow a hydrophone at slow speed while manoeuvring and still benefit from an undetected presence relative to the U-boat.[156] Trials throughout the spring and summer of 1918 demonstrated that towing hydrophone gear from an airship, even at slow speeds, produced almost insurmountable problems such as excessive water-noise generated from the equipment, drogue and cable failure, noise from the airship's own engines interfering with the operator's headset, and an inability to keep the drogue from breaking the surface of the water. By the closing months of the war experiments had finally found a combination of the right gear with the right technique but the war ended before the sets could be distributed.[157] Mullion Airship Station (in Cornwall) used some of the experimental sets operationally, but no submarine attack reports during the closing months of the war mention the use of hydrophones from airships.[158]

Although the use of hydrophones from aircraft during the Great War foreshadowed its current use by naval helicopters employing 'dunking sonars' to hunt submarines, the Admiralty wanted more than what existing technology could offer. The useful range of these early hydrophones was only about two miles from a towed system or four from a stationary set; directional accuracy was not much better than 20 degrees.[159] However, as Richard Compton-Hall relates, 'despite hydrophones of one kind or another, the most reliable A/S [anti-submarine] detection method on both sides remained, throughout the war, a sharp visual lookout for periscopes and torpedo wakes'.[160]

Submarines

If Winston Churchill's assessment of the U-boat threat was correct, that 'of all the tasks ever set to a Navy none could have appeared more baffling than that of sheltering this enormous traffic and groping deep below the surface of the sea for the deadly elusive foe', then the technical advances of British maritime air forces must be measured against the backdrop of German submarine capabilities and their ability to conduct their missions.[161] This final section will briefly assess these capabilities in order to provide context for the following chapters.

There were four distinct categories of German U-boats, each designed for specific tasks, which took part in the campaign against commerce during World War I.[162] The most numerous type of submarine was the patrol U-boat designed both before and during the Great War to operate with the fleet. Early pre-war classes used heavy oil and were limited in range and armament, but later models were superb performers on the high seas and had two diesel engines plus two electric motors. The later classes were well armed with large deck guns and a dozen or more torpedo rounds launched from four bow or two stern torpedo tubes. Over 200 feet long, these fleet boats could generally reach 16 to 17 knots while on the surface and a maximum submerged speed of 8 to 10 knots for short periods. With a crew of three dozen men, they carried enough fuel and provisions to be at sea for three to four weeks during a single cruise.[163]

Two smaller types of U-boats were the coastal minelayers (*UC* class) and coastal patrol submarines (*UB* class), both designed to operate in the waters around Britain. The earlier versions of these coastal boats were extremely small, about half the length of the fleet boats, and could reach surface speeds of only 6 to 8 knots on their single heavy-oil engine. Later versions, however, approached the size and performance of the fleet boats but carried fewer torpedoes. The *UC* minelayers carried 12 to 18 mines in six internal tubes. According to William Jameson, typical *UB* and *UC* patrols lasted between four and 14 days.[164] The final type of World War I U-boat was the U-cruiser, adapted from commercial cargo U-boats and designed for long-range patrol operations. These U-boats typically carried two deck guns, had large crews of 56 men, and were poor sea boats. Only seven were completed.

On the surface, U-boats were normally fast enough to chase down an individual merchant vessel or to manoeuvre into firing position against a convoy. Submerged, they possessed enough battery power for about one hour at a maximum of 8 knots or up to 20 hours at a much slower economical speed.[165] The time needed to dive varied with the capabilities of the specific type of U-boat and the training of the crew, but a typical fleet boat could reach a fully submerged state in 45 seconds.[166] Most classes could reach depths of 200 feet safely.[167]

A weakness was that the submarine was a complicated weapon system, relying on a number of fragile components, such as dive planes, depth-keeping gear, and periscopes, to operate effectively. Damage to any of these from gunfire, bombs, or depth charge attack could render the submarine useless in combat, even though the vessel did not sink outright.[168] Oil leaks would leave patches of oil on the surface and could give away the U-boat's position. Ventilation was important to clear the hydrogen gas generated from the battery cells; leaks in the hull could introduce seawater into the battery compartments, producing poisonous fumes, necessitating immediate surfacing.[169] Batteries had to be recharged from the main diesel engines while running on the surface. Finally, if visibility was suitable, an aircraft or ship could estimate the position of a U-boat after it launched a torpedo because this weapon left a clearly visible wake on the surface of the sea.

In August 1914, the Germans had 24 operational U-boats, all based with the High Seas Fleet in north-western Germany. A rapid expansion of the U-boat construction programme coupled with opportunities for service in other theatres meant that by February 1917, the start of the unrestricted campaign, the Germans had 105 operational boats: 46 of these served with the High Seas Fleet flotillas, 23 were in Flanders, 26 worked from the Mediterranean bases at Pola, Cattaro, and Constantinople, and 10 more served in the Baltic. If training units are added, the total number of U-boats in commission during that time was 152. This total U-boat strength peaked in mid-1918 with about 175 commissioned boats in German service.[170]

It is important to note that only about a third of available U-boats were on patrol at any one time; a high proportion were proceeding to or returning from their operational areas and some were undergoing repairs at any given moment. For example between March and July of 1917, the most effective period for the Germans with over 3 million tons of enemy shipping sunk, they possessed between 155 and 160 U-boats in commission per month. The average number of operational U-boats at sea, however, was only 46 over the same period.[171]

When operated by a trained and motivated crew, all classes of U-boats were formidable weapon systems. However, once they completely submerged below periscope depth, U-boats lost the ability to navigate and attack. Later chapters will show that forcing the U-boat down, through the credible threat of air attack and communication with surface vessels, was the true tactical value of aircraft technology in the First World War.

Summary

By 1918 maritime air power had made tremendous leaps in solving the technological problems related to anti-submarine warfare. Many, but not all, of the ingredients for success were in place by the critical final two years of the anti-submarine campaign. Air groups balanced advantages with limitations in using a wide array of aircraft for anti-submarine patrols. Engine power increased rapidly during the war years, producing high performance aircraft capable of flying extended patrols and carrying heavy bombs. As bomb sizes increased, advanced bomb delivery systems provided accuracy. Navigating out of sight of the coast and flying at night were challenges that became routine by the end of the war. Communications capabilities served as a force multiplier. Finally, detecting a submerged U-boat held promise for the future, but hydrophones did not develop sufficiently to have a significant impact on operations.

Combined arms teams do well on the tactical level of warfare because they take advantage of the capabilities of each weapon system. It will become evident in later chapters that aircraft rarely did well acting alone but nevertheless contributed measurably to the anti-submarine campaign. As a team member, working within an intricate intelligence and communications network, naval aviation enhanced the effectiveness of surface patrols and escorts, and mine barrages.

Although it played an important role in early maritime air power, technology could not defeat the U-boat threat alone. As in any era, innovative equipment required trained aircrews to operate it and a training system to continue the flow of qualified personnel to flying units. Also the new aircraft, and their engines, had to be produced in large enough quantities to make an impact on the naval war. Finally, these new weapon systems of 1917–1918, which were indeed extremely advanced by the standards of 1914, required organisation and doctrine to govern their employment if they were to be effective in the field.[172]

2   Training and production

Despite its competition with the RFC, British Army, Royal Navy, and industry for qualified personnel, Britain's maritime air arm never worried about the supply of superb volunteers for naval flying duties.[1] These volunteers, however, required flying training and aircraft in order to be productive to the war effort; the growth of the RNAS caused tremendous strains on both the training infrastructure and Britain's ability to either produce or purchase aircraft for use in the field.

Both systems – training and production – experienced significant organisational changes and rapid leaps in technology and methods while Britain's war machine continued to demand higher volumes and faster output. This chapter summarises the challenges, changes, and results of the twin problems of training naval aircrews and producing maritime aircraft within the context of both the anti-submarine campaign and the growth of British air services during World War I. The impact of the independent RAF on these interrelated subjects also deserves special attention.

The evolution of the RNAS training system

Although the Admiralty paid civilian instructors to train the first four naval aviators at the Isle of Sheppey in early 1911, its own initial naval pilot training system consisted of two separate establishments. The first was the Central Flying School (CFS) at Upavon, which opened in June 1912 under Captain Godfrey Paine, RN. Jointly financed by the Admiralty and War Office and employing a small staff of naval and military instructors, the CFS provided basic flight training for pilots of the Royal Navy and Marines and of the British Army. The first course commenced on 17 August 1912; trainees learned how to fly aeroplanes and accomplished coursework and examinations in map reading, engines, both military and naval operations, signalling, and aerial reconnaissance. The Admiralty soon established its own separate Naval Flying School at Eastchurch, and this facility, under Commander C. R. Samson, conducted both initial and advanced flight training of a particularly 'naval' character. The Airship Service, which only employed seven airships at the start of the war, trained its small aircrew force at Farnborough. By May

1914, the Naval Wing of the RFC had trained 28 pilots at the CFS, 16 pilots at Eastchurch, and 19 airship officers at Farnborough.[2]

Early flight training was extremely primitive during the pre-war years. At the time, the Royal Aero Club flight examination, required for all naval pilots, consisted of three parts; in order to earn their certificate the applicant had to fly a set of figure eights around posts in the ground, attain a height of 50 metres, and land within 50 metres of a point chosen by the examiner. Thus, flight training was geared towards passing this exam and usually saw students soloing after only a few hours of dual instruction. Students and instructors flew on Bristol Boxkites and early Shorts and Farmans. These aeroplanes had only the most basic instruments: a glass to monitor oil flow to the engine, an airspeed pointer on the wing, and a piece of string to coordinate turns. With 50 HP engines, they reached maximum speeds of only 40 miles per hour.[3] After this initial training, new pilots joined their operational squadrons and subsequently learned how to fly machines in service with their units.

The start of the war brought rapid expansion of the flying services and quickly overwhelmed this minuscule training establishment. The Admiralty immediately turned to contracting civilian flying schools, such as those at Bristol, Hendon, and Eastbourne, in order to increase the volume of its initial pilot training programme. The RNAS also recruited civilian pilots who had already earned their Royal Aero Club Aviator's Certificate, offering them advanced seaplane training at Calshot.[4] By the end of 1914, the Admiralty had established a selection and training system for pilots that reflected the Royal Navy's traditionally high standards for obtaining new officers. After approval by an Admiralty selection committee, which considered education, sporting ability, fitness, and of course, social background, a medical examination determined the applicant's physical suitability for flying duty.[5]

Candidates who passed the selection process were graded as Probationary Flight Sub-Lieutenants and began a three-stage training programme. The first element was a very short basic military training course at White City or, later, Sheerness. C. P. O. Bartlett, who later became an RNAS bomber pilot, mentions that the basic course lasted for one week and was limited to training in military drill and discipline.[6] Basic flying training – which included classroom instruction – at the CFS, Eastchurch, Farnborough (airships only), or a civilian flying school immediately followed. Those candidates attending civilian aeroplane schools earned their civilian pilot rating and then transferred to the CFS or Eastchurch to complete the naval basic flying course.[7] Students then progressed to advanced flying training at Fort Grange or Eastchurch for aeroplanes, Calshot for seaplanes, and Kingsnorth for airships. In this higher stage of learning, the student flew aircraft of increased performance and learned advanced flying concepts such as cross-country navigation, bomb dropping, and gunnery – all skills required in a combat pilot.

September 1915 witnessed a change in Admiralty and RNAS leadership and a subsequent reorganisation of the training system. The sweeping

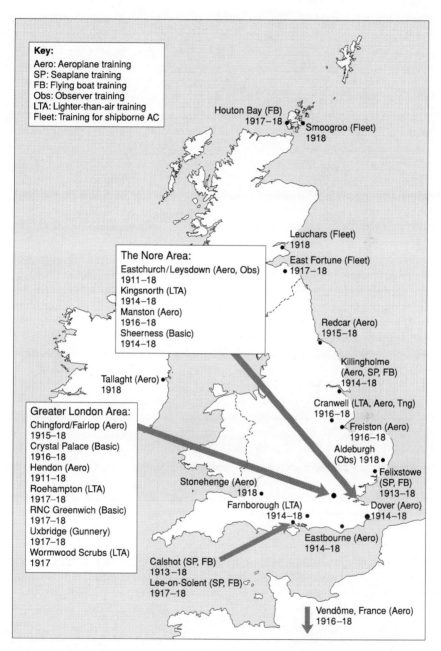

Key:

Aero: Aeroplane training
SP: Seaplane training
FB: Flying boat training
Obs: Observer training
LTA: Lighter-than-air training
Fleet: Training for shipborne AC

Houton Bay (FB)
1917–18

Smoogroo (Fleet)
1918

Leuchars (Fleet)
1918

East Fortune (Fleet)
1917–18

Redcar (Aero)
1915–18

Killingholme
(Aero, SP, FB)
1914–18

Cranwell (LTA, Aero, Tng)
1916–18

Freiston (Aero)
1916–18

Aldeburgh
(Obs) 1918

Felixstowe
(SP, FB)
1913–18

Dover (Aero)
1914–18

The Nore Area:

Eastchurch/Leysdown (Aero, Obs)
1911–18
Kingsnorth (LTA)
1914–18
Manston (Aero)
1916–18
Sheerness (Basic)
1914–18

Tallaght (Aero)
1918

Greater London Area:

Chingford/Fairlop (Aero)
1915–18
Crystal Palace (Basic)
1916–18
Hendon (Aero)
1911–18
Roehampton (LTA)
1917–18
RNC Greenwich (Basic)
1917–18
Uxbridge (Gunnery)
1917–18
Wormwood Scrubs (LTA)
1917

Stonehenge (Aero)
1918

Farnborough (LTA)
1914–18

Eastbourne (Aero)
1914–18

Calshot (SP, FB)
1913–18
Lee-on-Solent (SP, FB)
1917–18

Vendôme, France (Aero)
1916–18

Map 2.1 RNAS and RAF maritime air training establishments.

changes that brought C. L. Vaughan-Lee into the Air Service directorship also included a new supervisory position, the Inspecting Captain of Training, to oversee the rapid expansion of the RNAS training establishment. The new regime instituted standardised training programmes for all aircrew members. A stream of RNAS memoranda spelled out exactly what subjects trainees would study and how they would be examined. Since one of the objectives of the Balfour-Jackson administration was to bring the RNAS back into the fold of the regular Navy, it approved a new finishing course for all officers under aircrew instruction, which included pilots and observers in aeroplanes, sea-planes, airships, and kite balloons. This course was to be conducted at HMS *Daedalus*, the new 'RNAS Training Establishment Cranwell' in Lincolnshire, which opened under Commodore Godfrey Paine's command on 1 April 1916. Additionally, the Admiralty established a policy that called for new pilots initially to remain at home stations in order to increase their flying experience prior to going overseas.[8]

Pilots were not the only crew position requiring training, however. The observer aircrew position at this time was a new concept for the RNAS, and the nature of the aircraft and mission often determined the type of training the observer received, if any at all. An enlisted gunner or W/T operator, with little or no training specific to aerial operations, often occupied the rear seat in early two-seat aeroplanes and seaplanes. Gradually the RNAS began to train these ratings at Eastchurch and other training facilities in more thorough courses.[9] The Admiralty also began to commission Royal Naval Volunteer Reserve Officers as aircraft observers in seaplanes. Fears of having no naval aircraft observer officers on active service after demobilisation forced the Admiralty to recognise the RNAS observer as an official crew position.[10] After March 1916, officer and enlisted observers received flight pay, an RNAS perk previously offered only to pilots.[11] By mid-March 1916 the RNAS had 78 observers, 48 of those in training![12]

The year 1916 saw further changes regarding training flow, rank of train-ees, and command of the training establishment. The RN training centre at Crystal Palace opened during the spring of 1916 and became the basic train-ing establishment for new RNAS officers and most ratings. All new entrants attended a three-week course of instruction there. All aeroplane and seaplane pilots then went to a basic flying training course at one of four RNAS schools. Lighter-than-air pilots did their basic flight training during a free ballooning course at Roehampton. Advanced flight training was accomplished at Cran-well for aeroplane pilots; Calshot, Felixstowe, or Killingholme for seaplane pilots; Kingsnorth for airship pilots; and Roehampton for kite balloon crew-members. Naval observers attended a single four-month course at Eastchurch. After these courses, all flying officer trainees attended the Cranwell finishing school for further classroom instruction and a series of flying and written examinations.[13]

The initial rank system in the RNAS, which gave new entrants immediate rank as Probationary Flight Sub-lieutenants and experienced civilian pilots the rank of Acting Flight Sub-lieutenants, gave its officers an advantage over the rest of the Royal Navy, where officer candidates entered as midshipman. After training, RNAS officers rapidly rose to the rank of Flight Lieutenant, equivalent of a Lieutenant, RN, which otherwise would have taken many years. This system attracted the best candidates; the RNAS was especially successful at recruiting Canadians during this period.[14] The Balfour-Jackson administration found this an unfair head start and in August 1916 changed entry rank for all new RNAS officers to Probationary Flight Officer, equivalent in status and pay to a Midshipman, RN. Finally, the Admiralty placed Commodore Paine – in addition to his directorship of Cranwell – in charge of all RNAS training establishments and abolished the short-lived post of Inspecting Captain of Air Training effective September 1916.[15]

This system of training remained in force in its basic form until early 1918. The only major revision was the opening of a basic officer training course at RN College Greenwich during the summer of 1917, which increased the level of classroom instruction and written examinations than had previously been the norm. Additionally new schools opened in order to increase training output, such as a new airship pilot school at Wormwood Scrubs (early 1917), another basic flight training school at Vendôme (late 1916) in France, another seaplane training base at Lee-on-Solent (early 1918) and a few specialised courses such as the Manston Fighting School, where new pilots learned air-to-air gunnery tactics.[16]

A few personal accounts serve to demonstrate further the evolution of the training system. George Meager attended Wormwood Scrubs for his SS airship training in late 1915 after the free balloon course at Roehampton. The RNAS sent him to navigation, engineering, and gunnery courses at Portsmouth before being posted to his active duty station, Anglesey. He finished training before Cranwell opened.[17] When he later upgraded in other types of non-rigid airships, he simply reported to the depot and flew the new aircraft. There appeared to be no formal training for experienced airship pilots upgrading to new types.[18]

C. P. O. Bartlett entered in April 1916 and was thus caught between training system changes. After only a week of drill and military lectures at White City, he immediately transferred to Chingford for basic flight training. Ground school included lectures on aerodynamics, engines, navigation, and meteorology; students still flew initial flight training on Farman Longhorns and Bristol Boxkites. After soloing (with just under four hours of instruction), he and his fellow students flew more advanced trainers such as the Avro 504K and the BE2C. After four months and eight and a half total flying hours, he graduated and proceeded to the RNAS two-week gunnery course at Eastchurch. He then went to the finishing school at Cranwell, further flight training at Dover in service aircraft, and reported to Dunkirk on 28 September 1916.[19]

The advantages of this system was standardisation; all new pilots and observers would be indoctrinated, step by step, as the Admiralty saw fit and would achieve a minimum standard of proficiency and knowledge. For example, all aeroplane pilots were trained in bomb dropping – in the advanced flying course at Cranwell – in the same manner. All trainees flew the same number of practice bomb runs and were examined to the same standard.[20] Finally, changes to existing syllabi for the various courses could be made relatively easily since each facility focused on a certain aspect of training.

The weakness of the RNAS's system of course was volume. The RNAS lost more officers in combat in 1917 than it did during the period 1914 to 1916 combined and needed to make good its losses as well as provide more personnel for new units.[21] In order to increase the number of trained aircrews the RNAS needed to provide more experienced instructors; thus it had to balance its experienced personnel between training establishments, combat units, and forming squadrons.[22] The finishing course at Cranwell actually served as a bottleneck since facilities to house and educate trainees were physically limited. In early 1916, all of the basic flying schools were graduating a total of 64 pilots per month. By mid-1917 Cranwell was graduating only 90 officers per month for all types of aircraft and the goal for 1918 would be 200 per month.[23] During the first five months of 1917, the RNAS produced only 250 pilots of all types, or an average of 50 per month; poor weather and engine shortages for training aircraft were to blame for the dismal output.[24] At this time Dunkirk's RNAS commander was asking for 60 pilots per month just to maintain the complements of his own squadrons.[25] Field units also complained of a lack of trained observer officers; seaplane pilots flying offshore anti-submarine patrols needed more than just a W/T rating in the back seat.[26] Commanders quickly recognised the requirement for more multi-purpose observers with skills in navigation, ship recognition, bombing, gunnery, and communication.

By the beginning of 1918 – again, with new leadership at the Admiralty – the RNAS was forced to abandon the finishing school concept for its naval aviators. Cranwell continued as an advanced flying training station for aeroplanes and airships, however.[27] At HMS *Daedalus* aeroplane students learned cross-country navigation and aerial photography and other advanced skills in Sopwith Pups and 1½ Strutters and in Bristol Bullets.[28] Airship trainees learned similar skills in small Sea Scout non-rigid airships, which by this time had mostly been relegated to training duties, being replaced by more advanced types in the field.[29]

Finally, as the Royal Navy expanded its use of kite balloons with the fleet, and subsequent use of these tethered 'aircraft' with anti-submarine flotillas, it needed to provide training for such crewmembers. According to Richard Bell Davies, the kite balloon service 'attracted members of the stage and police'.[30] Nevertheless the course for kite balloon observers at Roehampton reflected the Admiralty's high standards of training. Trainees studied the theory of ballooning, naval operations, and communications. In addition to 'flying' their tethered lighter-than-air craft, they also learned how to build and maintain their balloons on land and at sea. Their course called for an extensive battery of examinations prior to qualification.[31]

The RAF training system

The aircrew training system faced two major problems in early 1918: a continued high demand for trained aircrew for active service squadrons and the approaching amalgamation of the RFC and RNAS into an independent air arm. The RFC had a much larger training organisation, but was itself in the process of reorganising its training system. In early 1918 the RFC began to eliminate the distinction between preliminary and advance flying training units, instead adopting 'all-through' training squadrons where both programmes would be merged. Thus at a single location the student would fly basic trainers, proceed to advanced trainers, and finish with their service machine. Brief advanced flying courses in navigation, bombing, or gunnery would follow depending on the final assignment.[32]

The amalgamation therefore brought the smaller RNAS training scheme more into the flow of the RFC's programme. Initially, however, this meant that the RAF's new coastal air groups, which were under the operational control of local naval commanders, continued to conduct maritime flight training since the Air Ministry's new Training Directorate needed time to organise itself.[33] By and large the amalgamation of the training systems was a slow process with changes to maritime aviator training measured incrementally.

Naval aeroplane pilots benefited from the RAF amalgamation by gradually adopting the Gosport method of flight instruction, which had been widely accepted in the RFC by 1917. The RFC institutionalised the teaching techniques of Major Robert Smith-Barry, who had been an RFC combat flyer and became a training squadron commander in December 1916. Smith-Barry replaced older Farman and Short trainers with the relatively advanced Avro 504 aircraft as the students' initial training aircraft. He added an elementary speaking tube system in order to enhance verbal communication between the instructor and the student; engine noise had previously been a serious hindrance to teaching in the air. His instructional techniques were so successful that the RFC established the Gosport Special School of Flying in July 1917. Here new flying instructors were trained how to be effective teachers. Instructors learned what they were themselves doing with the controls and how to teach that to students. Complex aerial manoeuvres such as loops and spins, formerly considered 'stunting', were now encouraged and included during the latter stages of training. These manoeuvres taught students how to recognise their own limitations and those of their aircraft. They also promoted self-confidence and resulted in a better-trained pilot force.[34]

RNAS flight instructors began adopting the Gosport techniques early in 1918 but stopped short of implementing the full system due to a 'prohibitive' requirement for more instructors. The Gosport instructor school became mandatory for RNAS instructors a month prior to the amalgamation.[35] The Gosport system introduced three fundamental changes to previous flight instruction programmes. First, it focused on student confidence – hence the addition of aerobatics and practice forced landings to the syllabus. Second it called for more dual instruction prior to solo and occasional dual flights during the solo phase to 'correct faults and add finish in the later stages of instruction'. Previously, students flew with instructors only until they were safe enough to solo and then essentially learned how to fly on their own. The final, fundamental concept of the Gosport system was an arsenal of superior methods and skills for the instructor. Instructors now thoroughly pre-briefed manoeuvres on the ground prior to demonstrating them in the air. They were encouraged to allow students to recognise and correct mistakes on their own in order to enhance their learning experience. Instructors were reminded to stress the 'how and why' of aircraft control.[36] This system required a much greater investment in numbers of instructors and explains why the RFC had a training establishment of over 100 training squadrons by the end of 1917.[37] Students trained under the new 'all-through' system at the Central Flying School averaged 66.7 hours in less than five months of training during early 1918.[38]

Although advanced seaplane and flying boat pilot and observer training remained relatively unchanged after the amalgamation, with former RNAS officers still commanding training units and instructing students in their new RAF uniforms, the RAF benefited enormously from former RNAS Handley Page aircrew experience. In preparing for the amalgamation of the air services, the RNAS moved their Handley Page training squadron to Stonehenge in January 1918. There it merged with an RFC Training Depot Squadron to become the No. 1 School of Navigation and Bomb Dropping. Now the RAF would benefit from RNAS experience with navigation and long-range bombing – the school was commanded and staffed almost exclusively by former RNAS aircrews – in its build-up of bomber pilots and crewmembers for the projected Independent Force of 'strategic bombers'.[39] Likewise, the RAF's new all-through Handley Page Training Squadron was opened at Cranwell in June 1918.[40] Thus while naval aviation clearly gained from the training techniques and sheer volume of the RFC's training system, the RAF also benefited from the expertise of the former RNAS flyers.

Admiralty reservations – 1918

The loss of the RNAS to the RAF did not mean that the Admiralty surrendered its concerns about naval aviation. On the contrary the Naval Staff's own Air Division was designed to keep a close watch on the new service and liaise with the Air Ministry in the areas of operations, supply, and especially training. Since August 1917, when serious proposals for a new independent air service reached the Admiralty, the training of naval aviators stood out as a pressing matter to the Royal Navy's leaders. The growth of fleet cooperation and anti-submarine patrol squadrons demanded a larger output of naval aviators, requiring a particularly thorough course of training that in some specialties lasted twice as long as similar crew positions in the RFC.[41]

Within three weeks of the RAF's establishment, the Admiralty was already demanding 200 additional aeroplane observers immediately, and 50 per month after that, to be employed with the fleet and in anti-submarine units in Home Waters. In a letter to the Air Ministry, the Board of Admiralty further stated that it felt that anti-submarine training for pilots and observers needed to be improved and was willing to provide lectures by Royal Navy submarine officers for RAF coastal air units. The Air Ministry accepted the offer and patrol squadrons benefited from these lectures beginning in May 1918.[42] Additionally, the Admiralty proposed special anti-submarine courses for both observers and pilots to enhance aircrew effectiveness. As a result, the Air Ministry established courses at Dover (pilots) and Aldeburgh (observers). These advanced courses emphasised rapid signalling skills, low altitude bombing of moving targets, ship recognition, and advanced over-water navigation.[43]

The anti-submarine observer issue remained a concern for Captain F. R. Scarlett, director of the Air Division. Complaining that the RAF's system usually took observer candidates from those officers who had failed the pilot course, Scarlett felt that the importance of maritime observers in the U-boat war meant that these officers should instead be recruited from the 'most intelligent' cadets left after the best became fighter pilots. In his view, career inducements, such as promotion, honours, and command opportunities, were sorely needed to retain quality officers as observers.[44] There is, however, no evidence that these suggestions were heeded at the Air Ministry.

By July and August 1918 shortages of trained pilots and observers at coastal patrol squadrons became critical. Since the personnel demands of the anti-submarine squadrons left few trained observers for duty with the Grand Fleet, the Admiralty had to resort to using naval officers and ratings as temporary observers with ship-borne aircraft.[45] Shortages of flying boat pilots led to RAF proposals of converting Calshot, where both operational and training squadrons of flying boats flew side by side, to a purely training establishment. The Admiralty's Air Division would not agree until the area was reinforced with long-range aeroplane patrol units.[46] Likewise, the RAF investigated shortening the training course for flying boat pilots by skipping the intermediate float seaplane training phase. The float seaplanes, which were more numerous than flying boats and cheaper to maintain, were found to be a more economical way of giving trainees appropriate flight experience and the proposal was dropped.[47] In July, Scarlett voiced his concerns to the Assistant Chief of the Naval Staff over the shortages in RAF training output and the Admiralty passed on these concerns directly to the Air Ministry in early August. The Air Ministry defended the paltry training output by reminding the Admiralty that the importance of anti-submarine operations required the majority of Large Americas in commission, leaving few for training. 'Marine Observer' training was increased and improved as quickly as available facilities would allow, and the Air Ministry promised a higher output by September.[48]

The final training system

By October 1918 the RAF had established a thorough aircrew training programme to meet the needs of all of its missions.[49] The training system provided generalised training as well as applicable specialisation schools and was divided into a number of tracks, based on the student's final, assigned weapon system. From artillery observation aircraft to carrier-based torpedo bombers, the RAF laid out a set of courses to meet the needs of military and naval commanders in the field. A seaplane pilot, for example, would attend six different schools or courses before reaching his field service squadron. A brief review of these programmes, with emphasis on anti-submarine units, provides clear evidence of the RAF's commitment to preparing its aviators for field service.

The anti-submarine pilot programme called for between nine months and a year of training before posting to service units. Pilots experienced three distinct phases of training during this programme. The first phase, which was basically the same for pilots of all types, was strictly limited to ground training and began with eight to ten weeks of basic training at Cranwell. Here the 'cadet' experienced military drill, physical training, and classroom work in signalling, law and other basic subjects. The cadet then attended a six to seven week course at an RAF School of Aeronautics where he would continue with drill and physical training but would add coursework in aircraft engines and rigging, navigation, instruments, photography, and artillery and infantry cooperation. Classroom performance, as well as the specific needs of RAF field units, would determine the cadet's aircraft assignment at this stage. Most cadets then went on to the Ground Armament School at Uxbridge for a basic course in the use of machine guns and bombs. For bomber and seaplane selectees this course lasted three to four weeks. Upon the successful completion of this last course in the first phase of training, the cadet was promoted to 'flight cadet' and sent off to a flying training squadron, the second phase of training.

By late 1918 RAF training squadrons had completely transformed into the 'all-through' training system whereby a single squadron would train the flight cadet in both basic and advanced trainer aircraft types, completing the course by providing instruction in the actual service aircraft. Trainees continued to attend classroom sessions during this period of flight training. For day bomber trainees, the four to five month course included a minimum of 35 hours of flight instruction, eight of those mandated to be on the service aircraft. The Handley Page night bomber training squadron offered a course of the same length, but its syllabus required a minimum of five day and five night flying hours in the Handley Page itself. Seaplane pilots first attended a

Land Training Squadron for three months with a minimum of 20 flight hours followed by a six-week seaplane school for an additional 16 hours. Successful completion of this second phase resulted in the flight cadet being commissioned as a second lieutenant in the RAF. Training did not however end here.

Advanced flying schools, also known as finishing courses, comprised the third and final stage of pilot training. Day bomber pilots attended one of the three-week Aerial Fighting schools followed by a four- to five-week course at one of the three Schools of Navigation and Bomb Dropping. Handley Page pilots only attended the latter advanced course. Seaplane pilots attended a School of Advanced Gunnery for four weeks. Upon completing these finishing courses, the pilot would be awarded his 'wings' and posted to a field service unit. In the case of flying boat pilots, who had undergone the complete seaplane track of training and earned their wings, one final training course in Large America flying would be required prior to field service. Once the Large America pilot became experienced as a co-pilot (who in practice carried out the duties of navigator, bombardier, Lewis gunner, and occasionally relieving the pilot at the controls), he would upgrade to first pilot at the unit.[50]

Aircraft observers went through a shorter but no less rigorous course of instruction. Observer volunteers were initially graded as cadets and attended an eight-week course of basic training and ground school at an Observer School of Aeronautics (at Bath or Reading). Graduation from this single school meant a promotion to 'Observer Flight Cadet' and selection for a number of observer tracks. Cadets who had excelled in W/T performance were selected for anti-submarine observer duty. This track required attending Anti-submarine Observer School at either Aldeburgh (8–10 weeks) or Eastchurch (15–16 weeks). The course thoroughly familiarised observer trainees with the naval environment where they were:

> Taught high rate of visual and W/T signalling, elementary W/T theory, spark W/T sets, navigation chart reading, seamanship, recognition of ships, naval codes and procedure, sea reconnaissance, photography, Lewis gun ground and aerial firing, bombs, bomb-carriers and bomb dropping.

Successful completion meant a second lieutenant's commission, observer's wings, and posting to a service squadron; training time averaged five months. Bomber observers attended three different advanced schools to receive training in gunnery, bomb dropping and navigation, and signalling, but of course lacked the naval flavour of the maritime observer course.

Largely run by former RNAS personnel, airship pilot training retained a particularly naval orientation. Flight cadets attended six weeks of free balloon training at Roehampton. In addition to 45 hours of ballooning in seven flights, this course included 60 hours of ship recognition training, part of which was accomplished with scale models on a training lake, and 50 hours on the international signal code. Lectures on convoy work and submarine hunting prepared the airship pilot for his anti-submarine role. The trainee then attended the Uxbridge Armament School for two weeks. During the first week he studied bombing (to include sights, fusing, arming, loading, and dropping gear) and during the second he learned the vagaries of the Lewis gun. The trainee then attended airship flight training at Cranwell for nine weeks. Here he would receive dual instruction in non-rigid airships and accomplish a minimum of ten hours of solo flight. A number of courses on aircraft, navigation, naval operations, and signalling rounded out the curriculum.[51]

Finally, the RAF had by late 1918 established separate kite balloon courses for army and naval cooperation. The course for 'Kite Balloon Officers for work at sea' drew its recruits from officers and cadets. Since the course description for this track assumed that the trainee had already accomplished basic military training elsewhere, it must be assumed that he was recruited either from active service with the Royal Navy or from other incomplete RAF training programmes, perhaps resulting from a failed course. Nevertheless, a 12-week free balloon course at the No. 1 Balloon Training Depot (Roehampton), still demanding extensive ground schooling and examinations, was followed by four weeks at the No. 1 Balloon Training Base at Sheerness. This finishing course concentrated on kite balloon flying and coursework in naval operations; successful completion led to observer's wings, a second lieutenant's commission (if required) in the RAF, and an active service posting.[52]

How well were RNAS aircrews trained for the missions assigned them? Although anti-submarine patrol and bombing missions against U-boat bases required a specific range of skills, especially familiarity with naval operations and over-water navigation, maritime pilots generally performed well in the field. Monthly *RNAS Anti-submarine Reports* and later *Reports of Naval Air Operations*, which detailed the particulars of every known air attack on submarines between June 1917 and October 1918, rarely mention bombs dropped outside of 50 feet of the aiming point. Likewise, records of air combat between Large America flying boats and German seaplanes demonstrate a high level of air-to-air gunnery skill.[53]

Official reports and memoirs of combatants seldom mention aircraft getting lost owing to poor navigational technique. During a 17-month period at Felixstowe, witnessing 949 patrols from that base, only one pilot had to force land at sea owing to navigational error.[54] Only on limited occasions did field commanders complain of poorly trained new pilots.[55] For example, on the fourth Spider Web patrol in April 1917, Large America pilot T. D. Hallam could not attack a sighted submarine because his co-pilot had not yet been trained in the flying boat's bomb dropping gear.[56] This probably had more to do with the frequent changes to bomb dropping equipment in the field than to the fault of the training establishment.

Still, classroom time in the training environment was limited and senior RNAS officers were never completely satisfied with the level of naval knowledge new aircrew possessed after training. As late as March 1918, the

Director of the Air Division complained that aircrew knowledge of German submarine tactics was weak and proposed that a pamphlet be produced to make up for the lack of training in this area. The proposal resulted in a manual covering known U-boat capabilities and limitations.[57]

At the time of the Armistice, there were 199 RAF training squadrons of all types. This contrasts with 67 naval cooperation squadrons, 10 squadrons in the Independent Force, and 133 for Home Defence and Army cooperation.[58] There were 30,000 pilot pupils under various stages of instruction, including cadets, at the end of the war, and the total number trained in Britain amounted to 22,000.[59] Training aircrew was a costly endeavour in terms of pilots killed and aircraft wrecked in accidents; exact numbers are 'impossible to establish' from available records but some evidence shows that deaths in training were far fewer than had been assumed. Admiral Mark Kerr, who commanded the training-heavy South-west Air Force Area in 1918 as an RAF officer, recalled that 300 pilots were killed in only three months during his tenure, mostly through 'stunting low and other follies'.[60] If this was a standard accident rate, then the cost was heavy indeed.

However, historian Lee Kennett explains that one RNAS surgeon, stationed at a flying training base, recorded that he had seen only four training deaths in two years.[61] Surgeons' logs at other RNAS training bases show that aviation training deaths were relatively uncommon in the Royal Navy, with only 12 deaths each at Chingford and Cranwell in all of 1917.[62] It is difficult to determine an overall comparison of safety records among RFC, RNAS, and later RAF training units, but the advanced training methods and relatively faster aircraft in use by 1918 probably explains the apparent increase in training fatalities. Nevertheless, by 1918 the training of aircrew had become a high priority in the RAF, and pressure from the Admiralty ensured that anti-submarine pilots and observers received a thorough course to prepare them for flying duties.

Maritime aircraft and engine production

Trained aircrew would be useless, however, without sufficient numbers of aircraft to fly on active service. Before examining the specific issue of the production of maritime aircraft and engines, the supply of which was a critical factor in assessing the effectiveness of the air anti-submarine campaign, a brief summary of the British aircraft production in general is necessary.

Although the end of the war saw Britain with what historian John Morrow calls 'the world's largest aircraft industry', a number of factors hampered the nation's aircraft production effort. The first group of issues concerned the capabilities of the aircraft industry, a latecomer relative to other war industries and a field of production that saw expansion from a handful of British firms in 1914 to over 800 by the end of the war. The Admiralty's policy of encouraging civilian firms to design and produce war aircraft and engines, in order to promote healthy competition, often clashed with the War Office's early reliance on the Royal Aircraft Factory. The Admiralty wisely recruited engineer officers into the Royal Naval Volunteer Reserve to serve as quality controllers and liaison officers at the factories. Growth of the industry, where firms gradually learned mass production techniques, was a painfully slow process. By 1917 a dearth of skilled labour, in an industry that was new and reliant on high proportions of such workers (especially in the manufacture of aircraft engines), was exacerbated by the needs of the air services for skilled mechanics, the requirement for skilled workers in Britain's dockyards to replace losses to U-boats, and Army demands for infantrymen. Labour unrest was not uncommon in the aircraft industry either, especially over workers' wages. In mid-December 1917, for example, 50,000 striking aircraft factory workers seriously retarded aircraft production.[63]

The nature of the industry – where firms constructed aircraft of wood frames, fabric coverings, rubber tyres, sheet metal parts, and complicated engine, fuel, and armament systems – added to the complexity of construction and supply. Shortages of raw materials such as hardwood timber (most of which was imported), textiles, dope, ball bearings, and steel meant that aircraft production was especially susceptible to delays if only one of these components did not arrive at the assembly factories as expected.[64] The most critical component, and the one that had the largest impact on production, was aircraft engines, which John Morrow calls 'Britain's Achilles heel in aviation'.[65] During the last five months of 1914 Britain's aero engine firms produced only 99 engines; in 1918 alone the industry delivered 22,088 – an extraordinary rate of growth. Britain relied on imports of French and other foreign engines, especially during the first two years of the war, to make up the difference in engines for its aircraft.[66] However, engine production did not grow as quickly as airframe production; during June and July of 1918, 40 per cent of all aircraft accepted from manufacturers were delivered without engines.[67] Even as late as August 1918, 4,000 aircraft sat uselessly in storage depots awaiting engine deliveries.[68]

The second set of issues hampering production growth stemmed from the difficulties of standardisation. The evolution of aircraft roles, which required new types of machines with specific performance capabilities, and rapid advances in aircraft technology meant that designs changed almost continuously; 'machines became obsolete very quickly'. In January 1917 there were 76 different types of aeroplanes and 32 seaplane models being produced for the RFC and RNAS along with 57 different engine designs. A forced programme of standardisation by the Ministry of Munitions led to only 18 aeroplane, 12 seaplane, and 25 engine models in production by March of 1918 with further planned reductions in design types. Most of these however were proven models that had been around for years where improved performance was squeezed out of existing designs.[69] The Rolls-Royce Eagle engine, with eight versions, and the Large America flying boat, with five, serve to illustrate this concept.[70]

The third area of concern was in organisation; how did the ministries and services organise their efforts in producing aircraft? The early Joint War Air Committee (February to April 1916) and Curzon Air Board (May to December 1916) failed to resolve the issue of interservice rivalry over aircraft production priorities and methods, the responsibility for which initially rested individually with the Admiralty and War Office and not with the Ministry of Munitions. In December 1916, Lloyd George's new cabinet established the Cowdray Air Board, which controlled design and supply aircraft but left policy and operations to the services. By establishing a Department of Aeronautical Supplies (later, the Department of Aircraft Production), whose controller, William Weir, sat on both the Air Board and the Ministry of Munitions Council, the War Cabinet made great strides in consolidating the air production effort. Both Admiralty and War Office aircraft supply sections were absorbed into this new department. The establishment of the Air Ministry in January 1918 and an independent RAF three months later confirmed this arrangement but better linked production and operational policy under one ministry.[71] All of these organisational changes, along with the establishment of the Fifth Sea Lord position to oversee naval aviation, were initiated under Sir Edward Carson's administration of the Navy – leadership considered by one historian to be 'more pliant' than in previous administrations.[72]

Finally, the issue of America's entry in the war was a hindrance rather than a boost to British aircraft production. The planned expansion of American air services meant that the US was less willing to offer Britain her raw materials (such as spruce for aircraft construction) and finished aircraft and engines. The Americans also sought excess French production and now competed with Britain for contracts. With the exception of limited Large America deliveries and promises of new Liberty engines from American industry, Britain had to become largely self-sufficient with her own aircraft production after April 1917.[73]

These overall industrial and organisational factors shaped Britain's effort to produce maritime aircraft for the anti-submarine campaign. Although the general issues surrounding aircraft production are well known – adequately assessed in the air and munitions official histories as well as other recent studies – neither these texts nor any other secondary work make a clear evaluation of the production effort towards constructing the required number of anti-submarine aircraft.[74]

The realisation that aircraft were useful against submarines came too late, and this led to severe difficulties in the generation of adequate numbers of aircraft for this purpose. The Admiralty's requirement for more anti-submarine air units in early 1917, resulting from increasing merchant losses to U-boats and leading to an expansion of squadrons operating over Home Waters, called for increased maritime aircraft production at a time when the British aircraft industry was already overwhelmed and just when the establishment of the Cowdray Air Board meant that the Admiralty lost control of aircraft production priorities. This period also saw increased demands for air support from the BEF; during the last half of 1916 the RFC's planned establishment had been doubled to 106 service and 97 training squadrons![75] America's entry in the war and increased losses to the merchant fleet, as mentioned above, meant a further strain on *materiel* and labour for the aircraft industry. Added to this, the Admiralty, after careful study, had hoped to make the Large America flying boat the primary anti-submarine patrol aircraft – an aircraft which probably more than any other was susceptible to the difficulties of mass production.[76]

Flying boats required skilled craftsmen to build the hulls and their production was necessarily slow. Only a small number of firms – such as Saunders, Dick Kerr, and Short in Britain and Curtiss in America – had the necessary experience in building these designs. Additionally, the large size of these aircraft meant that only two engine types were suitable as power plants: Rolls-Royce Eagles or American Liberties. Even though the Air Board gave Large Americas first priority for Rolls-Royce engines, their meagre rate of production curtailed deliveries of flying boats severely. Eagle engine components had to be hand fitted by experienced specialists and were unsuited for mass production, and Rolls-Royce refused to allow other companies to produce its engines. Eventually Rolls-Royce agreed to allow American firms to mass-produce Eagle components, assembling the engines themselves in Britain, but bureaucratic delays led to failure; no components arrived in Britain prior to the Armistice. Likewise, promises of Liberty engines from America, suffering from its own production difficulties, did not materialise until the closing months of the war and even then on a scale much less than had been hoped. By the end of September 1918, only 980 Liberties had been shipped to England, and these engines were desperately needed not only for Large Americas but also for Handley Page and DH-9a bombers.[77]

A brief statistical review will provide scope to these production woes. Although the programme for the first half of 1918 called for 200 seaplanes and flying boats of all types per month, only 120 arrived on average. An adjustment for the second half of 1918 called for 190 per month; shortfalls continued and monthly deliveries averaged only 127 aircraft.[78] Taken separately, flying boat shortages were even more pronounced. According to one staff officer's diary, by 1 May 1918 flying boat deliveries were behind by 50 per cent, caused by strikes and labour shortages.[79] Ministry of Munitions records for deliveries of Large Americas of all models between October 1917 and July 1918 demonstrate a profound disappointment in the flying boat programme. Added to this was the fact that flying boat hulls typically had a useful service life of only six months due to the nature of operations and therefore required a faster rate of replacement for 'wastage' than was common in other large aircraft (see Table 2.1).[80]

The realisation that flying boat production would never reach desired levels in the immediate future meant that the Admiralty and Air Ministry were forced to rely on float seaplanes – which the Admiralty had hoped would eventually 'die out' as a class – and land-based aeroplanes for the

Table 2.1 Snapshot of maritime aircraft deliveries, October 1917–July 1918

	Oct	Nov	Dec	Jan	Feb	Mar	Apr	May	Jun	Jul
Lg Americas Expected	19	13	23	18	23	24	32	44	46	50
Lg Americas Delivered	4	17	8	5	13	16	18	32	32	22
Short 184s Expected	41	47	26	19	26	20	28	32	34	38
Short 184s Delivered	26	34	27	31	31	20	18	35	31	20

Source: Ministry of Munitions [C.R.R.(S)], Output of Seaplanes, MUN 5/212/1960/26.

Note: Short 184 production shown for comparison.

anti-submarine patrol mission.[81] During the spring of 1918 the Air Ministry agreed to provide as many Large Americas as production would allow and supplement this force with float seaplanes. It also suggested that the Admiralty consider replacing float seaplanes with twin-engine aeroplanes after August 1918. The Admiralty agreed in principle provided they receive their full requirement of flying boats, which was 169 Large Americas for patrol and reconnaissance plus 50 more for a planned bombing offensive of German harbours. The entire programme, as of April 1918, called for a force of 459 seaplanes and flying boats plus 726 aeroplanes for naval cooperation at home and anti-submarine work.[82]

About the same time that these negotiations were taking place, Wing Captain R. M. Groves, a senior RNAS officer seconded to the Department of Aircraft Production, produced a proposal to use DH-6 training aircraft for submarine patrols close to the coast. Groves surmised that even aircraft of such poor performance, unable to carry both an observer and a bomb, would act as a 'scarecrow' against German U-boats, which usually submerged upon sighting any type of aircraft. The Air Ministry and Admiralty accepted the proposal only as a stopgap measure since more suitable aeroplanes, such as the DH-9 bomber, were not yet available to meet naval requirements. Admiral A. L. Duff, the Assistant Chief of the Naval Staff, warned that these aircraft could never replace seaplanes in anti-submarine work.[83] By September 1918, over 300 DH-6s served in anti-submarine patrol squadrons in Britain.[84]

On 30 April the Admiralty returned to the question of their air programme for anti-submarine aircraft. In addition to the 27 planned flights (six aircraft each) of obsolescent DH-6 aeroplanes, they submitted a request to the Air Ministry for 27 submarine hunting aeroplane squadrons (almost 500 aircraft) of the latest design, which did not yet exist. Additionally they asked for 13 flights of the well-armed DH-9 aeroplanes for the south-east coast, where German seaplanes were a serious threat. They also requested an establishment of 180 flying boats and 180 float seaplanes, this second group to be replaced by a similar number of flying boats when available.[85] Although the Air Ministry tried to shrink this programme to provide more aircraft for the Independent Force in August, First Lord Geddes protested loudly, asserting that 'the country could not afford the risk' of predictions of successful bombing operations against U-boat bases and yards being incorrect.[86]

While delays were lengthy, flying boat production finally began to see progress by the close of the war. On 25 April 1918, about a year after their debut with RNAS units, there were only 68 Large Americas of all types in service; 25 July saw an increase to 135 with 238 by 31 October. On 31 October Air Ministry contracts in force called for further deliveries of 174 of H-16, F2a, and F3 Large Americas plus an additional 392 new F5s, a slightly more advanced 'mark' which did not reach field units by the Armistice.[87]

Even naval aeroplanes were susceptible to production problems. The Blackburn Kangaroo aircraft, which largely fulfilled the Admiralty's desire for a twin-engine submarine-hunting aeroplane, suffered from shortages of cypress timber, slowing production.[88] Only 11 were 'on charge' on 31 October 1918. Of the DH-9 and DH-9a aeroplanes that the Air Ministry hoped to offer as replacements for the DH-6, almost 250 of these were available to naval cooperation units by the end of the war, but 90 of those were assigned during the last week of October. Likewise, a squadron of Vickers Vimy bombers, designed as a replacement for the Handley Page O/400, was due to arrive with naval units in November 1918.[89] Seven squadrons of these long-range aeroplanes were programmed to serve with anti-submarine units at home, but the war ended before any arrived at coastal air groups.[90]

In 1918 alone, British industry produced 30,671 land aeroplanes and 936 float seaplanes and ship-borne aeroplanes. During the same period, Britain produced only 411 flying boats of all types. A further 100 flying boats were purchased from manufacturers abroad, mostly American.[91] Between June and November 1918, Eagle engines (of all models) on charge in all RAF units and depots hovered between 1,741 and 2,077 each month, with new production barely making up for losses in combat and flying accidents.[92]

Though used in far fewer numbers than fixed-wing aircraft, lighter-than-air weapon system production deserves mention here. It is important to note that due to its expertise in the field the Admiralty retained production responsibility for airships even after the Air and Munitions Ministries took control over aeroplane, seaplane, and flying boat production. The Admiralty rigid airship programme, witnessing changes in administration and accompanying shifts in policy, suffered from severe production problems. As Robin Higham asserts, these huge craft, as well as their bases, soaked up tremendous amounts of manpower and *materiel*, which the war economy could barely spare.[93] Sheds alone used 6,000 to 10,000 tons of steel over lengthy periods of construction – scarce resources due to the needs of other war industries, especially shipbuilding.[94] Only late in the war did the Admiralty finally get a few rigids, but these were plagued with performance problems.[95] The Admiralty was therefore never able to provide an adequate fleet reconnaissance rigid airship, like the Zeppelins of the German Navy, but instead employed a large force of non-rigid airships for anti-submarine patrol and occasional fleet work.

The Admiralty itself built most of the envelopes for these non-rigids at its own depots, while civilian firms provided the cars and engines. Always under Admiralty control, the production of non-rigid airships was never a particularly difficult issue; the Royal Navy contracted and built what it deemed necessary for operational requirements.[96] In one case, however, the Airship Department, rushed by lack of progress in rigid construction, went into full-scale production of the North Sea type non-rigid before it completed operational testing. Problems with the engine transmission gear, discovered only after 200 hours of flying, led to a fleet-wide modification after full production was underway.[97] However, the end of the war saw Admiralty depots in the process of replacing C and C Star airships with the new SS Twin design and no major problems appear to have affected production.[98]

The final area of naval aircraft production was the naval kite balloon. With the expanding roles of gunnery spotting and reconnaissance with the Grand Fleet as well as proliferation with anti-submarine flotillas and convoy escort forces, these weapon systems became increasingly important to naval operations. Naval kite balloons, which required 100 per cent spares due to their fragile nature, reached a production rate of seven per week by August 1917.[99] By the end of the year the demand was 23 per week. Once again the Admiralty turned to civilian firms to make up for shortages; Admiralty officials provided instruction to waterproof garment manufacturers in how to cut fabric for balloon envelopes. Even here, however, there was competition for *materiel*, since kite balloons were also used by the BEF in France for artillery spotting duties. The Admiralty controlled the design and supply of all balloons until February 1917, when the Department of Aeronautical Supply took responsibility for War Office production. Two months later the Admiralty lost control of its own naval kite balloon production but retained responsibility for supplying certain components such as cotton fabric, hydrogen tubing, and silk for parachutes. By February 1918, however, the total demand for kite balloons for both services had grown to 85 per week and yet again shortages – this time in fabric and proofing materials – slowed production.[100]

The Admiralty, however, appeared to be satisfied with the rate of naval kite balloon production.[101] The probable reason for the absence of complaints to the Air Ministry in the archives is the simple fact that the Admiralty had to provide the winches and other equipment necessary to employ kite balloons aboard their vessels, the fitting of which required time and resources not always available.[102]

Conclusion

This chapter surveyed the interconnected issues of providing trained aircrew and sufficient numbers of aircraft for the anti-submarine campaign in Home

Waters, and a number of conclusions may be drawn from the analysis above. First, training systems for naval airmen progressed rapidly and had reached a high standard early in the war. The RAF amalgamation added refinements but also spurred closer scrutiny from the Admiralty. A noteworthy characteristic of the training and production systems in the RAF was the use of field visits by home training units and production departments to obtain first-hand knowledge of service air unit requirements.[103] Second, the RNAS and RAF had to overcome tremendous difficulties of scale in producing trained men and *materiel*. Except in the case of lighter-than-air craft, demand always outstripped availability. The Admiralty employed civilian firms in both pilot training and aircraft design and production to help alleviate shortages. By the end of the war the Admiralty considered aircraft an extremely high priority in the anti-submarine campaign and fought tenaciously after April 1918 to maintain an effective naval air force in Britain, looking to flood the skies with aircraft in order to deter U-boats from attacking merchantmen. It was unfortunate that this realisation came too late. Specifically, had the Admiralty made more than half-hearted efforts to produce and employ land-based aeroplanes in place of seaplanes earlier, as they were forced to do in 1918 due to production difficulties, more of them might have reached coastal air units during the critical year of 1917.

A December 1917 report probably best summarises the difficulties of the seaplane production effort:

> The deliveries of machines during the year [1917] have been influenced by circumstances dating back to 1916, when the value of aircraft for anti-submarine work was not fully realised, and the production of seaplanes was allowed to fall until deliveries reached a very low figure at the commencement of 1917. Strong efforts were made early in 1917 to raise the production, but the results of these efforts will not be fully felt until 1918. It is hoped that the establishments of the majority of stations will be completed early in the coming year.[104]

Nevertheless, during the last six months of the war, aircraft specifically devoted to anti-submarine operations averaged 189 aeroplanes, 300 seaplanes and flying boats, and 75 airships each day.[105] These numbers, while impressive, must be placed within the context of the overall British air effort. Between 1 August and 11 November 1918 alone, RAF units supporting the BEF in France lost 2,692 aircraft and received 2,647 new aircraft during the same period.[106] Although naval aircrews were reasonably well trained, production of the most effective anti-submarine aircraft, such as flying boats and long-range Kangaroos, was plagued with problems and naval air units continued to rely on less than ideal types to carry out operations against U-boats. The next three chapters will now examine these roles: bombing U-boat bases, patrolling the waterways, and escorting convoys.

3 Attacking 'at source'

Bombing the Flanders U-boat bases

The absence of a coherent British maritime air doctrine – that is, an accepted method of applying the air power of the Royal Naval Air Service – at the start of the First World War comes as no surprise. Theory and history combine to form doctrine,[1] yet at the start of the war the RNAS possessed no combat experience to provide a guide for operating their tiny force of aircraft against the Germans. What roles and missions would the RNAS seek in order to contribute to the war at sea? As the U-boat threat emerged, the air bombardment of German submarine bases was one possible function, but a lack of clear doctrine and sharp disagreements over aircraft employment would limit the effectiveness of such efforts. This chapter will trace the role of maritime aircraft, from the start of the Great War through its closing months, in attacking the German U-boats 'at source' along the Belgian coast.

Attempting to attack German submarines in their own bases was natural for the RNAS, which like its parent Royal Navy was steeped in the mentality of offensive warfare.[2] Unlike the Royal Flying Corps, which first employed aircraft strictly for reconnaissance, the RNAS went beyond this useful yet benign role and experimented in attack capabilities from the start. Pioneers such as C. R. Samson, Arthur Longmore, and R. H. Clark-Hall conducted trials with aircraft armed with machine guns, bombs, and torpedoes even before the Great War erupted. By March 1912 Samson had dropped a 100-lb dummy bomb from a naval aircraft for the first time, to be followed by further experiments in bomb ballistics and sighting apparatus.[3] The Admiralty even went as far as ordering trials that determined the blast effect upon aircraft that dropped bombs from low altitude.[4]

The start of the war witnessed a rapid development of roles and missions for the RNAS. Since the majority of the Royal Flying Corps' operational strength deployed to the continent with the British Expeditionary Force, the Cabinet had no choice but to task the Admiralty with the responsibility for Britain's air defence. In addition to flying air patrols off the coasts and over the dockyards of south-east England, Churchill ordered the RNAS to Dunkirk to aid Royal Marines hastily deployed there and to establish air superiority in Flanders 'with a view to attacking any German airships on their way to England, and preventing any temporary airship base being established within the area defined [100 mile radius from Dunkirk]'. This force was projected to include three squadrons of 12 machines each plus 60 armed cars for ground reconnaissance.[5] The Admiralty correctly assessed the German Zeppelin as a potentially serious threat, perhaps based upon the 25 August 1914 Zeppelin raid on Antwerp, and acted accordingly; the first airship raid on England would be in January 1915. Again, this deployment reflected the offensive spirit of the Royal Navy through attacks against Zeppelins and their bases – before they could strike England. It also demonstrated an acknowledgement of the difficulties of airborne interception of enemy aircraft in the early days of aviation. The birth of over four years of British naval aviation's presence at Dunkirk therefore had little to do with German submarines.

In 1914 alone the RNAS conducted land- and seaplane carrier-based air strikes against Zeppelin sheds at Düsseldorf (22 September and 8 October), Friederichshafen (21 November), and Cuxhaven (25 December). These early offensive operations against the bases of Germany's only long-range air threat resembled later attempts to neutralise German U-boats in their submarine pens at Ostend, Zeebrugge, and Bruges. If one considers later RNAS bombing raids against German naval industries in 1917 and plans for a massive torpedo-plane assault on the High Seas Fleet in their home ports in 1919, it becomes readily apparent that the RNAS strongly believed in attacking enemy forces 'at source' by targeting infrastructure, bases, and centres of support. This philosophy reflected the strong British tradition, and hence naval doctrine, of attacking enemy naval bases during the pre-industrialised wars against Spain, France, and America – an option particularly attractive if threats were difficult to hunt down once at sea.[6] The RNAS therefore employed its parent service's doctrine to make up for its own lack of experience.

After the failure of their August offensive, and as a result of the inconclusive 'race to the sea', the Kaiser's forces occupied Zeebrugge and Ostend on 15 October 1914, the area eventually forming the right flank of the German trench system. The entire Flanders coast, from the front line near Nieuport to the Dutch frontier, soon became a massive coastal fortress dominated by the harbours of Ostend, less than nine miles east of the trenches, and Zeebrugge, a further 12 miles eastward. Eight miles inland from Zeebrugge was the port of Bruges, which was linked to both Zeebrugge and Ostend by a system of canals and would later earn the status of an Imperial Dockyard of Germany.[7] Threatening sea communications in the English Channel, these facilities would become a major thorn in the side of the Royal Navy, since the Germans would soon exploit them as forward bases for submarines, seaplanes, and destroyers. The benefit to the Germans was enormous; Zeebrugge was only 65 miles from Dover, and 2½ days closer (300 miles) for a U-boat travelling to its patrol areas than bases in Germany.[8]

In September 1914 the German Admiralty asked their U-Boat Inspectorate to examine the possibility of building small, rail-transportable submarines that could be produced rapidly, in order to take advantage of forward bases in

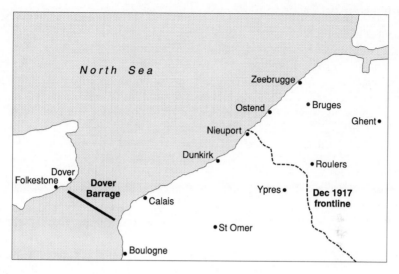

Figure 3.1 The Belgian coast.

Flanders and in the Adriatic. On the same day that the army occupied the Flanders ports, the German *Kaiserliche Marine* authorised a contract for 15 Type *UB* coastal submarines. Although the contracted building time was only four months, the first of these boats was completed in only 75 days.[9] Deployment to Belgium followed in early 1915, and by the last two years of the war the Flanders-based U-boat flotillas would account for one-third of all Allied shipping losses in the waters around Britain.[10] Thus, Ostend, Zeebrugge and Bruges would form the focus of effort for the British naval forces of the Dover Patrol. Four years of mining, net barrages, shelling the ports, blocking attempts, and air attack met with varying degrees of success, but the Flanders U-boats would persevere in their attacks on shipping until the advance of the Allied armies forced them to evacuate in October 1918.

The existence of the Flanders bases presented the RNAS at Dunkirk with an opportunity to take further offensive action. Other than random, disorganised patrol work during the first years of the Great War, early bombing attempts aimed at Ostend, Zeebrugge, and Bruges were the first systematic efforts to use British aircraft against German submarines. These initial air strikes may be characterised as mere raids inflicting limited damage to dockyards, support facilities, and vessels. As greater numbers of aircraft with improved carrying capability became available to the RNAS, and later the Royal Air Force, the opportunity to neutralise these bases from the air showed potential but was lost to conflicting aims. It is the thesis of this chapter that using aircraft to bomb U-boat bases was the least effective use of maritime aviation against German submarines because the British never made this bombing campaign a priority for resources, even when advancing technology offered promising tools.

Early attempts

The operational aircraft of the RNAS, which had deployed from their base at Eastchurch to Dunkirk during the opening months of the war, were an assortment of Nieuports, Farmans, Avros, Sopwiths, and other types. Typical bomb loads comprised a handful of 16- or 20-lb bombs; such limited capability did not deter the pilots of the RNAS. One advantage available to the naval airmen at Dunkirk was their proximity to the German facilities in Flanders. The closest target, Ostend, was less than 30 air miles from Dunkirk. Likewise, Bruges and Zeebrugge were each approximately 40 miles away. Additionally, the major cities of Ghent (60 miles), Brussels (87), and Antwerp (90) were easily within reach.[11]

The Eastchurch station commander, Wing Commander C. R. Samson, led the initial deployment of the RNAS to Dunkirk. Operations included attacks on Zeppelin bases, air and motor car reconnaissance of the Belgian coast, and cooperation with the British Expeditionary Force.[12] By late October 1914 the Admiralty had received reports of German plans to develop submarine bases along the Flanders coast. Samson's force attacked rail lines leading into Bruges in early November – possibly the first 'air interdiction' missions of the war – and conducted a number of air observation sorties over the harbours.[13] Throughout December and January the pilots and observers braved poor weather conditions and increasing enemy anti-aircraft fire in order to keep watch over a growing German naval presence in Belgium, and in late January conducted their first attacks against enemy U-boats temporarily berthed at Zeebrugge.[14]

Germany's announcement of a 'danger zone' around Britain in February 1915 led to increasing concern over the development of the Flanders submarine bases.[15] This concern was manifested in a 'maximum effort' of RNAS units from Dunkirk, Dover, and seaplane carriers. The Director of the Air Department, Captain Murray Sueter, was able to organise such a project because – as the reorganisation of February 1915 allowed – he now had personal control over all RNAS operations and reported directly to the Board of Admiralty.[16] This command arrangement gave Sueter unprecedented authority to lead and administer this infantile yet potentially powerful air arm.

Sueter planned to use forces from five naval air stations and a seaplane carrier for his assault on the German bases in early February. Dunkirk, Dover, Eastchurch, Hendon, Felixstowe, and HMS *Empress* each contributed contingents, a total force of 22 aeroplanes and 12 seaplanes. A key innovation of this planned raid was that each flight of aircraft was allocated a specific target of military value, with each group attacking from different directions.[17] Sueter launched his first attempt on 11 February, but snow and thunderstorms hampered all but three of the aircraft. The majority of the force landed at Dunkirk where Samson took over direct command. On the next day he led 21 aircraft over the German lines, and 15 succeeded in bombing their planned targets without a single aircraft being lost. Again on 16 February, this time with the help of eight French bombers, Samson attacked coastal gun positions and the Ostend harbour. Four British pilots – three killed and one interned in Holland – were lost to German anti-aircraft fire during this raid.[18]

Although the February 1915 raids might appear tiny when compared with modern air combat,[19] at the time they represented a tremendous leap forward in aerial operations. Damage to Ostend, Zeebrugge and their associated gun emplacements, rail lines and support facilities, was considered significant; however, only one submarine was reported as damaged.[20] RNAS aviators had learned the value of low altitude bombing, appreciated the need for larger bombs and aircraft with better payloads, gained a respect for German anti-aircraft fire, and discovered the weaknesses of seaplanes attacking targets ashore.[21]

Samson remained at Dunkirk with his Eastchurch force until March 1915, when Sueter ordered most of the command, now called No. 3 Wing, to the eastern Mediterranean for the Dardanelles expedition. Wing Commander Arthur Longmore and his No. 1 Wing, many of whom participated in the February raids, arrived at St Pol from England to continue the work of attacking aeroplane and Zeppelin bases, naval cooperation, attacks on 'Submarine Building Yards' and other facilities, and developing wireless and photo-reconnaissance techniques. Seaplanes were for the most part confined to anti-submarine patrols and over-water reconnaissance.[22] At a time when there was little distinction between 'bomber', 'fighter', and 'observation' aircraft, Longmore's shore-based aircraft concentrated their limited capabilities on U-boat bases and Zeppelin sheds through the rest of the year.[23]

In August 1915, Commander Charles L. Lambe, RN, took command of the RNAS units in the Dunkirk and Dover areas. Although not an aviator himself, Lambe had been the captain of HMS *Hermes*, the parent vessel of the RNAS and an operational seaplane carrier, when she was torpedoed and sunk by *U27* on 31 October 1914. He was a torpedo specialist who possessed both operational experience with the fleet and staff expertise from two tours in the office of the Director of Naval Ordnance.[24] Lambe would serve both the RNAS and the RAF as commander of British maritime aircraft in Flanders until the last month of the war.

Lambe took command during a period of modest expansion of the naval air forces at Dunkirk and Dover, with Longmore's No. 1 Wing soon to be one of three wings in the area. Indeed the change in the Royal Navy's top leadership, resulting from the controversial resignations of Fisher and Churchill over the Dardanelles fiasco in May, had also brought about a dramatic shift in policy and organisation of air units in late July 1915. As mentioned in the Introduction, the less colourful regime of A. J. Balfour and Admiral Sir Henry Jackson was intent on curbing the independence of the RNAS by taking away all of the air units from Sueter's Air Department and giving control directly to local naval commanders. Rear-Admiral C. L. Vaughan-Lee, who 'knew nothing about aircraft and flying' but was acceptable to their Lordships, became the new Director of the Air Service at the Admiralty.[25] In September he became responsible for administration and personnel in the RNAS, while Sueter was relegated to the position of Superintendent of Aircraft Construction.[26] This de-centralisation of operational control was a beneficial decision in terms of giving each regional admiral his own air support, with a clear command structure at the tactical level, but less helpful for coordinating air assets within an operational theatre, and in the end would hamper the air campaign against the Flanders U-boat bases.

The direct result for Lambe's force at Dunkirk was that it now became subordinated to the Vice-Admiral Dover Patrol – Sir Reginald H. S. Bacon. Lambe and Bacon had both served in the 1897 punitive expedition to Benin City and worked together again when Bacon commanded the Naval Ordnance Department.[27] The surviving correspondence between Lambe and Bacon shows that the two officers communicated regularly, though not always without disagreement, as the following pages will demonstrate.

Prodded by the Air Department, Lambe's first major task was to obtain permission to add two new wings and associated aerodromes in the Dunkirk area in order to attack German facilities in Flanders during the spring of 1916. Specific targets for this bomber force were to be objectives of naval and military importance in Belgium: canal locks, bridges, railway stations, airship sheds, and aerodromes. With the Dardanelles operations winding down and the Home air defence mission returning to the War Office in early 1916, Bacon and the Admiralty agreed to the expansion programme, stipulating that the new units would be used to aid the RFC in France when a lull in naval work permitted.[28] Lambe also revised the RNAS's wing and squadron organisation. Formerly wings consisted of six squadrons of six aeroplanes; the new scheme, bringing the RNAS more in line with the RFC's organisation and alleviating a shortage of qualified commanders, called for squadrons of 12 to 18 aeroplanes with wings of two to four squadrons.[29]

Lambe, however, faced a number of challenges in trying to build an adequate bombing force at Dunkirk. Although the Admiralty approved the plan for three wings at Dunkirk, it set out to establish a joint strategic bomber force with the French in eastern France. A new No. 3 Wing, RNAS, was formed at Luxeuil during summer 1916 and assigned the task of attacking economic targets, such as iron works and factories within Germany, that were related to naval production.[30] After a spell of poor weather, a lack of resources, and pressure from the RFC, this luxury of a naval strategic bombing force had to be disbanded by April 1917.[31] Lambe, however, pressed on with his own expansion by providing a nucleus of experienced flyers from established units to his two new wings. While No. 1 Wing continued operations with aircraft at St Pol, No. 5 Wing established its base at Coudekerke in March 1916. No. 4 Wing, now released from air defence duties at Eastchurch, moved its squadrons to Petit Synthe the following month.[32] The RNAS presence in France and Belgium would now comprise a complex of several aerodromes centred on Dunkirk.

Another challenge to Lambe's build-up was his own commanding admiral. As the Vice-Admiral Dover Patrol, with the German-held ports of Flanders on his immediate flank, Bacon was responsible for one of the most difficult districts in the Royal Navy. In early May 1916, his forces completed an extensive anti-submarine minefield off the coast of Belgium, consisting of 18 miles of mines and nets that were guarded during the day by surface patrols. According to Winston Churchill, an 'immediate dimunation[*sic*]' of losses to merchant ships and of U-boat activity followed, but the apparent success was due to Scheer's frustrated withdrawal of U-boats from the commerce campaign rather than Bacon's mine barrage.[33] Thus, as summer approached, Bacon thought he was gaining the upper hand against the Flanders U-boats.

As Neville Jones clearly proves in *The Origins of Strategic Bombing*, Bacon had little time for talk of independent bombing operations from Dunkirk. Again, when Balfour and Jackson rescinded the RNAS's brief operational independence in July 1915, they returned Dunkirk air units to the operational control of their local naval commander. The aircraft under Bacon's command were to be used to support naval operations, such as in support of monitor bombardments along the Belgian coast. Otherwise, he was committed to using his air assets to support the BEF as much as he reasonably could.[34] Even the short-lived Joint War Air Committee listed operations with Bacon's monitors first in Lambe's list of duties, with attacks on submarine bases and enemy aerodromes as secondary priorities.[35]

Meanwhile, the Germans prepared the Flanders ports against air attack. As early as March 1916, the Admiralty had received intelligence reports of hardened submarine shelters near the Mole at Zeebrugge. Actually built during the summer of 1915, these shelters were reportedly armoured with plate and concrete and were camouflaged to blend in with the surrounding stonework.[36] Additionally, anti-aircraft defences continued to mature.

While Lambe continued his build-up of forces around Dunkirk during the spring, he sent limited raids against German naval facilities and aerodromes. Most of these attacks, carried out by French-made Breguets and Caudrons and the new Sopwith 1½ Strutters and Short Bombers, were conducted at night in order to avoid German anti-aircraft fire.[37] Bacon was initially happy with the work of his air forces, reporting to the Admiralty that bombing 'had some value in producing unrest and causing special precautions to be taken which must prejudice the general work' and in increasing refit and repair times for German vessels.[38] In his testimony to the Air Board on 8 June 1916, Lambe also pointed out that his night bombing raids had a 'moral effect', which he thought to be 'considerable'. Additionally, Lambe had hoped that by attacking at night he could catch German aircraft in their sheds when raiding enemy aerodromes. A final benefit from his new bombing campaign was the diversion of German resources, both anti-aircraft guns and defensive aircraft, from other parts of the front.[39]

However, by late May Bacon's opinion of the RNAS at Dunkirk was taking a turn for the worse. Crews sent to bomb Mariakerke Aerodrome, near Ghent, on 21 May 1916 could not see the target due to poor weather conditions and instead dropped their bombs on Ostend Docks. Bacon saw this type of raid as counterproductive to his overall scheme of operations. Three days later he wrote to the Admiralty that he was

> determined to stop this useless and most pernicious promiscuous bomb-
> ing which inevitably leads to the strengthening of anti-aircraft guns and
> searchlights and to no useful results. The consequence is that when the
> time arrives for serious military operations the assistance of the air craft is
> compromised by the defences having been strengthened and the anti-
> aircraft crews practised, whereas if they had been left alone their own
> weaknesses would never have been discovered by the enemy.[40]

Two weeks later, in a report on air operations in Belgium, Bacon stated that his aviators were just starting to understand that air operations were to be subordinated to land and sea campaigns. He also warned that these 'indis-criminate bombing' missions were 'useless' and even 'harmful to well thought-out Military operations' because they provoked enemy retaliation, caused a strengthening of German defences, and were ineffective unless massed.[41] As a result of this frustration with his airmen, Bacon banned bomb-ing operations from Dunkirk, unless necessary to support the BEF.[42]

Although Bacon's decision stemmed from purely tactical reasons, he may have been influenced by the intensifying debate within the Royal Navy con-cerning the RNAS. The First Sea Lord, Admiral Sir Henry Jackson, thought the RNAS was poorly disciplined and had grown too quickly. He clearly preferred a smaller, efficient RNAS in order to reduce expenditure, which he thought had previously been 'wasteful'.[43] Some members of the Admiralty Board even questioned the usefulness of bombing operations from Dunkirk.[44]

Throughout the rest of the summer, Lambe's Dunkirk squadrons flew defensive patrols over the front and above Bacon's ships, but these were hindered by poor weather. The bombers flew even less often.[45] The lull in operations had served to increase Lambe's pilot pool and available aircraft by protecting them from combat losses. His pilot force had tripled in size since he took command, and numbers of new Sopwith 1½ Strutters grew steadily.[46]

Haig's Somme Offensive, which began on 1 July 1916 and would come to an exhausted end in November, initially saw only limited RNAS participa-tion due to the distances involved, poor weather conditions, and the lack of a coordinating infrastructure between the RNAS and RFC. On 29 August, Lambe visited HQ 2 Brigade of the RFC to discuss RNAS cooperation with the upcoming 15 September push on the Somme. Bacon subsequently approved a plan to allow RNAS aircraft to bomb enemy aerodromes at the northern end of the front.[47] On 3 September, Lambe launched his first of many attacks on Ghistelles Aerodrome, south of Ostend, in order to draw German air assets away from the Somme. Additionally, in October the RFC asked for Admiralty assistance in providing a full squadron of RNAS fighter aircraft for service with the BEF. Lambe responded by drawing a flight from each of his three wings in order to create No. 8 Squadron, RNAS, which he promptly sent to the RFC.[48]

The autumn of 1916 brought closure to the first phase of the RNAS's campaign against the German U-boat bases in Flanders. Attacks were limited by the capabilities of the available aircraft, shifting Admiralty policy, and the reservations of the Vice-Admiral Dover Patrol. In November 1916, Lambe reorganised his wings into numbered 'fighter' and 'bomber' squadrons in order to mirror RFC organisation.[49] During the following month, he managed to gain the Admiralty's approval for a further expansion to five fighter squadrons, two bomber squadrons and a reconnaissance squadron to be distributed among his three wings. His reason for the high proportion of fighter squadrons was the need for air superiority through almost constant offensive fighter patrols, in order for the bombers and spotters to operate safely.[50] Such increased growth would have never happened under Jackson's regime; it was only possible through Jellicoe's succession as First Sea Lord in December 1916. These organisational changes, along with the loosening of Bacon's ban on bombing, would provide the opportunity for Lambe to begin operations against Ostend, Zeebrugge, and Bruges in earnest in 1917.

1917: Bacon, Bruges and the BEF

After Jutland the German Navy, frustrated by inactivity, began to send High Seas Fleet destroyer flotillas temporarily to Zeebrugge in order to harass Bacon's surface patrols. On 26 October 1916 German destroyers surprised a group of British patrol craft, sinking a destroyer, six drifters, and an empty transport without loss to themselves. Between late January and mid-April 1917, these destroyer forces tried repeatedly to wage what historians have called a 'guerrilla war against the British in the Straits of Dover' by sending destroyers on night raids into the English Channel, but they ultimately failed to upset the strategic balance.[51]

These attacks were just what Lambe needed to persuade Bacon into resuming bombing attacks against the Flanders bases. In reaction to the first German destroyer raid, Bacon allowed Lambe to attack Zeebrugge and Ostend in early November 1916. Lambe's orders to his bomber squadrons specified that the object of the attacks were to destroy German naval craft – to include submarines – and 'render these bases unsafe'.[52] In November his pilots conducted six raids on Ostend and five against Zeebrugge.[53] These November raids against German destroyers were the heaviest of the year and, according to Canadian official historian S. F. Wise, succeeded in forcing the Germans to withdraw one of the raiding flotillas back to Germany. 'Here RNAS Dunkirk had made one of its most useful contributions of 1916.'[54] Poor weather and extremely cold temperatures grounded the bombers through December and January thus limiting further attacks.

On the second day of February, Lambe issued specific orders to attack

Bruges, new to the target list; an air reconnaissance the day before had shown that German destroyers and submarines had been trapped in the harbour there as a result of the cold temperatures freezing the lock gates of the canal system.[55] From 3 to 9 February, Lambe's Sopwith and Short bombers flew five raids against Bruges Harbour, damaging ammunition sheds but failing to destroy any vessels. The sub-zero temperatures hampered the bombers by freezing the oil in their engines. During the 3 February raid, for example, five of eight Short bombers had to abort the mission for engine problems, while only two of eight Sopwiths that had launched reached the target area.[56] The Germans retaliated with air raids against Dunkirk, but RNAS bombers continued attacks against Bruges in mid-February, adding a German bomber base near Ghent to their list of objectives.

March saw no operational flying due to continuing poor weather – a thick bank of fog enshrouding most of Flanders. Thus, during the first quarter of 1917, the RNAS bomber units around Dunkirk dropped a total of 348 bombs, over six tons of munitions, on naval objectives and German aerodromes in Flanders – all during the month of February.[57] Not a single submarine was destroyed. Weather had severely curtailed operations and intense anti-aircraft fire had forced the bombers to attack from higher – and therefore less accurate – altitudes and usually at night.[58] The bombs themselves were relatively light; other than a few 65- and 100-lb bombs, most of the ordnance dropped were the readily available 16-lb and Le Pecq (20-lb) munitions which, while good for destroying wooden buildings, were simply too light to damage naval vessels armoured with steel plate. Frustrated with the weather and his bombers' poor performance, Lambe once again reorganised and prepared for a renewed campaign in the spring.

Meanwhile, the RFC had continued its demands on Lambe's fighter force and by April had 'borrowed' no fewer than four naval fighter squadrons for service with the BEF.[59] Nevertheless, Lambe pressed forward with a new scheme of organisation whereby his three wings were arranged functionally with No. 1 Wing working with the Dover Patrol, No. 4 Wing maintaining fighter patrols over the fleet and providing fighter escorts, and No. 5 Wing serving as a bomber force with two squadrons (No. 5 and No. 7). The disbandment of No. 3 Wing, the long-range strategic bomber force at Luxeuil, provided Lambe with an influx of trained pilots to aid his efforts.[60] Although the reorganisation allowed the wings to focus on training and operations in their functional areas, new aircraft designs arriving during the spring of 1917 made it essential. Advances in technology, which produced fighters of increased agility and bombers of increased speeds, ranges, and payloads, would no longer allow the survival of general-purpose aircraft.

Radical improvements in performance enabled two important bomber aircraft to specialise in this manner. The DH-4, first introduced to No. 5 Squadron in April 1917, could outrun most German fighters then in service and defend itself admirably if any caught up. Its speed allowed No. 5 Squadron to return to day bombing operations, after being forced to bomb mainly at night with the less capable Sopwith 1½ Strutter.[61] The DH-4's respectable bomb load, at 460 lbs, was a welcomed addition to the striking power of the RNAS.

The more important innovation, however, was the introduction of the mammoth Handley Page twin-engine bomber. With two 250 HP Rolls-Royce engines, it could carry a 'normal load of 14 112-lb bombs'. By early April, No. 7 Squadron had already acquired five Handley Pages to supplement its seven Short bombers.[62] In late April, Lambe sent his new Handley Pages against German destroyers off the coast, but after losing a Handley Page to a German seaplane during a daylight raid he confined them to night flying in order to minimise losses to these precious machines.

During the second quarter of 1917, superb flying weather combined with easing restrictions on bombing led to a tremendous increase in ordnance delivered on German targets. Even though the phasing-in of new bombers was a gradual process, the increased carrying capacity of the new DH-4s and Handley Pages also contributed to a quarterly total of 1,801 bombs dropped on German objectives of all types for a weight of 48 tons.[63] This represented an eight-fold increase from the first quarter of 1917, and demonstrates the importance of good weather for early air operations. During the second quarter of 1917, the RNAS at Dunkirk conducted 13 raids on Bruges, 14 on Ostend, and 16 on Zeebrugge.[64] These figures represent the importance of naval targets at a time when losses to unrestricted submarine warfare, a German tactic begun in earnest on 1 February 1917, were at their peak. Additionally, if one examines the period between 24 April 1916 and 17 June 1917 it is evident that of the raids that Bacon allowed, the majority of targets were naval objectives. During this period Bruges absorbed over 22 tons of bombs, with Ostend and Zeebrugge receiving 21 and 13½ tons respectively. With the exception of the aerodromes at St Denis Westrem and Ghistelles, which received 10 and 3½ tons respectively, the RNAS devoted about a ton or less to all other targets they attacked.[65] It is also noteworthy that during the months of May, June, and July 1917, Dunkirk squadrons did not lose any bombers to combat losses.[66]

The introduction of the Handley Page nearly coincided with the deployment of Germany's own heavy bomber, the Gotha, which was designed to carry out raids against England. In March 1917 the *Luftstreitkräfte*, or German Army Air Force, established aerodromes – mostly in the vicinity of Ghent – for these bombers to carry the war to England's home front, just as the unrestricted submarine campaign had done.[67] Gotha raids on the southeast of England in May, followed by shocking attacks against London in June, led to two major developments that would affect the RNAS at Dunkirk significantly. The first was a public outcry for defence of the homeland; Lambe's major role in this development would be a shifting of effort to bombing German bomber aerodromes at the expense of attacking the Flanders ports. Apparently, direct attacks on British civilians were seen as more of a threat to England's war effort than the U-boat menace during the summer months of 1917. The second development was the eventual establishment of an independent air service, the new Royal Air Force under an independent Air Ministry, which would officially come into being on 1 April 1918.

Just as Lambe's bomber strength reached a full squadron of DH-4s and almost two of Handley Pages, the campaign was diverted again by Haig's 31 July 1917 offensive near Ypres. In addition to hampering the ability of the Gothas to attack England, helping the BEF was now a second reason for bombing German aerodromes, which the RNAS took on with vigour. The Handley Pages helped to push up the quarterly tonnage during July through September to over 185 tons, 160 of those dropped by the big bombers.[68] While the DH-4s of No. 5 Squadron attacked by day, the Handley Pages of Nos. 7 and 7a Squadrons attacked at night for a round-the-clock campaign designed to check the bombing against England and draw German air defences away from the Ypres front.[69] These squadrons also bombed German rail stations and ammunition dumps behind the lines in order to hamper the movement and supply of enemy troops opposing Haig. Additionally, as of July 1917 five of Lambe's fighter squadrons were serving under direct orders of the RFC further to the south, a severe drain on his pilot pool.[70] While Major-General Hugh Trenchard, commander of the RFC in France, complained about the shortages of pilots for the naval fighter squadrons under his command, he should have welcomed Lambe's bombing efforts, most of which were devoted towards non-naval objectives.[71]

Although German night Gotha raids on England and the Passchendaele Offensive made aerodrome attacks a high priority, RNAS bombers did occasionally fly against naval targets during the third quarter of 1917. Out of 137 bombing raids during the quarter, 79 were aimed at aerodromes, 15 at Bruges, 12 at Ostend, and 9 at Zeebrugge. The remaining two-dozen attacks sought various military targets including railway centres and ammunition dumps. The RNAS employed an average of 4.5 aircraft per raid.[72] The end of the quarter serves to illustrate the new priorities clearly: during the last two weeks of September, Lambe sent only three raids to Zeebrugge with none against Bruges or Ostend. Twenty-one attacks were made against other targets.[73]

By August 1917, the Handley Page had proven its worth as a night bomber with the RNAS. Pilots and observers had grown accustomed to the local landmarks in northern Belgium and could easily navigate at night regardless of the moon's illumination.[74] Up to this point, no Handley Page bombers had been lost to German fighters, except the aircraft lost to a German seaplane in April, during either day or night bombing missions.[75]

The Germans, however, did not remain idle as the RNAS attacked their aerodromes; Lambe's attacks generated a severe response. The *Luftstreitkräfte* conducted a series of night aerodrome raids against the British around Dunkirk during the summer and autumn of 1917, using parachute flares to illuminate their objectives.[76] Attacks were persistent and effective. A raid on 6/7 July damaged 12 aircraft at Bray Dunes, while a full week of attacks against the depot at St Pol in late September caused severe damage. On 24 September, a direct hit on a hangar destroyed 140 aircraft engines, while a raid on the night of 1 October, during which the Germans dropped over 100 bombs, destroyed 23 aircraft, three engine test sheds, and a bomb dump. These attacks put the depot 'out of commission' and as a result Lambe had to distribute depot level work on aircraft and engines to the squadron aerodromes.[77] British night bombers returning from missions often had to orbit overhead or land on alternate landing strips on the beach while their own aerodromes were being bombed.[78] Such attacks gave the RNAS's own counter-air bombing campaign much more impetus.

Additionally, German anti-aircraft defences of the naval facilities had become imposing by summer 1917; even the night bomber crews feared their reach. After the war, one squadron commander wrote that 'officers were often heard to say that they would rather carry out long distance raids into Belgium or Germany than do a short flight over Bruges'.[79] Although Bacon's naval forces could shell Ostend and Zeebrugge, Bruges could only be attacked from the air due to its inland position.[80]

The autumn of 1917 witnessed a continued emphasis on supporting Bacon's monitor bombardments, occasional bombing raids on targets in northern Germany and Antwerp, and the now regular attacks on German aerodromes, especially after a new series of night Gotha attacks against England started in September. Bacon had hoped, yet ultimately failed, to destroy the lock gates at Zeebrugge with gunfire from his monitors in order to empty the Zeebrugge-Bruges Canal, which was above sea level.[81] Handley Page bombers also attempted to knock out these gates in late September but succeeded in only damaging them. The monitor attacks throughout the autumn were a poor substitute for a naval landing, officially cancelled in October, that Bacon had been planning in conjunction with Haig's Ypres Offensive.[82] The offensive near Ypres had made only slight gains along Passchendaele Ridge and failed to break through to Roulers and Bruges beyond.

November 1917 brought poor winter weather and allowed Lambe more time to rest his aircrews and plan for the upcoming bombing operations during the spring. As he received his loaned fighter squadrons back from the RFC, he began to rotate them back to the Dover area for two to three months' rest. This he could not do with his handful of bomber units, but he encouraged his commanders to grant leave liberally during the winter months 'with a view to preparing for the increase asked for by next Spring'.[83] The increase Lambe referred to was his proposed expansion of the three wings under his command to include eight fighter, one reconnaissance, two light bomber (DH-4), four heavy bomber (Handley Page) and one training squadrons. On 30 November, the Secretary of the Admiralty informed Vice-Admiral Bacon that the Board had approved an increase to the Dunkirk air forces to Lambe's requested establishment.[84]

The last quarter of 1917 brought little change to the lack of emphasis on attacking U-boat bases. RNAS bombers flew only 12 raids against Bruges between 1 October and the end of the year, with one attack on Ostend and three against Zeebrugge.[85] The total tonnage of bombs delivered on German targets of all types decreased to 101½ tons, down from 186 tons the previous quarter.[86] Weather had hampered the bombing raids, but the increased tempo of operations since the spring had taken its toll. Indeed, the RNAS at Dunkirk even requested that Bacon approve a sharp decrease in bombing raids due to pilot shortages in mid-November. Bacon approved, commenting that 'military targets assigned to you when our Army was on the coast [awaiting the aborted landing] must be discarded, and aerodromes attacked when possible. The monitors on patrol will still require support.'[87]

In *The War in the Air*, H. A. Jones summarises the RNAS effort at Dunkirk in 1917 through a tally of bombing objectives listed with their respective tonnage. Of a 344½-ton annual total, 80 tons were aimed at Bruges, with 30 tons on Zeebrugge and 10 tons on Ostend. Railways bore a total of 88½ tons while the German aerodromes of Flanders absorbed 114 tons.[88] An Air Historical Branch summary of the campaign paints a slightly different picture: '211 tons were released over targets of military importance and 123 tons on objectives pre-eminently of naval interest'.[89] Sir John Jellicoe's later assertion that 'aerial bombing attacks . . . had as their main objective the destruction of enemy vessels lying in these [Flanders] bases' during 1917 therefore represented a common misperception.[90] As one RNAS staff officer wrote in December 1917, 'The opinion is held by many officers, and particularly by those best qualified to judge, that the submarine activity on the Belgian coast might have been affected adversely in no small measure if the whole Naval bombing resources available in 1917 had been devoted to this single purpose.'[91] Although it is unclear whether this remark criticised the brief deployment of bombers to No. 3 Wing in eastern France or the overall disjointed nature of Bacon's air policy, Lambe's efforts to combat the submarines of the Flanders Flotilla were nevertheless interrupted by poor weather, limited resources, and an almost constantly changing focus. Not a single U-boat was destroyed in port during 1917 and the tempo of German submarine operations remained unchallenged. Lambe's best opportunity for success for bombing Bruges, Ostend, and Zeebrugge – with good weather and plenty of bombers available during the summer months – was squandered on the hopes of a Flanders ground offensive and the public reaction to German Gotha raids. The new year would initially offer promise through a more offensive-minded naval commander, but once again organisational changes, this time resulting from the RAF amalgamation, would pull Lambe's bombers in many different directions.

Lambe, Keyes, and the RAF in 1918

On 1 January 1918 Sir Roger Keyes replaced Bacon as the Vice-Admiral Dover Patrol. The change in command resulted from disagreements throughout the autumn of 1917 between Bacon and Keyes, then the Admiralty Director of Plans and Chairman of the Channel Barrage Committee, over the effectiveness of the Dover Mine Barrage. The offensive-minded Keyes raised strong objections concerning Bacon's patrol and maintenance policies, but Jellicoe staunchly defended the latter officer.[92]

By late December Sir Eric Geddes, the First Lord, had become convinced that both Jellicoe and Bacon had to go.[93] Sir Rosslyn Wemyss, the Deputy First Sea Lord, replaced Jellicoe in the top naval position, while Keyes was afforded the opportunity to carry out his suggested improvements for the Dover Patrol as Bacon's replacement. Keyes, who before the war had been the Inspecting Captain of Submarines (1910–15), later served as chief of staff to Admiral Sir John de Robeck during the Dardanelles campaign. Keyes had also commanded one of the escort forces during the Cuxhaven Raid at the end of 1914.[94] In addition to strengthening the Dover mine barrage with better minefields and more effective patrols, Keyes planned to attack the German submarine bases directly, since the Ypres Offensive had obviously failed to clear the coast of Belgium. Finally, the new Vice-Admiral Dover Patrol removed his predecessor's restrictions on bombing attacks and encouraged the RNAS at Dunkirk to begin 'a most ruthless and ceaseless assault on everything German that could be attacked'.[95]

Shortly after assuming command of the Dover Patrol, Keyes asked Lambe to write a detailed report of the effects of his bombing operations, to include his views on attacking naval objectives with aircraft. The subject was to be considered 'urgent' and he implied that the report would be forwarded to the Admiralty.[96] The resulting document was a critical piece of evidence to be used in later debates between the Admiralty, the War Office and the Air Council.

Lambe's report provided few surprises but valuable insights from the senior RNAS officer at Dunkirk. He admitted that bombing attempts in 1915 and 1916 were 'negligible' in their effects on the enemy, but that better aircraft in 1917 had shown promise. Lambe praised his well-trained aircrews for losing only three Handley Page machines to enemy action and one to a landing accident during eight months of operations. Aerial photographs and intelligence had shown that attacks against enemy aerodromes had been effective in forcing the Germans to abandon at least three raids against England and making them move to new aerodromes. Finally, Lambe lamented that had his bombers not been diverted by 'Military requirements of the moment', he might have been able to render Bruges 'untenable'. Lambe concluded that attacks had to be continuous to be effective, especially regarding the effects on enemy morale.[97] The report was in essence a scathing indictment of Bacon's air policy.

Poor weather and re-equipment efforts with new Handley Page O/400s had slowed bombing operations during the first two months of 1918. During this period Lambe had two day and two night bomber squadrons under his command; the new units approved in late 1917 had not yet arrived. In mid-February, however, the new Air Ministry had arranged with the Admiralty and War Office a complete change in organisation for the Dunkirk Command in preparation for the air force amalgamation in April. As a result of these changes Keyes's air contingent would include only No. 5 Group, RAF, under F. C. Halahan, formerly Lambe's second-in-command. Along with seaplane and airship units near Dover, No. 5 Group would possess only one land-based wing, the 61st, comprising one reconnaissance squadron (No. 202, DH-4s), one anti-submarine squadron (No. 217, DH-4s), and three fighter squadrons (initially Nos. 201, 210, and 213) for air cover.

All of the remaining fighter and bomber squadrons at Dunkirk would be handed over to the BEF's control as of late February in a separate unit under Lambe's command. The agreement stipulated, however, that Haig should keep one Handley Page squadron in the Dunkirk area to bomb the 'submarine bases at Bruges and Zeebrugge . . . and it is requested that the C-in-C may be informed that the Admiralty and Air Council attach the utmost importance to the bombing of these submarine bases, which should be carried out continuously'. Additionally, new squadrons would be added to the Dunkirk force in order to add weight to the bombing offensive and Keyes was permitted to petition Haig directly for additional air support when necessary.[98] Thus on 22 March 1918 Keyes made a standing request for day and night bombing attacks on Bruges and Zeebrugge.[99] The timing of this request could not have been worse; on the previous day the long-awaited German Spring Offensive crashed into the British lines.

Lambe's bombers thus became embroiled in supporting the desperate defence of the British Army in France. During the last week of March his pilots flew between two and four missions daily, sometimes while their aerodromes were being shelled, in order to bomb bridges, aerodromes, and troop concentrations.[100] The Royal Air Force was thus born in battle, the formal establishment date being 1 April 1918.

Lambe, now a Brigadier in the RAF and commander of its 7th Brigade, controlled all air units near Dunkirk except for the naval cooperation squadrons of the 61st Wing. Between his two wings, the 64th and 65th, Lambe had five bomber and two fighter squadrons, all engaged in supporting the BEF's repulse of German attacks.[101] Other than minimal support to the famous Zeebrugge Raid of 22/23 April, Lambe's attacks on the submarine facilities had been severely curtailed due to Haig's requirements and the seasonally poor weather.[102] The attack on Zeebrugge, with block ships supposedly 'bottling-up' many destroyers and submarines in harbour, directly led to a crisis over control of Lambe's bombers.

By the end of April the bomber strength of Lambe's brigade had been drawn down to one night and two day squadrons, due to the demands of the Army and the necessity of building up the Independent Force under Trenchard – a command intended to be a long-range, strategic bomber force.[103] Keyes, who had received photo-reconnaissance information revealing the blockage of 'a large number of Torpedo Boat Destroyers, Submarines and Floating Docks at Bruges', complained directly to the Admiralty that the RAF was not sufficiently following up his Zeebrugge Raid with bombing attacks on the German bases. Due to the tremendous opportunity to attack these enemy forces and the requirement to work with supporting air forces directly, Keyes demanded that the Air Ministry put additional bomber squadrons immediately under his command, with Lambe as his senior air adviser. The Admiralty forwarded Keyes's complaints to the Air Ministry, adding that the requested bomber support was of the 'utmost urgency' and that aircrew with previous flying experience along the Belgian coast should be employed. The Air Ministry allowed the organisational change – giving Lambe command of a larger, amalgamated No. 5 Group as of 16 May – but could not further reinforce the bombing effort due to 'extreme urgency of the demands for long-distance bombing squadrons elsewhere'.[104]

These organisational changes meant that Lambe could employ even his limited number of bombers in a focused effort against the German bases. In May 1918 his aviators dropped almost 70 tons of bombs on Zeebrugge and Bruges.[105] Twenty-three days of the month saw raids against naval installations. During the night of 9/10 May, Keyes had Lambe send Handley Page bombers to attack German coastal batteries as the crew of HMS *Vindictive* attempted a blockage of Ostend. The Ostend attack generated another barrage of complaints over the lack of bomber support and unsuitable aircraft types offered; on 28 May Keyes lamented that the Air Ministry had displayed 'a complete failure to appreciate our requirements' and that Haig's RAF commanders did 'not seem to understand the elements of the Naval requirements on the Belgian Coast or the great importance of the bearing on the general conduct of the war'.[106] A week earlier Major General Sir John Salmond (GOC, RAF in the Field, and Trenchard's replacement) wrote to Haig's headquarters that 'all available squadrons have been placed at the disposal of the Vice-Admiral, Dover Patrol, for the purpose of bombing Bruges Docks and Zeebrugge. Eighteen raids have been carried out since the attack on Zeebrugge in spite of the fact that until the last few days the weather was very unfavourable'. During the first week of June 1918, Keyes, Haig, Salmond and a number of subordinate flag officers became embroiled in an almost constant exchange of telegrams regarding the trading of squadrons between No. 5 Group and the BEF's air contingent.[107] This correspondence clearly illustrates the senior officers' high regard for air operations by the end of the war. During June and July the Air Ministry, finally reaping the fruits of increased aircraft production and pilot training and under increasing pressure from the Admiralty, added the 82nd Wing to reinforce No. 5 Group.

The first secret operations order that Lambe issued as commander of No. 5 Group, RAF, was a call for his bomber squadrons to conduct two bombing raids daily on Bruges Docks. Beginning on 27 May, his bombers were to bomb the harbour 'continually by day and by night and by this means hinder the work which is in progress on enemy submarines and destroyers and also wear down A.A. [anti-aircraft] defences'. During the first two weeks in June, No. 5 Group dropped 60 tons of bombs, which destroyed the electrical works at Bruges and damaged the lock gates at Zeebrugge.[108] Lambe finally had the forces and senior support to carry out a continuous bombing campaign against the German bases.

No. 217 Squadron, the only anti-submarine patrol squadron of No. 5 Group, also contributed to the effort. Converting from seaplanes in March 1918, the squadron was equipped with DH-4s using 375 HP Rolls-Royce Eagle engines, enabling them to carry two 230-lb delayed action bombs for use against submarines. They also had inflatable air bags under the wings to keep the aircraft afloat as long as possible in case of ditching.[109] Although their primary mission was U-boat patrol, the crews of No. 217 Squadron were allowed to attack naval targets, including Ostend and Zeebrugge, at the conclusion of each patrol mission, as it was inadvisable to land with a heavy bomb load still onboard.[110] In June Lambe formalised this role by ordering No. 217 Squadron to bomb the Zeebrugge lock gates with a daily 'bombing raid of three or four machines'.[111]

Between mid-June and the end of August, No. 5 Group dropped over 86 tons of bombs on Zeebrugge, Ostend, and Bruges, with other RAF squadrons adding 49 additional tons.[112] During this period the Germans stepped up their air strength in northern Belgium and once again the Dunkirk bombers had to devote some of their energy toward German aerodromes.[113] Lambe concluded that his bombing raids must have been inflicting damage in order for the Germans to make such a determined defence and sought to continue his 'attacks with the utmost vigour'.[114] Luckily the weather had improved since the spring, and day and night attacks on the German naval installations continued incessantly.

In July and August 1918, No. 5 Group lost a total of 28 aircraft to combat operations.[115] Although this represents a much higher rate of losses than experienced during the previous summer, Dunkirk's losses were considerably less than the average of 180 planes per week for all RAF units supporting the BEF during the last 15 weeks of the war.[116] One serious consideration for Lambe during this period was the concern for limiting Belgian casualties during bombing operations. Targets were carefully chosen to reduce the effects of collateral damage.[117] In fact, since late 1917 Belgian civilian casualties from British bombing had become a concern of Field Marshal Haig's headquarters. However, mistakes did occur and Salmond defended a case of No. 5 Group's bombing error at Bruges in August 1918 by explaining that although regrettable, casualties to civilians were 'inevitable if the docks were to be bombed, owing to the necessity of bombing from a great altitude and the consequent wide margin of error'.[118] Likewise, No. 5 Group's efforts were defended at the highest levels of government; in late June 1918, the Chief of the Air Staff assured the War Cabinet that 'rigorous instructions' to bombing units called for avoiding Belgian casualties as much as possible, but important targets in Belgium, such as naval facilities and aerodromes, must be attacked 'by maintaining a continuous and sustained offensive attitude'.[119] In any event, Lambe made the Imperial Dockyard at Bruges the primary target for all bombing efforts in early September.[120] Later in September, No. 5

Group abandoned raids on naval installations in order to support the advance of Allied ground forces in Flanders. The subsequent German evacuation and Allied re-occupation of the Belgian ports had rendered further bombing unnecessary, and on 20 October Allied land forces reached the Dutch border.

The termination of the bombing campaign against the Flanders Triangle was planned well before the advance of British, Belgian, and French army forces along the Belgian coast in late September 1918, however. Three factors influenced the proposed cessation of British bombing operations against Ostend, Zeebrugge, and Bruges for 1919 and beyond. The first was the arrival of the US Northern Bombing Group, which represented the primary focus of the fledgling US Naval Air Service. The second influence was a massive expansion of the Independent Force, designed to use strategic bombardment directly controlled by the Air Ministry to devastate the German economy. Finally, Grand Fleet plans to attack the High Seas Fleet 'at source', through the use of towed flying boats and carrier-based aviation, showed promise and developed a great deal of momentum during the summer of 1918. The combination of these three plans, and their drain on limited resources, meant that there was no future for British bombers engaging in a bombing offensive against the Flanders submarine bases. It is also interesting to note that all of these schemes were developed before the final successes of Allied armies in France made them irrelevant.

The Americans entered the Great War with a naval air service that had a strength of one air station, 48 pilots, one airship, and 54 aircraft. Expansion would take time. Initial discussions between the Admiralty and the US Navy focused on defeating German submarines through the addition of American patrol vessels and a new North Sea Mine Barrage. During the spring of 1917 Jellicoe presented US Rear-Admiral H. T. Mayo with naval air policy papers that called for using aircraft for fleet reconnaissance and anti-submarine patrols. Bombing German bases on the Belgian coast was only mentioned as a minor role. Jellicoe proposed that anti-submarine patrols from Ireland should form the focus of the initial US naval air effort.[121]

As the Americans studied the U-boat menace more closely, they gained an appreciation of the offensive qualities of directly bombing Ostend, Zeebrugge, and Bruges. By February 1918 their Planning Section, working closely with the Plans Division at the Admiralty, proposed that the primary effort of American naval aviation should be an 'offensive against enemy bases' with aircraft anti-submarine patrols clearly stated as a secondary function. The air attacks had to be continuous, 'avoiding sporadic offensives'.[122] This preference for attacking German submarine bases reflected President Wilson's desire to destroy 'the "hornet's nests" rather than chasing individual hornets'.[123] By July 1918 the Americans had established forward bases and provided an initial cadre of aviators and ground crew for what was called the Northern Bombing Group. This group would comprise eight US Navy and Marine squadrons of day and night bombers 'with the distinct mission of destroying enemy Naval Bases on the Belgian Coast'.[124]

Engine problems with their Italian-built Caproni night bombers and delayed deliveries of American-built DH-4 day bombers postponed independent operations of this force. In the meantime, the US naval aviators augmented RAF squadrons near Dunkirk in order to gain familiarity with the local flying area and profit from combat experience. Independent operations, under overall command of the Vice-Admiral Dover Patrol through No. 5 Group, RAF, began in September 1918.[125]

The key feature of the American involvement in bombing the Flanders bases was that they would continue the assault into 1919 *alone*. On 17 September US Navy, Admiralty, and RAF representatives agreed that it would be 'extremely desirable' for the joint naval air policy for 1919 to include handing over the task of bombing from Dunkirk entirely to the Americans, with a final goal of 12 US Navy and Marine bombing squadrons.[126] On 17 August 1918, Brigadier General R. M. Groves, RAF, the new Director of the Admiralty's Air Division, wrote in his diary that 'obviously No. 5 Group will contain such a preponderance of Americans that we shall only be auxiliaries'.[127] The Admiralty welcomed the American contribution simply because they had no choice in the matter. The Air Ministry's plans for 1919 would strip away all RAF maritime units from Keyes's control, except for one reconnaissance squadron, in order to provide the Independent Force with an overwhelming concentration of bombers to attack Germany directly.

The chief result of the formation of the RAF as it affected the Dunkirk-based bomber force was that Lambe and Keyes had little say in the future nature of bombing operations. As early as July 1918, the Air Council had begun to push for a massive increase in the size of the Independent Force. The Secretary of State for Air, Sir William Weir, proposed stripping 50 squadrons from naval and army cooperation in order to bring the Independent Force to a strength of 104 squadrons. This strategic bombing force would destroy the German ability to bomb England, divert defensive fighters from the front, and devastate the German economy. Dunkirk's five bombing squadrons would of course be needed for the build-up.[128] The concept of strategic bombing, so forcefully supported by the Admiralty in 1916 and 1917, had by summer 1918 transformed into the concept of the Independent Force of the RAF, directly controlled by the Air Ministry and free of Admiralty and War Office interference; it was also a drain on limited resources of bombers and trained aircrews.[129] In July 1918, Lambe confided to Captain Hubert Lynes, RN, formerly the Commodore Dunkirk, that the Independent Force 'no doubt irritate[s] the enemy, but at the present stage of the development of aircraft will not lessen the duration of the war by forty-eight hours'.[130] Thus at least one senior RAF officer opposed the strategic bombing philosophy of the Air Ministry. In fact, Trenchard himself, as the commander of the Independent Force during the closing months of the war, devoted less than 20 per cent of his bombing sorties to targets of 'strategic' nature, instead choosing to attack targets that directly supported the army, such as supply centres, aerodromes, and railroad yards.[131] Nevertheless, in August the Air Council acknowledged that the American naval bombing squadrons would serve to replace the British bombing efforts in northern Belgium, thus releasing bombers for the Independent Force.[132]

The final diversion of interest in bombing from Dunkirk stemmed from Grand Fleet plans to use aircraft to attack the High Seas Fleet at its moorings. The Tondern raid in July 1918 was aimed at Zeppelin sheds and showed promise as an experiment in what shipboard aircraft could do against both land and naval targets. Trials with towing flying boats atop lighters and the continued development of aircraft carriers with new 'naval' aeroplanes demonstrated that Beatty and his admirals thought highly of the potential of naval aviation.[133] Although Jellicoe and the Admiralty disagreed with such schemes in 1917, due to reasons of inadequate equipment and the impossibility of achieving surprise in the Heligoland Bight, Jellicoe's departure at least returned an air attack on the High Seas Fleet back into the realm of possibility.[134] HMS *Argus*, the Royal Navy's first flush-deck carrier, was built to carry a squadron of Sopwith Cuckoo Torpedo Bombers precisely for this purpose.[135] However, along with the planned American effort and the build-up of the Independent Force, such projects overshadowed the efforts of the Dunkirk bombers.

Conclusion

In late October 1918 Lambe reported the results of his air attacks on the Belgian bases to both the Air Ministry and Keyes. Forgetting the earlier problems with Vice-Admiral Bacon, Lambe stated that Bruges Docks had 'been bombed more or less continuously' and that the objectives of these attacks were to interfere with repair work and effect the morale of the submarine crews and dock workers, in addition to damaging facilities. The German base there was a difficult target because of its close proximity to the historic city and the extremely thick defences. Anecdotal evidence – from interviews of civilians remaining after the German evacuation – suggested that the bombing lowered the morale of German naval personnel. Also, Lambe repeated the classic argument that forcing the Germans to devote resources to defending the area had justified, at least in part, his efforts. His final conclusion was 'that the value of systematic bomb dropping on any given objective can scarcely be over estimated'.[136]

By the end of the Great War Lambe had devoted over three years of service to commanding the air units at Dunkirk; he naturally justified both his own and his subordinate's efforts during that period. What he failed to mention in his report was the lack of any evidence showing that even a single U-boat was destroyed by the bombing campaign. Other than inflicting limited damage and possibly motivating German submariners to get back out to sea, the impact of the bombing campaign had been slight.

The RNAS units around Dunkirk and their RAF successors had, however, fully developed the required infrastructure for a modern bomber force by the end of the war. Maintenance depots performed mandatory inspections and repairs and provided frontline aerodromes with replacement and spare aircraft. Intelligence officers at Lambe's headquarters not only scoured photographic reconnaissance to obtain 'valuable evidence . . . of [the] results of our Bombing Raids', but also maintained thorough records of the tonnage dropped on specific targets in Flanders.[137] Likewise, they compared aircrew reports of what they thought they had hit to other available intelligence, such as agent reports, Dutch and German newspaper articles, and prisoner interrogations, in an attempt to gain a clear picture of the effects of the attacks.[138] The Admiralty produced a set of detailed target maps of most towns and cities in occupied Belgium, which identified individual buildings and structures.[139] Finally, Lambe's wing and squadron commanders codified operating technique in order to provide standardisation for their air and ground crew-members. Manuals provided guidance for preparing aircraft and crews for raids; navigating to and approaching targets; communicating during departure from and return to the aerodrome; and other necessary details.[140]

As an Air Ministry historian would later state, it is ironic that the naval aviation resources of Dunkirk, whose *raison d'être* was, arguably, to make the German submarine bases untenable, devoted 'a far greater weight of bombs on military objectives than on the nerve centre of the German naval organisation [Bruges] in Belgium'. If the Dunkirk bombers dropped 75 per cent of their weight of bombs on Bruges, instead of only 25 per cent, Bruges might have been rendered useless as a submarine base.[141] Yet this opinion was the exception rather than the rule. Most historians ignored the fact that the campaign was continuously interrupted. Admiralty and Air Ministry staff studies, stating that attacks against the bases were 'frequent' and 'unremitting', helped to mislead other historians of the period.[142] Later accounts went as far as to view the bombing campaign as a misuse of naval aviation resources.[143] The Admiralty, responsible for allocating air resources until 1918 and then fighting for their return in 1918 and beyond, clearly was willing to base bombers at Dunkirk, but on the other hand chose not to dictate to the commander on the spot how to employ his air assets. Evolutionary changes in organisation and command structure in the Royal Navy and the RAF as well as the novelty of air operations meant that doctrinal development – that is, an accepted set of operational beliefs – was severely curtailed. In modern parlance, Bacon failed to choose between 'target sets', or groups of targets such as naval facilities (anti-submarine) or aerodromes (anti-air) or railway systems (transportation), because no doctrine at the operational level of war existed and none was forthcoming from the Admiralty. Instead, the bomber forces at Dunkirk actually conducted three bombing campaigns simultaneously – one against naval bases, one against aerodromes, and one against Army-support objectives – because the Admiralty's lengthy list of responsibilities for Dunkirk aircraft provided no specific targeting advice for Bacon.

The problem was of course a matter of priorities. Bombing the German naval bases did not become a priority for the Admiralty Board until the Air Council took over responsibility for all aerial operations in 1918; some justification had to be presented in order to prevent the RAF from working completely under the BEF in France. The Air Council favoured the idea of bombing U-boat bases, in order to demonstrate the usefulness of independent air power on the war at sea, but the BEF came first and the investment in Dunkirk was too little and too late. Bombing Bruges, Ostend, and Zeebrugge did not reach 'continuous' status until May 1918. By this time the combination of mines and patrols of Keyes's Dover Barrage had made the Flanders bases practically useless to the Germans anyway.[144] Had the war continued into 1919, there is little reason to believe that British bombers would have had anything to do with an assault on Bruges from the air. In the end, this role was the least effective way of using aircraft against submarines, not because of an absence of technology, but because the commanders responsible for employing this innovative new capability failed to understand its nature.

4 Hunting the enemy

Air patrols in Home Waters

The advantages of height and speed made First World War aircraft of all types valuable contributors to naval operations. In the reconnaissance role, they had the potential to be useful in many ways. Broadly speaking, aircraft could act as a screen for the fleet – as the German Zeppelins had demonstrated in August 1916 – while it was at sea. They could patrol the coasts of Britain in order to spot enemy raiding forces of any type (surface ships, Zeppelins or Gotha bombers) and attempt to warn defensive forces for the purpose of interception. Finally, aircraft could patrol the waters around Britain in an attempt to defend mercantile trade. In this case, the German U-boat would be the primary quarry of the airborne hunters. The potential of these three roles – of fleet, coastal, and anti-submarine reconnaissance – in addition to commitments to Dunkirk, the Dardanelles, and the Adriatic, meant that the Admiralty had to make some difficult choices regarding the operational focus of available resources.

This chapter analyses the effort British maritime air units made in conducting anti-submarine air patrols in Home Waters. This effort has been widely deprecated both in Naval Staff studies during the 1950s and in the secondary historical literature that followed. The general thrust of these criticisms is that air patrols, as opposed to convoy air escort, wasted precious air resources since they were ineffective in sinking U-boats. The famous Barley and Waters 1957 staff study, entitled *The Defeat of the Enemy Attack of Shipping 1939–1945*, makes the convincing argument that convoy was the supreme antidote for the U-boat threat and that any diversion of resources to 'hunting patrols' was simply a wasted effort. The initial pages cover the experience of the First World War and praise the British effort to use aircraft in the close and distant convoy escort role. Schemes to use aircraft in the hunting patrol role are dismissed as ineffective.[1] Likewise, Arthur Marder, strongly influenced by Waters in writing *From Dreadnought to Scapa Flow*, goes a step further and offers that 'All this busy work [1917 air patrols] was singularly unproductive' and 'As patrols they [aircraft in 1918] proved ineffective.'[2]

The major problem of this critical interpretation is that it looks at World War I air patrol operations through the experience of the Second World War. During the latter conflict, ship and shore-based Allied aircraft accounted for as many as 381 German and Italian submarines, with an additional 53 shared with naval vessels, out of 870 total U-boat losses.[3] This vast difference in aircraft effectiveness stemmed from a number of factors, mostly related to advanced technological capability. World War I aircraft did not benefit from high performance engines to extend range and speed or from powerful explosives, radar, and illuminating devices to enhance attacks. World War I aircrew instead relied on their own eyesight for detection and simple weapons for attack, supported by an Admiralty and RAF forced to create airpower doctrine from scratch in the midst of a very different sort of war.

Although convoy escort was the most effective role of aircraft in the anti-submarine campaign, making the assumption that aircraft were completely ineffective in the hunting patrol role is inaccurate. These hunting patrols were effective in forcing U-boats commanders to submerge when they did not want to, losing valuable time on their relatively short cruises and restricting their ability to operate freely. When viewed as part of a larger anti-submarine system, which eventually included patrolled mine barrages, the convoy system, air and surface hunting patrols, and bombing U-boat bases, the use of aircraft to seek out U-boats and submarine-delivered minefields was a valuable contribution. It must be remembered that the unrestricted U-boat campaign of 1917–1918 was largely a coastal operation; 1,623 of the 1,971 Allied and Neutral ships of over 500 gross registered tons (GRT) lost in Home Waters were sunk within 100 miles of the coast;[4] this fact highlights the opportunity of relatively short-ranged aircraft to make a contribution from their bases ashore. An analysis of this patrol effort must no longer be viewed only in light of the experience of the Second World War, but should instead be assessed relative to what is important to today's historians, such as questions of organising forces to deal with asymmetric threats and of using untested technology to counter equally new technology and tactics. The key issues for the First World War air patrol experience were the growth of an organisation and infrastructure to conduct operations, the evolution of thought processes, policy and policy-making organs within the Admiralty and Air Ministry, and the development of operational technique by units in the field.

Pre-war development and early attempts: 1912–1916

In August 1912, Captain Murray Sueter, the first director of the new Air Department at the Admiralty, suggested a wide range of purely naval reconnaissance and defensive duties for aircraft, which included scouting for the fleet and British submarines as well as protecting surface forces, harbours and naval facilities from enemy air attack. Sueter's suggestions regarding trade defence demonstrate his extraordinary vision: aircraft were to assist 'destroyers to detect and destroy submarines', find 'mine layers at work or mines already laid', and locate 'hostile craft in waters which have to be kept clear for our war and merchant vessels'. In November the Admiralty acted on Sueter's proposals by ordering the establishment of a 'regular chain of stations along the Coasts of the United Kingdom within easy flight of each other'. Enemy submarines, universally used only for coast defence at this time and thus justifiably not considered a serious threat to Home Waters, were not seen as a concern of the Sea Lords who instead wanted bases 'for naval aircraft working with the Squadrons and Flotillas at sea'.[5]

The primary role pushing early RNAS expansion was not anti-submarine warfare but defensive reconnaissance against raids by enemy Zeppelin and surface forces against the British coast. Nicholas Lambert states that the Admiralty War Staff considered 'giving a major role to the embryonic Royal Naval Air Service' along the east coast of England in 1914 before the out-break of the war. The Admiral of Patrols was to have 50 wireless-equipped aircraft in addition to destroyers and submarines to guard the coastline.[6] Specifically, however, the Admiralty was concerned with the protection of naval facilities, and a 1913 committee – established to ascertain the best way to protect oil tanks and 'other vulnerable points' from air attack and chaired by Sueter – concluded (naturally) that an air offensive against the threat should be the first objective with air interceptors and anti-aircraft artillery as 'a second line of defence'.[7]

The need for coastal reconnaissance nevertheless drove the establishment of a chain of eight seaplane, aeroplane, and airship bases located along the coast between the Humber Estuary and Portsmouth by August 1914. The opening of the war highlighted the need for more bases; for example, Jellicoe asked for and received a new seaplane station in the vicinity of the Grand Fleet base at Scapa Flow, and the deployment of the BEF to France necessitated the need for seaplane bases at Dover and Dunkirk. The departure of most of the Royal Flying Corps to France with the BEF meant that the RNAS would now undertake the important role of defending British airspace, which it grudgingly assumed on 3 September 1914, requiring even more air stations. Further growth was needed to base Admiral Fisher's SS airships – small non-rigids of 'quick construction' useful for a sustained air patrol – after October.[8]

Early, multi-purpose air patrols were poorly organised and supported at first, relying on any aircraft a given air station could get into the air. H. C. G. Allen flew some of these patrols along the Yorkshire coast in Bleriots, Caudrons, and Avros.[9] Arthur Longmore recalls taking the 80 HP Bristols of his squadron to the Newcastle area for a two-week period in November 1914 to conduct anti-invasion air patrols.[10] The first months of the war were a time of rapid growth and uncertainty for the RNAS, and home stations were often stripped of aircraft and pilots for overseas service, leaving few resources for the air defence of Britain and reconnaissance flights along the coastline. These early patrol flights did, however, serve to provide RNAS aircrews with much need flying experience in all weather conditions, an investment that would reap benefits later in the war.[11]

The first German Zeppelin attack on English soil, against Yarmouth and King's Lynn on the night of 19/20 January 1915, was the probable motivation

Figure 4.1 Naval geography of Britain.

behind an Air Department inquiry at the end of the month. The air attack threat, recognised in 1912, had finally appeared. On the 29th Sueter ordered all RNAS commanding officers to forward narratives of their air patrol schemes. The responses were disappointing. Only two stations, Newcastle and Great Yarmouth, carried out regular patrols; as one staff officer minuted, patrolling was curtailed simply by a 'lack of machines'.[12] Indeed by the spring of 1915, the needs of the RNAS operating from Dunkirk and the contingent sent to the Dardanelles seriously strained the limited resources of the RNAS, specifically of seaplanes, aeroplanes, and pilots.

The replacement of the Churchill/Fisher regime with that of the Balfour/ Jackson administration could not have immediately prevented the first Zeppelin raids against London at the end of May 1915. The change in leadership did not alter the fundamental Admiralty policy of offensive bombing against Zeppelin bases in order to help prevent air attacks on Britain, as evident from the build-up of RNAS bomber forces in France, and a continued lack of emphasis on defensive air patrols at home. After a year of generally poor results from RNAS defensive patrols, the Cabinet War Committee finally agreed in February 1916 to return the air defence mission to the RFC, but with the caveat that the RNAS would 'undertake to deal with all hostile aircraft attempting to reach this country' with the Army taking responsibility once they reached the shore. The RNAS was also required to 'watch the coast' and work with the fleet and surface patrol flotillas.[13] Admiralty support of operations around Dunkirk and a renewed effort to build rigid airships, potentially a superb reconnaissance platform for the fleet, thus remained justified.

This is not to say that the patrol role was completely ignored during the first years of the war, but it must be noted that patrols had more than one purpose. Admiralty orders to all eastern and southern Home naval districts in late October 1915 called for air patrols along the coastline under their respective areas of responsibility. These patrols, which were a matter 'of the greatest importance', were aimed at locating attacking Zeppelins.[14] The initial purpose for new long-range flying boats was offensive patrols off the Heligoland Bight and by summer of 1916 the Rear-Admiral, East Coast of England, still considered the importance of anti-submarine patrols third in priority to air patrols searching for German surface vessels and Zeppelins.[15] Shortages still plagued operations; the commander at Killingholme, for example, complained that only two BE2Cs could do little in patrolling for Zeppelins while he had no trained seaplane pilots to fly his handful of Sopwith floatplanes.[16] In other words, the demand for aircraft, with their relatively good ability to search the coastline, rapidly outpaced the supply of airframes and pilots.

The RNAS Airship Service made the most important effort to use aircraft patrols against submarines during the first half of the war. Regular SS airship patrols began during the summer of 1915. At first these flights were limited to approximately three hours duration, due to a lack of hydrogen production and a lack of 'confidence in the airships themselves'. By early 1916, however, conditions had improved and patrol flights lasted six to seven hours on average.[17] The increased level of experience, after a year of flying operations, meant that SS airships, soon to be joined by the new and larger 'Coastal' class, were able to expand their role in the anti-submarine war. During the summer and autumn months of 1916, airship stations began to patrol key waterways extensively. For example, Pembroke Airship Station took up the St George's and Bristol Channels as its primary areas of operations while Howden in Yorkshire concentrated on the mouth of the Humber.[18] Despite the growth of this effort, there were nevertheless very few occasions during the first two and a half years of the war when aircraft of any type sighted a U-boat.

In summary, the important pre-war thinking of considering the use of aircraft to search for submarines was overcome by other priorities and shortages of resources for the variety of tasks taken on during the first two years of the war. The demands of war generated new roles and missions for aircraft, severely taxing the RNAS. As one Air Historical Branch historian wrote, 'the whole period may be said to have been one of development rather than achievement', since the airship service rapidly expanded while seaplane performance and numbers gradually increased.[19] Between the start of the war – when the airship complement of the RNAS comprised seven airships and a handful of men based at two shore establishments – and the end of 1916, the Royal Navy's lighter-than-air force had grown to 58 non-rigids in commission and over 4,000 officers and men, based at 20 stations (four overseas). Likewise, after a period of rapid growth in 1914 and 1915, the seaplane establishment reached just under 500 aircraft in commission during the summer of 1916, a significant growth rate from the two-dozen seaplanes in the service in August 1914. Total RNAS personnel figures perhaps best illustrate the level of expansion during this period: 15 August 1914 – 140 officers and 708 men; 15 August 1915 – 1,346 officers and 9,370 men; and a year later – 2,401 officers and 20,355 men.[20] These resources were still not adequate for all of the missions the RNAS sought for naval aviation, but the stage was now set for the employment of aircraft in a role first envisioned in early 1912.

1917: Jellicoe, Duff, and the Anti-Submarine Division

Admiral Sir John Jellicoe's assumption of the top professional position in the Royal Navy was a critical event in the use of aircraft in the anti-submarine patrol role. The key decision of Jellicoe's early administration, which began when he officially replaced Jackson as First Sea Lord on 5 December 1916, was the creation of the Anti-Submarine Division (ASD) on the Admiralty Staff. This new branch would manage and coordinate all measures to defeat German submarine attacks on British shipping; the decision to form this organisation, as proposed by a conference of senior naval officers,[21] demonstrates the widespread shift of opinion regarding the U-boat threat from one of mere nuisance to real concern.

Jellicoe wanted the new branch to work under the direction of a flag officer and brought a trusted subordinate with him from the Grand Fleet to develop the ASD into an effective organisation. Rear-Admiral A. L. Duff had been second in command of the Grand Fleet's 4th Battle Squadron and became the Director of the new division. With reference to German U-boats, Jellicoe charged Duff with the task of considering 'new *methods* of dealing with them *offensively* and also defensively'.[22] Specifically, the ASD's duties included keeping track of 'all anti-submarine appliances', to include *materiel* and training, as well as managing the Auxiliary Patrol of small surface craft. In February, Duff's responsibilities expanded to include determining policy for Home Waters minesweeping, air patrols, Q-ships, and destroyers detailed for anti-submarine work.[23]

Duff immediately submitted a number of proposals designed to minimise losses to increasingly active German submarines. A major reorganisation, for example, of shipping lanes and surface patrols was required along the heavily traversed waters of the English Channel and Western Approaches, areas too large to be thoroughly patrolled given the available resources. Duff therefore established a single inshore lane, heavily patrolled by British warships, from the Scillies to the Thames Estuary.[24] Grouped with a number of these organisational and technical proposals, however, was an important recommendation to expand air patrols in order to continue the policy of using every available means to counter the growing U-boat menace.

On 15 December 1916 Duff submitted a minute to Jellicoe that proposed a significant growth of RNAS operations in Home Waters. This initiative – only ten days after Jellicoe took the helm of the Royal Navy – called for anti-submarine air patrols, already organised in the North Sea, to be expanded to include the English Channel, the coasts of Cornwall and Wales, the south and west coasts of Ireland, and the approaches to these areas as far out to sea as possible. Thus, the flag officer responsible for coordinating all aspects of anti-submarine warfare explicitly supported the idea of expanding the air station network by focusing the role of patrolling aircraft on anti-submarine warfare as opposed to counter-air or general reconnaissance.[25] In response to the increasingly costly U-boat campaign against commerce, the primary objective of air patrols would now be locating German submarines instead of the diminishing Zeppelin threat. Official naval historian Henry Newbolt later reflected that these new air patrols were 'the most important of these complementary measures' emanating from the ASD.[26]

Duff's initiative – in cooperation with the RNAS and the Operations Division, and with Jellicoe's full support – led to the construction of a number of new air stations, especially in south-western England where pre-war assumptions had not considered the need for air bases. Within a few months, new seaplane bases opened at Cattewater (Plymouth), Newlyn (Land's End), the Scillies, and Fishguard (south-western Wales). In April 1917 Wing

Commander E. L. Gerrard, one of the four original naval aviators in Britain, took command of these stations as well as the airship bases at Mullion (near Lizard Point) and Pembroke. During the spring months, three aeroplane flights were also established to supplement the seaplane patrols, but the needs of the Western Front necessitated a withdrawal of the pilots by the end of the summer. Headquartered at Plymouth, this new 'South-western Group' worked directly for the naval district commander at Devonport (also known as the C-in-C Plymouth) and immediately established a scheme of anti-submarine patrols that became a model for the rest of the RNAS.[27]

Gerrard codified his patrol system into three categories. 'Routine' patrols either covered a designated box of airspace for airships or a standardised route for seaplanes and aeroplanes. 'Emergency' patrols would be launched, from a pool of aircraft readied for such a contingency, when intelligence or a reported U-boat sighting sufficiently justified an immediate hunt. Finally, 'contact' patrols were ordered when arrangements were made with aircraft to work with surface craft. In all cases Group Headquarters sent precise, abbreviated instructions to the individual air stations regarding specific routes to be flown or ship rendezvous points to meet – all coordinated to provide maximum patrol coverage and based on the latest intelligence.[28]

Similar patrol schemes and expansion of air stations occurred in the other home commands. The Portsmouth Group, headquartered at Calshot under Wing Commander A. W. Bigsworth, opened new bases at Portland, Bembridge, and Newhaven during the first half of 1917. This group patrolled the central portion of the English Channel and in July 1917 opened a seaplane sub-station at Cherbourg. The RNAS units of the Dover Patrol continued to patrol the eastern channel and Belgian coast. In March 1917, the Admiralty set clear limits on patrol areas for the east coast commands to avoid overlap and maximise the coverage of air patrols extending from the Thames Estuary to Scapa Flow.[29] Thus by the summer months of 1917, Duff's single-page memorandum and the increased losses from the German unrestricted submarine campaign being waged since February had led to, as one staff historian put it, 'a frantic effort to increase the air patrol coverage off our coasts'.[30] In essence the infrastructure of bases, units and operating methods for a comprehensive air patrol system was now in place covering the Irish Sea, Bristol Channel, English Channel and the entire east coast of Britain. From 22 airships and 120 seaplanes and aeroplanes available for patrols in Home Waters at the end of 1915, the passing of 1916 saw a growth to 47 airships and 160 heavier-than-air craft; and 1917 witnessed a further 'leap up to 63 airships and 314 flying boats, seaplanes and landplanes' on submarine patrols at home by the end of the year.[31] The airship flying hour rates tell the true story of expansion: 7,078 total airship flying hours in 1916 compared to 22,389 in 1917.[32]

Although the start of the unrestricted U-boat campaign highlighted the fact that the RNAS was spread too thin and was performing too many different missions, submarine patrols now became the priority for Home air stations. The War Office took advantage of this turn of events and forced the Admiralty to cease nascent strategic bombing operations from Luxeuil (near Nancy) during the spring of 1917, arguing that the effort was an expensive luxury while Home patrol units, Dunkirk squadrons, and fighter units attached to the BEF suffered from pilot shortages.[33] Patrol units at home also contributed to economising the forces devoted to the many RNAS missions listed earlier; specifically, air patrols in search of submarines could also serve to spot and at times intercept German Zeppelins during daylight hours as they approached the British coastline. This was especially true of the long-range Large America flying boats stationed at Felixstowe (near Harwich), Great Yarmouth (near Lowestoft), and Killingholme (at the River Humber), which possessed the range to approach the coast of Holland during their patrol flights.[34] Yarmouth aircraft alone shot down five Zeppelins during the war, the last one within 20 miles of the German coast.[35]

Although Felixstowe's Spider Web patrol scheme has received some measure of fame in *The War in the Air*, T.D. Hallam's memoir and other secondary texts, it would be useful to point out some of the lesser known aspects of these operations, which due to the range of these aircraft was somewhat unique to the generally accepted patrol systems in place in other regional commands. The Spider Web pattern of patrols, which generally took the shape of an eight-slice 'pie' with its centre at the North Hinder Light Vessel, was not derived randomly. From the start it was based upon signals intelligence, from two intercept stations in eastern England, which fixed the signals of U-boats sent while traversing the area between Holland and the Thames Estuary. The spokes of the 'pie' were only 30 miles long, but the web system was designed in such a way that one-quarter of the 4,000 square mile area could be thoroughly searched by one of the long-range flying boats in five hours. The truly novel concept employed, however, was not the search pattern itself but the intelligence picture maintained at Felixstowe. All wireless intercepts were plotted on a chart at the base's War Flight headquarters, allowing for the despatch of flying boats to areas of the web where known U-boat positions had been recently recorded.[36] It is no wonder that this system yielded one-quarter of all U-boat sightings for 1917.[37]

The Spider Web patrols did face a few challenges that limited their success. The precise navigation required to the fly the web routes, especially in accounting for the significant effect of wind drift relative to a great number of course changes, initially overloaded the aircrews and hampered their ability to keep up a visual scan of sea and sky. The Chaplain of the Felixstowe station developed a drift table – by which pilots could adjust their compass course to allow for wind drift – to ease the workload of the pilot team, but the major difficulty lay in the fact that wind speeds at cruise altitudes could not be measured with certainty at that time and pilots relied on educated guesses for accuracy. Eventually, the aircrews decided to forgo any drift corrections whatsoever in exchange for imprecise navigation. The patrol area – that is, the actual path over the ground that was flown – would thus shift by a few miles,

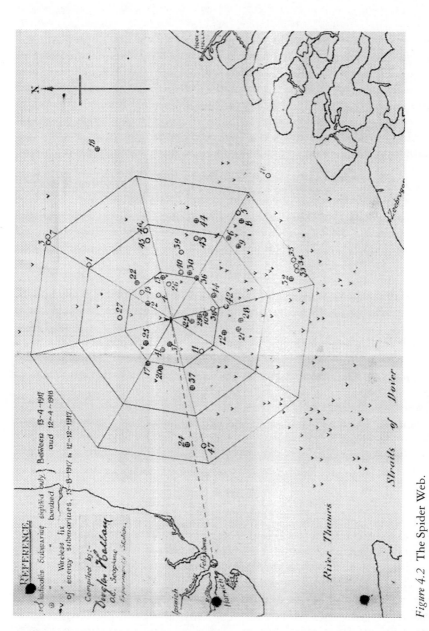

Figure 4.2 The Spider Web.

Source: Hallam Papers, AIR 1/6A/4/29.

depending on the winds, from day to day but the pilots could now devote more energy to visually scanning for the enemy.[38]

In addition to maintenance and weather challenges mentioned earlier (in Chapter 1), the flying boats had to be prepared to face enemy seaplanes, which by summer of 1917 became increasingly active in the waters off Belgium and Holland. Although their production never reached the level required to gain air superiority in the southern North Sea, high-performance German float-planes based in occupied Belgium and the fleet bases in north-west Germany posed a serious threat to Large Americas from Felixstowe and Great Yarmouth as well as other seaplanes from south-eastern England and Dunkirk. During the summer of 1917, Felixstowe flying boats began to fly two or three ship formations in order to maximise the volume of defensive Lewis gun fire against enemy seaplanes – a concept not unlike B-17 formations in the next world war. In 1918 a defensive sweep system was developed as an alternative to the Spider Web patrol. Two or more flying boats would fly on patrol abeam of each other, at the limit of visual range, in order to extend the searchable area as much as possible; if enemy seaplanes approached, the aircraft would close up and form a tight formation in order to defend themselves with interlocking fields of fire from their Lewis guns.[39] The German seaplane threat also hindered the operations of airships off the south-east coast of England. By January 1918 the Admiralty had ordered Pulham airships to discontinue patrols in this area due to the presumed loss of two Coastal airships (*C-17* and *C-27*) to German seaplanes.[40] Dunkirk seaplane units, which required fighter escorts when they flew, finally re-equipped with DH-4s in February 1918 specifically because of the German seaplane threat. The poorly armed floatplanes of the Dover Air Station were limited to patrolling to the west of the Dover Mine Barrage, while better, defensively equipped land planes (DH-9s and Camels) took on the patrols over and to the east of the Barrage.[41] Despite the danger of German seaplanes, the British adapted to counter them effectively and continued with anti-submarine patrols.

By May 1917 the Admiralty demonstrated its enthusiasm for the use of aircraft in the anti-submarine campaign by ordering all district commanders to report patrol activity of aircraft under their orders on a weekly basis. Commanders were to provide full details of all submarine attacks and were to include 'recommendations for the improvement of the methods employed by aircraft against submarines'.[42] The Anti-Submarine Division compiled this information into monthly *RNAS Anti-Submarine Reports* in order to distribute a record of accomplishments and 'lessons learned' amongst the commands.[43] Additionally, the Admiralty ordered that all naval centres receiving intercept information concerning U-boat wireless transmissions were to share this data with nearby air stations.[44] The following month the Admiralty placed an RNAS officer on the Anti-Submarine Division staff for the first time in order to coordinate and report on 'air operations in connection with Anti-submarine work'.[45] The use of aircraft against the U-boat had thus taken on a new level of importance as evident not only through new bases and operating techniques but also through infrastructure, staff support, and communications.

The success of the Large Americas at Felixstowe led to further interest in expansion of that system. As early as May 1917 the Operations Division recognised the superiority for Large Americas in anti-submarine patrols because of their 'reliability, speed and facilities for accurate bomb dropping'.[46] During an August conference between the First Sea Lord, the C-in-C Grand Fleet, and their staffs, Jellicoe and Beatty set a goal of 150 Large America flying boats for use with the Grand Fleet and patrols of the northern North Sea, especially over the planned Northern Mine Barrage.[47] This resulted in a plan to increase the RNAS presence at Houton in the Orkneys by turning it into a flying boat base housing 18 Large Americas. The intention was to have a sufficient force in place to be prepared to fly a high volume of sorties during the summer months of 1918 when better weather could be expected.[48] By January 1918, six stations (including Felixstowe, Yarmouth, Killingholme, Calshot, Cattewater, and the Scillies) were operating a total of approximately 50 Large Americas, with Houton preparing to begin flying operations.[49]

Before moving on to a narrative of the effect of RAF independence on the air patrol system, a brief sketch of the contribution of kite balloons would be useful. These weapon systems are usually associated with convoy escort, which was one of its better-recognised roles by the end of the war. There were occasions, however, when ships carrying kite balloons were employed on hunting patrols. The most celebrated of these instances was the Grand Fleet's Destroyer Kite Balloon Force, which was established in July 1917 with five destroyers. These destroyers succeeded in severely damaging, and possibly sinking, *U69* in a depth charge attack, subsequent to it being spotted at a distance of 28 miles by the kite balloon observers aboard one of the vessels, HMS *Patriot*.[50] Kite balloons therefore saw service not only as an extended crows nest for gunnery spotting (their original purpose) and as convoy escorts, but also as U-boat hunters.

A change of command: The RAF

Plans to form an independent air force, which developed rapidly during the second half of 1917, forced the Admiralty to consider seriously its air organisation once again. Establishing the Air Division of the Admiralty War Staff provided an office that would serve as a coordinating body between the Royal Navy and the Air Ministry. The Air Division's chief role was to 'study the anti-submarine work carried out in each [RAF air] group, comparing results obtained in one group with those in another. It is considered that by central supervision, and careful analysis, a great improvement can be obtained in the use of aircraft for anti-submarine purposes'.[51] This charter resulted in the continuation of the former monthly *RNAS Anti-Submarine Reports* as monthly

Reports of Naval Air Operations, published and compiled not by the RAF but by the Admiralty's Air Division.[52]

The establishment of the RAF on 1 April 1918 added two benefits to the anti-submarine patrol system: improved organisation and the employment of greater numbers of aeroplanes.[53] The amalgamation of the RNAS with the RFC into a new RAF and Air Ministry did not bring immediate, revolutionary changes in operating routines or even command; on the contrary, the routine continued as before. RNAS group and squadron commanders retained their commands under the new service, the Admiralty and Air Ministry negotiating for months prior to the official commencement date over the organisation of naval air contingents and the commanders of the naval air groups. For example, the South-west Group under Wing Commander Gerrard, RNAS, became the No. 9 Group under Colonel Gerrard, RAF, and so on, as of 1 April 1918.[54]

The RAF did, however, universalise the Home Waters air contingent organisation, ensuring that each naval SNO had an air group assigned to him, with the RAF Group Commander acting as his chief air adviser. Some areas were streamlined; whereas the C-in-C The Nore, SNO Harwich, and Commodore Lowestoft, had to deal previously with unclear lines of command regarding their air assets, RAF units were now under one overall commander, Colonel C. R. Samson of No. 4 Group. Other areas, such as northern Scotland, where the RAF contingents working with the Grand Fleet complicated command and administrative matters, were reorganised. Admirals continued to issue operational orders directly to their air contingents, such as when, where, and how to conduct anti-submarine patrols, but the personnel came under the local RAF district commander for administration and discipline.[55] Additionally, RAF intelligence officers were ordered to coordinate with Admiralty intelligence, and the Air Ministry soon created an office dealing with air intelligence for naval contingents.[56] Nevertheless, the Royal Navy kept full operational control of its air contingent in Home Waters, albeit through a better organised system and helped by inputs from an external intelligence agency.

The other benefit to the air patrol system stemming from RAF independence was a heavy investment of aeroplanes to the overall effort. This initially appeared as a suggestion from R. M. Groves, a senior RNAS officer seconded to the Air Council staff, to use obsolescent DH-6 training aircraft to patrol shipping lanes close to shore until more suitable aircraft became available. The advantages of this scheme were that 851 of these aircraft were immediately available for service, and pilots could be easily scrounged from personnel deemed medically unfit or technically incompetent for overseas service but skilled enough for this relatively simple mission in a very forgiving aeroplane. Since U-boats had consistently demonstrated that they immediately submerged upon sighting an aircraft, the scheme was promising since 'even slow and obsolete machines carrying a pilot and without any bombs at all are better than nothing; they will prevent submarines from operating'.

Challenges to the scheme included a shortage of mechanics and a severe lack of facilities for basing the aircraft and housing the pilots and ground crews.[57] In service, the DH-6 proved that it was incapable of carrying both a bomb and observer and tended to suffer from frequent engine malfunctions. It did, however, serve as an airborne 'presence' along the inshore lanes. By 1 May 1918 the RAF had established 27 independent flights comprising 100 DH-6s around the coasts, especially in the south-west and north-east of England.[58]

The DH-6 scheme required a further increase in bases, but this investment had clear advantages. More bases meant shorter distances to patrol areas and shorter flight times for emergency patrols to reach their designated search areas. When the Air Ministry was finally able to provide well-armed DH-9 and Blackburn Kangaroo bombers in mid-1918, an infrastructure already existed to employ these units. By the summer of 1918 the RAF had provided the Admiralty with a powerful naval contingent in Home Waters whose primary duties were trade protection and cooperation with surface forces. The Admiralty did have cause for complaint; as mentioned above, deliveries of Large America flying boats and aeroplanes designed specifically for anti-submarine patrol (the Blackburn Kangaroo) fell behind due to labour and *materiel* shortages as well as lagging engine production. The future looked promising, however, since a proposed RAF order of battle for 1919 (dated August 1918) called for an increase of at least 40 further naval cooperation squadrons, many of which were slated for Home Waters anti-submarine patrol work.[59] Between April and October 1918, the RAF added 35 additional anti-submarine bases to the maritime air infrastructure in Home Waters.[60]

The Allies

Although the focus of this study is on the British experience in air anti-submarine operations in Home Waters, it would be useful at this point to mention briefly cooperation with the other two naval air services operating within or adjacent to British air forces in this region: the French and the Americans. Due to their heavy investment of pilots and machines on the Western Front, the French did not begin a coastal patrol system in earnest until early 1917. In May 1917, representatives from the Admiralty and the Dunkirk and Portsmouth air groups met with French Naval Air Service officers to discuss methods of coordinating the air effort against U-boats. The meeting, which was convened essentially to work out a mutually supporting system for the English Channel, produced an agreement which defined patrol areas (in order to avoid overlap and ensure maximum coverage) and kept aircraft on both sides of the channel ready for emergency patrols in the event of a U-boat sighting. Signals arrangements were simplified, and the services agreed to share statistics, methods, and observations. The Admiralty staff supported the initiative, and by July French summaries appeared at the end of each monthly *RNAS Anti-Submarine Report*.[61]

The French patrol scheme was in theory similar to that of the British, with an air commander working for the regional commanding admiral. The French, however, devoted most of their naval flying resources to the Mediterranean Theatre. In January 1918, for example, naval air stations in North Africa conducted the most anti-submarine patrols of any French coastal command.[62] Patrols conducted along the Biscay and Channel regions suffered from poor intelligence distribution and a lack of interest from senior commanders. As one visiting British staff officer commented, the system which he 'had been sent to investigate [in March 1918] did not exist'. The relatively few U-boat sightings in the coastal waters of northern France can be explained not only by a mediocre flying effort and organisation, but also by a simple lack of U-boats operating these areas.[63] The hunting was better in the approaches to, and coastal waters of Britain.[64]

The entry of the United States brought an eager partner to the war against U-boats in April 1917. Despite a dearth of personnel and aircraft at the start of its involvement, the US Navy planned to expand its air service and use it aggressively to combat the U-boat threat, which after all was – arguably – the primary reason for the declaration of war against Germany. The Admiralty welcomed the contribution, and the Americans acknowledged their 'junior partner' status. As Stephen Roskill put it, 'although there was a useful exchange of ideas . . . it was in general the British who were the teachers and the Americans who were the learners'.[65]

On 4 May 1917 a division of US destroyers arrived in Queenstown, signalling the initial American naval involvement in the war. Deployment of the scratch-built naval air service, however, would require a much greater investment in time, since aviators and mechanics had to be trained and equipment had to be purchased. In September 1917 the Admiralty proposed to the Admiral Mayo Mission that the US Naval Air Service take over the three main seaplane bases in Ireland to be 'equipped, manned, and controlled entirely by their personnel'.[66] The admiral commanding at Queenstown, Sir Lewis Bayly, had earlier demonstrated a lack of interest in naval aviation and a shift of this effort to the Americans, who got along well with their Irish hosts, seemed to provide an appropriate solution.[67]

As a result, the US Navy finally established a plan for air expansion in October that called for over 1,700 aircraft and 600 kite balloons. Early in November, the Navy's Air Board declared that this force would primarily be used offensively against U-boats.[68] In addition to the bombing effort mentioned above, the Americans would establish a group of patrol bases in England, Ireland, France, and Italy to aid the Allied naval effort against U-boats. The patrol bases assigned to work with the Admiralty, eventually through RAF oversight, included four seaplane bases in Ireland (Queenstown, Lough Foyle, Wexford and Whiddy Island), one Irish kite balloon base at Berehaven, the Dunkirk Seaplane Station, and the Killingholme seaplane base at the mouth of the Humber. It is interesting to note that a much greater American naval air effort was established along the French Atlantic coast, with 15 stations in operation or under construction at the time of the Armistice. Here, counter to the Planning Section's advice, the French and Americans agreed that escorting convoys would be the primary role of seaplanes; this is not surprising since American troop transports normally put into port in this area.[69]

Analysis of effectiveness

Both the Admiralty and the RAF went to great lengths to record the contribution of their airmen to the anti-submarine campaign, especially in regards to the numbers of patrols, flying hours, and attacks on submarines. The following analysis – based on a comparison of statistics compiled by the services during the war and on post-war staff studies, along with a number of previously overlooked Admiralty and Air Ministry files – will demonstrate that the contribution of air hunting patrols, relative to both air escort of convoys and surface hunting patrols, made a significant contribution to the containment of the U-boat threat. The key elements of successful patrols were organisation and persistence. The contribution was not singularly decisive, however. It was only important as an adjunct to other schemes and not an independent formula for success.

Area denial

The value of aircraft in an anti-submarine role was not necessarily in their limited ability to attack U-boats, but rather in forcing the U-boat to submerge. This fact was recognised and generally accepted during the war years.[70] U-boat commanders would generally dive their boats upon sighting any British or Allied aircraft; it was a precaution that was necessary in order to protect themselves from a lucky hit by an aircraft bomb that might damage critical operational equipment such as the periscope, depth sensors, dive planes or fuel tanks.[71] Even the slightest leak from a fuel tank would leave a deadly trail of oil on the surface, easily spotted in calm seas. Additionally, cases of U-boats attempting to fire at approaching aircraft were extremely rare; out of 47 U-boats spotted by Felixstowe flying boats between April 1917 and April 1918, only two attempted to fire at the approaching aircraft. Forty-four of these submarines submerged in order to escape the threat of air attack.[72]

Submerging would hinder the U-boat's ability to operate. Submerged speeds were generally limited to between 2 and 8 knots depending on the type of U-boat and the extent to which the captain risked discharging his batteries. The speed required to travel to the patrol area efficiently or to position the submarine for a torpedo attack could thus not be attained while submerged; U-boat commanders generally had to wait until the aircraft or accompanying surface vessels had left the area before coming to the surface and continuing at higher speeds. Also while submerged, navigation was temporarily hindered due to a lack of available landmarks, light vessels or celestial bodies with which to check the boat's position and course. The inability to navigate accurately in the often-dangerous coastal waters of Britain was a serious handicap to a U-boat captain.[73] Again, due to the lack of visibility while under water convoys and individual merchant vessels could not be found or, if discovered, could not be followed or attacked. The relatively short duration of the time a U-boat had in its patrol area – two weeks for a fleet boat or a few days for a coastal U-boat – meant that losing even a few hours of hunting due to being forced to dive at the approach of an air patrol would significantly reduce the effectiveness of the cruise. Moving from one operating area to another, either due to a lack of targets or to the threat of British patrol forces nearby, was also made difficult by these air patrols. As one RAF Staff College lecturer stated, 'The threat of attack by aircraft forced the enemy to remain submerged, which imposed serious disadvantages upon him.'[74] Chapter 7 below will further illustrate the German view of air patrols.

In 1917 British seaplanes, aeroplanes, airships, and kite balloons based in Home Waters sighted 169 U-boats resulting in attacks on 106 of those occasions. The first ten months of 1918 saw a modest increase to 192 sightings with 131 attacks.[75] It is evident from captured U-boat logs and diaries that at least a few German submarines were forced to dive on multiple occasions during a single cruise due to aircraft in the vicinity.[76] It is probable that in many instances U-boats dove before patrolling aircraft had the opportunity to spot and report them; the number of reported U-boat sightings, as mentioned above, is most likely a conservative judgment of the operational effect of the air threat and hence the impact of air patrols on hampering U-boat operations.[77]

As mentioned in Chapter 1, aircraft made surface hunting patrols more viable due to their advantage of visibility. For example, Felixstowe flying boats were able to sight U-boat conning towers (that is, while they were surfaced) as far away as 15 miles with good visibility, while a periscope wake sighting was recorded at four miles in misty weather.[78] Other accounts demonstrate the typical visible range of sighting a periscope, in normal seas, at five miles, ten miles in calm seas.[79] The speed of seaplanes and aeroplanes over surface vessels was an additional advantage, offering efficiency in sea area coverage. Although a First World War destroyer could achieve well over 30 knots, it typically patrolled at slower speeds to conserve fuel. Likewise, the P-boats, drifters and trawlers of the surface patrol flotillas normally had maximum speeds of 20, 9, and 10 knots, respectively, and cruised yet slower on patrol to increase range.[80] Typical patrol aircraft, such as the Short 184 float seaplane or the Felixstowe F2a flying boat cruised at 50 to 60 knots with airships achieving approximately half this speed.[81] Although limited endurance and susceptibility to poor weather conditions were a hindrance to aircraft patrols relative to those of surface craft, the combination of visibility and speed was a powerful supplement to the patrol flotillas.

The efficient exploitation of intelligence, as mentioned earlier, played a vital role in making the air patrol system more effective. By the end of the war, each air group had its own intelligence centre, 'usually in or adjacent to the Naval Operations Centre' of the parent Naval Command. Precise information from reports of sinkings and attacks as well as from wireless intercepts was collated and charted. Intelligence received from adjacent commands and the Admiralty itself further supplemented this data. One RAF aviator recalled that in north-eastern England (No. 18 Group), specific intelligence regarding the U-boat commanders known to be operating in their area – such as previous methods of attack and probable arrival time and location, as derived from espionage and other sources of intelligence – was passed on to the aircrews conducting patrols 'in time to be of real value to pilots and observers'.[82]

The following anecdote further illustrates this point. Flying airships from Anglesey in northern Wales for over 17 months, Captain T. B. Williams noticed definite patterns in how the U-boats conducted attacks. Working with his station's intelligence officer, the two men discovered that a German submarine appeared along a coastal steamer route at dawn at regular intervals.

> I decided that when this date and time next appeared I'd be there first . . . So in the middle of the night I had three airships – myself included – over this particular place in line ahead in equilibrium with engines just ticking over [i.e., hovering] . . . and absolutely at the first stroke of dawn there we had a report from a ship we could see that was being fired at by a German submarine. Simultaneously I had a message from the middle one of the three ships to say that it had sighted this submarine and actually as I was reading the message he was diving for it. We kept clear and he dropped his bombs and then I came up behind him you see and dropped mine . . .

The episode ended with destroyers arriving at the scene, which 'blew the bottom out of the sea', allegedly crippling the U-boat.[83] The use of intelligence thus served to focus patrols at points where they would be most useful, and 'such information enabled considerable economy to be effected' by forces patrolling in search of U-boats.[84]

At the end of August 1918, Sir Roger Keyes, the Vice-Admiral Dover Patrol, wrote to Brigadier General C. L. Lambe of No. 5 Group, RAF, complaining of delays between the time a U-boat was reported and the time No. 217 (Anti-Submarine) Squadron was notified, a few of which were just over four hours, during July and August 1918. The typical time between reporting and notification during the spring had been approximately 30 minutes and this correspondence demonstrates how important the use of intelligence had become by summer 1918.[85]

The ability to communicate completed the picture. By April 1918, 83 per cent of naval two-seat aircraft and 100 per cent of airships had been fitted with wireless sets. In order to support the aircraft and to intercept U-boat transmissions, there were 30 permanent and 23 'semi-permanent' wireless stations adjacent to Home Waters.[86] Patrolling aircraft, especially airships, would maintain wireless communications with home stations and surface patrols in order to report U-boat sightings immediately. Airship crews were instructed not to fly if their wireless equipment was inoperable and to return to base if it failed in flight, circumstances permitting.[87] Even without wireless, most aircraft observers had the option of communicating with surface vessels by Aldis Lamp and in the case of airships by semaphore and megaphone.

Through W/T, commanders could send reinforcements when possible in order to attack the U-boat when it resurfaced or at least to keep it down. By October 1917, a clear majority of air attacks on U-boats were followed up by surface hunts or air reinforcements – especially in waters in the immediate vicinity of the coast – due to the widespread availability of small patrol craft and the ability of aircraft to communicate with wireless, Aldis Lamp, flares, or semaphore. It is also interesting to note that the majority of these air attacks were conducted by aircraft on patrol as opposed to those on convoy escort duty.[88]

As mentioned previously, aircraft were at times specifically assigned to work with surface patrols. In these circumstances, the visibility and speed advantages of aircraft complemented the staying power and killing capabilities of surface vessels. In the South-west Group, seaplanes began to work with hydrophone flotillas regularly, flying triangular patterns around the ship formation.[89] These air-sea hunting patrols normally searched a specific area upon the receipt of intelligence of a U-boat sighting or wireless intercept. By summer 1918, schemes existed whereby seaplanes would work with surface vessels until they ran low on fuel, at which point airships would take over the scouting role for the force.[90] There were even cases recorded of patrolling airships being called in to assist with submarine hunts that were not pre-planned; on 2 January 1918 a P-boat flotilla summoned *SSZ-5* to help guide a depth charge attack.[91]

After considering the points above, the air patrols were in essence a powerful contributor to an area denial strategy against the U-boats. The evidence strongly indicates that in certain areas, when weather conditions and adequate numbers of aircraft permitted, U-boats were literally forced to operate elsewhere due to these patrols. In May 1917, six war cruises of Flanders U-boats accounted for only 3,138 tons of shipping off the Dutch coast, a failure largely resulting from extensive air patrols originating from Dunkirk, Felixstowe (Spider Web), and Great Yarmouth.[92] Examples of aircraft patrols frustrating U-boat operations abound in the German sources from spring of 1917, and wartime British commanders were aware of the contribution of aircraft from captured documents. One captured report confirmed that airship patrols off the Scottish coast 'were most unpleasantly active', 'repeatedly compelling the boat [*UB35*] to submerge for long periods'. The commander of *UB34* confessed in his war diary that the combination of three airships, calm seas, and clear weather forced him out of his patrol area, while *UC77*'s skipper explained that air-sea patrols north of the Firth of Forth 'hampers our operations in the same way as the centralisation of ocean-going shipping had done'.[93] Spindler's official history of the U-boat war and war diaries support this argument; air patrols frustrated U-boat operations often, especially from summer months of 1917 and 1918.[94]

Airship operations from Anglesey Airship Station during the summer of 1918 further bears out the area denial nature of aircraft operations. In May 1918 a new admiral commanding at Holyhead reorganised his anti-submarine efforts by *reducing* convoy escorts (both air and surface) to a bare minimum and using airships and patrol vessels to maintain a sustained presence over the area of a submarine attack, sighting, or wireless intercept. Better intelligence distribution, through a new web of wireless radios and telephone lines between headquarters and stations, combined with an improved U-boat tracking centre at Holyhead, produced a system whereby airships and patrol craft could be instantly directed from their patrol areas to a U-boat fix or the scene of an attack.[95] The resulting decline in Irish Sea sinkings, from 15 to 16 ships lost per month between February and April 1918 to a *total* of six sinkings during the period June through August (or an average of two per month), demonstrates the effectiveness of such a system.[96]

Arthur Marder offers that the primary factor in the increasing number of U-boat attacks against shipping conducted at night during the last 18 months of the war was the threat of air attack during the day. However, in steering the argument in support of the efficacy of the convoy system, and its accompanying air escorts, Marder misses the contribution of air hunting patrols to this shift in German tactics.[97] The area patrols of the Portsmouth air group, the busiest anti-submarine air unit of this period, provide a case in point. A staff officer summed up this effort in a December 1917 memorandum:

> [I]t should be realised that in the Portsmouth Command, an area of approximately 9,000 square miles, with water most suitable to submarine operations, there is a monthly traffic of 2,000 vessels passing East and West, and a cross channel traffic exceeding 600 per month, yet the average losses have not been above five ships per month in the last half year. It would of course be erroneous to ascribe this success wholly to aircraft, but it is unquestionable that the comparatively small force available, roughly 30–40 seaplanes and 6 airships, has contributed in a large measure to the success achieved.[98]

Between January and March 1918, the area between St Alban's Head and Beachy Head (mid-Channel) witnessed 53 night U-boat attacks on shipping out of 65 total attempts, or 81.5 per cent.[99] U-boats were forced to operate at night because the airspace in the mid-Channel was flooded with aircraft hunting patrols of the Portsmouth Group. The Portsmouth Group accounted for approximately one-quarter of the total home station flying effort, concentrated in a relatively small area.[100]

German U-boats tended to be more active when weather prevented aircraft from launching. An intelligence office snapshot of operations at East Fortune Airship Station (Firth of Forth) demonstrated that in August 1918 U-boats were active in the area only on days that the airships were grounded.[101] Although a further statistical examination does not directly point to aircraft patrols as the sole reason for success against the U-boats, the data does suggest that they had a positive impact. May of 1918, a month that witnessed a record destruction of nine U-boats in the Eastern Atlantic and Home Waters as well as a significant reduction of shipping losses in the same area, also happened to be the month that RAF air patrol flying hours and U-boat sightings substantially increased from previous periods (see Appendix 1). During May, the second month of the RAF's existence, sinkings in British coastal areas fell from an average of 56 per month to 35 ships lost. The average between May and October 1918 fell to 29 per month. The flying effort of all home-based anti-submarine air units doubled during this period – from 7,787 hours in April to 15,701 in May – and remained at high levels until the Armistice. Significant increases in the number of patrol sorties during this period led to a drastic increase in submarine sightings and attacks by aircraft.[102] The absence of any important changes in convoy tactics, other than a gradual improvement in efficiency, marks the increased flying effort of May 1918 as an important contributor in the anti-submarine campaign.

Mine detection

There is one further point worthy of consideration regarding the positive impact of air patrols. The improved visibility afforded to aircraft by their height was not only an advantage in spotting submarines and their periscopes, but it also contributed to the ability to detect German mines. German mine-laying submarines, particularly the *UC* classes based in Flanders, had the potential to wreak havoc on busy shipping lanes by laying small fields unexpectedly along mercantile routes and at the entrances to busy harbours. Although the threat of mine-laying submarines was not discovered until July 1915,[103] the Admiralty recognised the usefulness of air patrols in spotting mines, albeit as a lower priority to enemy submarine and aircraft searches, as early as March 1916.[104] Arthur Marder explains convincingly that it was not until the widespread use of the convoy system that the mine threat was really defeated. Controlled by the Royal Navy, which had access to the latest mine threat information, convoys were easily able to avoid these danger areas. In 1917 mines accounted for 404,000 tons of British, Allied, and neutral shipping; the total losses to mines in 1918 was only about 60,000 tons with only 12 ships being lost in areas under British mine sweeping responsibility.[105] These figures demonstrate a clear defeat of the German mine-laying effort, but the question of how these mines were initially detected remains unexplained in the literature. The contribution of aircraft patrols may shed light on this issue.

According to the Admiralty's staff study on the minesweeping effort during the Great War, mines were located by three primary methods: by using the minesweepers themselves to sweep up unknown mines in suspected areas, such as the approaches to a port or in front of a convoy; through 'scouting by means of aircraft or shallow draft craft at or near low water'; or simply by a vessel striking a mine or otherwise sighting it. Although aircraft could not spot submerged mines in clouded waters, such as those found around most coastal areas in eastern Britain, they were certainly useful in spotting these systems when they appeared on the surface after breaking free of their moorings or at low water. Aircraft had the advantage of speed and safety over surface vessels which hunted for mines; the British alone lost 214 mine-sweepers and small patrol craft to mines during the war – all but nine of those in Home Waters.[106]

Airship crewmembers, likely to spot mines due to their aircrafts' slow speeds and extended patrol durations, were instructed to treat mines seriously. In addition to photographing mines they spotted, pilots and observers were required to report and mark the position of the threat immediately. The importance was stressed with the following admonition: 'No mine is to be left until assistance had been obtained or it has been destroyed by the airship's own machine gun fire.'[107] Evidence from Admiralty airship statistics, crew memoirs, and logbooks bear out that these aircraft were active in detecting and reporting mines. Between June 1917 and October 1918 airships detected 134 mines and destroyed 73 of them.[108] Although this seems like a miniscule contribution, given that German submarines laid about 11,000 mines in 1,360 small fields during the course of the war, sightings led to detection of further mines and their neutralisation. For example, air reconnaissance led directly to the sweeping of 215 mines in the Dover area alone 'without accident' in 1918.[109] A total of 26 mines were detected by Capel airships of No. 5 Group during the period 1–15 June 1918 alone, of which eight were sunk by the airships themselves and the rest dispatched by follow-on surface vessels.[110] Even in northern waters, airship W/T operator Dixie Kidd recalled that mine searching was an important mission for North Sea airships operating from RNASS Longside, near Aberdeen. In this district, crews dropped buoys on detected mines in order to warn surface vessels of their location.[111]

Seaplanes also made a significant contribution to mine detection. Although total figures for mine detection by seaplanes and aeroplanes are not available, monthly *RNAS Anti-Submarine Reports* demonstrate that between July 1917 and March 1918 seaplanes and flying boats spotted 23 mines; airships detected 32 during the same period. Flying from Westgate, a seaplane base adjacent to the Thames Estuary, C. Phillip Bristow recalled that searching for periscopes and mines were his primary duties while on area patrol. Mines freed from their moorings would float to the surface revealing the presence of larger minefields in these heavily traversed waters, often a target of German

UC minelayers. This no doubt explains the typically high mine reporting figures from Westgate seaplanes in the monthly reports.[112] Even flying boats, conducting sweeps ahead of Dutch beef convoys, patrolled at 500–600 feet above the sea specifically to be in a position to spot periscopes or mines.[113]

Late in the war, the Admiralty considered equipping airships with mine-sweeping gear – 'either with a light sweep or by controlling a surface-borne [unmanned] sweep by electric cable'.[114] Although this proposal did not seem to develop into actual operations, airship and seaplane units continued patrolling after the Armistice in order to search for mines while the aircrews awaited demobilisation.[115] Their contribution to the post-war task of sweeping up almost 2,000 unaccounted German mines and thousands of defensively-laid British and American mines in Home Waters further demonstrates the value of aircraft in spotting these weapons.[116]

Challenges to operations

It must be emphasised, however, that air patrols were at the mercy of the weather and equipment failures. One seaplane commander estimated that his aircraft at Portland experienced an engine failure 'once in three patrols' during 1917.[117] During the last sixth months of the submarine campaign (May–Oct 1918) over 8 per cent of fixed-wing and 14 per cent of airship anti-submarine missions had to be curtailed due to weather conditions. In September 1918 alone, one in ten heavier-than-air and one in four airship sorties were similarly cut short.[118] The period between 1 July and 30 September 1918 saw only 35 days (out of 92) where weather was suitable for No. 18 Group's airships to operate along the Yorkshire coast.[119] The typical monthly total of flying hours during the last six months of the submarine campaign was between 10,000 and 12,000 hours per month for all types of aircraft (except kite balloons). May and August witnessed superb flying weather, however, and monthly totals during these months jumped to 15,701 and 21,574 hours, respectively (see Appendix 1).[120] Such variations prove how dependent these early aircraft – susceptible to fog, low clouds, and high winds – were on good weather.

Anti-submarine patrols also presented a challenge to aircrew morale. Long hours of monotonous patrols, often conducted in foul weather, strained pilots and observers mentally and physically. Airship unit commanders soon discovered that the eyestrain added to the monotony of patrolling and learned that limiting missions to eight hours duration served to maximise efficiency.[121] By meticulously recording numbers of sorties and hours flown, air commanders used statistics in an attempt to promote rivalry among the units, thus enhancing morale. It was further necessary to keep the aircrew 'interested and well informed, and explain that the better they were doing their work the fewer submarines would be sighted'.[122] The 'utter boredom' of these patrols may have indeed been, in the words of one airship veteran, 'the greatest difficulty to contend with'.[123] Another seaplane pilot referred to a certain 'temperament' that was required to fly these missions over water: 'The soul destroying monotony of flying hour after hour and day after day, month in and month out over apparently endless expanses of gray[*sic*] heavy sea with nothing whatever in sight appears to demand different qualities from those which go to make the dashing fighter pilot.'[124]

It was not until October 1918, however, that the Admiralty finally realised that RAF pilots and observers assigned to naval contingents were not being encouraged in their work in an official capacity. The Board therefore urged regional naval commanders to recommend deserving individuals for honours and awards, which the Admiralty would then forward to the Air Ministry for approval.[125] Fortunately, the lowering of morale caused by the daily, arduous conditions did not appear to appreciably affect actual operations.

Conclusion

Air patrols made an important contribution to anti-submarine warfare from mid-1917 until the end of the war. A synergistic effect, of leveraging the height and speed advantages of aircraft with the endurance and weaponry of surface vessels, developed dramatically during this period and denied the U-boats the use of certain operating areas. The RAF's improvements to infrastructure and intelligence networking served to increase the effectiveness of these patrols despite the limitations of weather and equipment and the challenges of defending against German seaplanes and of sustaining morale.

The new RAF seemed to embrace its responsibilities to provide air units for naval cooperation in this role. Former RNAS men found themselves accomplishing the same missions but in new uniforms and under new organisations. In May 1918, R. M. Groves wrote that 'the general feeling amongst the ex-Naval men (and indeed I believe amongst the ex-Military men also) of the Royal Air Force was that it was up to us to give the Navy even more than they would have got under the old regime.'[126] According to S. F. Wise, the Admiralty was at this time 'clearly interested in making the new service a success', with senior officers such as Wemyss and Beatty supporting the amalgamation.[127] Although Air Ministry-Admiralty relations suffered over the supply of adequate naval aircraft, the younger service never challenged the Admiralty's operational oversight of its RAF maritime contingents.

What is important to realise from the air patrol effort was not the number of U-boats destroyed during these operations but the effect that aircraft had on U-boat cruises. In today's defence terminology, these operations would be characterised as Effects-Based Operations (EBO), an approach that does not necessarily target enemy forces for destruction but intends to achieve only the desired effect on that target, such as neutralising enemy activity through limiting or hindering their actions.[128] Thus, air patrols helped to hinder the ability of U-boats to find merchant vessels and convoys by forcing them to dive when they did not want to. With well over 200 anti-submarine attacks to their credit, mostly during area or hunting patrols, aircraft played an important role in the overall anti-submarine effort.

The most valuable contribution from these weapon systems, however, is the subject of the next chapter: air escort of convoys. It was not convoy alone that 'defeated' the U-boats. The U-boats were defeated only in the sense that their ability to inflict damage was curtailed severely by a larger anti-submarine system of convoys, surface patrols, mine barrages and air patrols. Anti-submarine air patrols were useful when viewed as part of this system.

5   Aircraft and convoy escort

The decision to adopt convoy as an anti-submarine method was clearly the key event in the war at sea between 1914 and 1918. A failure to contain the U-boat menace, especially after the adoption of unrestricted submarine warfare in February 1917, would have meant severe food shortages at home, the paralysis of trade and its war-feeding profits, the absence of shells and supplies at the front, and the potential for defeat. The heavy shipping losses of the early months of 1917 provided the necessary incentive to attempt convoy as an alternative anti-submarine method. Although the decision to adopt convoy for overseas trade in late April 1917 has met with much historio-graphical controversy over the course of the last nine decades,[1] convoy tactics nevertheless contributed decisively to a strategic defeat of the unrestricted submarine warfare campaign and ensured that Britain and her Allies would continue to fight and win the war. At its peak in April 1917, the German offensive cost the Allies 226 ships of over 500 tons GRT in all theatres; in September 1917, the worldwide losses amounted to only 87 ships.[2] As the meticulous Barley and Waters staff study states, during the unrestricted submarine campaign only 257 out of 83,958 ships (over 500 tons GRT) sailed under convoy escort were lost to U-boats in Home Waters. Out of 1,757 total losses during the period, the vast majority (1,500 or 86 per cent) occurred when ships sailed independently.[3] Convoys completed the Admiralty's array of anti-submarine methods and tactics – which also included surface, sub-marine, and air patrols, mine barrages, and assaults on U-boat bases – but the convoy system was the most important contributor to thwarting the U-boats.

The decision to adopt convoy escort as an anti-submarine method added yet another task to naval aviation units operating in Home Waters. In order to supplement their surface escorts, regional naval commanders ordered sub-ordinate air units to carry out convoy protection missions. This new role for aircraft met with immediate success and was without question the most effective use of air power in countering the U-boat threat. No U-boats attacked a convoy that had air escort to supplement its warship protection until December 1917. The first recorded attack on an air escorted convoy occurred on the 19th when a Newlyn seaplane observed a torpedo wake approaching a steamer. Luckily the torpedo missed its target, the seaplane commencing an immediate counterattack with its own bombs and guiding surface ships to the submarine's position. The second case of a U-boat attack on an air-escorted convoy was more troubling. On Boxing Day, a U-boat sank two merchantmen as they left Falmouth under the protection of an airship, which was seven miles from the scene of the attack since the convoy was still forming. A third torpedo missed another ship; the U-boat skilfully attacked three times in a period of less than one hour and escaped unharmed.[4] This success was short-lived. British sources reported that in 1918 there were only six occasions when U-boats attempted attacks on convoys, which had both air and surface escort, resulting in a loss of only three ships.[5] Thus, during the First World War U-boats were able to claim a mere five vessels sunk out of the thousands of ships accompanied by both air and surface escorts. Judging by these statistics, the use of aircraft to protect convoys was an extraordinary development in naval warfare.

The concept of air escort developed rather haphazardly, however, and techniques and emphasis varied from region to region. Again, the Admiralty's refusal to organise the RNAS centrally, instead relying on naval district C-in-Cs to exercise operational control, meant that the air escort concept was not universally accepted around the coasts of Britain and there were clear regional variations in technique. Depending on the personalities of the naval and air group commanders, the tactical considerations of the specific area, and the operational experience accrued, air escort doctrine, especially regarding the allocation of air weapon systems, differed tremendously.

While most historians are content to highlight aviation's contribution to the World War I convoy system, they do so without explaining how aircraft escort patrols were conducted in order to provide such immunity. Likewise, a close examination of Home Waters air contingent operations demonstrates that not all naval commanders were convinced of the air escort idea, as many of the secondary accounts would lead readers to believe. The Barley and Waters convoy study, which heavily influenced Arthur Marder's more public and hence more well-known and oft-quoted volumes, states that by the middle of 1918 anti-submarine air units 'shifted from area patrol to convoy close and distant escort'.[6] Marder failed to recognise that much of the evidence provided in the Barley and Waters study came from one area: the north-east coast of England, an area that led the way in air escort but by no means typified a widespread, accepted policy.[7] Likewise, other historians generalise the role of aircraft by 1918 and imply that air units spent most of their time escorting as opposed to patrolling.[8] The purpose of this chapter is to examine the operational technique employed by airship, seaplane, aeroplane, and kite balloon units in order to discover the reasons for success. Additionally, the voluminous statistics left by the Admiralty's Directorate of Statistics and Air Division Staff will expose the extent to which the operational techniques of the various air groups diverged.

Tactics and operational technique by geographic area

World War I convoys may be generally grouped into four categories, all of which had fruitful support from aircraft. The first group included the short-distance convoys in Home Waters to European Allies and neutrals and included commercial convoys to Holland and Norway and coal convoys to France.[9] The threat of German submarines and other warships on either flank of the Thames–Holland route meant that protection was vital to its success and convoys began here in July 1916. These small 'Beef Trip' convoys, so named for their high proportion of foodstuffs, became the responsibility of Harwich Force destroyers and – eventually – Felixstowe flying boats. Like-wise, commercial convoys to Norway (beginning in late January 1917) and coal convoys to France (as of February 1917), both crossing U-boat infested waters, benefited from escorts of Scotland-based airships and Channel coast aircraft, respectively. These convoys were organised either locally or by the Admiralty, while the control and allocation of their escort forces was directed locally.[10]

The second and probably most overlooked category of convoy was warship escort. Destroyers and cruisers escorted troop transports from the very start of the war, especially those vessels carrying soldiers from the Dominions. Airships in western England escorted these valuable ships into port when weather conditions permitted. The most obvious benefactor of convoy, how-ever, was the Grand Fleet, which always sailed with a screen of destroyers. Again, long-range airships, such as the Coastal and North Sea classes, escorted the fleet in the North Sea on a number of occasions.

The third category of convoy was overseas trade, also known as ocean convoys. The first experimental convoy sailed from Gibraltar on 10 May 1917, and a flying boat from the Scillies escorted it during the final leg of the journey. Trans-Atlantic convoys began on a trial basis in late May and into June, leading to a gradual expansion of the ocean convoy system. The Admir-alty controlled these convoy sailings through the Convoy Section and Mercantile Movements Division and issued escort orders directly to the C-in-C Plymouth regarding escort forces.[11] Admiralty orders for escort forces of ocean convoys included rendezvous arrangements and details of the ships in the convoy and their sailing order. It is noteworthy that the Wing Captain of the South-west Air Group was included in the distribution list for these orders, although no direct air escort orders emanated from the Admiralty.[12] The role of aviation in support of the ocean convoys was to escort them as they approached the western ports of Britain when possible. Kite balloons flown from escorting warships also served to protect convoys through the danger zones.

The final category of convoy was the coastal trade of Britain, known as coastal convoys. The first of these set sail on 29 April 1917, originating in the Shetlands (from Lerwick, also the terminus of the Norway convoy route) and proceeding down the coast of Scotland to the Humber. From the start, the

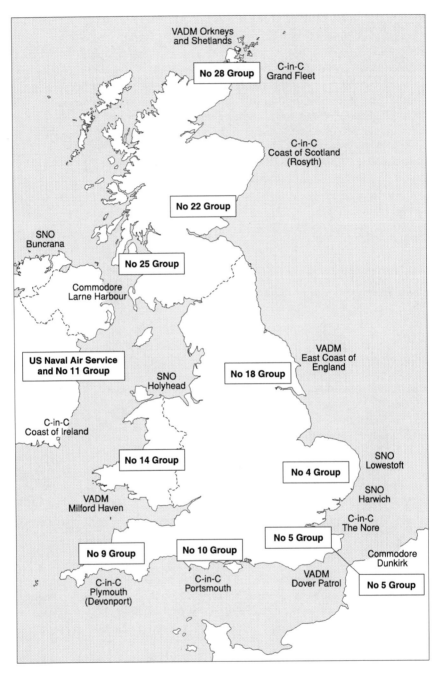

VADM Orkneys
and Shetlands

No 28 Group

C-in-C
Grand Fleet

C-in-C
Coast of Scotland
(Rosyth)

No 22 Group

SNO
Buncrana

No 25 Group

Commodore
Larne Harbour

VADM
East Coast of
England

**US Naval Air Service
and No 11 Group**

SNO
Holyhead

No 18 Group

C-in-C
Coast of Ireland

No 14 Group

SNO
Lowestoft

No 4 Group

SNO
Harwich

VADM
Milford Haven

C-in-C
The Nore

No 5 Group

Commodore
Dunkirk

No 9 Group

No 10 Group

VADM
Dover Patrol

No 5 Group

C-in-C
Plymouth
(Devonport)

C-in-C
Portsmouth

Figure 5.1 RAF (Naval) Air Groups and major naval districts, 31 October 1918.

Lerwick-Humber convoys benefited from the protection of airships based in Scotland and Yorkshire. At that time, these convoys represented only a tiny proportion of the coastal traffic, however. As the coastal convoy system developed further, especially after June 1918, the role of aircraft expanded tremendously as the convoys increasingly enjoyed the protection of aeroplanes as well as seaplanes and airships, which could easily reach the convoys from their bases ashore. By the summer of 1918, control of these convoys with their escorts appears to have been delegated from the Admiralty to local naval commanders.[13]

General aircraft tactics

In general the overall tactical benefit of the convoy system, derided by many as 'defensive' instead of 'offensive',[14] was that it forced the U-boats to attack a relatively well-defended area. The shipping which formerly stretched out across the trade routes was now concentrated in small groups, providing fewer targets for submarine commanders. If a U-boat sighted a convoy, it would normally have to proceed on the surface at high speed in order to position itself for the attack. Even if the U-boat was able to gain an adequate firing position, it usually only had one attempt to fire a torpedo, since the escorts' counterattack would normally be so powerful that a subsequent attack would generally be extremely difficult.[15] Knowing therefore that the Germans would be searching for convoys and attempting to manoeuvre in order to intercept them, 'the area in which the submarine is to be hunted is narrowed to the least possible limits', as the December 1917 RNAS *Anti-Submarine Report* stated.[16]

Aircraft were a nearly perfect complement to the surface escorts of a convoy. Airships, seaplanes, and kite balloons brought increased visibility to the tactical picture. As one Admiralty Technical History reported, the track of a torpedo was easily seen from the air even in a rough sea; the beginning of the track would deliver the position of the submerged U-boat to aircraft observers and pilots.[17] The inability of aircraft to deliver more than a couple of depth bombs, however, was offset by the availability of dozens of heavier depth charges onboard the surface escorts. Finally, aircraft orbiting further away from the convoy – as a distant escort a few miles ahead, behind, or on the flank – would most likely be able to observe a surfaced U-boat manoeuvring to gain a firing position. Thus, as Arthur Marder neatly concludes, 'air escorts deprived U-boats of their chief advantage – surprise attack after unobserved approach'.[18]

An Admiralty manual outlined the Air Division's recommended procedures for air escort by seaplanes, which in essence provides the accepted employment views during the closing months of the war. *Notes on the Co-operation of Aircraft with Surface Craft for Escorting Convoys of Merchant Ships* began with an admonition to air station commanders to keep in close touch with local SNOs and port convoy officers in order to coordinate rendezvous times and locations. After providing examples of convoy air escort requests and relay schemes for multiple seaplanes escorting a convoy over a long distance, the manual set out specific guidelines for aircraft crewmembers. If only one seaplane was available for escort, the pilot was to 'remember the golden rule for aircraft: KEEP CLOSE TO CONVOY'. Relying on known U-boat attack tactics, the advice was fairly straightforward: take station between the sun and the convoy to simplify observation; venture out to ten miles on either side of the convoy when escorting a slow-moving formation in fine weather in order to thwart a U-boat's attempt to manoeuvre into firing position on the surface; with a fast convoy only scout ahead of the formation since the U-boat must be ahead to make a successful attack; with a brisk wind stay to the windward of the convoy where the U-boat captain knows the ship lookouts will not be as effective with wind in their eyes; and finally, attempt an immediate counterattack at low altitude if the periscope is still visible – if not, circle the area to keep the submarine down and call for surface escort help. The manual concludes with a technical discussion of estimating the bomb aiming point based on the U-boat's assumed speed and depth.[19]

Airship crewmembers received similar guidance. The endurance of non-rigid airships meant that they could remain with the convoys for many hours at a time. An extreme case from April 1918 demonstrates the endurance advantage of airships; East Fortune's *NS-3* flew a 55-hour mission in which it escorted three different merchant convoys (over 28 hours), in addition to three groups of minelayers and minesweepers, between the Moray Firth and the Tyne. The airship easily maintained contact with the convoys during the night.[20] A more typical example was a 16-hour patrol by airship *C-9*, which devoted almost nine hours to convoy escort.[21]

The airship lacked speed, however, and this fact made it vital to keep close to the formation. Pilots were warned to keep to the upwind side of the formation; the relatively slow maximum speed (40–50 miles per hour) of the airship would be drastically reduced if it had to manoeuvre into a strong headwind in order to investigate a possible periscope sighting or make a bombing run. In the event of a submarine attack on a convoy, airship trainees were instructed to search for the U-boat at the start of the torpedo track, attack immediately, and communicate the threat to the escort leader.[22]

There were only two cases during the war in which convoys escorted by airships were attacked: one as mentioned above in December 1917, and another in 1918.[23] One of the keys to the success of airships in this role was that they conducted these escorts in areas where there was no threat from German seaplanes. With nothing to fear from enemy air attack, the airship crew could devote their entire attention to visual scanning for surfaced U-boats, periscopes, and mines. There were a very small number of cases in which a U-boat attempted to fire at an airship, but Lewis gun fire from the observer normally forced the U-boat gun crew below decks.[24]

For all of these reasons, the airship was well suited for convoy escort, although high winds could offer a challenge, especially in the winter months.

As an indication of the growth of the air escort role for airships during the course of the anti-submarine campaign, it is interesting to note that between June 1917 and October 1918 airships flew 2,210 escorts but only 210 of these took place in 1917.[25]

The final airborne weapon system available as an escort to convoys was the kite balloon – a system that was essentially an elevated observation post for the escort vessel, benefiting from a voice telephone system to communicate with the bridge. The early thinking concerning kite balloon employment called for an offensive posture, with the kite balloon ships sailing 30 miles ahead of the convoy, searching for manoeuvring U-boats planning to get in front of the convoy along its course.[26] Leading up to the end of 1917, there was extensive debate in the Admiralty over the use of kite balloons as convoy escort. The main disadvantage of employing kite balloons with convoys was that it enabled a hunting U-boat to spot a convoy at a longer range since the balloon could be viewed from a considerable distance, rising well above the horizon. The Anti-Submarine Division estimated that a submarine could spot a convoy at 15 miles range if it had no kite balloon escort; with the kite balloon flown near the formation of ships, the range increased to 20 miles. Nevertheless, it was obvious that a surfaced submarine would usually be able to see the kite balloon at a distance before the balloon could spot the submarine. On the other hand, the advantages of using the balloon in company with the convoy were immense – outweighing the liability of five extra miles visibility to a searching U-boat – due to the extended visibility afforded to the observer. The December *RNAS Anti-Submarine Report* listed these benefits as:

1   The ability to spot a torpedo approaching the hosting warship.
2   Detecting the submarine as it manoeuvres into attack position.
3   Seeing a surfaced submarine at relatively long range.
4   Compelling the U-boat to dive through fear of observation/detection, causing it to lose sight of the convoy and the opportunity to calculate its course.
5   To deceive the submarine as to the position of the convoy by sailing the kite balloon vessel many miles ahead of the main formation.[27]

By early July 1918, the official Air Division recommendation on kite balloon employment was that two balloons should be ideally used and be placed ahead of the convoy on either bow at three to five miles distance. If only one balloon were available, it was to steam the same distance ahead of the convoy by zigzagging across the path of the formation.[28] This appears to be the standard operating method by the end of the war. These basic 'rules of thumb' for air escorts provide only a tactical-level view of why aircraft were so effective. The following examination, however, will serve to illustrate the differing priorities and operating techniques among the various air contingents serving senior naval officers in the Home naval commands – that is, at the operational level of strategy.

The barrage areas: Dover and the Orkneys and Shetlands air groups

The purpose of a World War I mine barrage was to force U-boats to dive into a series of nets and minefields, hopefully destroying or at least disabling the submarine. In all cases, a strong patrol was required in order to force an approaching U-boat to dive into the fields. There were two mine barrage areas that received air support from RNAS and RAF Home air contingents, again with the purpose of forcing the U-boat to dive into danger. The earliest was the Dover Barrage, supported by the air forces of the Dover Patrol and later No. 5 Group, RAF. This line of minefields crossed the Dover Straits between Folkstone and Cape Griz Nez and was heavily reinforced under Sir Roger Keyes in 1918. Also, the Northern Barrage project, meant to employ a series of minefields from the Orkneys to the coast of Norway, had a group of seaplane and airship stations devoted to its patrols. This massive effort would require a large number of surface and air patrols to make it effective. The North Sea class of airships were specifically designed for this patrol mission and were based at nearby Longside and East Fortune for this purpose. Air units in these areas generally avoided air escort as a specific task due to the requirements of barrage patrolling and offensive sub-hunting, but a review of each area will show that there were exceptions, especially during the closing months of the war.

The Dover air station, established in November 1914, used two seaplanes and six aeroplanes at the opening of hostilities to escort troopships and transports across the Channel.[29] Airships from south-eastern England accomplished similar missions. When aircraft took on more of an anti-submarine role during the spring of 1917, the Admiralty recommended that Sir Reginald Bacon, the Vice-Admiral Dover Patrol, use his air units to protect the coastal shipping routes as their first priority.[30] Monthly flying reports demonstrate that the Dover air contingent escorted shipping sparingly during the remaining months of 1917 and early 1918. Aeroplanes, seaplanes and airships of Dover and Dunkirk instead concentrated on area patrols over the mine barrages and over the Belgian coast; few convoys crossed the operational area until very late in the war anyway. The airship station at Folkstone (also known as Capel) flew only 22 escorts during the last seven months of 1917. It did not employ its non-rigids in the escort role significantly until March 1918, when approximately one out of three patrol missions flew a convoy escort, this rate being sustained until the end of the war. Many of these escorts were for the cross-Channel steamers en route to Boulogne.[31]

The first significant jump in escort rates for fixed-wing aircraft in the Dover command occurred in July 1918, with 26 escorts out of 241 air patrols flown. This resulted from new No. 5 Group orders, on 1 July 1918, for its DH-9 patrol flight to provide a two-aircraft formation for each convoy scheduled to proceed through the Dover Straits. In the meantime, the other flights of seaplanes and Camels would conduct offensive patrols but also keep a reserve of aircraft ready to assist in any submarine sightings.[32] No. 217

Squadron, located near Dunkirk, avoided escort work in favour of hunting patrols and bombing attacks on Belgian ports, its high speed and well-armed DH-4s being less suited to orbiting above convoys.[33] The still relatively small number of convoys traversing the heavily mined and U-boat infested area meant that air escort remained a secondary mission in the Dover command.

The primary role of aircraft in the Orkneys and Shetlands area, on the other hand, was to work with the Grand Fleet when it was present at Scapa Flow – an anti-submarine mission for aircraft considered as early as 1913.[34] The airship station at Caldale, near Kirkwall and hence close to Scapa, was a small facility and had room only for a few airships at a time. In early June 1917, Beatty issued orders to the Caldale Airship Station to carry out daily patrols, the object of which was to be convoy protection, submarine search, and mine detection. The only convoys supportable from the Orkneys and Shetlands were the Scandinavian convoys running between Lerwick and Bergen. The key to this order was that the Admiral Commanding, Orkneys and Shetlands, was 'requested to supply the Airship Station with information regarding the movements of convoys, in order that airship patrols may be arranged with a view to scouting ahead of convoys and affording them as much protection as possible'. Upon spotting a submarine, the airship pilot was instructed to notify the convoy immediately both by visual signal and a wireless message.[35] Airships at the station were relatively active during the late summer and early autumn of 1917, conducting a few escorts of Norwegian convoys, but the airship facility at Caldale was closed down in January 1918. The strong gales of the Orkneys, the base's limited capacity (only one airship could be inflated at a time), and the desire for more kite balloon support for the Fleet and Northern Barrage led to Caldale being converted into a kite balloon base by summer 1918.[36]

The RNAS maintained a small seaplane station at Scapa Flow itself since August 1914, reinforced by seaplane carriers from the Grand Fleet (such as HMS *Campania*) in conducting a limited number of submarine patrols.[37] Seaplanes and aeroplanes in the Orkneys and Shetlands did not undertake convoy escorts of merchant convoys until September 1918; instead they were employed as escorts and reconnaissance forces with the fleet with occasional searches for reported U-boats ('emergency' patrols). So, in the sense that these aircraft escorted battleships, it may be considered that their screening role, in search of German ships, Zeppelins, and submarines, was a useful deterrent to U-boats. The Admiralty also opened two flying boat stations in the area – at Houton Bay, Orkneys, in July 1917, and at Catfirth, Shetlands, in November 1917 – in order to provide patrols for the planned North Sea Mine Barrage's western sectors. The acquisition of these precious aircraft was slow and by mid-February 1918 the two bases could only report one flying boat on charge.[38] Thus, these bases did not contribute significantly to the anti-submarine campaign until the spring of 1918, when increased aircraft production provided more flying boats and hence a greater number of patrol sorties. Nevertheless, seaplanes (aeroplanes only worked with the fleet) in the

Orkneys and Shetlands area flew a total of six convoy escorts during the entire course of the war.

The Northern Isles possessed one other resource in their array of anti-submarine systems: the kite balloon. In July 1917, the Admiralty requested that Beatty experiment with kite balloon escorts for the Lerwick-Bergen convoy route. Beatty's chief air adviser at this time, Vice-Admiral Sir John de Robeck, commander of the 2nd Battle Squadron of the Grand Fleet, recommended that the kite balloons for the convoy experiment be drawn from the Grand Fleet Destroyer Kite Balloon Force, then in use conducting intensive hunting patrols of northern waters.[39] These destroyers did not return to Scapa until the end of the summer, and when they finally attempted the experiment on 18 September 1917 the weather proved 'unsuitable for kite balloon work'. With the onset of winter weather, the experiments were postponed until the following spring.[40] A November letter from de Robeck, where he advised against the kite balloon escort concept for the Norwegian convoys because 'fitting out a separate kite balloon convoy service appears to be a somewhat complicated matter involving the use of less effective vessels, new organisation and additional equipment', probably discouraged Beatty from attempting the experiments again.[41] As a result kite balloons operating from the Orkneys and Shetlands appear never to have been used as convoy escorts.[42]

The air contingents operating adjacent to the barrage areas of Dover and the Northern Isles thus failed to conform to the myth of widespread air escort employment. Their priorities rested elsewhere. The experience of the air stations of East Anglia further demonstrates that the role of aircraft operating with convoys has been misrepresented by over-generalisation in the literature of World War I naval operations.

East Anglia coastline

The south-eastern coast of England represented the frontline of the naval war; this area faced Holland and was the easternmost portion of British territory in the southern North Sea. The air stations of East Anglia and the Thames Estuary had been some of the first in existence in Britain. Eastchurch (established in 1911, but from 1916 was for training and experimental use only), Felixstowe (1913), Yarmouth (1913), and Westgate (1914) played important roles in the employment of aircraft in the anti-submarine war, but the aircraft in this region had many other duties. Close proximity to German Zeppelin bases and their expected flight paths meant that all of these stations took part in anti-Zeppelin defence patrols. The threat of German seaplanes based in Flanders and along the north-west coast of Germany added 'hostile aircraft patrol' missions to their duties, where formations of flying boats and aeroplanes ventured out into the Hoofden to seek combat with German naval aviators in an attempt to gain air superiority over the area.[43]

Offensively laid British minefields in the Heligoland Bight benefited from long-range flying boat patrols in order to observe German minesweeping efforts. The Spider Web U-boat patrol scheme, beginning in April 1917, added yet another role to scarce flying boat resources and meant that few aircraft were available for convoy escort. Airships based at Pulham, in East Anglia, were not available for convoy escort either; they had been forbidden from flying patrols after January 1918 because of the threat of German seaplanes.

Luckily for the south-eastern air stations, there was only one primary convoy operation being conducted in the area: the Dutch food convoys between the Thames and Holland. Commodore Reginald Tyrwhitt and his Harwich Force escorted these small convoys, beginning in July 1916, approximately twice per week with as much of the journey as possible sailing at night.[44] During the spring of 1917 Felixstowe flying boats commenced air support operations of the 'Beef Trips'.[45] According to T. D. Hallam, the Large Americas would patrol the route on the day prior to the sailing, and relays of flying boats would provide a distant escort, 10 to 15 miles ahead of the formation, during the journey.[46] In October 1917 day sailings began, offering opportunities for direct escort. The 11-hour voyage required two to three flying boat sorties per convoy on the day of the sailing, and the aircraft flew at 500 to 600 feet in order to spot periscopes and mines ahead of the formation.[47]

The relatively small number of these convoys – some 1,861 vessels escorted during the entire war with the loss of only seven ships[48] – meant that this mission made up only a small percentage of Felixstowe's flying effort. Between August 1917 and February 1918, the station never flew more than five escort sorties per month, which statistically meant that a maximum of two convoys per month received air escort during this period. Under No. 4 Group's tenure (during April–October 1918) the East Anglian flying boats increased their escort effort slightly, flying only 68 escorts of a total of 2,804 patrol missions by all aircraft types in the group, but it is clear that air escort stood at a low priority in comparison with other roles.[49] The fact that units of No. 4 Group, under C. R. Samson, served under the orders of three different senior naval commanders – C-in-C The Nore, Commodore Harwich, and Commodore Lowestoft – would have made convoy coordination efforts difficult, had the need been more pressing in this area.[50]

Finally, kite balloons in the South-east area, with their bases at Shotley, Lowestoft, and Sheerness, were employed only for offensive anti-submarine patrols and Harwich Force cooperation. The statistics demonstrate that commanders in this region apparently did not value the role of kite balloons as convoy escorts.[51]

The English Channel

The air group in the English Channel, centred on air stations in the Portsmouth area and serving the C-in-C Portsmouth, provided air escorts for a number of convoy systems, including cross-channel transports, some coastal escorts, and part of the French Coal Trade.[52] This extremely active air group patrolled for U-boats as they passed through the Channel on their way to the better hunting grounds of the South-west Approaches early in the unrestricted submarine campaign. The Portsmouth area, however, saw a great deal of coastal merchant traffic (some 2,000 vessels per month) as well as approximately 600 cross-Channel passages per month travelling through the sector, and U-boats often took the opportunity to sink some of this traffic on their cruises.[53] After the institution of ocean convoys, and the subsequent shifting of German attacks away from the South-west Approaches towards the coastal areas, losses in the Channel remained high until spring 1918, where the numbers of independent sailings (i.e. good hunting for U-boats) were commonplace. The aircraft of the Portsmouth area provided escorts for cross-Channel convoys beginning in September 1917.[54] The high volume of independent shipping in this area meant that area patrols remained an important priority for the aircraft of No. 10 Group until the coastal convoy system extended to the area in earnest in mid-1918.

The C-in-C Plymouth, commanding just to the west of the C-in-C Portsmouth's area, recommended in November 1917 that convoys be organised for all Channel traffic. One of the advantages Admiral Bethell listed was 'the greater protection afforded by aircraft', an appreciation he must have gained through his own experience in the south-west.[55] Channel losses declined sharply in May 1918, largely from the switch of Flanders U-boat cruises to the east coast of England, although this period also coincided with a rapid increase in the number of air escorts for the command.[56]

Personal experiences serve to further illustrate the general rise in escort missions in the region, but the increase was measured and a greater proportion of missions remained as area patrols. J. K. Waugh, who commanded the seaplanes at the Portland air station, recalled that not a single U-boat attack occurred during his squadron's 304 escort missions during the last four months of the war. In August 1918 alone, his seaplanes and DH-6s flew 400 hours on convoy escorts out of 1,100 hours flown.[57] The chief mechanic's log at the Newhaven seaplane station shows that the majority of 1918 sorties were area patrols with only a small proportion of convoy escorts. Likewise, C. S. Mossop, who flew 24 sorties in floatplanes from Calshot between 9 July and his death on 12 August 1918, conducted 16 area patrols but only three escorts during the period.[58]

Airships and kite balloons, present in relatively large numbers in the Portsmouth area, devoted only a small proportion of their sorties to escorts. Again, the high level of independent sailings in the mid-Channel until very late in the war may explain this lack of emphasis on escorts. The Portsmouth area, however, contrasted with the south-west region of the English coast, where the presence of more convoys provided greater opportunities for air escort.

The south-west

The south-west region was an important area for ocean convoys; a large proportion of the 1,134 ocean convoys conducted during the war travelled through the area. Falmouth and Devonport especially saw a large number of convoy arrivals and departures, and many convoys approaching the south-west of England required escorts from Plymouth surface escorts and Wing Captain Gerrard's air group. The first ocean convoy experiment from Gibraltar was escorted by a flying boat from Scillies during its final inbound leg to England in May 1917.[59] During the same month the C-in-C Devonport issued orders to Gerrard and his flyers instructing them that they might 'from time to time' be required to escort convoys and important individual vessels.[60]

One example of air escort of ocean convoys from this early period stands out as an ideal case of air-sea cooperation. In August 1917, Gerrard ordered that the homeward bound New York convoy, led by the USS *Cleveland*, be afforded a maximum effort air escort due to the importance of its cargo. Thus, at first light on 9 August a flying boat from the Scillies launched to rendezvous with the convoy and escorted it towards the coast. Later in the morning a Newlyn Short seaplane relieved the flying boat. At 0900 two airships took over escort duties from the seaplane. Then at 1035, HMAS *C-2*, a Coastal class airship, spotted a submarine on the surface seven miles away, a position approximately 15 miles south-west of the Lizard. The submarine was manoeuvring at high speed to intercept the convoy, but soon submerged to escape detection. Five minutes later, *C-2* dropped bombs on the submarine's suspected position and later signalled four destroyers from the convoy escort force to search the area. They depth charged an oil patch suspected to be emanating from the U-boat, while the other airship and a new seaplane arrived to maintain watch over the area. The air and surface escorts kept the U-boat down, while the convoy continued up the Channel unharmed.[61] The U-boat was almost certainly *UC33*, which reported being attacked by airships on the same day in the western English Channel.[62]

Gerrard codified the air escort concept in his September 1917 standing orders. Escorts were to be specifically ordered from group headquarters; airships were at times diverted from routine patrols for this duty, but seaplanes always began their escort missions specifically with the convoy in mind (due to their relatively short endurance). In either case aircraft were ordered to arrive at the rendezvous point 15 minutes early in order to search the area for submarines, and then to escort the ships as specifically directed. The other types of patrols in the south-west, such as routine, contact, and emergency patrols, appeared to possess significantly more importance, however.[63] By September 1917 airships of the South-west Group were conducting an increased proportion of escort missions, but seaplanes and aeroplanes flew only a small number of escorts. Even flying boats from the Scillies, in a relatively superior geographic position to escort convoys passing through the

South-west Approaches, spent a clear majority of missions in the routine patrol role.[64]

The airship station at Mullion (Cornwall) and its three substations contributed a large number of sorties to the submarine war and led the Airship Service in flying hour rates during 1918.[65] Even within the region, airships from the four stations would hand off convoys as they passed through each area of responsibility, ensuring continuous coverage for many journeys.[66] The French Coal convoys originating in Falmouth, which lost only 53 ships out of 39,352 sailed from all ports, also benefited from air cover, a success the Rear-Admiral in command at Falmouth attributed 'first and foremost' to air escort.[67]

With fixed-wing aircraft being reserved for routine patrols and 'offensive' uses such as contact and emergency patrols, the airships in the south-west assumed the bulk of the responsibility for convoy escort, but that was far from their sole purpose. Even as late as June 1918, Gerrard still maintained an emphasis on area patrols and contact work between destroyers, seaplanes and airships.[68] This view was confirmed by Gerrard's successor, Brigadier General H. D. Briggs, RAF, who in September reported that he intended to deny U-boats the ability to operate along the 'Coastal Traffic Routes' through heavy area patrols by both airships and heavier-than-air craft. Convoys were to be protected mostly by airships, backed up by seaplanes during periods of unsuitable weather.[69]

The south-west, however, employed kite balloons in greater numbers than any other Home command, which added protection to the convoys as they sailed through the danger zone but beyond the effective range of seaplane and airship patrols. The Plymouth Command – specifically, the 4th Destroyer Flotilla at Devonport – had actually led the way in experimenting with kite balloons during the spring of 1917 at the instigation of Jellicoe himself.[70] By 1918, operating from the detachment at Merifield (Devonport) and later reinforced by another base at Torquay, the kite balloons were very active and had flown the most escorts of any command during the final six months of the submarine campaign.[71]

The Irish Sea

The Irish Sea was an extremely challenging area for local naval and air commanders alike due to the high volume of traffic proceeding to and from the ports of the Clyde, Mersey, and Severn areas – especially arriving from overseas – and the numerous sailings between Ireland and the west coast of Britain.[72] By August 1917, the Admiralty realised that the U-boats intended to concentrate near the entrances to the Irish Sea as one method of countering the new ocean convoy system.[73] By autumn the previously quiet area became a popular hunting ground for U-boats, and losses increased dramatically in the area, peaking in early 1918.[74]

An additional challenge for the Irish Sea area was the divided command arrangements. There were four major regional naval commands operating forces in or near the Irish Sea; these were C-in-C Coast of Scotland, C-in-C Queenstown (also know as C-in-C Coast of Ireland), Vice-Admiral Milford Haven, and SNO Holyhead.[75] Other semi-independent regions also exercised command over local naval forces and included Rear-Admiral Buncrana and Commodore Larne Harbour, both located in north-eastern Ireland. Only the two commands in Wales (Milford and Holyhead) and the Coast of Scotland area had airship or seaplane units directly under their orders. Kite balloon detachments operated at Buncrana (Rathmullen-Lough Swilly) and for a time at Berehaven. Commodore Larne worked closely with the Luce Bay airship station in escorting convoys across the North Channel between Scotland and ports in northern Ireland.[76] Finally, US naval air units flew seaplane patrols from four stations in Ireland during the closing months of the war, under the operational orders of C-in-C Queenstown.

During the RNAS period, air units in southern Wales had been under Gerrard's South-west Air Group until December 1917, while the Luce Bay airship station was grouped together with stations on the east coast of Scotland. The lack of centralised command in the Irish Sea was not a problem until losses increased dramatically in early 1918 and the convoy system necessitated improved communication and cooperation. Needless to say, it was a great feat of coordination for the air units of the Irish Sea to work as closely as they did with the naval commanders and with each other. The entire region was finally put under one RAF group commander in September 1918.[77]

The communication system worked well, but the differing command relationships of each air station meant that air escort employment varied from region to region. SNOs, such as Gordon Campbell at Holyhead, would advise local air units, such as the Anglesey airship station, of inbound convoys, which would then be met by air escorts. This station also cooperated with airships from Pembroke and Luce Bay in handing off convoy escort duties from area to area.[78] As mentioned in the previous chapter, Campbell stripped his surface and air escorts to a minimum and preferred an area saturation strategy to prevent U-boats from operating in the mid-Irish Sea. In the northern areas of the Irish Sea, on the other hand, the North Channel saw a large number of small convoys supported by the airship station at Luce Bay. Extremely hazardous winter weather made airship escorts difficult, especially when operating from the substation at Larne in northern Ireland, but escorts were provided whenever possible.[79] In the south, Pembroke airships and Fishguard seaplanes flew relatively fewer escorts in the Bristol Channel. Airships in this area were routinely hampered by periods of high winds common to the region.[80] The Irish Sea thus witnessed a mix of employment philosophies for aircraft.

The east coast of England and Scotland

The presence of three large airship stations along the east coast of Scotland and England meant that the early Lerwick-Humber convoys and the later coastal convoy system would benefit from a relatively generous amount of air protection. Under the orders of the C-in-C Coast of Scotland (also known as C-in-C Rosyth), seaplanes at Dundee complemented airships at Longside, near Peterhead, and East Fortune, at the mouth of the Firth of Forth. The Rear-Admiral Commanding East Coast of England (RAECE) could call on airships of Howden, located along the banks of the River Humber, and seaplanes at Killingholme, South Shields, and other bases to aid in convoy escort missions. In 1918, substations would expand the reach from these primary bases. Although the two commands cooperated in the escort of coastal convoys,[81] which sailed through these adjacent areas on a daily basis, conflicting demands on the aircraft and differing employment philosophies saw a contrast in the use of aircraft to escort convoys. By the end of the war, the Scotland command used a balanced approach, with both seaplanes and airships flying a moderate proportion of escorts to patrols. The East Coast command on the other hand vigorously employed all aircraft available for convoy escort and, as the only region doing so, demands closer scrutiny in this study below.

Due to its proximity to the Grand Fleet, which had units stationed at Rosyth, the Coast of Scotland area often fell under the influence of the C-in-C Grand Fleet, commanded by Admiral Sir David Beatty during the last two years of the war. Admiral Sir F. T. Hamilton got along well with Beatty but died in office and was replaced in October 1917 by Admiral Sir Cecil Burney, a less highly regarded officer.[82] In both cases Beatty was pleased to offer suggestions as to the use of all types of aircraft in convoy work.

Hamilton ordered his airships to cooperate with the early coastal convoys from the start in April 1917. Although not specifically assigned on convoy escort missions, airship units were instructed to protect convoys they may spot while on daily patrol, protection to be regarded 'as the most important part of their duty', and to sweep ahead of the formation 'for as long as possible'. A new convoy sailed each day, which kept the airships extremely busy. Pilots were instructed to inform escorting warships of any submarine sightings immediately. Airships from Longside were to pay particular attention to the outer Moray Firth and the coastal route, which varied between 5 and 30 miles from the coast.[83] Seaplanes from Dundee, on the other hand, did not begin flying convoy escorts until February 1918, with hunting patrols consuming the majority of missions.[84]

In February 1918, Burney published specific orders for all aircraft operating as convoy escorts in Scotland. If an aircraft spotted a submarine it was to immediately drop a bomb on the position. Likewise, if a mine was spotted, it was to open fire on it with machine guns until attracting the attention of a surface escort. As soon as conditions permitted, the aircrew was to contact the Convoy Leader by Aldis Lamp and provide details.[85]

Beatty, who appeared to support the convoy concept earlier than most Royal Navy flag officers,[86] took advantage of his senior position by offering advice to his colleague at Rosyth: 'East Fortune airships should patrol the coast and screen convoys as far South as the Tyne' and 'While the co-operation of airships with the Fleet may be most valuable, their principal duty at present must be the protection of convoys proceeding up and down the coast.'[87] The relatively small number of fleet escorts by airships during the last two years of the war illustrates this emphasis: during 1917 there were six cases of fleet escorts with a further ten in 1918. Fleet escort operations, typically flown by as many as five airships from East Fortune and Longside, lasted for many hours and accompanied the Grand Fleet, or parts of it, as the ships patrolled the North Sea.[88] A major focus for the airships of Scotland by this time, however, was trade defence, with a relatively large proportion of convoy escorts making up the daily missions. Airships typically flew zigzag routes above the coastal convoys, with single airships relieving others in shifts.[89] Between May and October 1918, the airships of Longside and East Fortune, along with their substations at Auldbar and Chathill, flew 249 escorts out of 697 total sorties. During the same period, seaplanes from Dundee and its substations averaged fewer than 20 escorts per month, maintaining a high rate of hunting patrols as an alternative to escorts.[90] When either the Short 184 or Large America aircraft at Dundee flew escorts, missions tended to last approximately four hours.[91] The Scottish command had no kite balloons under direct orders; the balloon unit at North Queensferry fell under the command of the C-in-C Grand Fleet and was never employed in the convoy escort role.

Thus the C-in-C Scotland tended to employ airships as the primary aircraft escort weapon system with seaplanes occasionally escorting but usually hunting. This approach differed from that seen further to the south, in the U-boat infested waters between the Tyne and Humber Rivers.

The air group under the Rear-Admiral (later Vice-Admiral) Commanding East Coast of England was responsible for the area between the Wash and the Scottish Border – some 250 miles of coastline. The Lerwick-Humber convoys enjoyed support from Howden airships, which escorted northbound convoys as far as Scarborough and attempted to return in company with the southbound convoy if daylight permitted.[92] Otherwise, air escort of convoy was limited until the RAF amalgamation in spring 1918 simply because there was still a great amount of shipping sailing independently and area patrols were a more efficient use of limited numbers of aircraft than trying to escort individual ships. During the months under RNAS command, with Wing Commander C. R. Finch-Noyes as the senior RNAS adviser to the RAECE, the area was starved of resources with only 47 seaplanes, five flying boats, five airships and no kite balloons in commission by January 1918.[93] Although losses to U-boats along the east coast were heavy during 1917, higher rates of sinkings in other areas, especially the English Channel, meant that the RAECE area had a lower priority for resources. Thus the effort to provide coastal convoys along the east coast with air escort – operating from only six air stations – met with difficulty during 1917 and early 1918.

The RAF amalgamation was a key event for the east coast because it allowed the numerous former RFC landing grounds along the coastline to be used for naval contingents, especially by flights of DH-6s that were being established in the command. Additionally, the amalgamation coincided with a change in command of the air group, now styled as No. 18 Group, RAF. As in all naval contingents, the RAF was happy to keep former RNAS officers in command, but the relief of Finch-Noyes in late March 1918 left an important position unfilled. The Admiralty nominated H. A. Williamson to take the position.[94] Williamson's experience in studying U-boat countermeasures while on the Admiralty Staff equipped him well for this command.

Williamson's philosophy was simple; he maximised the use of aircraft to escort convoys and maintained area patrols only in order to prevent U-boats from manoeuvring on the surface along the coastline. In a report on the employment of convoy air escorts in No. 18 Group, Williamson surveyed the successful combined-arms operating methods that he used. His general goal during daylight hours, and when weather permitted, was to have between two and four heavier-than-air craft plus two airships constantly over the coastal convoy as it passed through his area. Air escorts would provide both a close-in watch over the formation (generally the airships would do this) and a roaming search ahead of the convoy (heavier-than-air) from five to ten miles distance. The airships assigned to the convoy would normally stay with it the entire journey in the Group's area until handing it off to another command, while the seaplanes and aeroplanes would work in shifts, their endurance capabilities being much less. Between the Humber and the Tweed, Williamson had a dozen air stations to support his operations. Williamson rated the coordination between surface and air escorts as 'excellent', lauding the use of Aldis Lamps for quick communication and highlighting the periodic conferences held between pilots and escort captains as a cause for such success.[95]

The increased use of land-based aeroplanes in No. 18 Group probably stemmed from the limited ability of Howden airships to operate in poor weather. For example, between 1 July and 30 September 1918, airships were able to fly on only 34 days of the quarter.[96] Instead of using his DH-6s exclusively for Scarecrow Patrols, Williamson employed these aircraft increasingly for coastal convoy escort missions.[97]

Kite balloons contributed only marginally to the air escort effort along the east coast due to a lack of resources. The Rear-Admiral Commanding East Coast of England pushed for kite balloons in his area during the summer of 1917, but priorities for these new systems fell to the Grand Fleet and C-in-C Plymouth. Also, few surface vessels were available to be fitted out for this duty. Only three small gunboats could be spared for use as kite balloon vessels.[98] The single kite balloon detachment at Immingham did not commence operations until May 1918 and by October had only accomplished 20 patrols, with most of them serving as convoy escorts.[99]

Threatened by an increasingly dangerous Dover Barrage, the Flanders U-boats switched their emphasis to attacks along the east coast during spring

1918.[100] They were met by an average daily strength of 100 aircraft employed largely in the convoy escort role.[101] In Williamson's own words, the result 'was highly successful, and by the summer of 1918 when, as expected, the number of U-boats sent to attack the convoys increased to a maximum, the sinkings fell to a minimum, and losses in convoy to nil'.[102] The Captain (D) 7th Flotilla, also serving in the East Coast Command, confirmed this assessment reporting that 'extensive use of aircraft, whenever the weather permitted', and the protection of hydrophone flotillas combined to add 'enormously to the safety of the convoys passing along the coast'. Another report by the convoy intelligence officer for the east coast concluded that airships were seen as offering a 'very valuable' service in escorting the coastal convoys at night as well as day and observed that the east coast air stations carried out continuous convoy escorts and distant supporting air patrols, weather permitting.[103]

The Americans in British Waters

Before moving on to the overall results of the air escort effort, the operations of American naval aviators briefly deserve mention since they served under the orders of some of these coastal commands. The Americans assumed responsibility for the seaplane bases at Dunkirk and Killingholme as well as four stations in Ireland. They also operated airships and seaplanes along the west coast of France, but here they generally served under French orders. The emphasis of the American effort under British orders was initially thought to be bombing U-boat bases from the Dunkirk area, with a secondary role of offensive anti-submarine patrols. By the time the seaplane patrol stations began operations during the summer of 1918, the air escort role had been firmly established and these stations carried out the orders of their respective regional admirals. The seaplane station at Killingholme, under the VAECE, officially became an American base on 20 July 1918, while operations from the Irish bases (Aghada/Queenstown, Lough Foyle, Wexford, and Whiddy Island) did not commence until September 1918. The Americans also operated a kite balloon detachment at Berehaven, mostly flown aboard the US battleship division based at Bantry Bay.[104]

The Americans did not operate airships in Ireland, at Dunkirk, or at Killingholme, but did in France. The American chief of naval aviation forces in Europe disagreed with a proposal for USN forces to abandon completely the use of airships for shipping protection. Captain Cone, USN, stated, 'It is very well to give preference to offensive operations [i.e. the USN Planning Section's dismissal of convoy protection in favour of bombing U-boat bases and hunting patrols]; but where we have troop transports and supply vessels constantly making the French West Coast ports, it is unsound to discard the dirigible – an instrument that certainly has merit from a defensive standpoint, as it can in certain weather go well out to sea and escort convoys into port.'[105] Thus the Americans would use airships provided by the French for convoy escort only along the approaches to western France. Although 1919 would have witnessed a decisive role for US naval aviation, its late start contributed only marginally to the anti-submarine campaign in 1918.

Overall statistical analysis and conclusions

Although the Admiralty generally supported the air escort of convoys, it refused to issue specific orders to district commanders regarding air policy in this role. A September 1917 Admiralty letter to all district commanders at Home demonstrates this phenomenon clearly. The letter discussed methods for protecting convoys as they entered or departed a harbour, a vulnerable period for every convoy. Aircraft were considered valuable in this role, 'in order to immobilize all submarines as far as possible and sight any submarine that may be unwise enough to remain on the surface', but no directives regarding their employment were issued.[106] In May 1918, the Admiralty strongly recommended the use of aircraft generally in the convoy escort role, which explains the overall statistical rise in air escorts during the summer 1918. The Air Division certainly supported this policy.[107] Unfortunately, Scarlett and his Air Division staff possessed no command function. Their role was simply to advise the Admiralty on the use of aircraft and to liaise with the Air Ministry regarding naval air matters. The DAD recommended doctrine, but could not enforce it across the commands. Except for cases of special projects, such as the proposed air attack on the High Seas Fleet, the Admiralty Board itself was hesitant to provide specific operational orders, instead allowing regional SNOs to employ aircraft as they saw fit.

The following statistical analysis will serve to summarise the differences between the Home commands regarding the use of aircraft in the escort role. The following three tables (Tables 5.1, 5.2, 5.3) are based on information provided in the Air Division's monthly *Naval Air Operations Reports*.[108] The 'ASW Missions' columns indicate the number of single-aircraft sorties flown from the air stations within the designated operational area. The 'Escorts' column represents the number of occasions when a single aircraft escorted a convoy; a single patrol may have escorted more than one convoy and this could have

Table 5.1 Aeroplane and seaplane patrols and escorts, May–October 1918

Area	ASW missions	Escorts	Ratio
Orkneys/Shetlands (No. 28 Grp and Grand Fleet)	255	6	2%
Coast of Scotland (No. 22 Grp)	537	119	22%
East Coast of England (No. 18 Grp)	6509	3434	53%
East Anglia Coast (No. 4 Grp)	2542	55	2%
Dover/Dunkirk Area (No. 5 Grp)	1127	72	6%
Portsmouth (No. 10 Grp)	5107	846	17%
Plymouth (No. 9 Grp)	5356	109	2%
Irish Sea (Nos. 14 and 25 Grp)	1189	29	2%
Overall total	22622	4670	21%

Table 5.2 Airship patrols and escorts, May–October 1918

Area	ASW missions	Escorts	Ratio
Orkneys/Shetlands (No. 28 Grp and Grand Fleet)	nil	nil	–
Coast of Scotland (No. 22 Grp)	697	249	36%
East Coast of England (No. 18 Grp)	470	241	51%
East Anglia Coast (No. 4 Grp)	nil	nil	–
Dover/Dunkirk Area (No. 5 Grp)	657	301	46%
Portsmouth (No. 10 Grp)	1002	82	8%
Plymouth (No. 9 Grp)	859	341	40%
Irish Sea (Nos. 14 and 25 Grp)	1491	347	25%
Overall total	5176	1561	30%

been logged as two or three 'escorts' in one 'ASW Mission'.[109] The ratio figure on the right of the table is a direct percentage of escorts relative to total missions and must therefore be regarded as an approximate figure valuable only for comparative purposes. Finally, the last five to six months of active anti-submarine flying will serve to highlight the fact that the use of aircraft for convoy escort was not the predominant role by the end of the war.[110]

For fixed-wing aircraft, including aeroplanes, floatplanes, and flying boats of all types, Table 5.1 demonstrates the sharp differences from area to area. Williamson's No. 18 Group outpaced the other areas in using fixed-wing aircraft as escorts. Much of this increase was due to the use of DH-6s as escorts rather than as 'Scarecrow patrols'. The Coast of Scotland and Portsmouth Commands, both strong in seaplane complements, made efforts to fly more escorts, but in no way can this work be considered a primary emphasis. Finally, the remaining five coastal areas clearly preferred fixed wing aircraft for routine patrols, contact patrols, and 'emergency' hunts.

Airships appeared to produce a much more consistent rate of escorts across

Table 5.3 Kite balloon patrols and escorts, June–October 1918

Area	ASW missions	Escorts	Ratio
Orkneys/Shetlands (No. 28 Grp and Grand Fleet)	21	nil	0%
Coast of Scotland (No. 22 Grp)	14	nil	0%
East Coast of England (No. 18 Grp)	15	15	100%
East Anglia Coast (No. 4 Grp)	7	nil	0%
Dover/Dunkirk Area (No. 5 Grp)	32	nil	0%
Portsmouth (No. 10 Grp)	44	9	20%
Plymouth (No. 9 Grp)	58	53	91%
Irish Sea (Nos. 14 and 25 Grp)	19	19	100%
Overall Total	210	96	46%

Note: The kite balloon figures for the Irish Sea include the bases at Lough Swilly (Rathmullen) as well as Milford Haven. Additionally this chart is based on returns beginning in June 1918, since numbers of patrols were not reported by base prior to this month.

the commands. It is surprising, however, to observe that the number of escorts generally (except for No. 18 Group) gave way to non-escort patrols, that is, area patrols. Thus, the convoy escort role was not 'the principal use of the airships' as mentioned by one popular historian.[111] It is interesting to note the small number of airship escorts in the Portsmouth Group. Also, the three major airship stations serving the Irish Sea varied in their emphasis; Pembroke's ratio was 18 per cent, Anglesey's 20 per cent, and Luce Bay's a much greater 39 per cent. Thus even within an area, the focus of missions was not consistent.

Finally, the statistics regarding kite balloons appear to be the most surprising. This weapon system, which appears to have been perfectly suited for convoy escort, was employed in drastically different methods from area to area. The figures below demonstrate that Marder's assertion that kite balloons were employed 'frequently to provide air escort to convoys' did not paint a complete picture.[112] Three commands stand out as clear supporters of the kite balloon escort philosophy: East Coast of England, Plymouth and the Irish Sea. It comes as no surprise that Williamson's small kite balloon detachment at Immingham Dock would devote all of its effort to convoy escort. The Plymouth and Irish Sea kite balloon units supported inbound and outbound ocean convoys, a suitable role when protection at a greater distance from shore was needed. The remaining commands obviously chose to employ their kite balloons in the hunting role with patrol flotillas. Finally, between June and October 1918, kite balloons escorted convoys on only 96 occasions. Given a finite number of kite balloons available and with differing methods of employment from command to command, there were hundreds of daily convoys, as part of the ocean-going and coastal systems, that *did not* benefit from the protection of kite balloons. During the entire year of 1918, kite balloons made only 131 escorts.[113] R. D. Layman's assertion that kite balloons 'added to the deterrence that was the greatest contribution of aircraft to the defeat of the U-boats' is an incomplete analysis, since a relatively small proportion of convoys enjoyed this protection.[114]

To conclude, the convoy system was the key innovation in the anti-submarine war and aircraft generally contributed to its success. Air escort of convoys was an effective means of employing aircraft, but the percentages of aircraft allocated to this mission differed from region to region – differences ignored by many historians. At least 37 squadrons of naval cooperation aircraft – amounting to 285 flying boats and floatplanes, 272 landplanes, and 100 airships – participated in trade protection in Britain by the end of the war.[115] Tactical philosophies and operational requirements for the use of these resources differed from region to region. Only in north-east England did airship, seaplane, and aeroplane escort missions outnumber other forms of patrol work. The absence of a centralised organisation to command all naval air contingents operating in Home Waters, such as RAF Coastal Command of later years, led to a situation where the benefits of air escort would not be equally enjoyed in all regions.

6   British official assessments

Governments and defence establishments conduct official studies of past conflicts for three principal reasons. First, recording the course of recent operations offers planners a set of lessons and concrete examples useful in preparing for the next war. Staff studies are a class of literature published specifically with this in mind. The second purpose behind publishing official studies is to educate military and naval officers not only in the heritage of their respective service but also to offer anecdotes in decision making, battle-field conditions, and strategic considerations. Finally, official histories, a more general form of literature, are usually written for the benefit of the public in order to highlight the accomplishments of the services during the last war.

An examination of official studies is important to this monograph because much of the secondary literature concerning the use of aircraft against submarines during World War I is based on them. Popular writers such as Arthur Marder, John Terraine, and, most recently, Dwight Messimer cite evaluations and evidence from these official publications; these interpret-ations form the basis for our current understanding of the issues associated with air anti-submarine warfare during the Great War. Lee Kennett's com-ment on *The War in the Air*, that 'it has become the custom among historians to cite the work as indispensable, which it is', highlights the importance of this and other establishment-generated works.[1] It is important to analyse these staff studies and official histories in order to uncover any potential errors in judgment or outside influences in their publication. This chapter employs a chronological approach in examining these works.

The early staff studies

Most modern military organisations attempt to publish studies of recent conflicts in order to learn specific lessons that may apply to future conflict. Three staff studies, one sanctioned by the Admiralty, one by the Air Ministry, and one produced as a multi-service venture, made a direct evaluation of the use of aircraft against submarines and their bases during the Great War, and all of these saw publication by the summer of 1920.

The first examination of the use of aircraft against submarines was a comprehensive technical study published in March 1919 by the Admiralty's Technical History Section. As part of a multi-volume series concerning naval 'lessons learned' from the Great War, *Technical History 4: Aircraft v. Submarine* [*TH4*] evaluated the use of all types of aircraft employed against U-boats during the war, concentrating on methods and tactics of employment, armament and equipment, and results.[2] The study was most likely drafted by the Admiralty's Air Division, whose monthly Reports of Naval Air Operations examined the same issues and tracked the same statistics.[3]

The authors of *TH4* devoted a great deal of effort to statistical analysis but took pains to qualify their conclusions carefully. For example, a tabular summary of anti-submarine patrols shows that the Blackburn Kangaroo aircraft sighted a submarine every 50 hours of flying time during the period from 1 May to 12 November 1918. This compared extremely favourably to the overall averages for aeroplanes (352 hours), seaplanes (351 hours), and airships (1,278 hours). The authors then explained that the Kangaroos principally flew only when U-boats were reported to be in the vicinity, and that they were based in a 'position of maximum submarine activity'. Another example of qualifying the statistics regarded airship patrols; although airship flying activity more than doubled in 1918 from the previous year, airships actually sighted fewer U-boats. The reasons were fairly straightforward. By 1918 the Germans had realised that they had to maintain diving trim during daylight hours, lying lower in the water and therefore less visible from an aircraft. Additionally, airships were 'more conspicuous and slower' and thus 'easily avoided by the submarines'.[4]

Regarding the roles of aircraft in the anti-submarine campaign, the authors lauded both the use of area patrols and convoy escorts, portraying these missions as complementary and equally effective at hampering U-boat operations. At no time in *TH4* were these two roles measured against each other, either statistically or in the text. The authors mentioned bombing U-boat bases only briefly, and concluded that results were a 'matter of conjecture' but it was certain that the Germans were willing to go to great lengths in defending these bases from air attack. Finally, the authors claimed that 'all evidence points to the sapping of the "moral" of submarine crews by persistent bomb attacks' and that 'compelling submarines to remain submerged is in itself of great value'.[5]

TH4 therefore appears to have taken a balanced view of naval aviation. Although the authors regretted the insufficiency of investment in air resources during the anti-submarine campaign, they explained that the needs of other theatres necessitated adaptation on the part of maritime air units at home (hence the extensive employment of the DH-6). This neutral, blameless stance applied to matters of technical and production problems, while the authors applauded the final organisation and communication structure in place by the end of the war. The authors made it clear that in 1918 excellent working relationships between the RAF coastal air groups and local naval units served to enhance operations.[6] This 19-page report provides any reader with a solid grasp of how the RAF dealt with the U-boat menace by November 1918 and would have provided future maritime aviators with a superb guide to begin their own operations, based on the lessons of the Great War. It must be remembered, however, that *TH4* was an Admiralty publication which at least initially was a classified document;[7] the RAF on the other hand devoted its own post-war examinations of the anti-submarine campaign strictly to the employment of long-range bombing against U-boat bases.

Upon the cessation of hostilities, the RAF established a committee to examine the effects of bombing the German naval and military facilities in Flanders. Due to the limitations of available records, the study evaluated only the efforts of No. 5 Group and its RNAS predecessors from 3 February 1917 through 31 October 1918, a time frame that curiously coincided with the period of German unrestricted U-boat warfare. After four months of interviewing Belgian civilians, examining and cataloguing damaged and destroyed buildings in the ports, translating captured German documents, and scrutinising RNAS and RAF bombing reports and aerial photographs, Majors Erskine Childers and E. N. G. Morris of the RAF published their study.

Although the authors of this report were not pilots, both had significant experience with air operations. Both Childers and Morris had held Royal Navy Volunteer Reserve commissions and had served in the RNAS, later joining the new Royal Air Force in April 1918, as most RNAS officers did. Childers, the well-known author of *The Riddle of the Sands* (1903) and post-war Sinn Feiner, had been a seaplane observer and an intelligence officer in the eastern Mediterranean and at Dover and later served at the Air Ministry on the Air Intelligence Staff. As an observer, he took part in the Cuxhaven Raid of December 1914. Morris, on the other hand, was a technical officer who served at the Dunkirk Naval Air Depot – part of Wing Captain Lambe's command prior to the RAF amalgamation.[8] The combination of air intelligence and technical expertise made the team well qualified to carry out this study.

The report noted that during the last 21 months of the war, Dunkirk aircraft dropped over 1,085 tons of munitions on German targets. Just over 48 per cent of these (523.6 tons) fell on the bases of Bruges, Zeebrugge, and Ostend, while almost 5 per cent (51 tons) of the total was aimed at submarines or shipping caught outside the ports. Railways and roads (280 tons), aerodromes and dumps (130 tons), and 'various' other targets (101 tons) absorbed the remaining tonnage.[9] Thus approximately half of the total weight of munitions expended by the Dunkirk air forces fell on objectives related to the anti-submarine campaign.

Childers and Morris closely examined such subjects as bombing accuracy and its influencing factors; German methods of shelter construction and other defensive measures; destructive effects of the various British bomb types; and even wandered into questions of doctrine. The bomber crews had achieved 'good' results given the imperfect equipment and the activity of German anti-aircraft fire and intercepting fighters. German ferro-concrete shelters made submarines, ammunition stores, key equipment, and personnel impervious to all but the heaviest of British bombs. It is interesting to note that not a single bomb struck a submarine shelter until September 1918, and only three submarines were damaged as a result of aircraft bombs during the period in question. Regarding the overall effectiveness of the campaign, the authors concluded in a brutally honest fashion that

> bombing was at best a secondary and very imperfect method of attack. It would no doubt, in any event, have accompanied naval operations as an auxiliary method of attack, but to sprinkle a thousand tons of explosives in something under two years over a multitude of objectives, in not one of which (individual ships excepted) anything vital could be subjected to more than temporary injury, could not have a decisive effect, or anything approaching such an effect by itself.

The authors continued that the bombing of individual objectives was not concentrated and sustained sufficiently due to the 'various and pressing' needs of the Army and Navy. On the contrary, the 'bombing was of a rather diffuse and desultory character, annoying enough to induce the enemy to invest largely in ferro-concrete, but not sustained enough in any one area to dislocate his organisation or demoralise his personnel'.[10] The overall implication was that an independent air arm, thoroughly acquainted with the methods of air warfare, would have concentrated its efforts in a sustained bombing campaign in order to achieve decisive results.

The focus of the Aircraft Bombing Committee's report thus reflected their purpose – to examine the effects of air bombardment against a fixed set of targets over an extended period of operations. This was not the only examination of C. L. Lambe's bombing campaign against the Flanders U-boat bases, however.

In November 1918 the Admiralty coordinated with the Air Ministry and War Office to form a joint committee of officers from the three services to examine the German defences along the coast of Belgium. The committee included members from the Royal Navy, Army and Marine Artillery, Royal Engineers, and Royal Air Force and was clearly an independent project from Childers's Bombing Committee, which was solely an RAF undertaking. Led by Captain E. Altham, RN, who had been a light cruiser captain by the end of the war, the committee included a single RAF representative – Major R. J. Bone. Bone was a maritime pilot who had flown with the RNAS and RAF in the eastern Mediterranean during the last three years of the war.[11] In July 1920, under the auspices of the Admiralty's Gunnery Division, the committee published its findings.[12]

The report based its conclusions on surveys of the area, interviews with civilians and prisoners of war, and captured German documents. It also included an extensive collection of photographs. The all-encompassing study examined the organisation and methods of the defending German naval flotillas, infantry forces, coastal artillery, anti-aircraft and searchlight batteries, and air forces. In general, the committee concluded that the Germans invested an extraordinary level of effort in most of these areas, the primary objective being the repulse of any attempted landing along the Belgian coast. Although the possibility of collaboration cannot be dismissed, the joint committee independently reached similar conclusions to those formulated by Childers and Morris regarding the bombing of naval facilities by British aircraft. The report praised persistent bombing campaigns, such as the German raids against Dunkirk in September 1917 and July 1918 and British raids against German aerodromes in August and September 1918, while condemning 'desultory' bombing as ineffective. The committee assumed that the 'moral' effect of air attacks was strong, although it only provided a single anecdote of heavy drinking by U-boat officers as evidence. A more convincing argument concerning 'the success of our air operations' was the fact that the Germans invested heavily in concrete shelters and anti-aircraft artillery to counter the bombing raids. On the other hand German night interceptor capability and the use of barrage balloons did not meet with the success the British experienced in the defence of London.[13]

These three post-hostilities reports – *Technical History 4* and the reports by the Aircraft Bombing Committee and the Joint Belgian Coast Defence Committee – sought and found different lessons. The authors of the Admiralty's *Technical History 4* appeared to focus on efficiency – in weapons, in weapon systems, and in organisation. Childers and Morris were more concerned with scrutinising how a force of bombers best attacks a set of hardened targets. Finally, the Joint Committee stressed enemy organisation and appeared to provide context for methods of attacking a thoroughly defended coastal area – in this case, the Belgian Coast – by sea, land, and air forces. These examinations reflect the differing organisational climates found in the services immediately after the war, and serve as an excellent source of material for historians. Oddly enough, these documents are seldom found in the bibliographies of the secondary literature of World War I air and naval operations. More common sources for these later texts, on the other hand, are the British official histories.

The British official histories

Since the British official histories played such a dominating role in the secondary literature of this topic, a thorough review of their writing and publication is necessary. In a general sense, the British government was conscious of the need for official histories as early as 1907, when the Committee of Imperial Defence established a Historical Section to write a history of the Boer War, soon followed by a study of the Russo-Japanese War.[14] These earlier works were aimed at educating military professionals and were to be used at staff colleges as textbooks.[15] The official histories of the Great War served a different purpose; although the services and government agencies would use them for instruction and future planning,[16] they were also intended to satisfy 'a strong public demand' for information about the achievements of the services during the course of a very costly and painful war. These works were actually begun while the war was still in progress. For example, by the end of 1917 Sir Julian Corbett had nearly completed a draft of Volume II of the Navy history, while the Army, Trade, and Merchant Navy histories had progressed at least through the events of 1914.[17]

It is important to note that the four official histories that address Britain's struggle with German U-boats were all published prior to the public release of official Admiralty, Air Ministry, and Cabinet records – which did not happen until 1966.[18] Sanctioned by the Historical Section of the CID, Corbett and Newbolt's *Naval Operations*, Raleigh and Jones's *The War in the Air*, C. E. Fayle's *Seaborne Trade* and Archibald Hurd's *The Merchant Navy*[19] examined various aspects of the anti-submarine campaign as part of their overall scope. The official historians did enjoy access to pertinent records and cooperation with respective government ministries and armed services. At times the authors also received cooperation with foreign governments, including France and Germany, in collecting data of a given campaign or wartime issue, but this was not always the case.[20] Thus on many occasions the official history represented only the British extent of knowledge on a given subject. For example, H. A. Jones used British reports to contend that a Felixstowe flying boat patrol destroyed a small mine-laying submarine from the Flanders Flotilla (*UC1*) on 24 July 1917.[21] More recent studies, based on German records, indicate that this U-boat was most likely sunk by a mine off the coast of Flanders six days earlier.[22]

Regarding the use of aircraft to combat U-boats, the least helpful of the four official histories mentioned above are *Seaborne Trade* and *The Merchant Navy*. Both works are excellent sources of information and statistics on the economic and trade aspects of the war at sea, but do not mention the use of aircraft for trade defence. While Fayle focused on the general effects of the war on commerce, Hurd concentrated on organisation and inter-agency cooperation among Admiralty branches and the mercantile marine.[23]

The Admiralty's official history did not shed much light on the subject either. Julian S. Corbett, the first author of *Naval Operations* and a well-known naval thinker in his own right, did not significantly mention air operations in his three volumes and died soon after submitting the manuscript of the contentious Jutland volume (Volume III) in September 1922.[24] In November 1923, the newly created, permanent Official History Sub-Committee of the CID appointed Henry Newbolt, a well-known poet and author, to succeed Corbett.[25] Although at least one recent historical account of World War I maritime air operations complained of the almost complete lack of material on naval aviation in *Naval Operations*,[26] there is a very good reason for this apparent oversight. The CID's earlier, temporary Official History Sub-Committee, chaired by Admiral Sir E. J. W. Slade, had agreed with the

Cabinet's Historical Section and the new Air Ministry in May 1918 that the official history of the Royal Air Force would include 'the war history of the Royal Naval Air Service and Royal Flying Corps'.[27] Thus the naval official historians and their staffs had every reason to expect that naval air operations would be covered in the air history, these expectations being fulfilled in *The War in the Air*, and their own coverage of the naval air war could therefore afford to be truncated.

While Corbett's focus (Volumes I to III) was the surface actions of the naval war through Jutland, Newbolt (Volumes IV and V) concentrated on British efforts to subdue the submarine menace. Regarding the role of aircraft in the struggle with U-boats, Volume IV of *Naval Operations* contains only passing references to the Anti-Submarine Division's attempts to organise air patrols.[28] The final volume, however, goes into more depth with positive comments concerning air patrols of coastal routes (pp. 35–36), aircraft escort of the first convoy (p. 50), kite balloon experiments (p. 121), and, finally, airship and seaplane attacks on U-boats (pp. 198–99). Newbolt's appreciation of the air contribution to the submarine war is perhaps best expressed in a comment concerning 'a remarkable and most hopeful fact' that during July and August 1917, the British assessed that one-third of the German submarines they had destroyed had been through air attack. Appendix E of the volume supports this statement by showing that three of ten U-boat losses during that period were due to aircraft, plus an additional assist by a kite balloon working with a destroyer.[29]

The final British official history germane to the use of aircraft in combating U-boats is by far the most vocal of the four regarding this issue. *The War in the Air* and its treatment of the subject deserves special attention; a brief background to its authors and the mechanics of its writing is necessary since the air official history plays such a leading role in the historiography of World War I naval aviation.[30]

The Air Council actually considered the author for the official history of the RAF as early as mid-April 1918, and Sir Walter Raleigh, Professor of English Literature at Oxford, won out over Erskine Childers, a former RNAS and RAF officer mentioned above.[31] Raleigh went to work in 1918, with the Air Historical Branch – at that time an office within the CID's Historical Section – providing prepared notes. Raleigh was unfamiliar with the subject of the air services when he began his work, and he relied on a staff of 13 historians, archivists, and clerks, as well as seeking inputs from serving officers such as Hugh Trenchard and Sefton Brancker.[32]

The influence of senior RAF officers is obvious to the reader of Raleigh's volume. The new air service's mantra of the offensive appeared halfway through the book where Raleigh compared the strengths of offensive and defensive warfare in land, sea, and air operations; Raleigh had accepted the theory that the best defence in the air was a strong offensive capability. A separate section addressed the merits of a separate naval air service, a heated debate in the government and services at the time, but concluded that due to the nature and 'temper' of air operations, completely different from those on land or at sea, an independent RAF was necessary.[33] Raleigh interviewed many senior RAF officers and retired servicemen; for the naval air portions of Volume I, he relied on Murray Sueter, Godfrey Paine, and C. R. Samson – all former RNAS men who supported the idea of an independent air force.[34]

The influence did not end there. Typescript drafts of chapters went to Trenchard for review prior to going to the publisher for the production of galley proofs. The Chief of the Air Staff often suggested additions, which Raleigh accepted cheerfully but with private reservation. In October 1921 he confided to Lady Trenchard that it was 'really wrong' that the drafts should go to her husband since 'no man can judge what is written about himself . . . the position is impossible'.[35] The galley proofs themselves were later distributed to Air Council members, the Admiralty and the War Office, returned to the Air Council for final comment, and finally sent back to the CID's Historical Section for publication through Oxford University Press, the Stationery Office's contractor for the air history.[36] The book was released in June 1922, two months prior to Lloyd George's decision to raise the RAF's Home Defence Force to 23 squadrons and one year prior to Baldwin's call for a 52 squadron 'deterrent' force, increases largely sparked as a counter to France's air capabilities.[37] The 'help' Raleigh received from Trenchard, Brancker and others in drafting Volume I may have paid huge dividends to the RAF's survival.

Regarding the use of aircraft against submarines during the war, Raleigh argued that the work of the maritime air forces at least deserved some of the credit in defeating Germany's U-boats. Perhaps he overstated the case when he suggested that 'the submarine learned to fear aircraft as the birds of the thicket fear the hawk'. Since the first volume only served as an introduction to the series, covering pre-war progress and the air combat only through the end of 1914, Raleigh provides no hard evidence of the effectiveness of aircraft against the U-boats during the unrestricted submarine warfare phase of 1917 to 1918.[38]

After completing the first volume, of an expected three-volume work, Raleigh unfortunately died of typhoid fever, which he contracted while touring the Middle East in 1922. Most historians would have us believe that H.A. Jones, who had directed the Air Historical Branch from February 1920 until April 1923, simply picked up where the first author had left off.[39] There was much more to the story of Raleigh's replacement, however. The CID actually chose D. G. Hogarth to continue the work of the official air history after Raleigh's death. Hogarth was a well-known archaeologist and scholar, with ties to Oxford University, the British Museum, and the Royal Geographical Society. During the war he served as director of the Arab Bureau in Cairo, where he employed a former student, T. E. Lawrence, leading to quite famous consequences.[40] Unfortunately Hogarth's work on the air history, which began in October 1922, was short-lived because he 'was compelled, through ill-health and pressure of other work, to give it up'.[41] He resigned in February 1924.[42]

By March 1924 the Air Ministry feared that they would face allegations of wasted funds in the preparation of the official history, since no significant work had been accomplished since Raleigh's death. Although the Air Ministry was permitted to forward names for consideration, responsibility for the final appointment rested with the Prime Minister, 'on the recommendation of the Committee of Imperial Defence'. During spring and summer months of 1924 the Air Ministry and Historical Section actively sought out a replacement for Hogarth and approached four well-known public figures. T. E. Lawrence declined the offer in May 1924, and Maurice Baring – an accomplished columnist, author, and playwright who also served as Trenchard's aide during the war years – refused a request from his former boss the following month. P. R. C. Groves, a recently retired RAF general officer and new air correspondent for *The Times*, declined in July, while E. D. Swinton, renowned for his wartime work with tank development, was too busy with other projects to take up the air history. The Air Ministry and Historical Section finally recommended H. A. Jones, who had left the Air Historical Branch for a civil service posting with the Department of Overseas Trade in 1923. Jones, very familiar with the work of his former branch, was granted a generous leave of absence from his trade work and was confirmed as the official air historian in December 1924.[43] Jones had served in the infantry, RFC, and RAF during the war, being severely wounded in the Balkans as an aircraft observer in August 1917. He initially joined the Air Historical Branch, 'on loan' from the Air Ministry, in November 1918. He also wrote a history of his flying squadron, *Over the Balkans and South Russia*, published in 1923.[44]

The story of the search for a suitable air historian demonstrates not only the Air Ministry's concern with answering to Parliament but perhaps a more critical anxiety over public opinion. This they needed to help win the political war waged by the War Office and the Admiralty, which called for the disbandment of the RAF and the return of air components to the two senior services. As Phillip Meilinger relates, the 'seemingly endless' series of committees and commissions to determine the RAF's fate during the early 1920s taxed the fledgling Air Ministry yet ultimately confirmed the need for an independent air service.[45] This was not a time for Trenchard to take the decision of the air historian lightly, and getting a favourable official history in the hands of the public was an important component of this political war.

Jones had quite a bit of unfinished work to continue. Raleigh's first volume was published in June 1922, and Jones's successor in the Air Historical Branch, Captain J. Morris, had by the following year directed his staff to proceed with gathering materials and writing short accounts of operations in preparation for the future appointment of an official historian. By 1924 the Air Historical Branch employed three historians, in addition to Morris, to prepare these narratives. J. C. Nerney, Morris's 'senior assistant', was charged with writing monographs of 'naval air development and operations', while A. J. Insall and W. F. Cliffe compiled information on military air operations, squadron histories, statistics, and biographies.[46] Many of these useful narratives currently reside in the AIR 1 series at the Public Record Office at Kew and were based on available RNAS, RFC, and RAF documents as well as staff histories, memoirs, and other evidence.[47]

Although Raleigh's critically acclaimed volume of *The War in the Air*[48] was published in 1922, Jones's Volume II did not appear in print until 1928. There are a number of possible reasons for the lengthy delay of six years between volumes. Apart from the narrative production, little work had been accomplished during the more than two years between Raleigh's death and Jones's appointment. As early as November 1924 the extremely industrious staff historians at the Air Historical Branch had completed approximately half of the narratives for Volume II.[49] Staff narratives were far from finished products, however, and had to be edited and considerably shortened for inclusion in the final drafts of the official history. Second, collecting official records and unit documents from scattered locations – to include the Admiralty, War Office, Air Ministry, and worldwide RAF stations – took much time. These materials then had to be collated and notes made from them. Third, the Air Ministry had taken over direct control of the Air Historical Branch from the CID in 1919. This meant that work on the official history was further decelerated by Air Staff and government inquiries regarding wartime casualties, personnel issues, and claims of air-related inventions, in addition to helping writers of squadron histories and service training manuals and textbooks.[50]

There was perhaps also a political side to the delay. Although the RAF won the fight to confirm its independence during the early 1920s, the decade witnessed increasing Admiralty pressure over control of naval air assets – another political war that finally ended in the Royal Navy gaining back the Fleet Air Arm from the RAF in 1937–39. This interservice conflict may serve to explain the high 'naval air' content of Volume II, which included naval air operations in the Dardanelles and Home Waters operations in 1915 and 1916.[51] Additionally, the Air Ministry continued its policy of closely reviewing official history chapters, and Jones grew increasingly frustrated over the 'time wasted consulting this and that department to make sure their feelings are not being hurt'.[52] Chapters mentioning retired or serving officers by name were often sent to those officers for review and comment. Arthur Longmore, for example, reviewed Volume II text referring to his own service during the war. As expected, Trenchard had final editing authority in these cases and at times overruled his subordinates.[53] Despite the delays, Jones and the Air Historical Branch staff pressed ahead, publishing Volume II in 1928 and continuing at a steady pace until the final volume (VI) reached the public in 1937.

Jones formed his philosophical views concerning the air official history during his earlier tenure as director of the Air Historical Branch. Raleigh's work, he wrote in a memorandum, was to be aimed at the general public, 'to provide an antidote to the usual unofficial history which, besides being generally inaccurate, habitually attributes all Naval and Military failures to the ineptitude of the Government'.[54] Thus in Jones's own volumes, accounts of interservice rivalry and political squabbling are normally treated with neutrality, and names withheld in passages expressing criticism. In fact, Jones was 'anxious that his history should not stimulate controversial statements about air power – which are nowadays very numerous and reckless'.[55] Yet like Raleigh, Jones was fully immersed in the rhetoric of the contemporary RAF. His 1925 review of J. M. Spaight's *Air Power and War Rights* demonstrated his acceptance of RAF doctrine; Jones criticised the author for his focus on limiting future bombing operations to military targets, thus robbing a potential strategic bombing effort of its 'moral effect'.[56] Jones took care to not overstate the RAF's case in the official history; his approach was much more subtle than Raleigh's. Phrases such as 'entirely frank', 'vivid directness', and 'dispassionately treated' appeared in contemporary reviews of his *The War in the Air* volumes, but the reviewers still noted Jones's hints of the doctrine of offensive air warfare and the potential of a larger air force.[57]

Jones's subtleness is evident in his description of the disagreements between Admiral Keyes, Field Marshal Haig, and the Air Ministry over bomber availability for attacking the Flanders U-boat bases in May 1918. In Volume IV Jones recounted the various demands on the Dunkirk air services, in supporting the Fleet, the BEF, attacks on Gotha bases, and the anti-submarine campaign. In Volume VI he confessed that Bruges should have been attacked more energetically in May 1918, immediately after the Zeebrugge raid. But in both volumes he suggested that had there been a truly independent air force – that is, a force free from slavishly supporting either service and their constantly changing demands – it would have made these kinds of targeting decisions beforehand and been able to 'formulate a real policy'.[58]

Of the entire series, Volumes IV (1934) and VI (1937) contain the most material concerning the use of aircraft against submarines during the war, and during this time Jones would have been free from the guiding hand of Hugh Trenchard, who retired in early 1930. Jones devoted the first three chapters of Volume IV to naval air operations where he traced the development of maritime air policy, shipboard aviation, coastal anti-submarine patrols, and the efforts of the Dunkirk air services. This volume had actually grown by 36,000 words during the departmental review process; Jones received voluminous commentary from officers who had reviewed the draft, forcing the historical section to shelve plans to finish the series in five volumes.[59] These chapters show that Jones lauded advances in air anti-submarine warfare, such as improvements in intelligence distribution and the expansion of coastal air bases and patrol areas. He was not, however, willing to hold back fair criticism, such as the premature fielding of North Sea airships or anti-air prejudices by some officers within the Admiralty. In the end, Jones leaves the reader with an even-handed assessment of aircraft at the close of 1917: aircraft were valuable for their deterrent effect on U-boats, thus 'not by "doing", but by "being" they saved many vessels'.[60]

Volume VI, where Jones devoted a chapter to Mediterranean air operations and another on naval air developments in Home Waters in 1918, continued with similar themes. Jones did not hide the interservice disagreements over naval air requirements during the final months of the war, nor did he with-hold criticism of the Air Ministry's failed policies. One finds, however, that these critical passages are gentle, such as a description of employing the unsuitable DH-6 for anti-submarine patrols – a training aircraft incapable of carrying both a bomb and an observer, prone to engine failure, yet simple to fly and an opportunity for inexperienced or medically unfit pilots to contrib-ute to the war effort. Relying on the data provided in *Technical History 4*, Jones concluded again that aircraft should not have been judged by a rela-tively small number of submarine kills but 'by the effectiveness of their prevention', just as police officers should not be judged by the number of criminals captured but by the crimes prevented.[61]

Nevertheless both volumes employed official documents such as patrol reports and monthly summaries to provide detailed accounts of air U-boat kills. Jones claimed that eight U-boats were probably destroyed by aircraft acting alone, with an additional five destroyed by aircraft and surface ships working together. This is an increase by two kills from what Newbolt claimed in *Naval Operations* and what *Technical History 4* reported. Robert Grant's later work (1964), based on German documents and other wide-ranging sources, revised the total number of unassisted kills to only one, a figure accepted by most historians today. Oddly enough, a recent Fleet Air Arm history provides the earlier, inflated claims, which attests to the powerful influence of Jones's work.[62]

Although Volume VI of the official history appeared in 1937, the year the government decided to give the Fleet Air Arm back to the Royal Navy, its healthy naval content – especially regarding commerce protection – lent historical support to the policy that the RAF would retain Coastal Command, the land-based command whose purpose was to patrol the Home Waters around Britain and cooperate with the Royal Navy. There appeared to be less professional and literary interest in the later volumes of *The War in the Air*, however.[63] A comparison between Jones's Volume VI and the War Office's Volume VI of the Western Front official history illustrates the level of indif-ference; during its first two months on the market, Volume VI of *Military Operations* (Western Front) sold 954 copies while Volume VI of *The War in the Air* sold only 880 copies in 1937 and 1938 combined![64] Throughout the 1930s, a number of important public issues occupied the RAF's attention: threats to the bomber force from the disarmament conferences early in the decade to the Ethiopia Crisis and the growing German threat soon after-wards.[65] By the end of the decade, the public and government focus upon rearmament schemes as well as the publication of numerous World War I memoirs most likely overshadowed Jones's contribution to the RAF's legacy.

To summarise the contribution of the official air history to the histori-ography of the present subject, Raleigh and Jones give adequate coverage of naval aviation throughout the six volumes of *The War in the Air*. Together the authors devote nine of the 51 chapters in the official air history exclusively to naval aviation topics, while six others contain sections on the RNAS or RAF naval cooperation units.[66] This share of coverage, approximately 20 per cent of the entire series, is a fair treatment given the relative level of effort between the RFC and RNAS; units, aircraft, and personnel involved with army cooperation and long-range bombing vastly outnumbered maritime aviation throughout the duration of the war.[67] Finally, as mentioned above, Jones devoted a fair share of text to anti-submarine operations in Volumes IV and VI of *The War in the Air*. Both volumes provided strong evidence – albeit inflated at times – of the usefulness of aircraft to both naval operations in general and anti-submarine operations in particular.

Staff monographs and post-World War II staff studies

Although the Admiralty re-established its own Historical Section after the Armistice, budget cuts led to a gradual reduction of its personnel to two officers after 1925. In keeping with Winston Churchill's original 1912 intentions, which called for using history and experience to develop guidance for future naval policy, the Historical Section wrote a series of 35 Naval Staff monographs to record the experience of the Great War at sea. The start of World War II brought this work to a close, and as a result, the series ended prematurely with a volume on Home Waters operations through 31 July 1917. As Eric Grove states, the critical final months of the anti-submarine campaign, 'when imminent defeat was turned into victory at sea, was never researched'.[68]

The head of the Historical Section, eventually a component of the Admiralty's Training and Staff Duties Division, was Captain Alfred Dewar; his brother and later fellow Historical Section member, Vice-Admiral K. G. B. Dewar, had been one of the founders of *The Naval Review*.[69] During the bulk of the interwar years the task of writing the staff monographs, a form of history useful to the staff and preferred by Alfred Dewar, fell to men like Oswald Tuck and A. C. Bell, also retired naval officers who had worked with Corbett and Newbolt in researching *Naval Operations*.[70]

At a time when the Admiralty was fighting and winning the battle to regain its air arm during the Interwar Period, the historians on the naval staff had curiously little to say about naval aviation in the staff monographs they were writing. The relatively limited role for naval aircraft prior to 1917 may justify this lack of attention. The final volume, covering a period when aircraft patrols became increasingly important in the overall anti-submarine campaign, only mentioned that the summer months of 1917 saw an increase in seaplane operations in the Hoofden area, which served 'in keeping the submarines down'. Otherwise, this volume carefully used German and British official sources to debunk all of the aircraft submarine kills claimed by aircraft in *The War in the Air* during this period.[71]

Service politics may also point to the reason for this oversight. The mission of anti-submarine patrol around the coasts of Britain was not one cherished by either the Admiralty, whose recently regained Fleet Air Arm was to work with the fleet, or RAF Coastal Command, which was left unprepared for trade defence as the German U-boat threat loomed.[72] The close of the Second World War nevertheless witnessed a new set of lessons to be learned, most of which had their roots in the earlier conflict.

A succession of well-known officers served in the Historical Section at various times during and after World War II: the Dewar brothers, Rear-Admiral R. M. Bellairs, Commander Frederick Barley, and Lieutenant Commander D. W. Waters. These men espoused a set of core beliefs that are immediately evident from their writing and may be summarised in three points. First, and most importantly, the key to anti-submarine warfare in both World Wars was the convoy system and any investment in 'hunting' patrols or protected lane operations were a waste of limited resources. Second, the careful study of history and operational research, largely based upon statistics, yielded lessons for future employment. Finally, the Admiralty was open to criticism since it did not follow these lessons of history, in both World Wars, until the war was almost lost and many lives and ships had been wasted.[73]

The most well-known document set forth by this school of thought was *The Defeat of the Enemy Attack on Shipping, 1939–1945: A Study of Policy and Operations*. Authored by Barley and Waters, this extensive work is 'the most powerful justification of the convoy system of warfare ever written' and was issued on 16 April 1957.[74] Its release was preceded by a 24-page summary, outlining the main points, in May 1953 entitled 'Historical Research Memorandum No. 1: Surface and Air Anti-Submarine Escort of Shipping in Convoy, and Anti-Submarine Transit Area Patrols in Two World Wars'.[75] In order to set the stage for the struggle of the Battle of the Atlantic (1939–1945), both of these works began with an analysis of the convoy system in World War I and devoted large sections to air operations. The appreciation of the air contribution to maritime air power was probably enhanced by the fact that D. W. Waters was a former Fleet Air Arm pilot, who crashed during a torpedo attack and was captured in August 1940 and allowed 'to study history deeply and widely' as a prisoner of war for almost five years.[76] Since important naval historians, such as Arthur Marder and John Terraine, quoted extensively from these studies in their own more popular writing, it is important to examine the Barley and Waters works because they form much of the basis of historical understanding today regarding the use of aircraft against U-boats in World War I.[77]

So what did Barley and Waters say about air anti-submarine warfare during the Great War? The authors devoted four pages out of a ten-page chapter on World War I to the use of aircraft against submarines. According to the authors, 'maritime aircraft had a decisive influence upon U-boat operations in the First World War'. Using statistics from *Technical History 4*, Barley and

Waters demonstrated that the use of aircraft in the convoy escort role made the convoy system even more effective, rendering them 'virtually immune from successful attack'. To this they added the testimony of two admirals who lauded air escorts in their respective sectors.

Barley and Waters stated, however, that 'from July 1918, therefore, the bulk of the airship, seaplane, flying-boat and aeroplane patrols were reorganised so as to provide air escort to convoys whenever light, weather conditions and performance rendered it possible' and that by mid-1918 'the emphasis of our A/S[anti-submarine] air effort had by now shifted from area patrol to convoy close and distant escort'. Here they ignored the statistics showing that convoy escorts occurred on less than half of all aircraft patrol missions and was fully integrated only in one coastal region, as asserted in the preceding chapter. Finally, Barley and Waters dismissed the bombing efforts against the U-boat bases because they did not destroy or significantly damage any U-boats nor did they 'influence U-boat operations'.[78] Perhaps the greatest fault of this school of thinking was the attempt to explain a distinctly grey area in black and white terms.

An extensive Air Historical Branch narrative, also published after World War II, also used the experience of World War I to set the stage for an eight-volume staff history of maritime air operations in the latter conflict. Written during the late 1950s, D. V. Peyton-Ward's first volume of *The RAF in Maritime War* covered the growth of maritime aviation from the First World War through 1939. Peyton-Ward had been a First World War Royal Navy submariner and was recalled from retirement to serve the Admiralty again during World War II – this time as Senior Naval Staff Officer at Coastal Command Headquarters. Thus the AHB staff historian could tap his own wealth of experience and knowledge in writing about a campaign he followed closely during the war. The author summarised information provided in *The War in the Air*, Nerney's interwar Air Historical Branch narratives, and monthly Admiralty reports in order to stress an overarching theme that 'by 1918 a full grown maritime air power had been developed' but was squandered by limited budgets and other priorities in the years leading up to 1939.[79]

Regarding the use of aircraft against U-boats, Peyton-Ward lauded the expansion of anti-submarine patrol squadrons during the course of the war but complained of the relatively low proportion of air escorts to total patrol missions. In his view, 'area patrol unrelated to convoy movements was useless.' Unfortunately the author's zeal at times led to conclusions that did not necessarily match the data. For example, Peyton-Ward charged that a high level of sinkings in the Bristol Channel area finally decreased after the introduction of coastal convoys in September 1918 and that aircraft were used more profitably in the escort role. Appendix II of his own study showed that Bristol Channel sinkings remained well below ten ships per month, with the exception of February 1917 (14 ships), May 1918 (13), and September 1918 (12). In fact during June and July of 1918, only three and five ships were lost, respectively. Another example occurred in Appendix III, where Peyton-Ward listed all First World War U-boat kills by aircraft, indicating whether the aircraft responsible was on patrol or escort duty for the given attack. This was the first, and probably last, attempt to analyse First World War air U-boat kills in this manner. Unfortunately for his argument, Peyton-Ward showed that out of 14 'U-boats probably sunk or shared sunk by aircraft in the First World War', aircraft on area patrol attacked ten of them and only four by those conducting convoy escort.[80]

Charging that both the Air Ministry and Admiralty shared the guilt in failing to learn valuable lessons from the Great War, such as the need for close convoy escort tactics, large anti-submarine bombs, and close cooperation between air and sea escorts, Peyton-Ward concluded that 'the last seven months of the maritime air war operations were under R.A.F. participation and the experience with their lessons should have been indoctrinated against a future emergency'.[81] Peyton-Ward thus applied the arguments set forth by Barley and Waters exclusively to maritime air power.

The staff historians in both the Admiralty and Air Ministry tended to profess that historical lessons were simply not learned when they should have been. It would probably be inaccurate to charge that these men were providing a justification for their own existence; it is more likely that they held deep convictions about the utility of history in general and the value of the convoy system in particular.

Conclusion

A close examination of Admiralty and Air Ministry staff studies and official histories provide the historian with fascinating insights and valuable factual information to the investigation of aircraft effectiveness against submarines during World War I. These studies must be considered in light of their authors' agendas before employing them as sources for historical examination.

The most valuable works of this genre are the early reports regarding the anti-submarine campaign and the Belgian bases. Although these documents provide a staff perspective, the overall thrust seemed to be a justification for air power and a testimony to the potential of more and better aircraft in the future. While they offer detailed information as to the contemporary thinking of maritime aviators, they are rarely used as sources in the histories of naval aviation.[82]

On the other hand, the official histories are referenced widely in the literature.[83] Their influence upon the understanding of the air anti-submarine campaign is undisputed yet their conclusions have rarely been challenged. Jones presented institutional arguments about naval aviation in a neutral manner; his position was simply that an independent RAF could be a very valuable asset to naval operations. Although other issues — such as fiscal stringency, imperial policing, and offensive bombing doctrine — led to the neglect of maritime air power early in the interwar years, Inskip's 1937 decision to keep RAF Coastal Command under Air Ministry control ultimately provided a vehicle for an even greater contribution to anti-submarine warfare during World War II.[84]

Finally the post-war staff studies used the experience of World War I maritime aviation only as a tool for greater arguments: the superiority of the convoy system and unlearned lessons of history. The comparison between the two World Wars was inappropriate and ignored political and fiscal limitations witnessed during the intervening years. The Admiralty saw convoy and area patrol as complementary operations, not opposing systems as the authors presented them.[85] The work of Barley and Waters, as well as that of Peyton-Ward, also tended to be a justification for peacetime readiness during the early Cold War, where Soviet submarines presented a similar challenge to British sea power.[86]

Whether these staff studies created an informed staff – or the official histories an informed public – is a matter of conjecture. Close scrutiny demonstrates that these works represented the institutions that produced them and must be judged with these agendas in mind. Although the reasoning was varied and at times flawed, these studies all reached the correct general conclusion: during the Great War maritime aviation was an important adjunct to surface forces in conducting anti-submarine warfare. Whether the Germans who conducted the submarine campaign would agree is a different matter and is the subject of the next chapter.

7   The German assessment

Out of 390 submarines built prior to November 1918, the Germans lost 192 to all causes during World War I. According to a 1922 German Naval Staff report, the U-boat arm suffered 515 officers and 4,849 men killed during operations. About 13,000 sailors had served in German submarines.[1] Suffering such a high loss ratio – to both boats and personnel – the U-boat service presents an interesting source of opinion regarding the use of aircraft as anti-submarine weapons.

In his recent study of First World War anti-submarine warfare, Dwight Messimer correctly argues that one way of assessing the impact of aircraft on the U-boat campaign is to investigate the opinions of the German submarine captains. Citing nine different commanders, whose reports were summarised in the German official history or the U-boat's war diary, Messimer concludes that 'measured by the Germans' reactions to the air patrols, the effectiveness of aircraft in the anti-submarine role increased steadily'. He later states that although aircraft did not destroy U-boats in large numbers, they did succeed in causing a 'steadily increasing concern' among U-boat captains, who had to dive or remain submerged to avoid them. Simply through the threat of air attack, aircraft therefore 'played an effective role in protecting shipping'.[2] While offering a respectable start, Messimer's brief survey barely scratches the surface of available German material.

Due to the scope of this project and the limited availability of German memoirs, an examination of the German viewpoint cannot be comprehensive in a single chapter. There is enough material available, however, to form a general picture of the German opinion. The sources for these judgements of the effectiveness of British anti-submarine aircraft may be categorised into four broad areas: 1 German reactions to aircraft operations during the Unrestricted Submarine Campaign, 2 wartime interrogations of captured U-boat crewmembers, 3 opinions set forth in German official histories,[3] and finally 4 viewpoints expressed in memoirs of German naval leaders and U-boat combatants. This chapter will analyse German opinion regarding maritime air patrols, air convoy escort, and air attack on U-boat bases.

German reaction during operations

One of the best methods of determining the German viewpoint regarding aircraft is to investigate how they reacted to British anti-submarine aviation. As mentioned in Chapter 4, one response to anti-submarine aircraft was the use of German seaplanes to intercept them in the area between Flanders and the Thames Estuary. Seaplane patrols, flown from bases in Zeebrugge and Ostend, would often land at sea in order to lie in ambush for approaching British flying boat anti-submarine patrols. This tactic extended the range of the German seaplanes. The summer of 1918 witnessed the arrival of high-performance, monoplane seaplanes which according to a British post-war survey 'made these patrol squadrons a really formidable menace to our comparatively slow-flying boats [Large Americas]'.[4] Seaplane ambushes were only one of many responses to aircraft, and the other measures may be classified as anti-aircraft defences at U-boat bases, modifications to U-boat equipment, and changes to strategy and tactics while at sea. Although some of these measures have already been mentioned in previous chapters, a comprehensive review serves to formulate an overall German assessment.

Admiral Ludwig von Schröder commanded most of the defending units in the vicinity of the Flanders Triangle, comprising all naval surface, submarine, air and ground units in northern Belgium. His organisation – the *Marinekorps Flandern* – held the right flank of the German armies on the Western Front. As Erskine Childers's Aircraft Bombing Committee report stated, defence of the Flanders bases fell into three main categories: defensive fighters, flak and related surface to air defences, and hardened shelters.[5]

German pursuit aviation offered the first line of defence against air attack. According to the Belgian Coast Committee report, German night fighter capability was extremely limited and did not even appear until a two-seater night fighter squadron arrived in the area in July 1918. Coordination with flak and searchlight batteries was never worked out in detail and the single night fighter squadron, which rarely achieved its established strength of 12 aircraft, scored no definite victories.[6] Day bombing raids on the other hand were often met with swarms of German fighters. First formed in early 1917, the naval pursuit squadrons gradually evolved a system of working with observation posts on the ground that signalled the aircraft with large white panels to indicate the direction and height of attacking bomber formations.[7] Naval fighter squadrons in the area were few and often under strength and the German *Marinekorps Flandern* had to rely on army pursuit units to help in air defence of the area. A significant reinforcement from the army occurred during the spring of 1918.[8] By 1918 large air-to-air engagements resulted between groups of German fighters and formations of British DH-4 and DH-9 bombers with their escorts. For example, on 30 June 1918 the Germans intercepted a day bomber formation with 30 fighters; on 12 August 1918, No. 218 Squadron (DH-9s) with No. 204 Squadron (Camels) escorting met 14 German fighters.[9] Between June and mid-October 1918, German naval fighters alone, a force of no more than 75 aeroplanes, claimed 128 British aircraft of all types destroyed or driven out of control.[10] These victories would have included other units besides those directly attacking naval facilities, but the figures illustrate that the Germans made strenuous efforts to prevent daytime attacks through an active fighter defence and lend credence to Childers's assessment that fighters 'affected it [day bombing] seriously'.[11]

Anti-aircraft artillery, searchlights, sound detectors, and wire barrages also afforded the Germans with a strong defensive capability. Of these various countermeasures, guns were the most 'carefully developed' measure and 'attained an exceptional degree of accuracy in comparison with that of any other nation', according to the Belgian Coast Committee.[12] The Flanders Triangle's establishment of 70 anti-aircraft guns in 1917 had grown to over 200 by the autumn of 1918.[13] Guns ranged in size from 37mm to 150mm but were mainly 88mm high angle anti-aircraft guns. A battery commander, protected in a hardened shelter and in direct telephone communication with a centralised *Flakgruppe* Headquarters in Bruges, controlled each 88mm flak battery around the city.[14] According to the German historian of the naval war in the North Sea, Flanders anti-aircraft batteries claimed 31 Entente aircraft between June and mid-October 1918.[15]

In order to support the flak guns, the Germans developed searchlight batteries, powered by petrol-driven generators, which were arranged throughout the Flanders Triangle. Bruges alone had 30 searchlights by the end of the war. Anti-aircraft guns typically fired pre-planned barrages into fixed sectors at the start of a night air raid, with battery commanders hoping to send up a wall of metal fragments to strike an enemy aircraft. Once the searchlights found an airborne target, however, barrage fire was switched to aimed fire, which proved to be extremely accurate. Listening posts and machine gun emplacements further enhanced the defence. A countermeasure that was particularly dangerous to night bombers was the wire barrage, which was kept airborne by kites or balloons as high as 3,000 feet. One Handley Page was probably lost to this almost invisible threat and it most likely served as a deterrent to pilots attacking at low altitude.[16]

The Germans built hardened shelters to protect vessels and facilities, and this was probably the first, albeit passive, defensive measure they employed. In 1915 the Germans constructed six large shelters (two each in Bruges, Ostend, and Zeebrugge) to house submarines, and layers of sheet steel, sand, ferro-concrete, and earth protected these structures. The shelters were thus completely immune from all but the largest of Entente bombs. Further shelters for submarines and vessels appeared as the air attacks became heavier, especially after 1917. One such shelter type, the *Kragunderstande* added during the summer of 1917, was simply a hardened, overhanging roof designed to limit bomb damage to vessels moored along the docks. With space in the more extensive shelters limited, the Germans hoped that the *Kragunderstande* would make the bomb explode as it struck the steel sheeting or concrete roofing, absorbing most of the explosion and limiting damage to the effects of bomb splinters. At least two U-boats were severely damaged, however, as a result of British bombs piercing the overhanging roof and exploding after passing through the structure.[17]

How did German commanders react to the air attacks against the Flanders bases? As early as February 1917, during a period of particularly heavy night air attacks, *Admiral* von Schröder ordered all non-essential munitions moved out of the Bruges Harbour area and began a complete reorganisation of the air defences.[18] The following month witnessed a period of poor weather, generating concern on the part of *Korvettenkapitän* Bartenbach, commanding *U-Flotilla Flandern* throughout its operational life, that too many of his U-boats would be trapped in port and therefore susceptible to air attack. Those U-boats not able to find space under protective shelters were moved to moorings in canals away from the targeted harbour areas.[19] During the spring of 1917, Bartenbach arranged to have German aircraft escort outbound submarines during day departures, a practice apparently tried in early 1916. Full moon periods invited strong British surface patrols at night, a hindrance to a surfaced U-boat attempting to avoid mines and nets during the hazardous journey from Flanders through the Dover Straits, and day aircraft escorts during these times appear to have been successful. High Seas Fleet U-boats used the same tactic to escort U-boats through the heavily mined Heligoland Bight.[20]

The alteration to U-boat equipment that directly resulted from the threat of aircraft was the altiscope, a periscope that offered the submarine commander the ability to vary the viewing angle vertically thus enabling him to search the skies for enemy aircraft prior to surfacing. Other than the fact that they were in widespread use by 1918, there are few details published in British sources.[21] A contemporary British intelligence report states, however, that at least one periscope per U-boat was 'fitted for use against aircraft' through the use of a lever that varied the top prism, enabling 'the sky to be searched, instead of the horizon'. The field of view for this periscope was reported to be 40 degrees wide.[22]

German sources provide little additional information with both Gröner and Rössler – the best sources available in print concerning German U-boat design and specifications – not even mentioning this type of periscope.[23] *Kommodore* Andreas Michelsen, commanding High Seas Fleet U-boats during the last 17 months of the war, only makes a general reference in his memoirs to *zenitsehrohren* (loosely translated as 'height periscopes') used 'for seeing upwards'. Max Valentiner, a veteran U-boat ace, also recollects that late in the war periscopes were improved so that commanders could spot aircraft.[24] The existence of such an innovation nevertheless illustrates the fact that the Germans respected aircraft enough to invest in its development, production, and installation.

On the other hand, the Germans did not appear to consider seriously specialised anti-aircraft armament for their submarines. Although most classes of U-boat had machine guns as standard equipment, with a machine gun being the only armament for the early coastal boats of the *UBI* and *UCI* classes (designed in late 1914), there is little evidence to suggest that these were initially installed as anti-aircraft weapons and were probably meant to provide a lightweight general defensive capability.[25] At least one U-boat commander is known to have installed his own machine gun as extra protection against aircraft.[26] On the other hand, some U-boat commanders found machine guns impractical and 'have returned it to store as a useless encumbrance'.[27]

The 88mm deck gun, found on most fleet submarines and later classes of coastal boats and used to shell merchant vessels, appeared to have had an anti-aircraft capability. In December 1917, the pilot of airship *SSZ-16* reported that a surface U-boat fired at him with the submarine's deck gun before submerging. Shrapnel from a deck gun actually brought down a seaplane in July 1916 and one historian believes that airship *C-25* was lost to a U-boat's deck gun in July 1918.[28] It is certain that on at least one occasion *Kommodore* Michelsen ordered one of his fleet U-boats to attempt to engage airships off the Scottish coast.[29] German submarines typically carried only high explosive shell for their guns with a choice of three fuses – nose, internal, or timed – available to the gun crew.[30] The timed fuse would have been best for targeting an aircraft but probably would have required a gunnery officer trained in the complicated geometry of firing against a fast-moving target to be effective. The deck gun was a known danger to British pilots, but attack tactics were developed, such as approaching the U-boat only in certain directions, in order to minimise its threat.[31] Nevertheless, in the vast majority of aircraft vs. U-boat engagements the German submarine captain chose to avoid tangling with British aviators by diving immediately upon sighting an aircraft.[32]

Operational activity at sea comprises the final category of German reaction to British aircraft. The start of the unrestricted submarine campaign in early 1917 saw German U-boats concentrating their efforts in the Western Approaches, where British and neutral merchant targets were plentiful and British naval patrols almost non-existent. The introduction of the convoy system forced the U-boats to focus their attacks on inshore shipping (where convoys dispersed and coastal traffic still sailed unescorted) or outbound traffic, which was not convoyed until August 1917. Then, according to *The Defeat of the Enemy Attack on Shipping*, German submarines demonstrated their respect for aircraft in three ways. The first was by steering clear of convoys with air escorts, a proven fact based on the extremely few cases of losses with this type of defence. The second claim was that attacks were increasingly made at night when aircraft lost their advantage of better visibility. Finally, Barley and Waters stated that U-boats returned to operating 'in the Western Approaches beyond the range of our existing maritime aircraft. The difficulties of interception in these wider waters were preferred to the danger of air attack inshore'. Marder repeats these arguments in *From Dreadnought to Scapa Flow*.[33] Are these last two claims correct?

Some evidence supports the argument that the Germans purposely sought engagements with convoys at night, away from coastal areas, and hence beyond the range of aircraft escort. Throughout U-boat command war diaries, Bartenbach and to a lesser extent Michelsen commented on the air activity reported by their U-boat captains. They noted the obvious trend that British air activity had increased dramatically since the summer of 1917, especially in the English Channel, but that poor weather was a severe limitation to British aircraft.[34] In July 1917 Michelsen noted *U86*'s report stating that it sighted airship patrols on eight separate occasions in one cruise; he later argued that the winter coastal campaign, beginning in December 1917, would meet with success because, among other reasons, aircraft and small patrol vessels would be unable to protect shipping during the notoriously poor winter weather conditions around the coast of Britain.[35] Bartenbach confessed that in March 1918 air escorts made day attacks 'substantially more difficult' and that Flanders U-boat commanders almost exclusively relied on night attacks. Over the course of the next two months he lamented a new British measure, the employment of kite balloon and airship patrols and escorts at night, which he feared would prevent attacks in calm weather under the cover of darkness.[36]

Although this evidence may appear conclusive, it is not overwhelming. If the U-boats shifted to offshore attacks in the first place, they clearly did not meet with a decisive success. According to Marder, attacks further than 50 miles from shore (and hence beyond the range of aircraft) accounted for only 11.6 per cent of all attacks between February and April 1918, 26.8 per cent for May–July, and 21.7 per cent for August–October. This is hardly 'resuming operations in the Western Approaches' as compared to the 1917 campaign. During the pre-convoy days (May–July 1917), sinkings beyond 50 miles from shore had accounted for 62.1 per cent of merchant losses, while between November 1917 and January 1918, offshore sinkings were only 1.7 per cent of the total.[37] The prevalence of night attacks was likewise less than overwhelming. Between 1 January and 23 October 1918, there were 102 attacks against convoys but only 35 were at night.[38] Thus the shift in operating technique for the Germans was in fact less than Barley and Waters wanted to imply.

Secondly, the original orders to U-boat forces for the unrestricted campaign in February 1917 called for night attacks from the start – at a time when aircraft were not a viable threat. U-boat commanders were specifically instructed to use 'all chances of attack by night', which was considered one of the 'principal advantages of the ruthless submarine warfare'.[39] This leads to a third point about night attacks. Losses to night U-boat attack peaked during the period of December 1917 to February 1918 with night attacks comprising over 60 per cent in December. When plotted against the number of hours of darkness per day, however, the trend of attacks during night hours closely followed the amount of darkness in each period.[40] In other words, during the winter months, when days were short, there were more night attacks probably because it was dark for the majority of the day, as opposed to any other reason.

Finally, the 'shift' to the Western Approaches probably had more to do with the introduction of a thorough coastal convoy system – albeit supported by aircraft – than anything else. This measure, along with a defensive mine-field along the east coast of England in June 1918, was the most likely reason for the modest increase in U-boat sorties to the Western Approaches during the summer of 1918. So, the claim that U-boats tried to prey on offshore targets increasingly at night because of the threat of aircraft is only partially substantiated by the evidence.

A final set of figures might serve to illustrate how aircraft made an impact on submarine operations against shipping. According to D. V. Peyton-Ward, the former British submariner who wrote for the Air Historical Branch in the 1950s, German records indicate that U-boats attacked ships with an air escort on only 23 occasions in all theatres of operation. Of these engagements, U-boat captains claimed ten ships destroyed, eight hits without sinking the target, and five misses. U-boat crews claimed that a further ten attacks were frustrated (that is, they could not fire torpedoes) due to air escort.[41] As mentioned earlier, British records demonstrate that only five ships with an air and sea escort were lost during the convoy period.[42] These figures provide the best proof that U-boat captains had a healthy respect for aircraft in the convoy escort role. On the other hand, the arguments about the prevalence of night surface attacks, designed to discredit the Admiralty's initial performance in World War II since they 'should have learned' from this earlier experience, were less conclusive. In the end, British air activity forced the Germans to protect their U-boat bases from air attack, to install special periscopes on their submarines, and – to a certain extent – change the way they operated at sea, especially in taking special care or completely avoiding attacks against air-escorted convoys.

Interrogations of captured U-boat crews

Although the accuracy of information gleaned during prisoner interrogations was often questionable, such investigations nonetheless provide an interesting source of opinion regarding the effectiveness of aircraft. Throughout the course of the Great War, U-boats yielded survivors only about one-third of the time after being destroyed; in other words the majority of German submarines lost during World War I went down with their entire crew complements. Of the 132 U-boats destroyed during 1917 and 1918 – the period when aircraft would have realistically been viewed as a threat to submarines due to increasing numbers and performance – British and French authorities captured prisoners on 35 occasions. Numbers of prisoners varied in each instance; sometimes the entire crew surrendered but more often only one or two submariners survived.[43]

The Admiralty produced and distributed interrogation reports on these prisoners in most cases, especially during the last two years of the war. In October 1917, the Naval Intelligence Division inaugurated a series of printed confidential books (CBs) which detailed information obtained from German

U-boat crewmembers, including the circumstances of the sinking, crew opinions of submarine conditions and morale, equipment, operating techniques, and knowledge of sister U-boat operations.[44] It is interesting to note that British naval interrogators usually questioned the Germans about their opinions of the various anti-submarine measures; as the war progressed, intelligence officers specifically sought evidence regarding the effectiveness of both anti-submarine patrol aircraft and the bombing of U-boat bases. Most of the later reports therefore contain specific information concerning this subject.

Individual crewmember opinions varied based on their own experiences with air attacks, but an overall flavour of their views is discernible. Interrogation reports from 12 destroyed U-boats in 1917 and 1918 specifically mention crewmember opinions of aircraft effectiveness. The three reports of U-boat crewmembers captured in the Mediterranean theatre may be dismissed as outside the scope of this study, leaving nine reports mentioning air anti-submarine activities in Home Waters.[45]

Of the five cases where prisoners commented on bombing attacks against the Flanders bases, all stated that no important damage was done to U-boats or facilities. The earliest feedback that RNAS bomber units would have received would have been from the two survivors from *UC26* – captured on 9 May 1917 after being rammed by a British destroyer – who stated that air attacks against Bruges affected no submarines or U-boat personnel.[46] The second Flanders boat to yield prisoners willing to comment on the bombing operations was *UC61*, blown up by its own crew on 26 July 1917. Captured by a French cavalry patrol after running aground near Calais, *Kapitänleutnant* Georg Gerth and his crew told French interrogators that a Flanders Flotilla U-boat suffered damage to its outer pressure hull during a bomb attack against Bruges in May 1917. *UB20*, docked in Bruges Harbour at the time, was still under repair eight weeks later when Gerth's boat departed on its last mission.[47] Seven prisoners from *UB35*, recovered after surviving a depth charge attack in the Dover Straits in January 1918, insisted that they were aware of no damage being done to submarines or lock gates and stated that U-boat crew morale was 'excellent'.[48]

It was not until the capture of prisoners from *UB110* and *UB109* during the summer of 1918, recovered from ramming and mining losses respectively, that the Admiralty obtained further first-hand evidence of the effectiveness of air attacks against the Flanders bases. Both crews stated that there was usually a 30 minute warning of an air attack, enough time to take shelter in an elaborate system of protective dugouts. According to Admiralty naval intelligence comments, 'no material naval or military damage worth mentioning had yet been done by the dropping of bombs on these ports' and the submariners offered the high attack altitudes of the bombers as the reason for inaccuracy. Morale was unaffected by the bombing. The crew of *UB110* confessed that after their boat had suffered damage by bomb fragments, dockworkers repaired it within a few hours.[49] These final accounts would have coincided with the peak of the RAF's bombing campaign against the bases.

This evidence, which was probably influenced by a certain unwillingness on the part of the Germans to provide intelligence to the enemy, counters later RAF claims of success.[50] A poor state of morale, due to the bombing or any other reason, would certainly have been evident to the interrogators, regardless of prisoner comments; if morale was low, the prisoners would have had little reason to mislead their captors. Only one report mentions suspected dishonesty – from a U-boat captain – and in this case he made no comments about the bombing.[51]

Further information may be gleaned from prisoner accounts regarding the threat of patrol aircraft at sea. Opinions of German crewmembers varied widely throughout the interrogation reports and captured document translations specifically referring to patrol aircraft. Although *UC26* crewmembers commented on bombing, as mentioned above, the only evidence regarding patrol aircraft came from the second-in-command's diary. *Leutnant* Heinrich Petersen, a reserve officer, mentioned three separate encounters with aircraft on 1 May 1917 alone. Two of these resulted in bomb attacks by seaplanes just beyond the Dover Barrage, one of which was a near miss. Petersen's frustration is evident in his final comment: '9 p.m. [7 May 1917], Sighted a convoy, which of course we do not bag. Vessels turn away.' Less than two days later the boat was rammed in the Dover Straits.[52]

Captured U-boat commanders tended to display a more cavalier attitude towards the threat of aircraft to their interrogators. The commander of *UC61* commented on aircraft patrols directly. Gerth stated that seaplanes and dirigibles were the least feared of British anti-submarine weapon systems. He considered aircraft 'tiresome mosquitoes which force the vessel to dive, but whose stings are only superficial'. Gerth had heard of only one case where a U-boat suffered damage from a bomb; an unidentified Flanders U-boat received a hit on the conning tower resulting only in a damaged periscope. Although he admitted to not being informed of all of the details of missing U-boats, he had never heard of a submarine being 'destroyed by the bombs of a seaplane or dirigible'.[53]

The interrogation of *Oberleutnant zur See* Alfred Arnold, the only survivor of *UC33*, rammed in the Irish Sea on 26 September 1917, yielded a similar attitude. Arnold told his captors that an airship bombed him six to eight weeks prior to his capture near Falmouth but the boat suffered no damage. He then stated, 'I do not mind the bombs as it is a very difficult matter to drop them right on top of me, and when they drop on either side they do not harm.'[54] Likewise, the captain and crew of *UB110* mentioned an air attack in late June 1918 in shallow water off the Belgian coast. Unable to dive, *Kapitänleutnant* Werner Fürbringer had his men use a machine gun to fire at the aircraft, which dropped their bombs wide before leaving the scene.[55] Finally, although most of the crew complement survived the ramming of *U103* in the western English Channel on 12 May 1918 the commanding officer, *Kapitänleutnant* Klaus Rücker, was unwilling to provide details about an air attack earlier in the month. His crew, however, recounted that despite a lack of damage, two bombs landed close and exploded 'very loudly'. They later found bomb fragments on the forward deck of the boat. According to interrogators, this air attack 'seems to have made a deep impression on the crew'.[56]

Two other U-boats yielded prisoners willing to comment on aircraft patrols. A German petty officer, the only survivor from *UC63*, lost in the Dover Straits on 1 November 1917 after being torpedoed by a British submarine, stated that in late May the boat endured a devastating air attack near the North Hinder Light Vessel. Bomb explosions caused extensive fuel leaks and the boat had to return to Ostend for repairs.[57] *U104* likewise yielded only one petty officer as a prisoner when a depth charge attack destroyed the boat in the St George's Channel on 25 April 1918. In this case the prisoner stated that crewmembers feared mines more than depth charge or air attacks.[58]

Prisoner interrogations, again not the most reputable source of information, thus yielded sketchy information regarding aircraft effectiveness. Bombing attacks appeared to have had a limited effect on morale and *materiel*. Submarine crews did not seem to fear air attacks as much as other countermeasures but had at least a measured amount of respect for what an aircraft might do to them.

German official histories

The two German official histories that deal with British aircraft as an antisubmarine measure are Arno Spindler's *Der Handelskrieg mit U-Booten* and Walther Gladisch's last two volumes of *Der Krieg in der Nordsee*.[59] Spindler had been a U-boat flotilla commander until 1915, when he was transferred to the Reich Navy Office and later to the U-Boat Training School.[60] He was 'violently anti-British' according to the Admiralty's Foreign Documents Section, and at least his first three volumes appear to have met with criticism from senior German officers for being inaccurate representations of the events.[61] Gladisch, mentioned in a British intelligence summary as a highly decorated naval officer who entered the Imperial German Navy in 1898, became a *Vize-Admiral* in 1931 and full *Admiral* in 1943.[62] Spindler's coverage of U-boat flotilla operations and Gladisch's sections on naval forces in Flanders provide a rich source of information on the effects of British air operations.

As the official historian of the German U-boat campaigns of World War I, Spindler focused his attention on the accomplishments of the submarine forces engaged in commerce warfare against the Entente. The bulk of his account may be described as a chronicle of each U-boat war cruise, theatre by theatre, with important details taken from war diaries to include the route of the cruise, targets engaged, and results obtained. Short narratives preceded major sections, but these focused on German submarine policy and generally avoided discussions of British countermeasures.[63] For example, Spindler's introduction to a section on Flanders U-boat operations during the summer of 1917 briefly mentioned that the effective range of British light anti-submarine forces, such as small patrol vessels and aircraft, was limited to coastal waters.[64] Otherwise Spindler offered no overall analysis of aircraft as a countermeasure to German submarines.[65]

The individual entries of the U-boat cruises, however, mentioned aircraft on numerous occasions and through Spindler's summaries of war diary reports a general view becomes evident. Comments concerning aircraft are especially prevalent in entries for the Flanders U-Boat Flotillas from the summer of 1917 and onwards; since these vessels usually operated in coastal areas where aircraft patrols became increasingly heavy, these reports make sense. These entries are almost exclusively found in the Spindler's final two volumes, published in 1941 and 1966 respectively. The trend of opinion, as Spindler related, was that air patrols were a hindrance in many coastal areas, especially in good weather where increased visibility and smooth seas provided the enemy with a better environment for spotting periscopes. German submarines withstood numerous air attacks, some of which foiled attacks on merchantmen or subsequent attacks against convoys. However, in almost every case, damage from bombs was minimal.

A few examples from Spindler serve to illustrate these themes. In only eight pages of narrative from his fourth volume, Spindler reports the following incidents involving aircraft and submarines during the summer of 1917:

> *UB18*, 5 June: ineffective aircraft attack against the submarine.
>
> *UB20*, 17 June: damaged by bombs in Bruges, out of commission until late July.
>
> *UB31*, 17 June: enemy air attack foils shelling of a steamer.
>
> *UB31*, 5 August: operations near the Lizard hindered by airships and kite balloons towed from destroyers.
>
> *UB32*, June, U-boat commander's general remark: prevailing good weather meant that enemy airships and airplanes strongly obstructed operations.
>
> *UB32*, September, Spindler's comment: based on British accounts, the boat was probably lost to air attack, but not absolutely certain; loss must therefore be considered 'unknown'.
>
> *UB35*, 3 September: attacked by airships and airplanes near the Isle of Wight.
>
> *UB35*, 6 September: after sinking a French steamer, attacked by escorting aircraft.
>
> *UB40*, early June, U-boat commander's general remark: airships appear frequently in the eastern English Channel.[66]

The entries above are unique to Spindler's work in that so many references to aircraft fall within only a few pages. Although such a concentration is an exception rather than the rule throughout the final two volumes, the type of information presented and the results obtained by the aircraft are generally similar. For example, Spindler recounts the outward journey of *U102* in December 1917, whose commander commented that destroyer, aeroplane, and airship patrols along the English Channel coast often attacked him. The mission nevertheless continued as planned.[67] Likewise, smooth water and 'lively' air patrols caused the commander of *UB77* 'considerable aggravation' off the Yorkshire coast in July 1918. His only attack during the cruise was against a heavily guarded convoy; the single torpedo he fired exploded, but he did not observe the result.[68] Spindler's value therefore lies not in his sterile commentary, but in the summaries of the U-boat commanders' war diaries. Through these individual accounts, the reader understands that the Germans did not fear destruction of their submarines through aircraft attack, but saw them as a hindrance to operations limiting their freedom of action.

The second German official history to deal with British naval aircraft operations was Gladisch's *Der Krieg in der Nordsee*, where he covers the air defence of the Flanders naval bases in detail. Gladisch highlights the accomplishments of the German defending fighter pilots and the flak batteries in countering British air raids against the Flanders Triangle and adds more interpretation to the narrative than Spindler allows. Although he does not list every air raid in detail, his narrative chronicles the major raids and their immediate results. The entries for February and May 1917 reveal that most of the British bombing attacks tended to result in no or only limited military damage.[69]

Attacks during the summer of 1918 increased dramatically in frequency and violence, however. Gladisch states that during this time, the air war in Flanders reached a 'highpoint'. In June alone, British aircraft bombed Bruges, Zeebrugge, or Ostend on 24 days of the month, some days seeing five or more attacks.[70] Despite this increase in intensity, Gladisch stressed – as was his purpose – that the impact of these raids on the larger naval war was the important indicator of success or failure.[71] The strategic theme, which he does not openly state, was that although the bombing damaged a few destroyers, U-boats, and support craft, along with destroying or damaging some vital facilities at the operationally important Flanders harbours, the overall result of these attacks was minimal in the greater course of the war.

Neither Spindler nor Gladisch sought to evaluate British countermeasures to U-boat operations, instead chronicling the accomplishments of German naval forces. Thus the reader must rely on the narrative content of the German official histories – and not the authors' commentary – to gain insight regarding the German opinion of British aircraft effectiveness.

German memoirs

German naval memoirs of the Great War, many of which have been translated into English, vary tremendously in their treatment of British air anti-submarine countermeasures. Reinhard Scheer, commander of the High Seas Fleet from early 1916 and later Chief of the *Admiralstab*, and Alfred von Tirpitz, architect of Germany's dreadnought programme, never mention British aircraft as a threat to U-boat operations.[72] Likewise, Herman Bauer, C-in-C High Seas Fleet U-Boats until mid-1917, makes no mention of British anti-submarine air patrols.[73] The absence of commentary regarding aircraft in these accounts probably stems from their emphasis upon the higher direction of the naval war and unrestricted submarine warfare as a naval strategy. This trend also supports Stephen Roskill's contention that naval aviation did not reach a level of *strategic* importance until World War II.[74]

Andreas Michelsen briefly mentions the effect of Allied aircraft in his memoirs, however. Serving as a High Seas Fleet destroyer flotilla commander earlier in the war, Michelsen replaced Bauer in June 1917.[75] He devotes a three-page section to Entente aircraft where he admits that aeroplanes were a 'real threat' to U-boats from early 1917 and acknowledges that a reliance on good weather weakened the value of airships. Surprisingly, Michelsen goes on to laud the American air effort against U-boats and practically ignores the contribution of British and French air patrols. Michelsen quotes extensively from Sims's memoir and summarises US air anti-submarine activities in particular.[76] His focus on the American effort may have stemmed from a report of one of his U-boat commanders, quoted in the German official history later, which states that French air patrols south of Bordeaux were weak, but American flyers near La Pallice were aggressive and attacked with bombs.[77] Beyond this brief section, Michelsen mentions anti-submarine aircraft only one other time, where he recounts the near loss of *U70* in September 1917 to a bomb and depth charge attack. With its batteries severely damaged, German air patrols afterwards found the crippled submarine, which had to be towed into Zeebrugge for repairs.[78] The limited amount of references to British aircraft in his memoirs – and in his command war diary for that matter – may stem from the fact that the fleet submarines under his command usually operated further out to sea and probably had fewer encounters with aircraft than the *Flandern* coastal boats experienced.

On the tactical level, a mixed reaction from the memoirs and published accounts of the U-boat skippers and crewmembers themselves is apparent. Accounts covering the early years of the war, such as von Spiegel's *U.Boat 202*, do not mention aircraft at all, since few aircraft would have been patrolling at that time.[79] Other accounts referencing the later years of the war vary significantly in their treatment of aircraft. Dönitz's memoirs mention only a kite balloon giving away the position of a convoy, which he then attacked and was captured during the ensuing action.[80] He fails to mention his other experiences with aircraft, recounted in Peter Padfield's biography of him, which demonstrated the dangers of air attack.[81] Werner Fürbringer, a Flanders U-boat skipper captured in July 1918 (*UB110*), mentions aircraft as only a nuisance; British bombers, attacking Bruges 'almost every night', were 'insufficient to disturb the slumber of a U-boat man'. Later, when surprised in shallow water by two British seaplanes, he and his crew laughed as the aircraft dropped their bombs wide of the mark; the bridge watch then took shelter in the conning tower from the aircrafts' machine gun fire as German coastal batteries chased the aviators away.[82] Max Valentiner, who commanded submarines in British waters, the Mediterranean, and the Atlantic, mentions one case of being surprised by the sound of explosions while his submarine was at periscope depth. Later realising that the explosions came from aircraft bombs, Valentiner comments that he did not fear aircraft; he was instead extremely wary of patrol ships equipped with hydrophones.[83]

Ernst Hashagen, Martin Niemöller and Johannes Spiess, on the other hand, demonstrate a healthy respect for anti-submarine aircraft. Hashagen (*U62*) suffered a close call in October 1917 when a bomb from an aeroplane forced his submerged bows and conning tower above the surface; he was relieved when the aircraft withdrew after running out of bombs.[84] Niemöller, serving in a number of submarines in the Mediterranean and during the journeys between Germany and the Adriatic, mentions aircraft throughout his book and had a healthy respect for aviators, who almost succeeded in sinking him in July 1918. Niemöller took the opportunity to visit the German naval airship base at Tondern, where he 'found it far more interesting and more useful to me, as a submarine officer, to learn something of this arm of the service, which we considered more in the light of enemies to us'.[85] Spiess, who commanded a number of U-boats in the High Seas Fleet flotillas and later helped to quell mutinous sailors in October 1918, complained that airship patrols off the coast of Scotland hampered his operations and were an 'unpleasant innovation'.[86]

Karl Neureuther and Claus Bergen, at the request of a U-boat veteran's organisation, published *U-Boat Stories* as a collection of first-hand accounts of these Great War survivors. Only two, of the over two-dozen entries, mention aircraft. Navigating Officer Grassl (*UC70*) recounts tangling with aircraft in April 1917 and escaping by steering into a bank of fog. Later, Boatswain's Mate Seidel jokingly mentions an Italian air raid on Cattaro that resulted in a number of dead fish from bombs dropped into the water. His crew collected the fish, which resulted in a hearty dinner.[87] Otherwise, this large group of U-boat veterans apparently did not feel the need to mention the aircraft threat any further.

Lowell Thomas's *Raiders of the Deep* is an account of the submarine war based largely on interviews of German and British combatants. Although Thomas claims that six U-boats succumbed to air attack in 1917 alone, he mentions that frequent air attacks on Bruges, as a U-boat commander told him, were ineffective and 'could not have been labelled an important military success'. Later he mentions the story of *UB20*, a Flanders U-boat thought to have been bombed and sunk by a British aircraft. Half of the crew was in hospital with influenza and passengers were aboard when this attack allegedly took place.[88]

Conclusion

In conclusion, the Germans did not learn 'to fear aircraft as the birds of the thicket fear the hawk', as Sir Walter Raleigh would have his readers believe, nor did they generally think aircraft were harmless 'mosquitoes' as a U-boat commander told his interrogators.[89] The common view is perhaps best described as being somewhere in between these opposing opinions. Participants and official historians alike understood the *limitations* of aircraft as a threat to U-boat operations, but also appreciated the potential danger of not keeping a careful watch of the horizon.

Aircraft were a hindrance, and perhaps a danger, to German submarine crews during the Great War, and this view is clearly reflected in the way the Germans reacted to aircraft in the field, in the interrogation reports published during the war, and in the post-war German literature of the campaign. This final category comprised the legacy of opinion as the Germans approached yet another submarine campaign over 20 years later. The air threat would be much more serious during World War II, where, as a German submarine admiral would later state in 1945, 'the aeroplane had proved itself to be the most dangerous and most successful opponent of our U-boat warfare'.[90]

8   Conclusion

On his first cruise in command of *U927*, a new Type *VIIC* U-boat, *Kapitän-leutnant* Jurgen Ebert set sail from Kristiansand, Norway, on 31 January 1945.[1] After more than three weeks of patrolling (despite his boat having the newest technology including a snorkel which allowed the intake of air and venting of engine exhaust enabling the use of diesel engines when submerged) he had still not accounted for any Allied shipping. On the evening of 24 February, Ebert was patrolling the English Channel at a shallow depth with only the snorkel breaking the surface.[2] This cruise was part of Germany's 'renewed' submarine war against the Allies in 1945, a campaign conducted primarily against shipping in the coastal waters surrounding Britain, similar to the situation in 1918.[3] By this time, the Germans had lost their U-boat bases in France, an advantage that vastly extended their operational reach from 1940 until the liberation, and were now limited to conducting operations from bases in Germany and Norway.

On the evening of 24 February Flight Lieutenant A. G. Brownsill took off with his crew in Warwick 'K' of No. 179 Squadron. The Warwick was a slightly enlarged version of the Vickers-Armstrong Wellington, a twin-engine aircraft flown by many squadrons of both RAF Bomber Command and RAF Coastal Command. In fact, No. 179 Squadron had been one of the first Coastal Command units to fly the Wellington against U-boats, and the unit's 'night-capable' aircrews brought this experience with them when they converted to Warwicks in late 1944.[4] As the following account demonstrates, Warwicks, Wellingtons, and other long-range anti-submarine aircraft of the second half of World War II had three principal advantages over their First World War counterparts: detection capability, weaponry, and range.

Brownsill's night patrol found him off the south coast of Cornwall, near the Lizard, when at 1930 hours his radar operator reported a contact immediately ahead at 2 miles range. The aircraft was heading south-east at an altitude of 600 feet; the sea was calm and visibility was 10 to 15 miles. Calm sea conditions made it much easier for the radar to detect the tiny target – a U-boat snorkel protruding above the surface of the English Channel. After descending and turning slightly to the south, Brownsill visually spotted the wake of a U-boat's snorkel, proceeding south-westerly at 5 to 6 knots. Instead of attacking immediately, Brownsill circled the area and approached the U-boat from behind, at an altitude of only 70 feet. Once over the snorkel wake, he released six Mark IX airborne depth charges and achieved a perfect straddle of the target. Ebert and the other 46 crewmembers of *U927* were doomed; an immediate search of the attack area with the Warwick's Leigh Light, an 80 million candlepower spotlight mounted under the aircraft, and a subsequent sweep by warships of the Third Escort Group found large oil patches and wreckage. No survivors were recovered. Brownsill patrolled the area for an additional 5½ hours before returning to base. The Admiralty's U-Boat Assessment Committee, a body that evaluated each claimed U-boat kill during World War II, later declared the 'U-boat probably sunk' and historians have since agreed.[5]

The Warwick, as well as many other anti-submarine aircraft of 1945, was equipped with ASV III search radar, a system that enabled its operator to scan the surface of the ocean in order to detect vessels, land masses, and most other large objects. The Mark III first arrived in Coastal Command units in March 1943, and the British official air historian of World War II marks this event as 'the opening of the decisive phase in this long drawn out battle [the Battle of the Atlantic]'.[6] An improvement on the Mark II 15 centimetre radar of 1942, which was soon rendered less effective by a German radar warning system, the Mark III decreased the radar's bandwidth to 10 centimetres. This meant that aircraft equipped with the undetectable Mark III and powerful Leigh Light could now find U-boat conning towers on the surface at night, sneak up on them undetected, illuminate the U-boat, and deliver their weapons accurately. The introduction of the U-boat snorkel, with an extremely small radar signature, made the Mark III less effective, but on a calm night it could still be useful.[7] According to John Terraine, by the end of the war aircraft equipped with Leigh Lights made 218 night attacks against U-boats in which 27 were destroyed and 31 damaged.[8]

In addition to this day and night detection capability, aircraft now had the ability to destroy submarines with powerful anti-submarine weapons as well as the range and payload to affect profoundly the Battle of the Atlantic. Early World War II anti-submarine bombs were too small to destroy submarines, but from mid-1942, Torpex, a lightweight high explosive, was used in new aerial depth charges that had effective fuses.[9] The Mark IX airborne depth charge used by Brownsill was one such weapon. Also, RAF Coastal Command's long-range aircraft extended the reach of these detection and weapon systems tremendously as compared to the Great War; the Warwick had an endurance of 11 hours at its cruising speed of 164 knots and could carry a 2,000-lb. load of weapons. Likewise the Sunderland flying boat could carry 2,000 lbs. for 13½ hours or 1,000 lbs. for 15 hours, while the Very Long Range (or VLF) Liberator could haul 2,000 lbs. of bombs and depth charges for 16 hours at 150 knots.[10]

Thus, less than 30 years after the first air anti-submarine campaign of 1917 to 1918, vastly better capabilities made aircraft not only effective U-boat hunters but also deadly U-boat killers during the last half of World War II. The Warwick engagement of 24 February 1945 highlights both the techno- logical and employment chasm between the two wars. In order to place the Great War experience within a proper historical context, the bulk of this chapter will briefly trace air anti-submarine developments during the inter- war years and World War II. This review will show that technological capability was not the only major difference between air anti-submarine warfare in the two world wars. Finally, this conclusion will close this study with a summary of findings from the preceding chapters.

The interwar years

Air anti-submarine warfare in 1945 indeed had come a long way since November 1918. The interwar period, however, was a difficult time for foster- ing the anti-submarine role within the naval aviation community. The immediate post-war lessons for naval air units seemed clear enough. A 1919 *Naval Review* article by Brigadier General Oliver Swann, RAF, the former captain of HMS *Campania* and an early pioneer of the RNAS, listed 'anti- submarine patrol work, escort of convoys, [and] searching for enemy mines' as the *first three* 'principle functions carried out by aircraft for the Navy'. Only afterwards did he mention tasks involving working with the fleet and operations against enemy ships, bases, and aircraft.[11] Rapid demobilisation after the war, however, led to a dearth of air units trained and equipped to carry out anti-submarine tasks that Swann thought so important. Traditional roles and missions for naval forces, such as those associated with battle fleet combat, returned to the forefront of naval thought. Indeed, only two years after Swann's article appeared, Squadron Leader C. H. K. Edmonds, RAF, who had also been a First World War naval aviator with extensive experience in the field and on the Air Division Staff, wrote an article for the *Royal United Services Institute Journal* in which he summarised the lessons of Great War maritime airpower. Edmonds concluded that the next war would probably not find Britain in such close proximity to its primary naval adversary and hinted that the Pacific would be the probable location of the next conflict. In such circumstances, he predicted that the real value of maritime aircraft would be in working with the battle fleet to help locate enemy warships over vast distances.[12]

Between 1918 and the mid-1930s, three primary factors shaped naval aviation. The first and most important factor was the lack of naval threats to Britain. After Versailles, Germany no longer had U-boats and its navy was relegated to a coastal defence role until Hitler came to power. France, Italy, and America were likewise unlikely enemies. The only existing threat during this period was Japan, whose powerful surface fleet might have jeopardised British trade in Asia but whose submarines were not considered a viable danger south of Hong Kong.[13] Within this environment, the development of ASDIC/SONAR further curbed the need for naval aviation to perform the anti-submarine role that it had developed during the Great War. Whatever its capabilities and limitations, the ASDIC/SONAR 'antidote' would severely limit the possibility of an adversary using submarines successfully against the Royal Navy and the trade it protected.[14]

The second factor stemmed immediately from the strategic situation: enforced fiscal stringency. In the aftermath of one of the most destructive and expensive wars in European history, the Treaty of Versailles, 'Ten Year Rule' and 'Geddes Axe' led to what Christina Goulter calls 'the virtual liquidation of the RAF.'[15] During the mid-1920s, the RAF deployed the bulk of its operational strength overseas, especially in India, Somaliland, and Iraq where bombers were useful in controlling indigenous populations at an extremely low cost.[16] The RAF establishment in Britain, however, was reduced to an absolute minimum; in April 1923, for example, there were only six fighter, bomber, and Army cooperation squadrons at home, while the Grand Fleet enjoyed the support of four ship-borne squadrons and the equivalent of one shore-based squadron. At the same time, overseas units could call on 22 land-based combat squadrons (one of them maritime) plus one flight of ship-borne aircraft.[17] The conclusions of the Salisbury Committee of March 1923, which recommended the establishment of home defence air units after considering a credible French air threat, initiated a period of steady growth in home RAF units.[18] Naval cooperation squadrons, however, did not witness the expansion that home RAF fighter and bomber forces enjoyed. By January 1929 there were three shored-based squadrons and 11 ship-borne flights to cooperate with the Royal Navy while the non-naval establishment at home had expanded to 39 squadrons.[19] Such limitations on available assets meant that the Air Ministry was forced to prioritise where its share of the budget would be spent, and maritime aviation was not high on that list.[20]

The final factor shaping naval aviation after the First World War was the RAF's commitment to strategic bombing, which absorbed the bulk of the RAF's attention and resources during this period. Whether or not this was a correct philosophy has been documented at length, but the fact remains that a large proportion of RAF officers, wishing to avoid another bloodbath of 1914 to 1918 in future wars, thought that strategic bombing was the quickest and most humane method to win the next war.[21] Even if a submarine threat did emerge in a future war, a bomber force in theory could temporarily divert its strikes away from enemy industry and morale and defeat commerce warfare 'at source' by bombing enemy submarine bases and yards. The RAF preferred this method of anti-submarine warfare since it was easier to hit a base than a moving submarine.[22]

Using hindsight to their advantage, many historians have blamed the Air Ministry for neglecting maritime air power prior to the threat of Germany's rearmament, but this criticism is unfair.[23] Defence establishments plan for current and real threats. Especially in times of fiscal stringency, they must prioritise their assets to meet those threats. Thus with few potential naval enemies, it is not surprising that the RAF placed maritime air power below other higher ranking priorities. Nevertheless, despite a severe shortage of maritime air assets, Fleet Air Arm and Coastal Area aircraft still participated in a number of anti-submarine exercises during the interwar years. Between 1927 and 1930, at least six Royal Navy exercises involved aircraft, all demonstrating the value of aircraft in screening a formation of ships against submarines.[24]

From the mid-1930s and onwards, the strategic situation changed rapidly and many previously held assumptions became invalid. German rearmament under Hitler, as well as the Rhineland reoccupation and Italy's Abyssinian War, led to parallel efforts to rearm in Britain. The expansion of the Luftwaffe helped to accelerate RAF growth, while the rebirth of Germany's U-boat fleet and resurgent German surface forces made trade defence a more important issue for the Admiralty. The combination of emerging threats and force growth in Britain necessitated a reorganisation; Sir Thomas Inskip's 1937 decision to enlarge defensive fighter forces at home and return ship-borne aviation completely to the Admiralty resulted from these pressures. Interestingly, although the Minister for the Coordination of Defence returned the Fleet Air Arm to the Royal Navy, Inskip kept shore-based maritime aviation under RAF Coastal Command, which itself had been established in 1936 under an RAF reorganisation. Coastal Command descended from Coastal Area, an organisation established in September 1919 to reassure the Admiralty that the RAF would not ignore its needs.[25] An acknowledgement of the potential German naval menace was evident through Coastal Command's substantial growth under the 1937 and 1938 air expansion schemes.[26]

Trade defence exercises continued in the face of German rearmament. Aircraft played important roles during these exercises. Aircraft, however, were not seen as independent killers but rather served as force enhancers for surface escorts and hunting flotillas.[27] By this time U-boats were not the only threat to trade because enemy surface forces as well as attacking aircraft had the potential to wreak havoc on merchant convoys, realities borne out by convoy experiences in the English Channel, Artic, and Mediterranean combat areas during World War II.[28] Nevertheless, George Franklin states that by 1934 air anti-submarine tactics with surface vessels had 'become largely standardised', and Admiralty correspondence during the two years preceding the war demonstrates that the Royal Navy considered air power an important adjunct to anti-submarine forces.[29] Moreover, by 1936 Admiralty trade defence doctrine not only appreciated the threats of mines, surface vessels, air forces, and submarines, but also pointed to a mixed force of carrier-based, shore-based, and flying boat aircraft to aid in the protection of shipping.[30]

RAF Coastal Command still faced many problems during the last three years of peace. As Christina Goulter explains, the 'vacillation in deciding what Coastal Command's proper war role' should be, along with the focus on rearming bomber and fighter forces, left it materially unprepared for the kind of war it would have to fight against Germany. By 1939, anti-submarine warfare was still second in priority to the North Sea reconnaissance role, with

Home Waters air search and the development of anti-ship strike forces additional areas of responsibility.[31] Indeed, as the First World War had shown, there were many potential roles for shore-based aircraft in naval warfare, all of them requiring different types of aircraft capabilities and weaponry. This conundrum, combined with the interwar period's initial lack of priority for maritime aviation, the RAF's focus on bombers and fighters, and an unexpected change in Britain's geographic position relative to her enemies, meant that Coastal Command initially would not be prepared to fight the Battle of the Atlantic.

World War II

Upon the opening of hostilities with Britain, Hitler immediately ordered his U-boats to begin a counter blockade of the British Isles. With only 39 operational U-boats, the Germans embarked on yet another world war and another campaign against British commerce. The early months of the war, characterised by V. E. Tarrant as 'little more than a nuisance' to the British due to limited numbers of U-boats and ineffective torpedoes, gave way to a more successful phase in mid-1940 known as the Germans' 'Happy Time'.[32] Each side introduced countermeasures, through improvements in tactics, technology, and organisation, but by mid-1943 the Allies finally gained the upper hand.

At first glance the submarine campaigns of the two World Wars appear to be similar. In both wars, Germany attempted to counter Britain's naval blockade with a U-boat blockade of their own, using submarines of surprisingly similar performance characteristics. Other than an expected improvement in efficiency, frontline U-boats of World War II possessed only marginally better speeds, ranges, and torpedo capacities as their 1918 predecessors.[33] In both conflicts, U-boats sank significant amounts of shipping (over 11 million tons during the First World War and over 14½ million tons in the Second[34]), and in both cases the sheer might of British and Allied economic power replaced merchant losses, kept home industries running, supplied both civilian populations and field armies, and expanded naval resources. Finally, in both wars Britain conducted an effective anti-submarine programme, centred on the convoy system, but supplemented by the use of U-boat hunting patrols and direct attacks on German submarine infrastructure.

Geography, U-boat numbers, and technology played major roles in shaping World War II's latter campaign, which in fact was fundamentally different from the experience of the Great War. The fall of France and Norway offered the Germans advanced submarine bases from which they assaulted merchant shipping deep into the Atlantic between 1940 and 1944; after the summer of 1940, the Allies could no longer attempt to close the exits of the North Sea in order to contain the U-boats. The ability to refuel at sea, with disguised merchant vessels or submarine tankers, meant that the Germans could now send their U-boats to harass the coasts of North and South America and Africa in addition to threatening Home Waters and the Mediterranean. Thus, the Battle of the Atlantic truly raged throughout the Atlantic Ocean, only reverting to British Home Waters during the last year of the war.[35]

Whereas the Germans commissioned 346 U-boats and lost 192 of them (55 per cent) during the First World War, they commissioned 1,113 and lost 821 U-boats (74 per cent) in the latter. The monthly total U-boat strength, including boats in training units and under repair, averaged between 152 and 177 U-boats during 1917 and 1918, with a peak strength reached in September 1918. About a third of these boats were at sea operationally at any time, with a maximum number of about 65 boats on patrol in March 1918. Between December 1942 and March 1945, total U-boat strength was never less than 400 boats each month, and the strength peaked in January 1944 with 456. About half of these boats were at sea operationally at any given time, reaching a maximum 239 U-boats on patrol in May 1943.[36] World War II British and Allied anti-submarine forces therefore had to protect shipping in a vast geographical area against a U-boat force that was numerically three to four times larger than in the previous conflict. And because of this, they could not be content with simply keeping U-boats away from merchant ships but had to destroy the attackers outright or face being overwhelmed by sheer numbers.

In World War II, however, anti-submarine forces had a considerably greater technological capability to aid in the detection and destruction of U-boats. By August 1942 the assets used to win the Battle of the Atlantic, in addition to ASDIC/SONAR capabilities developed during the interwar period, included a variety of naval vessels and aircraft with well-trained crews, microwave radar, radio direction finding equipment, new ASW weapons, and a vast network of code-breakers and intelligence gatherers.[37] Between September 1942 and May 1945 the Germans lost 713 U-boats, with over 32,000 U-boat crewmembers killed and a further 3,356 captured.[38] German technology, which included such innovations as the snorkel, radar detectors, homing torpedoes, and new U-boats designed for high submerged speeds, either did not fully develop or did not appear in sufficient quantities to alter the tactical or strategic balance.

Although maritime aviation had a slow start in its trade defence role, the contribution of aircraft during World War II was tremendously more important than in World War I. The British not only had a shore-based organisation, RAF Coastal Command, with which to defend trade but also could count on ship-borne aircraft of the Fleet Air Arm to aid in anti-submarine warfare. Between September 1939 and May 1940, RAF Coastal Command conducted 85 attacks against U-boats but sank only one. Coastal Command killed only two more U-boats in 1941.[39] The American entry into the conflict at the end of 1941 added USN and USAAF air assets and the backing of US industrial output. By May 1943, ship- and shore-based air escorts and patrols had accounted for 66 U-boats destroyed out of a total of 225 from all causes worldwide.[40] During the critical turning point of January 1942 through May 1943, 52 of the 96 U-boats that the Germans lost worldwide resulted from air attacks or aircraft working with warships.[41] As Clay Blair states, from this point the combination of radar and long range vaulted aircraft 'to top rank as U-boat killers'. By the end of the war, unassisted land-based aircraft had destroyed 204 U-boats, and another 30 with assists from surface vessels. Carrier-based aircraft accounted for 39 U-boats plus 12 more with warships.[42]

Once again technology was only part of the formula for success. Despite the interservice rivalry of the interwar period, RAF Coastal Command worked closely with the Admiralty in the prosecution of the Battle of the Atlantic. In February 1941 the Admiralty's Western Approaches Command, largely responsible for trade protection, moved from Plymouth to Liverpool where it could keep closer contact with escort forces. Coastal Command's No. 15 Group followed it there from Plymouth, where it maintained a close liaison with transatlantic convoy escort forces.[43] In April 1941, the RAF officially gave the Admiralty full operational control of Coastal Command.[44] By mid-1943, Admiralty Intelligence, Western Approaches Command, and RAF Coastal Command conducted a daily telephone conference to coordinate convoy escort operations based on known U-boat threats from various intelligence sources. Likewise the existence of Coastal Command allowed shore-based air units to reinforce each other depending on the situation. For example, in July 1943 Air Marshal Sir John Slessor, commanding Coastal Command, was able to order a concentration of long-range aircraft from around the British Isles to the south-west of England from where they prosecuted a vigorous campaign against U-boat traffic in the Bay of Biscay. At the same time, the Admiralty sent a surface group of five sloops to work with aircraft in the area. Likewise, in early 1944, following a switch in U-boat tactics, Coastal Command reduced Biscay patrols and reinforced the west coast of England and Scotland to hunt U-boats operating individually in these areas.[45]

Aircraft also attempted to bomb U-boats 'at source' during the war. Limited raids by RAF Coastal Command, increasingly assisted by RAF Bomber Command, sought to attack U-boat infrastructure targets in 1940 and 1941.[46] Other strategic targeting priorities overrode this effort from mid-1941 and through most of 1942.[47] But from late 1942 until mid-1943, submarine bases, pens, and construction yards 'became the chief target' of Allied bombers, though they 'accomplished little' and according to the United States Strategic Bombing Surveys (USSBS) were 'not heavy enough to be more than troublesome'.[48] Apparently learning the lessons of the Flanders Triangle, the Germans housed their U-boats in French bases using concrete shelters protected by 12-feet-thick roofs. In late November 1944 Allied bomber forces returned to the 'at source' philosophy and concentrated on submarine building yards in Germany. Responding to the threat of new Type *XXI* and *XXIII* U-boats, the more numerous bombers now met with better results. By early spring 1945 they were able to 'close, or all but close, five of the major yards' through bombing alone. The USSBS writers claimed that the threat of new U-boat production would have been eliminated if the war against Germany continued beyond mid-1945.[49] Allied bombers also dropped aerial mines targeting German surface as well as submarine traffic; according to Barley and Waters, aerial mines might have sunk as many as 15 U-boats.[50]

The Allied offensives against U-boat bases and yards were considerable, especially when compared to the effort of Lambe's bomber force of the previous war. In 1943 alone, Allied bombers flew 15,398 sorties delivering over 40,000 tons of munitions on U-boat facilities. The following year witnessed 10,652 sorties with almost 32,000 tons dropped.[51] Barley and Waters claimed that 63 completed U-boats were destroyed by bombing in port while a further 112 may have been destroyed during construction. Although criticising the RAF's effort as being too little and too late – with 37 of the completed U-boats destroyed after the Rhine Crossing in March 1945 – the staff historians nonetheless admitted that the bombing effort probably 'delayed the operational use' of the new and more dangerous Type *XXI* and Type *XXIII* U-boats.[52] Clay Blair offers the latest, revised view of the effect of 'at source' attacks: 39 U-boats destroyed from bombing or aerial mining.[53] Given the investment in sorties, this effort leads George Franklin to conclude that 'no great study of the war is needed to pass judgment' on the RAF's pre-war prediction that U-boats and their yards would be flattened by massed bomber attacks.[54]

In summary, Allied aircraft were involved in 324 U-boat kills during World War II; 42 of those were in cooperation with warships while the remainder were conducted by aircraft operating alone – either patrolling, escorting, bombing, or dropping mines. Warships, on the other hand, destroyed 240 U-boats when acting alone and, again, 42 when shared with aircraft.[55] D. V. Peyton-Ward provides a slightly inflated total of 343 'air action alone' U-boat kills with 40 shared with surface vessels, but his detailed breakdown of causes is interesting. Of these kills, 181½ were attributed to RAF Coastal Command, 15½ to the Fleet Air Arm, and 60 to US Army and Navy patrol aircraft. A further 50 succumbed to Allied bombers, and airdropped mines destroyed 17 U-boats.[56] Aircraft were thus more than just an adjunct to surface anti-submarine warfare forces in World War II; here they were a critical and necessary component of the campaign. As Stephen Roskill states, 'The only important difference in the application of the convoy strategy in the two world wars was that where as in the first one air escorts did no more than force enemy submarines to submerge, in the second one they finally became as effective U-boat killers as the surface escorts.'[57]

Thus after establishing the role during the First World War, and only barely sustaining it during the interwar years, air anti-submarine warfare blossomed during World War II. Using the latter conflict as a yardstick for success in the former is, however, less instructive than an analysis of the factors governing Britain's employment of aircraft against submarines and the way in which historians have presented the major issues concerning this role during the Great War.

Summary

This monograph significantly reassesses Britain's use of aircraft as an anti-submarine weapon in the First World War. After providing an original survey of how the RNAS and RAF overcame the difficulties of technology and resources, this study finds that extant operational histories arrive at a correct general conclusion – that aircraft were a valuable contributor to anti-submarine warfare – but for the wrong reasons. Hunting patrols were more useful than had previously been acknowledged in the historiography. Aircraft convoy escort, an extremely effective part of Britain's trade protection system, was not a role universally accepted across the Home commands. The reality was that both regional priorities and the nature of maritime air organisation did not allow for a unanimous air anti-submarine doctrine. The reason for this inaccuracy? Most historians have relied for their source material on staff studies and official histories that were subject to specific agendas and did not provide a clear and unbiased view of the role of aircraft in anti-submarine warfare.

Naval aviation was a new endeavour when the Great War erupted in August 1914. Anti-submarine warfare, one of many potential roles for maritime aircraft, saw some experimentation in the years preceding the war, but did not receive serious attention from the Admiralty until late 1916. Only then, when the increasingly dangerous threat of German submarines intersected with a recognition by senior naval officers that aircraft had achieved a measured anti-submarine capability, did the Admiralty seriously consider this function. Many of the primary technological difficulties of the anti-submarine role had been solved by the end of the war; aircraft perform-ance, driven by increasing engine power and reliability, developed in parallel with better weapons, communication equipment, and navigation methods. RNAS and Admiralty innovators made huge technological leaps in a short space of time to solve these daunting operational problems of maritime aviation. Still, despite the advantage of height to visibility, spotting and attacking U-boats from the air essentially depended on the vigilance and eyesight of the aircrew. Since U-boats relied on surface cruising for seeking out merchant vessels and closing with them to attack, patrolling aircraft remained a threat to their operations. Through wireless telegraph and other signalling systems, aircraft could summon deadlier surface vessels to the encounter.

The different types of aircraft available to maritime air forces – including aeroplanes, seaplanes, flying boats, airships, and kite balloons – gave local commanders the tactical flexibility to employ these systems in ways that took advantage of specific capabilities. The demand for aircraft and crews, however, always outstripped availability. Unfortunately for the Admiralty, its recognition of the usefulness of aircraft coincided with its loss of control of the naval aircraft production process to the Air Board – and later Air Ministry – as well as a simultaneous expansion programme for air forces serving with the BEF. Added to this, seaplanes, flying boats, and most naval bombers employed advanced Rolls-Royce and Liberty engines that, although extremely powerful, arrived at a painfully slow rate. Still, the RAF amalgamation served to add more aeroplanes for coastal patrol work to offset seaplane and flying boat shortages, and maritime aviators benefited from its massive training system – one that employed modern teaching techniques on a vast scale.

The British employed aircraft in three roles against submarines. Bombing U-boat bases and facilities – an attack 'at source' tradition of the Royal Navy – was the least successful method because it was a primary mission for Dunkirk bombers only for a limited period. Other regional concerns interrupted these efforts for most of the war because Vice-Admiral Bacon did not make the Flanders Triangle bases a targeting priority for bomber aircraft. In the end, the Admiralty would have been forced to rely on USN bombers to carry out this role into 1919, since by then the Air Ministry would have used the Dunkirk bombers in strategic roles elsewhere.

Aircraft patrol was another major role for aircraft in anti-submarine warfare. Here, the most important contributions were to interrupt U-boat cruises by forcing them to dive at inopportune times and to summon follow-on surface attacks against spotted U-boats. Aircraft flew routine area patrols, such as the Spider Web, or hunting patrols where they sought out U-boats reported to be in certain areas. The use of intelligence, the proliferation of patrol stations, and cooperation with surface craft all served to enhance these efforts and made aircraft an important force multiplier to surface patrols. Aircraft also contributed to minesweeping efforts in Home Waters and generally helped to minimise this threat, especially in 1918. Thus, Arthur Marder's interpretation, emanating from the influence of Barley and Waters, that air patrols were useless was incorrect. Air patrols were part of a larger anti-submarine system consisting of attacks on bases, mine barrages, surface patrols, and finally convoys. Moreover, there was no heated debate between a 'patrol school' and a 'convoy school'; the Admiralty, unlike many historians, saw patrols and convoys as complementary tactics, not opposing ones.

Nevertheless, convoy escort was the most effective role for aircraft against submarines. Although they were limited by weather, aircraft denied U-boats the ability to reach a favourable position to attack convoys. Convoys protected by sea and air were 'virtually immune' from attack. It is noteworthy that this logic would have been true of aircraft area patrols denying U-boats the opportunity to travel to their patrol stations on the surface or to hunt for convoys in the first place. Trade defence philosophies differed from region to region, however, and not all naval districts used their RNAS or RAF aircraft in the same ways. Sortie allocation to area patrol, 'emergency' hunting patrol, and convoy escort depended on the circumstances of the given area and the employment preferences of the local naval commander. Only in certain areas, such as the East Coast of England Command, did escorts exceed area or hunting patrols, and only then by a slim margin. Moreover, by the closing months of the war, the overall majority of the maritime flying effort in Britain was focused on patrols and not on escorts. These bombing and trade defence roles had reached a high level of operational maturity by 1918, with an extensive infrastructure and detailed *tactical* doctrine, and led by a group of progressive air commanders. These roles generally reflect the Admiralty's willingness to experiment with technology and tactics in order to counter the dangerous U-boat threat to commerce, Britain's lifeblood.

This study provides an original interpretation of the employment of aircraft in anti-submarine roles because it focuses on the underlying impact of *organisation* upon the effort. Both before and after the RAF amalgamation, regional naval commanders employed their air groups independently within their respective areas of responsibility. The Admiralty generally chose not to interfere with operational air matters, and except for a few months in 1915, no high echelon of command, such as RAF Coastal Command, existed to exercise command of all naval air forces within Home Waters during 1914 to 1918. Thus, even after the RAF amalgamation, no headquarters existed to enforce employment principles (tactical doctrine) while no doctrine at the operational level, such as targeting priorities for bombers or sortie allocation for coastal units, was developed. The Admiralty's Air Division created tactics manuals and intelligence circulars for the RAF but could not enforce their use. Short of direct Admiralty Board requests to the Air Council, no vehicle for rapidly reinforcing certain areas from other coastal air groups existed. Such flexibility only appeared during World War II. This capability and command and control structure would have been welcomed when the Germans shifted their attacks from region to region and ultimately would have made the air anti-submarine effort even more effective than it was.

These findings adjust the current understanding of the use of aircraft against submarines during World War I. Generalising to the point of inaccuracy, historians have misrepresented the role of aircraft in coastal patrols and convoy escort, the former task more important than previously thought and the latter less comprehensive and universal than assumed. The true problems of organisation have also been overlooked in favour of other arguments, such as the 'patrol vs. convoy' debate and the specific agendas of staff and official historians. The various staff histories reflected the purposes for which they were written, but all concluded that maritime aviation during the Great War was an important force multiplier to surface anti-submarine forces. *The War in the Air*, influencing generations of historians, offered a substantial amount of detail to demonstrate the usefulness of air power in naval warfare while defending the concept of an independent RAF.

The Germans perhaps demonstrated the most accurate view of air anti-submarine warfare: World War I naval aircraft had a limited ability to destroy

U-boats outright but their ability to communicate meant that surface forces would soon arrive to deliver the dreaded depth charge attack. Thus, they respected the overall contribution of aircraft to Britain's system of anti-submarine warfare.

As in most historical issues, specific circumstances dictated how people thought about this air campaign. Available resources, existing technology, and operational experience influenced the practitioners themselves. The staff historians and official history authors were guided by their own set of purposes. Historians of more recent years tend to include this campaign only as a component of surveys of larger issues and thus misinterpret some of the key facts. This study, subject to its own influences, has helped set this question in the light that it deserves. It also serves to highlight the likelihood that many other issues relating to the Great War – where historians had to sift through vast amounts of archival materials in order to interpret events – are also subject to reassessment and our understanding may need adjustment accordingly.

Appendices

Appendix 1: Merchant losses and aircraft sorties

Source: D. V. Peyton-Ward, *The RAF in Maritime War*, Vol. I, AIR 41/45, Appendix I and II. [Note: 'Allied Ships Lost-Coastal' includes ships lost in the North Sea, English Channel, East Coast of England, Bristol Channel, and West Coast of Ireland]

	Allied Ships Lost-Coastal	Allied Ships Lost-Total East Atlantic	Aero/SP/FB Area Patrols Flown	Aero/SP/FB Escorts Flown	Aero/SP/FB Total Sorties	U-Boats Spotted by Aero/SP/FB	U-Boats Attacked by Aero/SP/FB	Airship Patrols Flown	Airship Escorts Flown	Airship Total Sorties	U-Boats Spotted by Airships	U-boats Attacked by Airships	Total Hours-Airship plus Aero/SP/FB
Feb 1917	61	106											
Mar	85	136					Not Available						
Apr	51	145											
May	61	114											
June	42	134	518	46	564	13	7	318	46	364	0	0	2925
Jul	49	112	651	53	704	11	9	348	59	407	2	0	3694
Aug	62	102	333	77	410	12	6	210	33	243	2	1	1949
Sep	36	62	611	92	703	28	18	457	86	543	6	2	4596
Oct	56	82	514	75	589	14	10	240	44	284	4	2	2628
Nov	51	63	584	52	636	18	10	337	63	400	5	3	3482
Dec	69	78	747	68	815	9	7	302	59	361	5	5	3526
Jan 1918	45	56	433	34	467	6	2	127	47	174	1	1	1679
Feb	55	67	671	35	706	5	2	231	37	268	0	0	2794
Mar	65	78	1209	80	1289	19	14	470	132	602	3	1	6773
Apr	51	57	1526	176	1702	10	8	415	184	599	1	1	7787
May	35	49	2751	402	3153	34	26	846	269	1115	5	4	15701

	Allied Ships Lost-Coastal	Allied Ships Lost-Total East Atlantic	Aero/SP/FB Area Patrols Flown	Aero/SP/FB Escorts Flown	Aero/SP/FB Total Sorties	U-Boats Spotted by Aero/SP/FB	U-Boats Attacked by Aero/SP/FB	Airship Patrols Flown	Airship Escorts Flown	Airship Total Sorties	U-Boats Spotted by Airships	U-boats Attacked by Airships	Total Hours-Airship plus Aero/SP/FB
June	38	44	2364	453	2817	24	16	518	170	688	3	2	11894
Jul	21	38	2399	751	3150	22	16	345	179	524	2	0	10795
Aug	30	45	4485	1340	5825	32	24	785	454	1239	3	2	21574
Sep	34	45	2989	820	3809	5	3	351	144	495	2	1	10168
Oct	16	24	4100	921	5021	5	4	549	204	753	3	1	15746
	Ships Lost			Aero/SP/FB					Airship				Hours

From Above:

	Monthly Averages	
	Feb 1917-Apr 1918	May 1918-Oct 1918
Coastal Ships Lost	56	29
	Jun 1917-Apr 1918	May 1918-Oct 1918
Aero/SP/FB Area Patrols	709	3181
Aero/SP/FB Escorts	72	781
Airship Area Patrols	314	566
Airship Escorts	72	237
Total Flying Hours	3803	14313

Appendix 2: Officer Ranks of RNAS, RN, RFC, RAF, and Imperial German Navy

Sources: *Jane's*; Peter Cooksley, *The RFC/RNAS Handbook, 1914–1918*

RNAS	RN	RFC/early RAF/Army	RAF (after Aug 1919)	Imperial German Navy
–	Admiral of the Fleet	Field Marshal	Marshal of the RAF	*Gross-Admiral*
–	Admiral	General	Air Chief Marshal	*Admiral*
–	Vice-Admiral	Lieutenant-General	Air Marshal	*Vize-Admiral*
–	Rear-Admiral	Major General	Air Vice Marshal	*Kontre-Admiral*
–	Commodore	Brigadier-General	Air Commodore	*Kommodore*
Wing Captain	Captain	Colonel	Group Captain	*Kapitän zur See*
Wing Commander	Commander	Lieutenant-Colonel	Wing Commander	*Fregatten-Kapitän* and *Korvetten-Kapitän*
Squadron Commander	Lieutenant-Commander	Major	Squadron Leader	*Kapitän-Leutnant*
Flight Commander	Lieutenant	Captain	Flight Lieutenant	*Oberleutnant zur See*
Flight Lieutenant	Sub-Lieutenant	Lieutenant	Flying Officer	*Leutnant zur See*
Flight Sub-Lieutenant		Second Lieutenant	Pilot Officer	

Notes

Introduction: British naval aviation and the U-boat menace

1 Crew of Seaplane 8695, Report of Bombing Submarine, RN Seaplane Station Dunkerque, 22 Sep 1917, ADM 137/377, 311–12, Public Record Office, National Archives, Kew. [Hereafter collection references to all PRO documents will include only department lettercodes and applicable series numbers.]

2 Ibid.

3 Report of Operations, Dunkerque Seaplane Station and Seaplane Defence Flight, 22 Sep 1917, AIR 1/1880/204/221/8.

4 C. E. S. Lusk Logbook, 22 Sep 1917, FAAM.

5 Arno Spindler, *Der Handelskrieg mit U-Booten*, Vol. IV (Berlin: E. S. Mittler, 1941), 302.

6 SO RNAS Dunkirk to VADP, 30 Sep 1917 and 15 Oct 1917, AIR 1/71/15/9/124.

7 *UB31*, 2 May 1918, Airship *SSZ-29* and drifters forced her into a minefield; *UB83*, 10 Sep 1918, HMS *Ophelia*'s depth charge attack guided by kite balloon; *UB103*, 16 Sep 1918, attacks by Airship *SSZ-1* and surface vessels; *UB115*, 29 Sep 1918, Airship *R-29* with subsequent destroyer and trawler attack; and *UC70*, 28 Aug 1918, attack by a Blackburn Kangaroo aeroplane followed by depth charge attack from HMS *Ouse*. One further destroyer with kite balloon (HMS *Patriot*) attack may have been successful on 12 July 1917, but evidence of *U69*'s loss is sketchy. Robert M. Grant, *U-Boats Destroyed: The Effect of Anti-Submarine Warfare, 1914–1918* (London: Putnam, 1964); Dwight R. Messimer, *Verschollen: World War I U-Boat Losses* (Annapolis: Naval Institute Press, 2003).

8 VADP to SO RNAS Dunkirk, 4 Jan 1918, and Commodore Dunkirk to SO RNAS Dunkirk, 12 Jan 1918, AIR 1/71/15/9/124.

9 H. A. Jones, *The War in the Air*, Vol. IV (Oxford: Clarendon, 1934), 73.

10 Henry Newbolt, *Naval Operations*, Vol. V (London: Longmans, Green and Co., 1931), 425.

11 Grant, *U-Boats Destroyed*, 63.

12 John Terraine, *Business in Great Waters: The U-Boat Wars, 1916–1945* (London: Leo Cooper, 1989), 77. Although this attack occurred beneath the extreme southern boundary of the Spider Web area, to be discussed in Chapter 4, this statement misleads the reader to assume that a Spider Web patrol aircraft made the attack. See S. F. Wise, *Canadian Airmen and the First World War: The Official History of the Royal Canadian Air Force, Volume I* (Toronto: University of Toronto Press, 1980), 177n, for a summary of further historiographical errors.

13 For example, Paul G. Halpern, *A Naval History of World War I* (Annapolis: Naval Institute Press, 1995), 424–27; Dwight R. Messimer, *Find and Destroy: Antisubmarine Warfare in World War I* (Annapolis: Naval Institute Press, 2001), Chapter

15; Lee Kennett, *The First Air War, 1914–1918* (New York: Free Press, 1991), 189–97; John H. Morrow, Jr., *The Great War in the Air: Military Aviation from 1909 to 1921* (Washington: Smithsonian Institution Press, 1993), 245, 324–25.

14 Michael Howard, *The Lessons of History* (New Haven: Yale University Press, 1991), 13.

15 Simon Fowler, Peter Elliot, Roy Conyers Nesbit, and Christina Goulter, *RAF Records in the PRO* (London: PRO Publications, 1994), 24; Sir Walter Raleigh and H. A. Jones, *The War in the Air: Being the Story of the Part Played in the Great War by the Royal Air Force*, Vol. I–VI (Oxford: Clarendon, 1922–37).

16 Halpern, *Naval History*, 333; Terraine, *Business*, 150.

17 Robin Higham, *The British Rigid Airship, 1908–1931: A Study in Weapons Policy* (London: G. T. Foulis, 1961), 88–90; Ronald Spector, *At War at Sea: Sailors and Naval Warfare in the Twentieth Century* (London: Penguin, 2001), 60, 108.

18 Higham, *British Rigid Airship*, 39.

19 D. V. Peyton-Ward, Air Historical Branch, *The RAF in Maritime War*, Vol. I, nd, AIR 41/45, 1.

20 These events are covered extensively in the literature of the period. See ibid., 2–11; Maurice Dean, *The Royal Air Force and Two World Wars* (London: Cassell, 1979), 21–29; Malcolm Cooper, *The Birth of Independent Air Power: British Air Policy in the First World War* (London: Allen and Unwin, 1986).

21 Roy Jenkins, *Churchill* (London: Pan Macmillan, 2001), 269–76.

22 Higham, *British Rigid Airship*, 77. Between May 1915 and Dec 1916, airship policy was discussed more than any other naval aviation topic at Admiralty Board meetings. Admiralty Board Minutes, ADM 167/49[1915] and 50[1916]. The *Mayfly* would have been the first British rigid airship had it not been wrecked during trials. After Lloyd George's rise to power in Dec 1916, the rigid airship programme once again fell into neglect.

23 Higham, *British Rigid Airship*, 79.

24 S. W. Roskill, ed., *Documents Relating to the Naval Air Service: Volume 1, 1908–1918* (London: Naval Records Society, 1969), xi.

25 Extracts from Admiralty Weekly Order No. 166, 'Naval Air Service, Reorganisation', 5 Feb 1915, Doc. No. 62 in Roskill, *Documents Relating*, 193–94. Also in ADM 137/2237.

26 Cooper, *Birth*, 21.

27 Admiralty Weekly Order No. 1204/15, 'Royal Naval Air Service', 29 Jul 1915, Doc. No. 72 in Roskill, *Documents Relating*, 212–13.

28 Peyton-Ward, *RAF in Maritime War*, AIR 41/45, I: 18.

29 Roskill, *Documents Relating*, xi.

30 AHB historian D. V. Peyton-Ward reflects the positive viewpoint in *RAF in Maritime War*, AIR 41/45, I: 18–19. Roskill asserts that the Balfour/Jackson regime 'will surely stand for a long time as one of the least effective Boards ever to rule the Navy – at any rate in time of war' and that he 'found next to nothing to suggest originality of thought' in any of Vaughan-Lee's papers or memos. Roskill, *Documents Relating*, xi–xiii.

31 Extracts from Vaughan-Lee, AIR4, Joint War Air Committee, 3 Mar 1916, Doc. No. 106 in Roskill, *Documents Relating*, 309–15.

32 Higham, *British Rigid Airship*, 78.

33 John Winton, *Jellicoe* (London: Michael Joseph, 1981), 53.

34 Admiralty Secretariat, Distribution of Business, June 1917, AIR 1/279/15/226/127.

35 Roskill, *Documents Relating*, xi.

36 Admiralty Memos and Minutes, Dec 1917, Doc. No. 216 in Roskill, *Documents Relating*, 603–04.

37 F. R. Scarlett Service Record, ADM 196/44, 146; R. M. Groves Service Record,

ADM 196/45, 129–30; Groves Diary, 12 Aug 1918, Groves Papers, IWM/DD/P322.

38 J. R. Jellicoe, *The Crisis of the Naval War* (London: Cassell, 1920), Appendices A–D.

39 Admiralty Memo 1391: 'Air Force Organisation', 19 Mar 1918, Doc. No. 234 in Roskill, *Documents Relating*, 641–45. Details of the RAF system will be discussed in Chapters 4 and 5.

40 Naval Torpedo School, *Twentieth Annual Report on the Instruction and Practice of Torpedo Warfare, 1899*, 1 May 1900, ADM 189/19, 114; Report of HMS *Illustrious*, 8 Apr 1905, ADM 1/7825.

41 Christina J. M. Goulter, *A Forgotten Offensive: Royal Air Force Coastal Command's Anti-Shipping Campaign, 1940–1945* (London: Frank Cass, 1995), 2–3.

42 Lt H. A. Williamson, 'Aeroplanes for Naval Service', 2 Jan 1912, and associated minutes, AIR 1/626/17/88; H. A. Williamson Service Record, ADM 196/49, 135. Williamson joined the RNAS in Dec 1913, was wounded in the Dardanelles in 1915, served in Admiralty staff positions in 1916–17, and commanded No. 18 Group, RAF, in 1918.

43 Submarine Committee, Report on Hydro-aeroplane and Submarine Exercises, 18 Oct 1912, AIR 1/626/17/88.

44 C. D. Burney, 'Air Power', *Naval Review* I, No. 2 (May 1913): 110–11.

45 Higham, *British Rigid Airship*, 61.

46 Arthur Longmore, *From Sea to Sky, 1910–1945* (London: Geoffrey Bles, 1946), 34; Lt A. M. Longmore, Summary of Report, 1 Mar 1914, Doc. No. 38 in Roskill, *Documents Relating*, 126.

47 Halpern, *Naval History*, 425, 333.

1 Technology: Aircraft and U-boats

1 Macgregor Knox and Williamson Murray, eds, *The Dynamics of Military Revolution, 1300–2050* (Cambridge: Cambridge University Press, 2001), 10–11.

2 Jack K. Gusewelle, 'Science and the Admiralty During World War I: The Case of the BIR', in *Naval Warfare in the Twentieth Century 1900–1945*, edited by Gerald Jordan (London: Croom Helm, 1977), 106–07; RNAS Aircraft Requirements Paper, Nov 1916, AIR 1/146/15/63; RAF Technical Department, Draft of Aircraft and Engine Requirements to mid-1919, 3 Apr 1918, AIR 1/1084/204/5/1720; DAD Memo: Design of Submarine Hunting Aircraft, 12 Apr 1918, AIR 1/671/17/134/7.

3 For example, Owen Thetford, *British Naval Aircraft Since 1912*, 6th ed. (Annapolis: Naval Institute Press, 1991); Patrick Abbott, *The British Airship at War, 1914–1918* (Lavenham: Terence Dalton, 1989); J. M. Bruce, *British Aeroplanes, 1914–18* (London: Putnam, 1957); Ces Mowthorpe, *Battlebags: British Airships of the First World War* (Stroud: Wrens Park, 1998).

4 Richard Compton-Hall, *Submarines and the War at Sea, 1914–1918* (London: Macmillan, 1991), 11.

5 Knox and Murray, *Dynamics*, 12–13.

6 C. P. O. Bartlett, *In the Teeth of the Wind*, edited by Nick Bartlett (Annapolis: Naval Institute Press, 1994), 114–18; Leonard Doughty, 'The Effect of Depth Charges on Submarines', *United States Naval Institute Proceedings [USNIP]* 61, No. 3 (March 1935): 356; Alfred Price, *Aircraft Versus Submarines: The Evolution of the Anti-Submarine Aircraft 1912–1972* (London: Kimber, 1973), 16.

7 Norman Friedman, *Submarine Design and Development* (London: Conway, 1984), 9.

8 'The distance to the horizon, D, in nautical miles, may be calculated by the formula $D = 1.17 \times \sqrt{h}$, where h is the height of eye in feet.' Elbert S. Maloney,

Dutton's Navigation and Piloting, 14th ed. (Annapolis, Naval Institute Press, 1985), 62–63.

9   Kennett, *First Air War*, 189.

10 Report of Progress, N6 (Admiralty Kite Balloon Section), 28 Apr 1918, AIR 1/ 444/15/303/7. This report mentioned that maximum kite balloon visibility at 800 to 1,000 feet was approximately 40 miles.

11 GHQ, Home Forces, *Intelligence Circular No. 14: Aeroplanes, Seaplanes, and Flying Boats, Part II*, Oct 1917, AIR 1/720/36/1/14.

12 Unless otherwise specified, aircraft performance data for this discussion is derived from Thetford, *British Naval Aircraft*; John W. R. Taylor, *Jane's Fighting Aircraft of World War I* (London: Random House Group, 2001); and Tables of Performance, Air Board Technical Section, 24 Jan 1918 and 30 Jun 1918, AIR 1/2423/ 305/18/45.

13 Bruce, *British Aeroplanes*, 96; R. D. Layman, *Naval Aviation in the First World War: Its Impact and Influence* (Annapolis: Naval Institute Press, 1996), 83.

14 Price, *Aircraft Versus Submarines*, 17.

15 Ray Sturtivant and Gordon Page, *Royal Navy Aircraft Serials and Units, 1911 to 1919* (Tonbridge: Air-Britain Ltd, 1992), 15–17.

16 Captain Richard C. Knott, *The American Flying Boat: An Illustrated History* (Annapolis: Naval Institute Press, 1979), 22–33.

17 Capt A. E. Bolton, 'The Development of the Large America Flying Boat for Naval War Purposes, 1917–1919', nd, AIR 1/2397/267/5; Felixstowe RN Air Station, 'Report on Experimental Flying Boat Hulls, 1915–1916', nd, Miscellaneous Papers(B433), RAFM(H).

18 Flt Lt J. P. Coleman, Lecture: 'Aircraft v. Submarine', RAF Staff College, Oct 1924, AIR 1/2393/228/13/1, 20; Wg Capt C. L. Lambe to VADP, 3 Dec 1917, AIR 1/642/17/122/238.

19 Col F. Sykes, 'Aircraft in the Dardanelles', 9 Jul 1915, AIR 1/669/17/122/788, 24. Engine strain on takeoff was a problem common to all seaplanes in all theatres.

20 Lambe to VADP, 3 Dec 1917, AIR 1/642/17/122/238; No. 217 Squadron Record Book, 1 Oct 1917–31 Mar 1918, AIR 1/1878/204/221/4; Commodore Dunkirk, 'Air Notes for Belgian Coast Patrol', 1 Jul 1918, ADM 137/2277, 381–92.

21 Layman, *Naval Aviation*, 25.

22 G. E. Livock, *To the Ends of the Air* (London: HMSO, 1973), 41.

23 J. C. Nerney, AHB Narrative: 'RNAS in Home Waters: Submarine Campaign', nd, AIR 1/677/21/13/1902, 6.

24 Layman, *Naval Aviation*, 26.

25 Lambe to VADP, 3 Dec 1917, AIR 1/642/17/122/238.

26 DOD and DAS minutes, Nov 1917, AIR 1/642/17/122/238.

27 Lt Col L. H. Strain, 'Review of Aircraft Anti-Submarine Campaign, 1918', nd, AIR 1/726/137/4, 8; Lambe to VADP, 3 Dec 1917, AIR 1/642/17/122/238.

28 J. M. Bruce, *Felixstowe F.2A* (Berkhamsted: Albatros Productions Ltd, 2000), 12.

29 Higham, *British Rigid Airship*, 342–43.

30 Thetford, *British Naval Aircraft*, 476, 483; Abbott, *British Airship*, 102; Messimer, *Verschollen*, 226.

31 Abbott, *British Airship*, 22.

32 Walter Raleigh, *The War in the Air*, Vol. I (Oxford: Clarendon, 1922), 462–63.

33 Mowthorpe, *Battlebags*, 67.

34 F. W. Verry Transcript, IWM/SA/311, 34; T. B. Williams Transcript IWM/SA/ 313, 34.

35 Mowthorpe, *Battlebags*, Chapter 7.

36 Thetford, *British Naval Aircraft*, 476–77.

37 Coleman Lecture, AIR 1/2393/228/13/1, 20.

38 Capt J. S. Wheelwright, Report of *NS-3* Patrol, 24 Apr 1918, ADM 137/1955, 191–96.
39 George Meager, *My Airship Flights, 1915–1930* (London: Kimber, 1970), 25.
40 CO Capel RNASS to SO RNAS Dover, 9 Jan 1918, AIR 1/77/15/9/182.
41 Lecture Notes: 'Airships', RAF Staff College, 20 Jul 1924, Elmhirst Papers(ELMT8/1), CCA.
42 Lt Cdr R. C. Hayes, 'Instructions for Landing an Airship S.S. Type', 19 Jul 1916, ADM 137/1953, 139.
43 Ces Mowthorpe, *Sky Sailors: The Story of the World's Airshipmen* (Stroud: Sutton, 1999), 34; Technical History Section, *The Technical History and Index, Part 4: Aircraft v. Submarine, Submarine Campaign, 1918*, March 1919, NHB, 8. [Hereafter, *TH4*.]
44 Coleman Lecture, AIR 1/2393/228/13/1, 20.
45 Raleigh, *WIA*, I: 460–62; File entitled: 'Kite Balloons for the Co-Operation with the Navy and Army', *c.* Aug 1919, AIR 1/1951/204/258/1.
46 DAD Report: 'Appreciation of British Naval Operations: RNAS Aircraft Operations', Nov 1918, ADM 1/8549, 40.
47 DAD Memo, 11 Aug 1918, AIR 1/281/15/226/134 Part II, AD2164. Balloon height not mentioned.
48 Air Department, *RNAS Kite Balloon Training Manual*, Jan 1917, AIR 1/673/17/134/44, 163.
49 Weekly Kite Balloon Reports, 6 Jul 1918–11 Jan 1919, AIR 1/270/15/226/111; Air Department Memo, 'Use of Kite Balloons at Sea', nd, AIR 1/444/15/303/11.
50 *RNAS Kite Balloon Training Manual*, AIR 1/673/17/134/44, 138.
51 H. A. Jones, *The War in the Air*, Vol. II (Oxford: Clarendon, 1928), 338.
52 Raleigh, *WIA*, I: 208; Layman, *Naval Aviation*, 22.
53 Morrow, *GWA*, 366.
54 Tim Travers, *How the War Was Won: Command and Technology in the British Army on the Western Front, 1917–1918* (London: Routledge, 1992), 2–3, 181–82; Nicholas Lambert, *Sir John Fisher's Naval Revolution* (Columbia: University of South Carolina Press, 1999), 6.
55 David Edgerton, *England and the Aeroplane* (London: Macmillan, 1991), xv, 64–65.
56 Morrow, *GWA*, 252; J. K. Bradley, 'The History and Development of Aircraft Instruments, 1909 to 1919', Ph.D. Diss. (Imperial College of Science and Technology London, 1994), 215–18.
57 Morrow, *GWA*, 252.
58 J. C. Nerney, AHB Narrative: 'Development and Supply of Aircraft,' 5 Feb 1935, AIR 1/678/21/13/2186; Raleigh, *WIA*, I: 425; Morrow, *GWA*, 43–44, 78.
59 Records Department, Air Board, Engines used by the RNAS, 25 Apr 1917, AIR 1/1/4/18.
60 Morrow, *GWA*, 122.
61 Nerney, 'Development and Supply of Aircraft,' AIR 1/678/21/13/2186, 15.
62 War Experiences of Sqn Ldr J. K. Waugh, RAF Staff College, 29 Sep 1925, AIR 1/2388/228/11/67.
63 J. H. Bentham Logbook, B1898, RAFM(H).
64 C. S. Mossop Logbook, FAAM.
65 No. 7 (Naval) Squadron, *Notes on the Work And Organisation of a Handley Page Night Bombing Squadron*, May 1918, AIR 1/2684, Pt 4.
66 Bolton, 'Development of the Large Flying Boat,' AIR 1/2397/267/5.
67 *TH4*, 16.
68 Ibid., 5–6.
69 Lambe to Bacon, 15 Oct 1917, AIR 1/71/15/9/124.

70 Thomas Crouther Gordon, *Early Flying in Orkney: Seaplanes in World War One* (Kirkwall: BBC Radio Orkney, 1985), 17, 20.

71 Typescript Memoir: 'An Airman's Life', Elmhirst Papers(ELMT6/1), CCA, 34–5; War Experiences of Flt Lt J. B. Cole-Hamilton, RAF Staff College, 1 Nov 1922, AIR 1/2386/228/11/15, 4; Beatty to Admiralty, 19 Jan 1917, ADM 137/1953, 61.

72 Thomas G. Miller, Jr and Douglas H. Robinson, 'Nonrigid Airships in World War I', *Cross and Cockade* [US] 5, No. 2 (1964): 100; Mowthorpe, *Sky Sailors*, 17.

73 T. B. Williams Transcript, IWM/SA/313, 56; Meager, *Airship Flights*, 71–72; Mowthorpe, *Battlebags*, 79–80.

74 Air Division, Monthly Summaries, AIR 1/269/15/226/109; *TH4*, 16.

75 Jones, *WIA*, II: 335.

76 War Experiences of Flt Lt P. H. Mackworth, RAF Staff College, 23 Jan 1928, AIR 1/2389/228/11/117, 5.

77 Livock, *To the Ends*, 45–46.

78 T. D. Hallam, *The Spider Web: The Romance of a Flying-Boat Flight in the First World War* (London: Arms and Armour Press, 1979), 34–35.

79 Guy Hartcup, *The War of Invention: Scientific Developments, 1914–1918* (London: Brassey's Defence Publishers, 1988), 123–25; War Experiences II, Elmhirst Papers(ELMT8/1), CCA, 6; Notebook of J. Havers, 'Rules for the Guidance of Airship Flights', 145, FAAM; DAS Memo: 'Aerial Navigation by W/T Directional Apparatus', 7 Nov 1917, AIR 2/38.

80 Bradley Thesis, 'Aircraft Instruments', Chapter 5.

81 Bolton's 'Development of the Large Flying Boat', AIR 1/2397/267/5.

82 RAF Experimental Station, 'Night Bombing From Low Height', 3 Sep 1918, AIR 1/459/15/312/91; Air Department, *RNAS Course-Setting Bomb Sight Mark I*, 8 Jan 1918, AIR 1/2103/207/30/34.

83 Livock, *To the Ends*, 47–48.

84 Goulter, *Forgotten Offensive*, 12. C. R. Samson probably flew the first night mission of the war when he bombed a German gun emplacement near Ostend on 14 Dec 1914. Thetford, *British Naval Aircraft*, 437.

85 Director of Statistics, 'Charts Showing Enemy Attacks by Day and Night', 17 Apr 1918, AIR 1/306/15/226/166. These figures refer to ships of 500 GRT and above.

86 Wg Cdr P. Smyth Osbourne, GM Nos. 2 and 8, Apr 1916, AIR 1/147/15/72.

87 Air Department, *Compasses in Aircraft*, 22 Aug 1916, AIR 1/699/27/3/415.

88 W. E. D. Wardop Transcript, IWM/SA/029, 22–23; Pamphlet Entitled 'Notes on Night Reconnaissance and Bombing', Jul 1918, AIR 1/475/15/312/196.

89 RAF Pamphlet: *Jenkins Night Altitude Indicator*, 31 Jul 1918, AIR 1/700/27/3/563; *Notes on . . . a Handley Page Night Bombing Squadron*, AIR 1/2684; Sqn Ldr W. A. McLaughry, 'A Lecture on Night Flying', in Air Ministry, *A Selection of Lectures and Essays . . .* [FS Pub 956], Dec 1923, AIR 10/973.

90 Bruce, *F2A*, 30.

91 Goulter, *Forgotten Offensive*, 12.

92 T. B. Williams Transcript, IWM/SA/313, 32–34.

93 William Edward Fischer, Jr, *The Development of Military Night Aviation to 1919* (Maxwell Air Force Base: Air University Press, 1998), 51; C. R. Samson, *Fights and Flights* (London: Ernest Benn, 1930), 203–06.

94 Bartlett, *Teeth of the Wind*, 18–19.

95 HQ RNAS Dunkirk, Report on Night Bombing, Aug 1917, AIR 1/642/17/122/250.

96 *Notes on . . . a Handley Page Night Bombing Squadron*, AIR 1/2684; Paul Bewsher, *'Green Balls': The Adventures of a Night-Bomber* (London: W. Blackwood and Sons, 1919), 168–69.

97 VADP to DAD, 7 May 1915 and DAD minute 25 May 1915, AIR 1/635/17/122/124.

98 Adm F. T. Hamilton, 'Duties of C. Airships', 3 Sep 1916, and 'East Coast of Scotland Air Patrols and General Instructions', 13 Apr 1917, ADM 137/1953, 153 and 56.

99 Cable: C-in-C Grand Fleet to Admiralty, 30 Oct 1917, ADM 137/1955; R. Jelliffe Logbook, FAAM.

100 SO RNAS Dover to VADP, 18 May 1917, ADM 137/2274, 130.

101 Polegate RNASS, *Reminiscences*, *c.* 1919, RAFM(H), 36. This publication commemorates the accomplishments of Polegate during the war.

102 Newbolt, *NO*, V: 338–39.

103 Report of *NS-3*, 24 Apr 1918, ADM 137/1955, 191–96.

104 DASD and DAD Minutes, 19–23 Jul 1918, AIR 1/308/15/226/194.

105 DAD Memo, Aug 1918, AIR 1/291/15/226/140 Parts I and II, AD5039.

106 Director Air Armament Division to Controller Technical Department, 22 Apr 1918, AIR 1/305/15/226/163.

107 Wg Cdr J. N. Fletcher, *Lecture on Maintenance, Flying and Operations of Airships*, Cranwell, 1918. NMM(CL), 32.

108 Air Division, *Report of Naval Air Operations*, Apr 1918, AIR 1/626/17/59/1, 9. [Hereafter, *NAO*.]

109 Goulter, *Forgotten Offensive*, 1–3.

110 Richard Bell Davies, *Sailor in the Air* (London: Peter Davies, 1967), 113–15; Jones, *WIA*, II: 342; Air Department, *Lectures on Bomb Sighting*, 23 Apr 1917, AIR 1/673/17/134/42, 9–10; Air Department, *Gunnery Memorandum No. 31*, Apr 1916, AIR 1/2103/207/30/20.

111 Air Division, *Notes on the Co-operation of Aircraft with Surface Craft for Escorting Convoys of Merchant Ships*, Dec 1918, AIR 1/2321/223/41/885; Capt J. G. Struthers, Airship Department, *Notes on Aids to Submarine Hunting*, Apr 1918, ADM 186/415.

112 Air Ministry, *Details of Aerial Bombs*, Feb 1918, AIR 1/704/27/7/1–24; Anti-Submarine Division, *RNAS Anti-Submarine Report*, Dec 1917, AIR 1/2105/207/41/7, 9–10 [Hereafter, *ASR*]; Admiralty to Air Ministry, 29 Mar 1918 and 12 Apr 1918, AIR 1/274/15/226/124 Pt I; Col H. A. Williamson, 'Employment of Aeroplanes for Anti-Submarine Work', and DAD minute, Aug 1918, AIR 1/287/15/226/137 Pt II.

113 Director Air Armaments to Controller Technical Department, 22 Apr 1918, AIR 1/305/15/226/163; *NAOs*, Apr-Oct 1918, AIR 1/626/17/59/1–7.

114 Director Air Armament to Director Flying Operations, 7 Sep 1918, AIR 1/32/15/1/184.

115 *Details of Aerial Bombs*, AIR 1/704/27/7/1–24; *TH4*, 9.

116 'Recommendations of Conference', 14 Jun 1918, AIR 1/305/15/226/163; *ASR*, Aug 1917, AIR 1/2105/207/41/3, 4.

117 Messimer, *Find and Destroy*, 134.

118 Technical History Section, *The Technical History and Index, Part 40: Anti-Submarine Development and Experiments Prior to December 1916*, Sep 1920, NHB, 54–55.

119 'Recommendations of Conference', 14 Jun 1918, AIR 1/305/15/226/163.

120 Mines Dropped From Aircraft, Mar 1917–Jan 1918, AIR 1/72/15/9/141. One of Sir Reginald Bacon's many schemes, the aerial mining trials ended with his dismissal in December 1917.

121 'Recommendations of Conference', 14 Jun 1918, and Director Air Armaments to Controller Technical Department, 22 Apr 1918, AIR 1/305/15/226/163.

122 Air Department, 'Report of Experiments Carried Out at Grain During April 1916', AIR 1/436/15/228/2.

123 Technical Department, Ministry of Munitions, *Bomb-Sighting with a Short Account of the Chief Apparatus Now in Use*, 13 Aug 1918, AIR 1/701/27/3/656; Air Department, *RNAS Equal Distance Bomb Sight (Mark I)*, 1 Jul 1916, AIR 1/2103/207/31; Capt D. S. Murray, 'General Notes on Bomb Sights', 8 Feb 1921, AIR 1/674/21/6/77.

124 Air Department, *RNAS Drift Bomb Sights*, four releases: 28 Sep 1917, AIR 1/2103/207/31; 28 Feb 1918, AIR 1/2103/207/30/46; 28 Jun 1918, AIR 1/699/27/3/435; 13 Aug 1918, AIR 1/700/27/3/570.

125 Capt G. McKerrow, Report on Drift Sight, 27 Jul 1918, AIR 1/945/204/5/999; *Lectures on Bomb Sighting*, AIR 1/673/17/134/42, 14.

126 Murray, 'General Notes on Bomb Sights', AIR 1/674/21/6/77, 18.

127 Goulter, *Forgotten Offensive*, 27.

128 Director Air Armament to Controller Technical Department, 22 Apr 1918, AIR 1/305/15/226/163; CO RN Seaplane Base Isles of Scilly, Bomb Test Report, 11 Dec 1917, AIR 2/38; RAF Experimental Station Report, 3 Sep 1918, AIR 1/459/15/312/91; 'General Notes on Bomb Sights', AIR 1/674/21/6/77, 18.

129 *TH4*, 13–15; see Introduction, note 7.

130 *TH4*, 15.

131 *Notes on Aids to Submarine Hunting*, ADM 186/415, 12–15; Air Division, *Notes on the Cooperation of Aircraft . . .*, Dec 1918, AIR 1/2321/223/41/885, 10–13.

132 *ASR*, Aug 1917, AIR 1/2105/207/41/3, 4; *TH4*, 11; Air Department Pamphlet No. 41: *Aldis Signal Lamp*, Jan 1918, AIR 1/699/27/3/417; 'A Chronological Account of W/T and Signal Work Carried Out By Seaplanes and Aeroplanes Working With The Grand Fleet', Mar 1919, AIR 2/125.

133 'W/T and Signal Work', AIR 2/125.

134 Meager, *Airship Flights*, 81.

135 Arthur Hezlet, *The Electron and Sea Power* (London: Peter Davies, 1975), 72.

136 DAD Report, 'Appreciation of British Naval Effort: RNAS Aircraft Operations', Nov 1918, AIR 1/2415/303/31, 18.

137 Airship Department, *Handbook on the 'Coastal' and 'C Star' Airships*, May 1918, NMM(CL); Air Department, *Receiver Model Th*, Dec 1917, AIR 1/2103/207/30/32; Air Department, *CW Transmitter Type 57*, Jan 1918, AIR 1/2103/207/30/37; 'W/T and Signal Work', AIR 2/125.

138 Wg Capt E. L. Gerrard to C-in-C Plymouth, 10 Jan 1918, AIR 1/641/17/122/106; War Experiences of Sqn Ldr R. M. Bayley, RAF Staff College, 21 Sep 1923, AIR 1/2386/228/11/20.

139 A. J. L. Blond, 'Technology and Tradition: Wireless Telegraphy and the Royal Navy, 1895–1920', Ph.D. Diss. (University of Lancaster, 1993), 329.

140 VAECE, *East Coast Aircraft Orders*, 30 Sep 1918, ADM 137/2242; *TH4*, 10; VAECE to Admiralty, 27 Nov 1917, AIR 1/641/17/122/222; RNAS HQ Plymouth, *South-West Group Patrol Orders*, 1 Sep 1917, AIR 1/644/17/122/292.

141 *TH4*, 4; *ASR*, Sep 1917, AIR 1/2105/207/41/4, 4; *NAO*, May 1918, AIR 1/62617/59/2, 14; Meager, *Airship Flights*, 79.

142 Raleigh, *WIA*, I: 224.

143 Hartcup, *War of Invention*, 154–55; DAD Memo, 10 Aug 1918, AIR 1/286/15/226/137 Pt I. Wireless telephone had been demonstrated in 1916, would have enabled 'en clair' communication, but proved difficult to mass produce at the time.

144 This advantage was realised as early as 1912. Lt H. A. Williamson, 'Aeroplanes for Naval Service', 2 Jan 1912, Air 1/626/17/88, App I.

145 *Notes on Aids to Submarine Hunting*, ADM 186/415, 3.

146 *TH4*, 13.

147 BIR, *Report of Proceedings, 31 Dec 1916*, Jan 1917, ADM 293/7, 18–20.

148 Newbolt, *NO*, V: 124–27; Messimer, *Find and Destroy*, 114–16; Cdr F. Barley, Historical Section, 'Anti-Submarine Measures in World War I', S.5659, 30 Nov 1960, Searches, Vol. 29, NHB.

149 *TH4*, 11; Anti-Submarine Division, *Hydrophones in Flying Boats and Float Seaplanes* [CB865], Aug 1918, AIR 1/2321/223/41/865, 3. On 26 January 1917, Lord Fisher wrote to Sir John Jellicoe that 'If the direction finder can be so effectively used (as stated) by seaplanes to locate submarines, we have a mighty weapon!' Doc. No. 389 in Arthur J. Marder, ed., *Fear God and Dread Nought: The Correspondence of Admiral of the Fleet Lord Fisher of Kilverstone, Vol. III: Restoration, Abdication, and Last Years, 1914–1920* (London: Jonathan Cape, 1959), 424.

150 *ASR*, Jul 1917, AIR 1/2105/207/41/3, 3.

151 Technical History Section, *The Technical History and Index, Part 7: The Anti-Submarine Division of the Naval Staff, December 1916–November 1918*, July 1919, Technical History Volumes, NHB, 25–26 [Hereafter *TH7*]; Geoffrey Williams, *Wings Over Westgate* (Malling, Kent: Kent County Library, 1985), 106–07.

152 Lt Cdr G. Hilhouse, 'General Report Concerning Flying Boats and Hydrophones', 17 May 1918, and H. W. Metcalfe, 'Trials of Hydrophone Suspensions with "Nash" Type Hydrophone,' 16 May 1918, ADM 137/2717.

153 DASD memo, 'Hydrophones and Flying Boats', 17 Jul 1918, AIR 1/284/15/226/136 Pt I. A few sets would go to floatplane units in areas where flying boats were not based.

154 CB865, AIR 1/2321/223/41/865, 11–12.

155 *TH7*, 26–7.

156 F. B. Young, BIR Paper 40974/17: 'The Airship in Relation to Gear for Submarine Detection', 28 Dec 1917, ADM 137/1953.

157 Wg Cdr T. C. B. Cave, 'Present Position of Hydrophone Experiments', 20 Apr 1918, ADM 137/2710, 37–9; *TH7*, 27–8; Experiment Reports, 9 Jun–23 Aug 1918, AIR 1/645/17/122/300.

158 J. C. Nerney, AHB Narrative: 'Short History of the RNAS', AIR 1/682/21/13/2226, 8; *NAOs*, Apr–Oct 1918, AIR 1/626/17/59/1–7; Verry Transcript, IWM/SA/311, 32.

159 *TH7*, 27–8; *ASR*, Jul 1917, AIR 1/2105/207/41/3, 3.

160 Compton-Hall, *Submarines*, 98.

161 Winston S. Churchill, *The World Crisis, 1911–1918. Volume II* (London: Odhams Press, 1923), 1223.

162 Performance specifications below are taken from Erich Gröner, *German Warships, 1815–1945. Volume 2: U-Boats and Mine Warfare Vessels*, revised by Dieter Jung and Martin Maass, translated by Keith Thomas and Rachel Magowan (London: Conway, 1991), 4–35; Eberhard Rössler, *The U-Boat: The Evolution and Technical History of German Submarines*, translated by Harold Erenberg (London: Arms and Armour Press, 1981), 328–32; and John Moore, *Jane's Fighting Ships of World War I* (New York: Military Press, 1990), 124–27.

163 William Jameson, *The Most Formidable Thing: The Story of the Submarine from Its Earliest Days to the End of World War I* (London: Rupert Hart-Davis, 1965), 209–10.

164 Jameson, *Formidable Thing*, 209–10.

165 Churchill, *World Crisis*, II: 1224.

166 Gröner, *German Warships*, II: 11.

167 Compton-Hall, *Submarines*, 37.

168 Price, *Aircraft Versus Submarine*, 16.

169 Compton-Hall, *Submarines*, 28.

170 V. E. Tarrant, *The U-Boat Offensive, 1914–1945* (London: Arms and Armour Press, 1989), 7, 46, 164.

171 Ibid., 58, 164.

172 A concept that is well-argued in I. B. Holley, Jr, *Ideas and Weapons* (Washington, DC: US Government Printing Office, 1997), 175–78.

2 Training and production

1 Even by the end of 1917, more volunteers were being entered than could be trained in the RNAS. Copy of Admiralty letter to Air Policy Committee, 5 Dec 1917, AIR 1/678/21/13/2108.
2 First and Second *Annual Reports of the Air Committee on the Progress of the RFC*, 7 Jun 1913 and 9 May 1914, Doc. Nos. 31 and 41 in Roskill, *Documents Relating*, 96–107, 128–138; Longmore, *Sea to Sky*, Chapters 1 and 2; Colonel C. R. Samson, 'History of Naval Aeroplanes and Seaplanes', nd, AIR 1/724/76/2. Eastchurch was established as a naval aerodrome in late 1911, and the Naval Flying School started there in December 1911. John W. R. Taylor, *C. F. S.: Birthplace of Air Power* (London: Putnam, 1958), 22.
3 Christopher Draper, *The Mad Major* (Letchworth: Air Review Ltd, 1962), 29–35; Longmore, *Sea to Sky*, 12–14; Thetford, *British Naval Aircraft*, 410, 452; Nigel Steel and Peter Hart, *Tumult in the Clouds: The British Experience of the War in the Air 1914–1918* (London: Hodder and Stoughton, 1997), 82.
4 Raleigh, *WIA*, I: 359; H. A. Jones, *The War in the Air*, Vol. V (Oxford: Clarendon, 1935), 438–39. This practice was actually started before the war. RNAS leaders such as Richard Bell Davies (1911), Christopher Draper (1913), Oliver Swann (1911), and H. A. Williamson (1911) earned their civilian pilot rating at their own expense and only later transferred to the RNAS.
5 Livock, *To the Ends*, 4.
6 Bartlett, *Teeth of the Wind*, 3.
7 Livock, *To the Ends*, 14–18; J. C. Nerney, AHB Narrative: 'Summary of Notes on Training of RNAS Personnel, 1914–1918', nd, AIR 1/678/21/17/2082, 2–3.
8 Ibid., 2–4; Air Department, *GM No. 14*, 24 Feb 1916, AIR 1/660/17/122/632; Jones, *WIA*, V: 439; Office Memo, Admiralty Secretariat, 13 Dec 1915, ADM 1/8448/36.
9 Wardrop Transcript, IWM/SA/0029, 9–15.
10 Nerney, 'Summary', AIR 1/678/21/17/2082, 3–5; L. H. Kemp Interview, IWM/SA/0026, Reels 1–2, and Wardrop Transcript, IWM/SA/0029, 9–16; 'Status and Training of Observers', January 1916, AIR 1/688/17/122/773 (excerpts also in Doc. No. 96 in Roskill, *Documents Relating*, 277–78).
11 Admiralty Memo CW 22508, 24 Aug 1917, ADM 1/8494/174.
12 C. G. Jefford, *Observers and Navigators and Other Non-Pilot Aircrew in the RFC, RNAS and RAF* (Shrewsbury: Airlife, 2001), 25.
13 Nerney, 'Summary', AIR 1/678/21/17/2082, 4–10; Jones, *WIA*, V: 440–42; Gordon, *Early Flying*, 14.
14 Wise, *CAFWW*, I: 123, 126; Jones, *WIA*, V: 458–59.
15 Nerney, 'Summary', AIR 1/678/21/17/2082, 7–8. The ICAT position was later resurrected in early 1918 only to be dropped again after the amalgamation with the RAF.
16 Ibid., 8–11, 17–18.
17 Meager, *Airship Flights*, 22–23.
18 Ibid., 72–73.
19 Bartlett, *Teeth of the Wind*, 3–7.
20 Paine to DAS, 3 May 1916, AIR 1/66/17/122/631.
21 'Casualties to RNAS Officers and Ratings, 1914–1918', AIR 1/671/17/133/2. Officers killed (all causes): 1914, 5; 1915, 29; 1916, 68; 1917, 217; ratios of WIA and MIA annually were similar.
22 Memo by Naval War Staff, 16 Aug 1917, Doc. No. 178 in Roskill, *Documents*

Relating, 501–10. 'A Short History of No. 218 (Bomber) Squadron, Royal Air Force', nd, Sqn Histories(5/218), AHB. Formed at Dover on 24 April 1918 this DH9 squadron did not see service in France until 10 June; when it formed it only had two pilots with combat experience. Although this example was later in the war, it serves to illustrate the challenges of balancing experience.

23 Nerney, 'Summary', AIR 1/678/21/17/2082, 15–16.

24 Asst DAS Minute, 24 May 1917, Doc. No. 168(4) in Roskill, *Documents Relating*, 481–82.

25 Lambe to Bacon, 8 May 1917, Doc. No. 168(1) in ibid., 479–80.

26 Wg Cdr A. W. Bigsworth to DAS, 5 May 1917, AIR 1/660/17/122/625.

27 Memoranda on Method of Training, 18–22 Dec 1917, AIR 1/663/17/122/692.

28 Gordon, *Early Flying*, 14.

29 Peter Wright, 'Submarine Scout Pusher Pilots: Captain George E. Bungay and Lt John E. Hoskins RNAS', *Cross & Cockade Journal* [GB] 15, No. 4 (Winter 1984): 170–73.

30 Bell Davies, *Sailor in the Air*, 162.

31 CO RNAS Roehampton to DAS, 14 Jun 1917, AIR 1/663/17/122/683; Air Department, *RNAS Kite Balloon Training Manual*, Jan 1917, AIR 1/673/17/134/44. This textbook contains almost 200 pages of theoretical and practical subjects. Curiously, this edition contains nothing about spotting for enemy submarines, which reflects the relatively late adoption of kite balloons in the anti-submarine role.

32 J. C. Nerney, AHB Narrative: 'Notes on Training: Home, 1918', nd, AIR 1/676/21/13/1840, 1–7.

33 Ibid., 21.

34 Steel and Hart, *Tumult in the Clouds*, 88–93; Taylor, *CFS*, 76–85.

35 H. D. Briggs, RNAS Director of Training, Memo, 4 Mar 1918, AIR 1/663/17/122/686.

36 *Flying Instruction*, Mar 1918, AIR 1/700/27/3/521.

37 J. C. Nerney, AHB Narrative: 'Notes on Training: Home, 1914–1917', nd, AIR 1/626/21/13/1773, 69.

38 Maj M. H. Davies, 'RAF Training, 1917–1918', nd, AIR 1/2423/305/18/36. For comparison, RFC pilots were arriving in France with as few as 14 hours of total flying experience in early 1916. Ralph Barker, *A Brief History of the Royal Flying Corps in World War I* (London: Robinson, 2002), 145.

39 Air Department Acquaint No. 57, 8 Jan 1918, AIR 1/663/17/122/691; HQ Training Division, RFC, to Master General of Personnel, Air Board, 23 Jan 1918, AIR 1/122/15/40/136; Syllabus of Lectures: No. 1 School of Navigation and Bomb Dropping, RAF Stonehenge, 12 Apr 1918, AIR 1/457/15/312/64.

40 Peter Dye, 'Biffy Borton's Bomber', *Cross and Cockade Journal* [GB] 34, No. 2 (Summer 2003): 78 (note 9).

41 Naval War Staff Memo, 16 Aug 1917, and Admiralty Board Minutes, 23 Aug 1917, Doc. Nos. 178 and 183 in Roskill, *Documents Relating*, 501–10, 522–25.

42 Admiralty to Air Ministry, 19 Apr 1918, Doc. No. 245 in Roskill, *Documents Relating*, 657–58, and in AIR 1/274/15/226/124 Pt I; DAD Memo, 11 Aug 1918, AIR 1/289/15/226/139 Pt II.

43 DAD Minute, 31 May 1918, Doc. No. 256 in Roskill, *Documents Relating*, 676–77 and also in AIR 1/274/15/226/124 Pt I; Training Conference Minutes, 28 Aug 1918, AIR 1/289/15/226/139 Pt II.

44 DAD Minute, Jun 1918, AIR 1/283/15/226/135 Pt II, AD2774.

45 DAD Memo, July 1918, ADM 1/8494/174.

46 RAF Training Expansion Committee Minutes, 5 Aug 1918, AIR 1/28/15/1/132; DAD Minute, 30 Oct 1918, AIR 1/290/15/226/139 Pt II.

47 Training Conference Minutes, 28 Aug 1918, AIR 1/289/15/226/139 Pt II.

48 Admiralty to Air Ministry, 8 Aug 1918, and 16 Sep reply, Doc. No. 264 in Roskill, *Documents Relating*, 693–98.
49 The following paragraphs summarise: Directorate of Training, RAF, *Training Courses in RAF* [FS Publication 39], October 1918, AIR 1/2087/207/7/39.
50 Gordon, *Early Flying*, 18; Hallam, *Spider Web*, 42–43.
51 Airship Pilot Training Syllabus, 30 Oct 1918, AIR 1/724/75/18.
52 FS Pub. 39, 40–41.
53 *ASRs*, Jun 1917-Mar 1918, AIR 1/2105/207/41/1–11; *NAOs*, Apr–Oct 1918, AIR 1/626/17/59/1–7; 'Flying Boats v Hostile Aircraft', T. D. Hallam, nd but *c.* late 1918, AIR 1/6A/4/29. In 19 air to air engagements between Felixstowe and Yarmouth flying boats and German seaplanes (April 1917 to August 1918), the always-outnumbered Large America crews shot down nine of the more manoeuvrable German aircraft while losing eight of their own.
54 'Landings at Sea', T. D. Hallam, nd, AIR 1/6A/4/29.
55 For example, see Wg Capt Oliver Swann to DAS, 9 Aug 1917, Doc. No. 173 in Roskill, *Documents Relating*, 491–92.
56 Hallam, *Spider Web*, 49–51.
57 DAD Memo, 7 Mar 1918, Doc. No. 231 in Roskill, *Documents Relating*, 635–36; NID Manual: *German Navy: Part III, Submarines*, Apr 1918, AIR 1/2321/223/41/1182. A number of other handbooks and manuals were produced by branches of the Admiralty for the RAF's use; these are referenced in later chapters.
58 Major General The Right Hon. Sir Frederick Sykes, *From Many Angles: An Autobiography* (London: George Harrap, 1942), 244 and n.
59 Air Historical Branch, *A Short History of the Royal Air Force* [FS Publication 136], June 1920, AIR 10/164, 230.
60 Morrow, *GWA*, 318; Mark Kerr, *Land Sea, and Air: Reminiscences of Mark Kerr* (London: Longmans, Green and Co., 1927), 280.
61 Kennett, *First Air War*, 127–29.
62 Surgeon's Journals, Chingford and Cranwell, ADM 101/439. Surgeon H. R. B. Hull noted that 1917's 35,000 training sorties at Cranwell – yielding 1,000 new pilots – witnessed only 12 fatal accidents, 75 serious injuries, and 500 further crashes with serious damage to aircraft but without serious injury to the pilot.
63 Morrow, *GWA*, 329, 43, 121, 251–52; Ministry of Munitions, *History of the Ministry of Munitions, Volume XII: The Supply of Munitions, Part I: Aircraft* (1921), 169–71; J. C. Nerney, AHB Narrative: 'Development of Aircraft Production, 1917–1918', nd, AIR 1/678/21/13/2100, 2–6; H. A. Jones, *The War in the Air*, Vol. VI (Oxford: Clarendon, 1937), 28, 67. At the start of the war there were only 'about eight' British companies building aircraft, according to the Ministry of Munitions.
64 Ministry of Munitions, *Munitions, XII, I*, Chapters IV and V; 'Aeroplanes and Seaplanes: A paper in relation to Strategical Policy', H. A. Williamson, 26 Jan 1916, Williamson Papers(WLMN1/5), CCA, II-7; Cooper, *Birth*, 87.
65 Morrow, *GWA*, 44.
66 Ibid., 78, 328–29.
67 Minutes of Aircraft Supply Committee, 29 Jul 1918, AIR 1/2302/215/11.
68 Nerney, 'Aircraft Production', AIR 1/678/21/13/2100, 173.
69 Ministry of Munitions, *Munitions, XII, I*, 155–58; Raleigh, *WIA*, I: 426.
70 The Eagle had eight 'marks', while the Large America design evolved into the Curtiss H-12 and H-16 and the Felixstowe F2a, F3, and later F5.
71 Morrow, *GWA*, 178–79, 325; Ministry of Munitions, *Munitions*, II, I, 144–45. When Weir became Secretary of State for Air in April 1918, Sir Arthur Duckham took over as Director-General of Aircraft Production. The Ministry of Munitions still held responsibility for design of aircraft.
72 Cooper, *Birth*, 85.

73 Ministry of Munitions, *Munitions, XII, I*, 62–63.
74 Morrow, *GWA*; Edgerton, *England and the Aeroplane*; Cooper, *Birth*, Chapter 7.
75 Jones, *WIA*, VI: 29–30.
76 DOD and DAD Minutes, 26 Oct 1917, AIR 1/642/17/122/238.
77 Air Board Minutes (AB 167), 21 Nov 1917, AHB; Morrow, *GWA*, 252, 255, 328, 369; Jones, *WIA*, VI: 45–53; Ministry of Munitions, *Munitions, XII, I*, 78–81; Nerney, 'Aircraft Production', AIR 1/678/21/13/2100, 169–171.
78 Morrow, *GWA*, 326.
79 Diary, 1 May 1918, Groves Papers, IWM/DD/P322. Groves was serving as Deputy Chief of the Air Staff at this time.
80 Jones, *WIA*, VI: 338. For example, many of the first batch of Handley Page O/100 bombers, delivered in 1916, were still flying and serving in training units in 1918. Sturtivant and Page, *Serials and Units*, 76–78.
81 Admiralty to Air Ministry, 30 Apr 1918, Doc. No. 248 in Roskill, *Documents Relating*, 661–63.
82 Air Ministry to Admiralty, 30 Mar 1918, and Admiralty reply, 23 Apr 1918, Doc. No. 239 in Roskill, *Documents Relating*, 650–53; Jones, *WIA*, VI: 338–40.
83 Groves, 'Notes on Marine Aircraft Construction and Design Policy', c. 1st week of Mar 1918, ADM 116/1278; Groves, 'Inshore Patrol Work by Aeroplanes', 18 Mar 1918, AIR 1/6A/4/43; Jones, *WIA*, VI: 330–34; First Lord Memo for Cabinet: 'Anti-submarine Coastal Patrols by Aeroplanes', 12 Apr 1918, ADM 116/1278; DAD Memo, 27 Mar 1918, and ACNS Memos, 13 and 29 Mar 1918, ADM 116/1278.
84 'Land Machines on Charge of Home Anti-Submarine Units at 30 September 1918', 22 Nov 1918, AIR 1/427/15/312/86.
85 Admiralty to Air Ministry, 30 Apr 1918, Doc. No. 248 in Roskill, *Documents Relating*, 661–63.
86 Air Ministry to Admiralty, 13 Aug 1918, and Admiralty Memo, 31 Aug 1918, Doc. Nos. 266 and 269 in ibid., 699–703, 711–12.
87 *Disposition of Aircraft* returns for 25 April, 25 July, and 31 October 1918, AIR 1/670/17/124. Does not include construction of flying boats at Malta, which amounted to only a handful by the end of the war.
88 A. J. Jackson, *Blackburn Aircraft Since 1909* (London: Putnam, 1968), 113.
89 'Number of Machines on Charge of Naval Service Units at 31st October 1918', 22 Nov 1918, AIR 1/427/15/312/86; Air Ministry Order B.6251, 25 Oct 1918, AIR 1/290/15/226/139 Pt II; DAD Memo, 10 Sep 1918, AIR 1/289/15/226/139 Pt I, AD4341.
90 Admiralty to Air Ministry, 8 Aug 1918, Doc. No. 264 in Roskill, *Documents Relating*, 693–98; DAD Memo, 31 Jul 1918, AIR 1/286/15/226/137 Pt I.
91 Ministry of Munitions, *Munitions, XII, I*, 173.
92 RAF Forms 9a: 'Engines on Charge' for June through November 1918, AIR 1/162/15/124/7 and 9.
93 Higham, *British Rigid Airship*, 79–81; Higham, 'Peripheral Weapon'.
94 Mr John Hunter, Director of Steel Production, Memo for Admiralty, 20 Apr 1917, ADM 167/52; Higham, 'Peripheral Weapon', 95.
95 Jones, *WIA*, IV: 41.
96 'Authorities for Airships (Non-rigid) Orders', AIR 1/2315/222/6A.
97 Jones, *WIA*, IV: 40–41.
98 *Disposition of Aircraft*, 31 Oct 1918, AIR 1/670/17/124, 26; Admiralty to Air Ministry, 30 Apr 1918, Doc. No. 248 in Roskill, *Documents Relating*, 661–63.
99 Report of Naval Kite Balloon Programme, 13 Aug 1917, AIR 1/667/17/122/757; Weekly Report of RNAS Kite Balloon Section, 25 Aug 1917, AIR 1/444/15/303/7.

100 Ministry of Munitions, *Munitions, XII, I*, 148–52.
101 Admiralty to Air Ministry, 30 Apr 1918, Doc. No. 248 in Roskill, *Documents Relating*, 661–63.
102 Beatty to Admiralty, 10 Apr 1918, and Sqn Cdr S. Bell to VA2BS, 1 Jun 1918, ADM 137/1957, 102–3 and 379–83.
103 'HQ RAF "Q" Liaison, May–Dec 1918', AIR 1/1084/204/5/1730; Training Visit Reports, Aug–Oct 1918, AIR 1/454/15/312/27.
104 *ASR*, Dec 1917, 4.
105 Admiralty Historical Section, *The Defeat of the Enemy Attack on Shipping, 1939–1945*, edited by Eric Grove (Aldershot: Aldgate, 1997), 8.
106 Cooper, *Birth*, 151.

3 Attacking 'at source': Bombing the Flanders U-boat bases

1 Headquarters US Air Force, *Air Force Manual 1–1, Volume 1: Basic Aerospace Doctrine of the United States Air Force* (Washington, DC: US Government Printing Office, 1992), vii; Phillip S. Meilinger, 'The Development of Air Power Theory', in *Air Power Leadership: Theory and Practice*, edited by Peter W. Gray and Sebastian Cox (London: The Stationery Office, 2002), 91.
2 Raleigh, *WIA*, I: 370.
3 Goulter, *Forgotten Offensive*, 3–4.
4 Lts R. H. Clark-Hall and J. W. Seddon (Pilot), Report: 'Experiments to determine effect of explosions on stability of seaplanes in flight', 12 December 1913, AIR 1/645/17/122/324. This set of trials proved that aircraft could drop bombs as low as 350 feet above the water without experiencing any aerodynamic effects from the explosion.
5 Air Department, Orders for Dunkirk, 12 September 1914, AIR 1/2301/212/2.
6 Norman Friedman, *Seapower as Strategy* (Annapolis: Naval Institute Press, 2001), 83.
7 Lecture: 'Blockade of Zeebrugge and Ostend, April 1918', nd, AIR 1/2393/249/2/1. The Bruges-Ostend canal was shallower and narrower than the canal linking Bruges and Zeebrugge; destroyers and large submarines (the later *UCII* and *UBIII* class) could only use the latter. Mark D. Karau, 'Twisting the Dragon's Tail: The Zeebrugge and Ostend Raids of 1918', *Journal of Military History* 67, No. 2 (April 2003), 474.
8 Friedman, *Submarine*, 32.
9 Rössler, *U-Boat*, 40.
10 S. W. Roskill, 'The U-Boat Campaign of 1917 and Third Ypres', *Journal of the Royal United Services Institute [JRUSI]* 104, No. 616 (November 1959), 440.
11 Report: 'Dunkirk, Résumé of Operations, Period: 17th to 31st July 1917 for Naval Squadrons 2, 3, 4, 5, 7, 7a, 11 & Seaplane Bases', nd, AIR 1/629/17/117/1. An untitled report in AIR 1/271/15/226/118 also lists the distances.
12 Samson, *Fights and Flights*; Raleigh, *WIA*, I, 372–92.
13 Jones, *WIA*, II: 340.
14 Davies, *Sailor in the Air*, 113–15.
15 Jones, *WIA*, II: 341.
16 Extracts from Admiralty Weekly Order No. 166 of 5 February 1915: 'Naval Air Service-Reorganisation', Doc. No. 62 in Roskill, *Documents Relating*, 193–94.
17 Samson, *Fights and Flights*, 195–96.
18 Ibid., 200.
19 P. K. Kemp, *Fleet Air Arm* (London: Herbert Jenkins, 1954), 34.
20 Captain M. S. Sueter, Report: 'Air Attacks on Ostend-Zeebrugge-Bruges Districts', 22 March 1915, AIR 1/672/17/134/39. Edwyn A. Gray, *The Killing*

Time: The U-Boat War, 1914–1918 (London: Seeley, Service and Co., Ltd, 1972), 90, states that the damaged U-boat was *U14*.

21 Samson, *Fights and Flights*, 200–02.
22 Sueter, Orders for Naval Air Service Units Based at Dunkirk (Ops. Order A.D. No. 15), 21 June 1915, AIR 1/672/17/134/33. See also Longmore, *Sea to Sky*, 44–45 and Admiral Sir Reginald Bacon, *The Dover Patrol 1915–1917, Volume II* (London: Hutchinson, 1919), 528.
23 Extracts from 'Report on the Performances of No. 1 Wing R.N.A.S. during 1915', Doc. No. 93 in Roskill, *Documents Relating*, 262–66; see also Longmore, *Sea to Sky*, 45–51. During the last ten months of 1915, No. 1 Wing attacked ten submarines, claiming two destroyed, and bombed 10 Zeppelin sheds, destroying two and damaging one. They also accounted for two Zeppelins.
24 C. L. Lambe Service Record, ADM 196/44, 105.
25 Geoffrey Till, *Air Power and the Royal Navy, 1914–1945: A Historical Survey* (London: Jane's, 1979), 112–13. Quoted from Williamson Memoirs, CCA.
26 Roskill, *Documents Relating*, 56.
27 *The Naval Who's Who, 1917* (Polstead: J. B. Hayward, 1981), 16, 93.
28 Lambe to Bacon, 16 Nov 1915, AIR 1/629/17/122/13. Bacon endorsed Lambe's proposal on 21 Nov and forwarded it to the Admiralty for approval. JWAC Memo AIR4: Policy of the RNAS, 3 Mar 1916, AIR 1/2319/223/26, later states Dunkirk's roles for the spring: supporting Bacon's naval forces; attacking U-boats and their bases; and raiding enemy aerodromes and destroying enemy aircraft used to attack Britain.
29 Jones, *WIA*, II: 426–27.
30 Cooper, *Birth*, 18.
31 Ibid., 66; George K. Williams, *Biplanes and Bombsights: British Bombing in World War I* (Maxwell AFB, Alabama: Air University Press, 1999), Chapter 1.
32 'History of No. 205 Squadron, RAF', nd, Sqn Histories(5/205), AHB.
33 Churchill, *World Crisis*, II: 1238.
34 Neville Jones, *The Origins of Strategic Bombing: A Study of the Development of British Air Strategic Thought and Practice up to 1918* (London: Kimber, 1973), 81–83.
35 JWAC Memo AIR 4, 3 March 1916, AIR 1/2319/223/26.
36 Wg Cdr R. M. Groves, OC, No. 1 Wg, to Lambe, 8 March 1916, ADM 137/2269; Translations of German Documents, Majs Erskine Childers and E. N. G. Morris, *Report of the Aircraft Bombing Committee of Effects of Bombing in Belgian and Enemy Defensive Measures*, March 1919, AIR 1/2115/207/56/1.
37 DAD Report: 'Appreciation of British Naval Effort: RNAS Aircraft Operations', Nov 1918, AIR 1/2415/303/3.
38 Bacon to Admiralty, 23 May 1916, AIR 1/634/17/122/98.
39 Minutes of the 9th Meeting of the Air Board, 8 Jun 1916, 5–8. Air Board Minutes Binders, AHB.
40 Bacon to Admiralty, Cover Letter: Report of Attack on Mariakerke Aerodrome and Zeebrugge carried out on the 21st May 1916, 24 May 1916, AIR 1/633/17/122/83.
41 Bacon to Admiralty, Report: Air Service Operations in Belgium, 6 June 1916, AIR 1/633/17/122/90.
42 Roger Keyes, *The Naval Memoirs of Admiral of the Fleet Sir Roger Keyes* (London: Thornton Butterworth, 1935), 161–62; Jones, *Origins*, 82.
43 Report of a Meeting held in the First Sea Lord's Room, 3 August 1915, Doc. No. 75 in Roskill, *Documents Relating*, 216–18. See also Malcolm H. Murfett, ed., *The First Sea Lords* (Westport: Praeger, 1995), 92–94, on Jackson's conservatism.
44 Extracts from Memorandum of Meeting held in Second Sea Lord's Room, 21 March 1916, Doc. No. 115 in ibid., 333–34.

45 Daily Summaries, RNAS Air Stations, 9 April to 31 July 1916, AIR 1/343/15/226/284.
46 Lambe to Bacon, 8 May 1917, AIR 1/660/17/122/622; Wise, *CAFWW*, I: 147.
47 Lambe to Bacon, 29 August 1916, AIR 1/62/15/9/81.
48 'History of No. 205 Squadron', AHB. The Air Board supported the request. See Extract from Minutes of War Committee, 18 Oct 16, Doc. No. 139 in Roskill, *Documents Relating*, 388.
49 'History of 207 Squadron, 1916–1920', nd, 3, Sqn Histories(5/207), AHB.
50 'History of No. 205 Squadron', AHB.
51 Halpern, *Naval History*, 347–50; Newbolt, *NO*, IV: 361.
52 HQ RNAS Dunkerque, Secret Operations Orders No. 25 (9 Nov 16), No. 28 (5 Jan 17), and No. 29 (2 Feb 17), AIR 1/88/15/9/211.
53 Air Department, 'Bombing raids from Dunkirk Listed by Objective, 1916–17', AIR 1/296/15/226/145.
54 Wise, *CAFWW*, I: 162.
55 HQ RNAS, Dunkerque, S.O.O. No. 29 (2 Feb 17), AIR 1/88/15/9/211.
56 Reports of Bombing Attacks, Feb 1917, AIR 1/632/17/122/64; Bombing Statistics, S.163., AIR 1/61/15/9/72.
57 Table of Bombs Expended by RNAS Dunkerque Command, AIR 1/61/15/9/75.
58 Intelligence Report: Information on German Anti-Aircraft Batteries, 19 Jun 1916. ADM 137/2269. As early as summer of 1916, HQ RNAS knew of an integrated air defence system of 150mm and 88mm high-angle guns around the harbours and coastal artillery batteries of Flanders. The numerous batteries made the area between Ostend and Zeebrugge one of the most thoroughly defended coastlines – from land, sea, and air – in the world at the time.
59 Location of RNAS Units, 1 April 1917, RNAS Papers, AHB. The squadrons were Nos. 1, 3, 6, and 8, RNAS.
60 Sturtivant and Page, *Serials and Units*, 160–72, 244–50. Most Sopwith 1½ Strutters from No. 3 Wing subsequently went to RFC or French Air Service units. Also, by July 1917, the Admiralty acknowledged that Dunkirk squadrons and 'loaned' fighter units to the RFC would require 'all available aeroplane pilots'. Admiralty to C-in-C Coast of Scotland, 13 Jul 1917, ADM 137/1955, 172.
61 Bartlett, *Teeth of the Wind*, 39.
62 'History of 207 Squadron', AHB.
63 'RNAS Dunkerque Command Bombing Raid Statistics, 1917–1918', AIR 1/61/15/9/75.
64 Bombing Raids from Dunkirk, AIR 1/296/15/226/145.
65 Bombing Report, nd, AIR 1/271/15/226/118.
66 'Bombing Raids Carried Out by RNAS Machines in France during May, June, and July 1917', nd, AIR 1/271/15/226/118.
67 James S. Corum, *The Luftwaffe: Creating the Operational Air War, 1918–1940* (Lawrence: University of Kansas Press, 1997), 34.
68 Bombs expended, AIR 1/61/15/9/75.
69 'History of No. 205 Squadron', 6–7, AHB. By July there were 18 Handley Pages with No. 7 Sq., so Lambe split it into two squadrons: No. 7 and No. 7a; No. 7a was redesignated No. 14 Squadron in December 1917.
70 RNAS Unit returns, 19 July 1917, RNAS Papers, AHB.
71 Cooper, *Birth*, 110–11. Cooper incorrectly notes that the Dunkirk squadrons were too busy bombing naval objectives to release any additional pilots.
72 Dunkirk Résumé of Operations, July to Sep 1917 Summary, AIR 1/629/17/117/3.
73 Dunkirk Résumé of Operations, 16–30 September 1917, AIR 1/629/17/117/5.
74 W.E.D. Wardop Transcript, IWM/SA/029; Capt Paul Bewsher Reminiscences, AIR 1/9/15/1/21; McLaughry, 'A Lecture on Night Flying' in FS Pub 956, AIR 10/973, 45–47.

75 Minutes of the 122nd Air Board, 3 Aug 1917, Air Board Minutes Binders, AHB. Commodore G. Paine used this as a reply to the RFC's claim that long-range heavy bombers were vulnerable.
76 Corum, *Luftwaffe*, 33.
77 Lt Cdr W. Wright, 'Report of fire and damage caused at depot by hostile aircraft on the night of the 1st October 1917', 5 Oct 1917, AIR 1/96/15/9/268. Lambe also moved the RNAS aircraft acceptance park from St Pol to Dover as a result of these raids.
78 Major H. G. Brackley, RAF, OIC, No. 214 Sqn., 'Rough History of No. 214 Squadron, Royal Air Force', 18 Jan 1919, Sqn Histories(5/214), AHB.
79 Ibid.
80 Jones, *WIA*, IV: 103.
81 Lecture on Blockade of Zeebrugge and Ostend, AIR 1/2393/249/2/1.
82 For a balanced account of the Navy's role in planning the landings and supporting Haig's offensive, see Andrew A. Wiest, *Passchendaele and the Royal Navy* (Westport: Greenwood Press, 1995).
83 Lambe Memo, 17 Sep 1917, AIR 1/58/15/9/61. The Canadian official historian concludes that the rotation/leave policy was due to sagging morale of RNAS aircrews. See Wise, *CAFWW*, I: 174–75.
84 Lambe to Bacon, 4 Aug and 5 Sep 1917, and ADM to Bacon, 30 Nov 1917, ADM 137/2273.
85 Bombing Raids from Dunkirk, AIR 1/296/15/226/145.
86 Bombs expended, AIR 1/61/15/9/75.
87 Bacon to Lambe, 18 Nov 1917, ADM 137/2273.
88 Jones, *WIA*, IV: 106. AIR 1/61/15/9/75 shows the total for 1917 was just over 341 tons, slightly less than Jones's figures.
89 J. C. Nerney, AHB Narrative: 'Development and Operations of RNAS, Home Waters, 1917. Part III: Belgian Coast Operations', nd, AIR 1/677/21/13/1930.
90 Jellicoe, *Crisis*, 203.
91 Wg Cdr H. A. Williamson, 'Remarks on Memorandum from the Force Commander, United States Navy', Dec 1917, Williamson Papers(1/6), CCA.
92 Details of the debate, not essential here, can be found in Halpern, *Naval History*, 406–07 and in the memoirs of Bacon and Keyes themselves. See Keyes, *Naval Memoirs*, 118–26 and Bacon, *Dover Patrol*, II: 401–13. Halpern also argues that this episode served as a catalyst for Jellicoe's dismissal.
93 Paul G. Halpern, ed., *The Keyes Papers: Selections from the Private and Official Correspondence of Admiral of the Fleet Baron Keyes of Zeebrugge, Vol. I: 1914–1918* (London: Naval Records Society, 1972), 411.
94 Raleigh, *WIA*, I: 402.
95 Keyes, *Naval Memoirs*, 161–62.
96 Keyes to Lambe, 24 Jan 1918, ADM 137/2710.
97 Lambe to Keyes, Report: 'The general effects of Offensive Operations carried out by Bomb-dropping aircraft', 3 Feb 1918, ADM 137/2710. Roskill published only the Admiralty minute of this report, in which they strongly agreed with Lambe's views. See Admiralty Letter M.02426 of 23 February 1918, Doc. No. 228 in Roskill, *Documents Relating*, 633–34. Full text of this report is at Appendix 1C below.
98 Air Council to War Office, 22 Feb 18, AIR 1/2153/209/3/304. Keyes and Lambe concurred with the planned transfer in Air Council to Admiralty and associated minutes, 9 and 23 Jan 1918, ADM 137/2273. Admiralty concurred in: DAD Memo, 5 Feb 1918, ADM 1/8500/226; Air Council to Admiralty, 19 Feb 18; and Admiralty to Air Council, 21 Feb 18, ADM 137/2277. Also note that in the new RAF system, all former naval wings would have 60 added to their designation (for example, No. 1 Wing, RNAS, became No. 61 Wing, RAF) with 200 being

added to squadron designations (No. 5 Squadron, RNAS, thus became No. 205 Squadron, RAF).

99 Keyes to Haig, 22 Mar 1918, ADM 137/2277.

100 Lambe Memo, 25 Mar 1918, AIR 1/108/15/9/292; 'History of No. 205 Squadron', AHB. The logbook of J. M. Mason, a pilot with No. 5/205 Squadron, states for his 23 March 18 entry: 'set out to bomb anything we could find.' Mason Papers, LHCMA.

101 RAF Location List, 11 Apr 1918, AIR 1/108/15/9/293.

102 During the month of March only four night raids and two day attacks on Bruges, with none on the other facilities, were carried out. April saw no improvement in the weather or targeting priorities. Lambe to Keyes, 13 May 1918, AIR 1/95/15/9/264.

103 No. 215 Squadron, for example, initially formed in Flanders in Mar 1918, but moved back to England in April in order to re-equip with Handley Page O/400s. In August it was assigned to the Independent Force. 'The History of No. 215 Squadron, RAF', 1919, AIR 1/184/15/218/1.

104 Keyes to Admiralty, 1 May 1918, Doc. No. 249, and Admiralty to Air Ministry, 3 May 1918, with reply of 16 May 1918, Doc. No. 250 in Roskill, *Documents Relating*, 663–67. The new No. 5 Group comprised all air units at Dover and Dunkirk, with Halahan, again Lambe's second-in-command, in charge of all units on the Dover side. Further complaints by Keyes and Lambe convinced the Air Ministry to remove No. 5 Group from the RAF SE Area Command and put it instead directly under the Air Ministry for administrative purposes in August.

105 Wise, *CAFWW*, I: 207.

106 Keyes to Admiralty, 28 May 1918, ADM 137/2277.

107 Squadrons for Bombing Zeebrugge and Bruges Docks (Collection of Letters and Memos), AIR 1/537/16/12/140, including Salmond to GHQ BEF, 21 May 1918; Keyes to Admiralty, 5 June 1918, ADM 137/2277; DAD Memo, 4 Sep 1918, AIR 1/288/15/226/138, AD4148.

108 HQ No. 5 Group, Operations Order No. 1, 26 May 1918, AIR 1/88/15/9/213; Lambe, Notes for Sir William Weir, nd, Air 1/95/15/9/264. A travel claim in this file shows that Lambe spoke with Weir on 22 June 1918.

109 No. 217 Squadron Record Book, 1 Oct 1917–31 Mar 1918, AIR 1/1878/204/221/4; Air Notes for Belgian Coast Patrol, 1 July 1918, ADM 137/2277.

110 HQ RNAS Dover, Dover Air Force Secret Operations Order No. 2A, 22 March 1918, ADM 137/2277.

111 Lambe to OC 61 Wg, 15 June 1917, AIR 1/58/15/9/62.

112 Fortnightly Summaries of No. 5 Group, AIR 1/109/15/9/297. No. 211 Squadron was the primary non-5 Group contributor.

113 Wise, *CAFWW*, I: 208–10.

114 Lambe to Keyes, Requirements of 5th Group, RAF, 7 Jun 1918, AIR 1/669/17/122/789.

115 FO2 Air Staff to Capt Gibbs, RAF Staff School, 13 Sep 1918, AIR 1/455/15/312/41.

116 Derived from figures provided in Cooper, *Birth*, 151.

117 Lambe to Lt Col C. F. Kilnor, OC No. 82 Wg, 14 Aug 1918, AIR 1/95/15/9/264. Lambe: 'You can vary the objectives to shipping along the lower reaches of the Ostende-Bruges Canal . . . but do not go closer to Bruges than Scheep Staele Bridge as there is a hospital close to the canal.'

118 Salmond to Advanced GHQ, BEF, 17 Aug 1918, AIR 1/526/16/12/43.

119 Sykes Memo to War Cabinet, GT 4946, 26 Jun 1918, WO 32/5565.

120 In June there were 26 raids on the port facilities, 19 in July, and 25 in August. Daily Summaries of Operations in Home Waters, 1 May–31 August 1918, AIR

1/456/15/312/46; Lambe to Wing Commanders, 7 Sep 1918, AIR 1/73/15/9/150.

121 Jellicoe, *Crisis*, 168–77.
122 US Navy Planning Section Memorandum, 15 Feb 1918, ADM 137/2710. Also see Doc. No. 226 in Roskill, *Documents Relating*, 624–32. Many RNAS and RN officers thought the primary USNAS effort should be patrolling instead of bombing. L. H. Strain, Memorandum regarding USNAS effort in Europe, 8 Mar 1918, AIR 1/2415/303/33/17, and Plans Division Memorandum, 26 Mar 1918, ADM 137/2710.
123 Halpern, *Naval History*, 357; David F. Trask, *Captains & Cabinets: Anglo-American Naval Relations, 1917–1918* (Columbia, MO: University of Missouri Press, 1972), 131–32.
124 R-Adm W. S. Sims, USN, to Admiralty, 12 June 1918, ADM 137/2277.
125 Commander, US Naval Northern Bombing Group, to Lambe, 20 Sep 1918, AIR 1/62/15/9/79; Sims to Secretary of the Admiralty, 12 Jun 1918, ADM 137/2277; Sims to Commander, US Naval Northern Bombing Group, nd, AIR 1/62/15/9/79; Adrian O. Van Wyen, *Naval Aviation in World War I* (Washington: Chief of Naval Operations, US Navy, 1969), 80–87.
126 Minutes of a conference at the Admiralty on 17 Sep 1918 on British and American Naval Air Policy for 1919, 27 Sep 1918, ADM 137/2710 and AIR 1/273/15/226/124 Part I, AD98. See extracts from same in Doc. No. 272 in Roskill, *Documents Relating*, 734–38.
127 Diary, 17 Aug 1918, Groves Papers, IWM/DD/P322.
128 Air Council to the War Cabinet, Précis No. 176, July 1918, AIR 6/17, 101–200.
129 For early Admiralty views on strategic bombing see Memo by Rear-Admiral C. L. Vaughan-Lee, 4 April 1916, Doc. No. 120 in Roskill, *Documents Relating*, 342–44. At this time the Admiralty had to defend its ideas concerning No. 3 Wing and bombing from Luxeuil.
130 Lambe to Lynes, 21 Jul 1918, AIR 1/95/15/9/264.
131 Cooper, *Birth*, 134–35; Williams, *Biplanes and Bombsights*, 224–30.
132 Air Ministry to Admiralty, 13 August 1918, Doc. No. 266 in Roskill, *Documents Relating*, 699–700.
133 For a concise summary of these efforts see Halpern, *Naval History*, 441–44. Plans are outlined in: Notes by Admiralty Plans Division on Proposed Agenda for Conference on American Naval Air Operations, 11 Sep 1918, Doc. No. 233 in Michael Simpson, ed., *Anglo-American Naval Relations, 1917–1919* (Aldershot: Scolar Press, 1991), 307–08; and Beatty to Admiralty, 'Consideration of an Assault by Torpedo Planes on the High Seas Fleet', 11 Sep 1917, ADM 137/1938, 104–109.
134 Goulter, *Forgotten Offensive*, 16–17; Admiralty to VAECE, 29 Dec 1918, ADM 137/2241; Plans Division Paper: 'Aerial Operations against Ships and Bases', 28 Jan 1918, ADM 137/2707.
135 Thetford, *British Naval Aircraft*, 13; Admiralty to Air Council, 8 August 1918, AIR 1/2418/305/6. In this letter the Admiralty complained about production delays of torpedo carrying aircraft, which hampered plans of the Grand Fleet to attack the Germans in port.
136 Lambe, 'Report on the Effect of Bombing . . . with Relation to Enemy Submarine Activity on the Belgian Coast', 31 Oct 1918, AIR 1/343/15/226/282.
137 Air Division Memo, 'RAF No. 5 Group, Report for period 1st–15th June, 1918', 27 Jun 1918, AIR 1/283/15/226/135 Part II, AD2765; Bombing Raids, AIR 1/271/15/226/118.
138 Target lists and agent reports, c. early 1918, AIR 1/60/15/9/70 and AIR 1/61/15/9/71.

139 These maps survived in the WO 153 Series at the PRO. WO 153/1326 is a superb example of an RNAS target map of Bruges from February 1917.
140 HQ No. 7 (Naval) Squadron, *Notes on the Work and Organisation of a Handley Page Night Bombing Squadron*, May 1918, AIR 1/2684, and *Raid Control of Handley Page Squadron*, nd, AIR 1/72/15/9/135.
141 Nerney, 'Belgian Coast Operations', AIR 1/677/21/13/1930, 118–19.
142 Historical Section, *Defeat*, 10; Air Ministry, *Synopsis of British Air Effort during the War*, 1 Jan 1919, AIR 8/13, 8.
143 Bill Finnis, *The History of the Fleet Air Arm: From Kites to Carriers* (Shrewsbury: Airlife, 2000), 31–40; Wise, *CAFWW*, I: 180; Terraine, *Business*, 126.
144 Grant, *U-Boats Destroyed*, 93.

4 Hunting the enemy: Air patrols in Home Waters

1 Historical Section, *Defeat*, 6–10.
2 Arthur J. Marder, *1917: The Year of Crisis*, Vol. IV of *From Dreadnought to Scapa Flow: The Royal Navy in the Fisher Era, 1904–1919* (London: Oxford University Press, 1969), 82; Marder, *Victory and Aftermath (January 1918–June 1919)*, Vol. V of *FDSF* (London: Oxford University Press, 1970), 91. In his preface to Vol. IV, Marder thanks Waters as well as RNAS veterans for their advice (vii). The anti-patrol arguments are repeated in Tarrant, *U-Boat Offensive*, 42–43, and elsewhere.
3 Peyton-Ward, *RAF in Maritime War*, AIR 41/79, VII: Table 32. See Chapter 8 below for alternative figures.
4 Notes of Capt D. V. Peyton-Ward: Statistics, 1914–1918 War, AIR 1/2420/305/17. Statistics taken from 'ADM NSC11 of 12 Jan 1921, Evidence for Sub-Committee of CID.'
5 Extracts from Paper by Captain Murray F. Sueter, Director of Air Department, 29 August 1912, Doc. No. 18; Admiralty to Admiral Commanding Coast Guard and Reserves, 2 Nov 1912, Doc. No. 20, in Roskill, *Documents Relating*, 56–62.
6 Lambert, *Naval Revolution*, 286–87. Lambert uses War Staff minutes from the Battenberg Papers to support this contention.
7 Report of the Oil Fuel Tank Camouflage Committee, 30 Apr 1914, ADM 116/1220. Making installations 'inconspicuous' and designed with fire prevention in mind fell third in priority relative to offensive and defensive airpower. The committee first met in August 1913. I am indebted to Dr W. Brown for bringing this report to my attention.
8 J. C. Nerney, AHB Narrative: 'History of the Anti-Submarine Campaign, 1914–1917', nd, AIR 1/675/21/13/1385, I: 3–7; Lord Fisher's Memorandum on Airships and Zeppelins, Doc. No. 307 in Marder, *FGDN*, III: 346–47.
9 Sqn Ldr Hubert C. G. Allen Interview Transcript, *c.* 1960, B2359, 12, RAFM(H).
10 Longmore, *Sea to Sky*, 42–43.
11 Raleigh, *WIA*, I: 367.
12 Sueter to all RNAS COs, 29 Jan 1915, and responses, 1–3 Feb 1915, and Minute by C. L. Lambe, 2 Mar 1915, AIR 1/147/15/65.
13 Conclusions of the 69th Meeting of the War Committee, 10 Feb 1916, Doc. No. 100 in Roskill, *Documents Relating*, 294–95.
14 Extracts from Admiralty Letter M.08235, 26 October 1915, Doc. No. 85 in ibid., 249, and AIR 1/650/17/122/434.
15 R-Adm C. L. Vaughan-Lee, JWAC 1: Present Deficiencies and Future Require-ments of the Royal Naval Air Service, 22 Mar 1916, Para. 2, Lord Douglas-Scott-Montagu Papers(I/M/7), LHCMA; RAECE Memo to SNO Tyne and COs of RNAS Stations, 16 Aug 1916, AIR 1/635/17/122/117.

16 CO RNAS Killingholme (R. Bell-Davies) to RAECE, 29 Jan 1916, AIR 1/631/
    17/122/42. The 18 Feb response informed Davies that seaplane pilots would be
    allocated when available.
17 War Experiences of Flt Lt J. B. Cole-Hamilton, RAF Staff College, 1 Nov 1922,
    AIR 1/2386/228/11/15, 4.
18 Pembroke and Howden Patrol Reports and Charts, Mar 1916–Apr 1917, AIR 1/
    436/15/275/1 and /292/1.
19 Nerney, 'History of the Anti-Submarine Campaign', AIR 1/675/21/13/1385, II: 1.
20 Development of Airship Service, 13 Nov 1918, AIR 1/2314/222/1; RNAS
    Machines in Commission, nd, AIR 1/146/15/42; Director of Statistics, Strength
    of RNAS Personnel, 1 Dec 1919, AIR 1/671/17/133/1.
21 Nerney, 'RNAS in Home Waters', AIR 1/677/21/13/1902, 1. The conference
    recommending the establishment of an Anti-Submarine Division took place in
    November 1916.
22 Jellicoe to Duff, 27 Nov 1916, Duff Papers(DFF/1), NMM. Jellicoe's underlining.
    The date of this letter means that Jellicoe had appointed Duff before he even
    officially assumed the office of First Sea Lord.
23 Office Memoranda, Admiralty Secretary, 16 Dec 1916 and 8 Feb 1917, ADM
    137/2715.
24 Nerney, 'RNAS in Home Waters', AIR 1/677/21/13/1902, 1–2b.
25 Duff to Jellicoe, Minute entitled 'Air Patrols', 15 Dec 1916, AIR 1/650/17/122/
    429.
26 Newbolt, NO, IV: 326.
27 Nerney, 'History of the Anti-Submarine Campaign', AIR 1/675/21/13/1385,
    II: 5.
28 Routine Patrols for the Plymouth Seaplane Station and Airship Routine Patrols-
    Mullion, Aug 1917, AIR 1/644/17/122/228 and /291; Gerrard to DAS, 23 Apr
    1917, AIR 1/644/17/122/283; SW Grp Patrol Orders, 1 Sep 1917, AIR 1/305/
    15/226/153.
29 Admiralty to East Coast C-in-Cs and SNOs, 15 Jan 1917, AIR 1/638/17/122/
    171; Nerney, 'History of the Anti-Submarine Campaign', AIR 1/675/21/13/
    1385, II: 7–8.
30 Peyton-Ward, RAF in Maritime War, AIR 41/45, I: 26.
31 Ibid., I: 26, 30.
32 Paper: 'Development of the Airship Services, 1914–1918', nd, AIR 1/726/122/3.
33 Haig to Admiralty, 24 Feb 1917, Doc. No. 162, and Admiralty to War Office, 23
    Mar 1917, Doc. No. 164, in Roskill, Documents Relating, 473–76.
34 Extracts from Admiralty Letter to East Coast SNOs, 26 April 1917, Doc. No.
    166 in Roskill, Documents Relating, 477–78. The Admiralty plotted Zeppelin
    positions by way of wireless intercepts and planned to communicate the locations
    directly to the station commanders by telephone.
35 Samson, Fights and Flights, 357.
36 Hallam, Spider Web, 32–34.
37 Hallam, Submarines Sighted by Felixstowe Flying Boats, AIR 1/6A/4/29. Felixs-
    towe FBs spotted 44 out of 168 reported sightings by aircraft in 1917.
38 Hallam, Spider Web, 36, 48.
39 John H. Morrow, Jr, German Air Power in World War I (Lincoln: University of
    Nebraska Press, 1982), 135–41; War Experiences of Wg Cdr J. L. Gordon, nd,
    RAF Staff College, AIR 1/2387/II/228/11/59, 2; Submarines Sighted, AIR 1/6A/
    4/29; ASR, Feb 1918, AIR 1/2105/207/41/9, 7.
40 Admiralty to Commodore Lowestoft, 4 Jan 1918, AIR 1/642/17/122/245; see
    also Mowthorpe, Battlebags, 52, 60.
41 Squadron Record Book, No. 17 Sqn, RNAS (Dunkirk), AIR 1/1878/204/221/4;
    Lambe to Scarlett, 20 Apr 1918, AIR 1/77/15/9/182.

42   Admiralty to all C-in-Cs and SNOs, 18 May 1917, AIR 1/669/17/122/779. Also in AIR 1/71/15/9/124.
43   H. A. Williamson was the primary author of these reports until spring 1918. Typescript memoir entitled *The Atlantic Failure . . .*, Grp Capt H. A. Williamson, Williamson Papers(4/1a), CCA, 118.
44   Nerney, 'History of the Anti-Submarine Campaign', AIR 1/675/21/13/1385, II: 24.
45   DASD Office Memo, 21 Jun 1917, ADM 137/2715. Again, this was Williamson of the Operations Division.
46   Operations Division Minute, 29 May 1917, AIR 1/71/15/9/124.
47   Notes of Conference Held Onboard HMS Queen Elizabeth, 24 Aug 1917, ADM 137/1939, 211–24.
48   Admiralty to Admiral Commanding Orkneys and Shetlands, 22 Sep 1917, Doc. No. 191 in Roskill, *Documents Relating*, 545, and in AIR 1/645/17/122/246.
49   RNAS *Disposition of Aircraft*, 10 Jan 1918, AIR 1/670/17/124.
50   J. C. Nerney, AHB Narrative: 'Operation "C.C." of the Destroyer Kite Balloon Force-Grand Fleet', nd, AIR 1/724/78/1; *TH4*, 8; Newbolt, *NO*, V: 122–23.
51   DOD, Proposed Establishment of Air Division of Naval Staff, 19 Dec 1917, ADM 1/8508/285; and Training Division Memo: Duties of Air Division, 22 Jan 1918, ADM 1/8504/255.
52   Located in AIR 1/626/17/59, Apr through Oct 1918.
53   These ideas are mentioned in general terms in Terraine, *Business*, 125, 148, and in V-Adm Sir Arthur Hezlet, *Aircraft and Sea Power* (London: Peter Davies, 1970), 100–01, but will be developed in detail below.
54   Admiralty to Air Ministry, 30 Mar 1918, AIR 1/276/15/226/125 Pt II, AD575. Williamson replaced Finch-Noyes at No. 18 Group, otherwise all other RAF group commanders had already been in place under the RNAS.
55   Extracts from Admiralty Weekly Orders Nos. 1391 and 1392 of 19 Mar 18, Doc. No. 234 in Roskill, *Documents Relating*, 641–45; VAECE to Admiralty, 3 Mar 1918, ADM 1/8517/70; Air Council Précis 19, 52, and 70, AIR 6/16.
56   Air Ministry to Admiralty, 12 Feb 1918, AIR 1/273/15/226/124 Pt I, AD73; Erskine Childers Diary, 29 Apr 1918, Childers Papers, IWM/DD/PP/MCR/C28: microfilm reel 1. The RAF's Director of Intelligence asked Childers to form a naval air intelligence section.
57   R. M. Groves, In Shore Patrol Work by Aeroplanes, Feb 1918, AIR 1/6A/4/43.
58   *TH4*, 5; Admiralty to Air Ministry, 30 Apr 1918, Doc. No. 248 and 8 Aug 18 (with Air Min reply of 16 Sep), Doc. No. 264 in Roskill, *Documents Relating*, 661–63, 693–98; Diary, 1 May 1918, Groves Papers, IWM/DD/P322. The Pierron Report of Mar 1918 may have influenced Groves into developing the idea of using obsolete aircraft and medically unfit pilots for anti-submarine patrols as the French had claimed was common in their scheme.
59   Geddes, Programme of the RAF to 30 Sep 1919: Allocation of Aircraft to the Navy, 31 August 1918, Doc. No. 269 in Roskill, *Documents Relating*, 711–12.
60   Air Historical Branch, Air Ministry, *A Short History of the Royal Air Force* [FS Publication 136], June 1920, AIR 10/164, 200. See Appendix 3 below.
61   Report of Conference, 11 May 17, and associated minutes, ADM 1/8488/102; *ASRs*, Jul 1917-Mar 1918, AIR 1/2105/207/41/2–10.
62   Air Division, Report on French Naval Air Service, Jan 1918, AIR 1/306/15/226/172.
63   Report of Visit to French Anti-Submarine Division, Mar 1918, AIR 1/458/15/318/75. No signature on the report but most likely Sqn Cdr Pink. Scarlett sent Pink to France to investigate the report's claims (AIR 1/274/15/226/124 Pt II, AD190), later finding that the French scheme was purely notional.
64   Tarrant, *U-Boat Offensive*, 55–56.

65 Roskill, *Documents Relating*, 612.
66 Air Policy Paper for Admiral Mayo, 23 Sep 1917, ADM 137/1437, 191–96.
67 VA Queenstown to Admiralty, 30 Dec 1916, AIR 1/650/17/122/429. Bayly 'wish[ed] emphatically to repeat that, if the seaplanes cannot be trusted to work by themselves, and to return safely, this area would be far better without them.' For a further discussion of Bayly's views, see Jones, *WIA*, IV: 46–47 and his own apologia in Admiral Sir Lewis Bayly, *Pull Together! The Memoirs of Admiral Sir Lewis Bayly* (London: George Harrap, 1939), 238, 247, 252. H. A. Williamson claimed that Commodore Paine initiated the suggestion that US Navy aircraft operate under Bayly's command in Ireland. HAW Memoir, Williamson Papers(4/1a), CCA, 105–08.
68 Noel Shirley, *United States Naval Aviation, 1910–1918* (Atglen, PA: Schiffer, 2000), 37.
69 Shirley, *USN Aviation*, 158, 113–16.
70 ASD Monthly Report No. 2: June 1917, 1 July 1917, ADM 186/394, 22: 'The number of submarines sighted is not necessarily a gauge of the efficiency of the patrol . . . and useful work is effected by compelling him to remain submerged.'
71 Doughty, 'The Effect of Depth Charges', 353–57; NID, 'UC–35: Translation of French Report on Interrogation of Survivors', June 1918, ADM 137/3897. Prisoners stated it was prudent to dive on the approach of an aircraft. See Chapter 7 below.
72 Hallam, Submarines Sighted by Felixstowe Flying Boats, AIR 1/6A/4/29. The 47th U-boat was not attacked because it was next to a fishing vessel.
73 At least five U-boats were lost after being stranded. Grant, *U-Boats Destroyed*, 159.
74 Coleman Lecture, AIR 1/2393/228/31/1, 5–6. According to the paper on his war experiences, as preserved in AIR 1/2387/228/11/24 (Sep 24), Coleman was the commander of the RAF station at Seaton Carew, Durham, during the war. For information on U-boat patrol durations, see Jameson, *Most Formidable Thing*, 209–10.
75 *TH4*, 14.
76 NID, Translations of *UB74* Diving Log Book and *UB110* Log Book, ADM 137/3900; NID, Translation of H. Petersen's personal diary, ADM 137/3897; NID, Translation of *UC47* Logbook, ADM 137/4813.
77 Again, see Chapter 7 below on the German opinion of patrols.
78 Hallam, Submarines Sighted, AIR 1/6A/4/29.
79 War Experiences of Sqn Ldr J. K. Waugh, RAF Staff College, 29 Sep 1925, AIR 1/2388/228/11/67, 6; Capt J. G. Struthers, Airship Department, *Notes on Aids to Submarine Hunting*, Apr 1918, ADM 186/415, 3.
80 *Jane's Fighting Ships of World War I*, 68–93.
81 Thetford, *British Naval Aircraft*, 198, 280–84, 479.
82 Coleman Lecture, AIR 1/2393/228/13/1, 11–12.
83 Williams Transcript, IWM/SA/0313, 40–41; T. B. Williams, *Airship Pilot No. 28* (London: Kimber, 1974), 73. NAO, May 1918, AIR 1/626/17/59/2, 19–20.
84 Coleman Lecture, AIR 1/2393/228/13/1, 12.
85 Keyes to Commodore Dunkirk and GOC 5 Grp, 30 Aug 1918, ADM 137/2274.
86 Col Grenfell, 'RNAS W/T: A Short Summary of Progress during the War', nd, AIR 1/109/15/29; War Experiences of Sqn Ldr R. M. Bayley, RAF Staff College, 21 Sep 1923, AIR 1/2386/228/11/20, 16.
87 Nerney, 'History of the Anti-Submarine Campaign', AIR 1/675/21/13/1385, III: 2–4; Col J. Fletcher, Duties of the Captain of an Airship, Feb 1918, AIR 1/306/15/226/167.
88 *ASR*, Oct 1917–Mar 1918, AIR 1/2105/207/41/5–10; *NAOs*, AIR 1/626/17/59/1–7.

89 *ASR*, July 1917, 2; *ASR*, Oct 1917, 2–3, AIR 1/2105/207/41/2,5.
90 Gerrard to Capt (D), 4th Destroyer Flotilla, 12 June 1918, ADM 131/64, 98.
91 Report of Flt Sub Lt WJ Pullen, Pilot *SSZ-5*, 3 Jan 1918, AIR 1/667/17/122/ 749.
92 Training and Staff Duties Division, *Naval Staff Monograph No. 35 (Historical), Vol. XIX: Home Waters, Part IX, 1 May 1917 to 31 July 1917*, Aug 1939, NHB, 84–5. The Flanders-based boats were *UC62, UC63, UC64, UB20*, and two cruises of *UC71*.
93 NID, 'Extracts from German Secret Instructions for War Against Commerce, November 1916–June 1917', Nov 1917, ADM 137/3886, 33–40.
94 Messimer, *Find and Destroy*, 131. See Chapter 7 below.
95 War Experiences of Flt Lt T. W. Elmhirst, RAF Staff College, 20 Sep 1924, AIR 1/2387/228/11/56, 3–6. Elmhirst commanded Anglesey from Apr 1918 until the Armistice.
96 Peyton-Ward, *RAF in Maritime War*, AIR 41/45, I: Appendix I. Ships listed include Allied vessels of 500 tons GRT and above. Losses during the period were Feb (16), Mar (16), Apr (15), May (9), Jun (2), Jul (0), and Aug (4). Newbolt states that this reduction in losses was due to the U-boats moving back to 'the outer approach routes [rather] than to the stiffening of our defensive system' but does not offer a reason for the shift. *NO*, V: 336.
97 Marder, *FDSF*, V: 94–96.
98 Cdr H. A. Williamson, 'Remarks on Memorandum from the Force Commander, United States Navy', Dec 1917, 5, Williamson Papers(1/6), CCA.
99 Dir of Statistics to ACNS and 1st Lord, Enemy Attacks by Day and Night, 17 Apr 1918, AIR 1/306/15/226/166. In the entire English Channel area, 58 per cent of attacks were at night during this period.
100 *ASR*s: Jan 1918, 6; Feb 1918, 5; and Mar 1918, 10, AIR 1/2105/207/41/8–10. The Portsmouth Group's bases were Portland, Calshot, Bembridge, Newhaven, Cherbourg, and Polegate (airships).
101 East Fortune Intelligence Office Report, Aug 1918, AIR 1/720/43/1; C-in-C Coast of Scotland to Admiralty, nd, AIR 1/642/17/122/253.
102 Peyton-Ward, *RAF in Maritime War*, AIR 41/45, I: Appendices I and II. Ships counted are of 500 GRT and above.
103 Training and Staff Duties Division, *Naval Staff Monograph No. 29 (Historical), Vol. XIII: Home Waters, Part IV, from February to July 1915*, Oct 1925, NHB, 268–69. Divers located the wreck of *UC2* on 2 July 1915 and found she had no torpedo tubes but only mine chutes.
104 JWAC Memo AIR 4: Policy of the RNAS, 3 Mar 1916, AIR 1/2319/226/26, 2.
105 Marder, *FDSF*, V: 79.
106 Training and Staff Duties Division, *History of British Minesweeping in the War*, Dec 1920, NHB, 123–28. [Hereafter, *Minesweeping*.]
107 Fletcher, *Lecture on . . . Airships*, NMM(CL), 30–1.
108 Development of the Airship Service, Nov 1918, AIR 1/2314/221/1, 22.
109 *Minesweeping*, 76.
110 Report for Period 1st–15th June 1918, RAF No. 5 Group, Dover, AIR 1/283/ 15/226/135 Pt II, AD2765.
111 Dixie Kidd Interview, IWM/SA/15714.
112 *ASR*s, Jul 1917-Mar 1918, AIR 1/2105/207/41/2–10; C. P. Bristow Interview, IWM/SA/13718, Reel 3; *NAO*s, the successors of the *ASR*s, only list mine sightings in Sept and Oct 1918, AIR 1/626/17/59/1–7.
113 War Experience of Wing Commander J. L. Gordon, nd, AIR 1/2387/II/228/ 11/59, 3. *Synopsis of British Air Effort during the War* also highlights the mine-spotting contribution of the south-east stations: AIR 8/13, 8.
114 *TH4*, 8; *Minesweeping*, 123.

115 Bristow Interview, IWM/SA/13718, Reel 4; Kidd Interview, IWM/SA/15714.
116 *Minesweeping*, 45.
117 Experiences of J. K. Waugh, AIR 1/2388/228/11/67, 3.
118 Director of Statistics, Monthly Summaries of Anti-Submarine Air Patrols Round British Coast, AIR 1/269/15/226/109.
119 H. A. Jones, *The War in the Air*, Appendices (Oxford: Clarendon, 1937), App. XVIII. This is despite the fact that in mid-September Howden and its two substations, No. 18 Group's airship force, had seven airships ready for operations with a further five undergoing repairs. *Disposition of Aircraft on Naval Duties*, 12 Sep 1918, AIR 1/670/17/124, 25.
120 Peyton-Ward, *RAF in Maritime War,* AIR 41/45, I: Appendix II.
121 War Experiences of Flt Lt T. W. Elmhirst, RAF Staff College, 20 Sep 1924, AIR 1/2387/II/228/11/56, 7.
122 Sqn Ldr E. B. Beauman, Précis of Lecture on 'Anti-Submarine Patrolling by Aircraft', RAF Staff College, Sep 1922, AIR 1/2385/228/1, 7.
123 Experiences of J. B. Cole-Hamilton, AIR 1/2386/228/11/15, 6.
124 Experiences of J. K. Waugh, AIR 1/2388/228/11/67, 3.
125 Admiralty Letter M024547/18, 20 Oct 1918, ADM 151/84, 134.
126 Diary, 1 May 1918, Groves Papers, IWM/DD/P322.
127 Wise, *CAFWW*, I: 194.
128 Lt Col Scott Lindsey, Comment and Discussion, *USNIP* 129, No. 2 (February 2003): 29; Phillip S. Meilinger, *AIRWAR: Theory and Practice* (London: Frank Cass, 2003), Chapter 9.

5 Aircraft and convoy escort

1 S. W. Roskill, *Churchill and the Admirals* (London: Collins, 1977), 68; Terraine, *Business*, 58.
2 Peyton-Ward, *RAF in Maritime War*, AIR 41/45, I: Appendix I.
3 Historical Section, *Defeat*, Table 1.
4 *ASR*, Dec 1917, AIR 1/2105/207/41/7, 15–23.
5 *TH4*, 19; Historical Section, *Defeat*, 8. These statistics do not specify whether they apply only to Home Waters or to all theatres, but they are nevertheless proof enough of the effectiveness of aircraft in this role.
6 Historical Section, *Defeat*, 8; Marder, *FDSF*, IV: vii.
7 Marder, *FDSF*, V: 92; Historical Section, *Defeat*, 5–10.
8 Morrow, *GWA*, 324–25; Halpern, *Naval History*, 426–27.
9 Halpern, *Naval History*, 351–54.
10 Newbolt, *NO*, V: 193–94; Admiralty to Commodore (T), 30 May 1917, ADM 137/2086, 17.
11 Newbolt, *NO*, V: 112–18.
12 Numerous examples of these orders are contained in Plymouth Station Records, ADM 131/100 through 102.
13 VAECE, *Standing Orders for Convoys and Escort Forces*, 20 Jun 1918, ADM 137/1553, 23–29.
14 Historical Section, *Defeat*, 4; William S. Sims, *The Victory at Sea* (Annapolis: Naval Institute Press, 1984), 164.
15 Messimer, *Find and Destroy*, 155.
16 *ASR*, Dec 1917, AIR 1/2105/207/41/7, 3.
17 *TH4*, 12.
18 Marder, *FDSF*, V: 93.
19 Air Division, CB885, Dec 1918, AIR 1/2321/223/41/885.
20 Report of *NS-3*, 24 Apr 1918, ADM 137/1955, 191–96.
21 Capt T. P. Moore, Convoy Escort Report, 26 Mar 1918, AIR 1/720/42/3/1.

22 J. Struthers, Draft: A Note of Aids to Submarine Hunting, 15 Apr 1918, AIR 1/
    308/15/226/90, 4; Airship Department, *Notes on Aids to Submarine Hunting*
    [CB01454], Apr 1918, AIR 1/2321/223/41/01454, 12; Fletcher, *Lecture on . . .
    Airships*, NMM(CL), 31–2; Fletcher, Duties of the Captain of an Airship, Feb
    1918, AIR 1/306/15/226/167.
23 *TH4*, 19.
24 The Work of Non-Rigids Airships During the War, nd, AIR 1/727/152/5. For
    example, *SSZ-16* (Pembroke) chased a deck gun crew below deck with machine
    gun fire on 7 Dec 1917. Seaplanes had similar experiences. For a German view,
    see Werner Fürbringer, *FIPS: Legendary U-Boat Commander, 1915–1918*, trans-
    lated by Geoffrey Brooks (Annapolis: Naval Institute Press, 1999), 114–16, and
    Chapter 7 below.
25 'Development of the Airship Service', nd, AIR 1/2314/222/1 and 1/726/122/3.
26 DASD (Duff) to C-in-C Plymouth (Bethell), 21 Jul 1917. Bethell Papers(VII),
    LHCMA.
27 *ASR*, Dec 1917, AIR 1/2105/207/41/7, 11–14. Not verbatim.
28 DAD minute, 4 Jul 1918, AIR 1/284/15/226/136 Part I, AD2921.
29 'A Short History of No. 233 (General Reconnaissance) Squadron', 17 Nov 1937,
    Sqn Histories(5/233), AHB, 1.
30 Admiralty to VADP, 28 Jun 1917, AIR 1/77/15/9/182.
31 *ASRs*, AIR 1/2105/207/41/1–10; *NAOs*, AIR 1/626/17/59/1–7; Nerney, 'RNAS
    in Home Waters', AIR 1/677/21/13/1902, 33. Dover Command warships
    escorted 624 vessels in Dec 1917, 584 cross-channel and 40 coastal. Director of
    Statistics Report: 'Escort Work Performed by the Navy in Home Waters', 30 Mar
    1918, ADM 137/1535.
32 *NAO*, Jul 1918, AIR 1/626/17/59/4; No. 5 Group Ops Orders, 1 Jul 1918, AIR
    1/682/21/13/2222; also in AIR 1/58/15/9/62.
33 No. 5 Group Fortnightly Summaries, Jul–Nov 1918, AIR 1/109/15/9/297.
34 Burney, 'Air Power',: 110–11.
35 Memo HF0036/267, 2 Jun 1917, ADM 137/1955, 175.
36 Admiral Commanding Orkneys and Shetlands to C-in-C Grand Fleet, 1 Jun
    1917, ADM 137/1955, 177; Nerney, 'RNAS in Home Waters', AIR 1/677/21/
    13/1902, 61i.
37 Davies, *Sailor in the Air*, 164–65.
38 Air Division, North Sea Air Forces Report, 13 Feb 1918, Air 1/308/15/226/188.
39 Admiralty to C-in-C Grand Fleet, 26 Jul 1917; VA2BS to C-in-C Grand Fleet,
    27 Jul 1917, ADM 137/1957, 456–57.
40 C-in-C Grand Fleet to Admiralty, 30 Sep 1917, ADM 137/1957, 468.
41 VA2BS to C-in-C Grand Fleet, 8 Nov 1917, ADM 137/1957, 472–73.
42 *ASRs*, AIR 1/2105/207/41/1–10; *NAOs*, AIR 1/626/17/59/1–7.
43 Samson, *Fights and Flights*, 358–60.
44 Halpern, *Naval History*, 351; Newbolt, *NO*, V: 31–32.
45 R-Adm Harwich to Commodore (T), 8 May 1917, ADM 137/2086, 56–58.
46 Hallam, *The Spider Web*, 79–81; Nerney, 'RNAS in Home Waters,' AIR 1/677/
    21/13/1902, 15a.
47 War Experiences of Wing Commander J. L. Gordon, RAF Staff College, nd, AIR
    1/2387/II/228/11/59.
48 Halpern, *Naval History*, 351; C. Ernest Fayle, *Seaborne Trade*, Vol. III (London:
    John Murray, 1924), 473.
49 *NAOs*, AIR 1/626/17/59/1–10; J. C. Grant Logbook, Jul–Oct 1918, FAAM.
50 Air Ministry to Admiralty, 4 Apr 1918, AIR 1/276/15/226/125 Part II. This
    letter outlines the regional RAF groups and the naval commands that they
    served.
51 *ASRs*, AIR 1/2105/207/41/1–10; *NAOs*, AIR 1/626/17/59/1–7.

52 Director of Statistics Report: 'Escort Work Performed by the Navy in Home Waters', 30 Mar 1918, ADM 137/1535. In Dec 1917, surface vessels escorted 157 French Coal Trade vessels, 324 cross-channel vessels (out of about 650 total), and 125 ships on coastal routes. These figures represent only about 30 per cent of all of December's traffic in the area.
53 Request Statement for the Air Force, 4 Jan 1918, AIR 1/483/15/312/255.
54 *ASR*, Sep 1917, AIR 1/2105/207/41/4, 3.
55 Bethell to Admiralty, 5 Nov 1917, ADM 137/1324, 194. An attached by R-Adm W. Fisher (DASD) states that although it was known that U-boats avoided air escorted convoys, his opinion was that this mission would leave few aircraft remaining 'for submarine hunting' and therefore a disadvantage. DASD Minute, 11 Nov 1917, ADM 137/1324, 195.
56 *NAOs*, AIR 1/626/17/59/1–7.
57 War Experiences of Sqn Ldr J. K. Waugh, RAF Staff College, 29 Sep 1925, 5, AIR 1/2388/228/11/67.
58 Log of F. Gurton and Logbook of C. S. Mossop. FAAM.
59 Jones, *WIA*, IV: 53.
60 C-in-C Devonport Memo, 10 May 1917, ADM 131/64, 109.
61 *ASR*, Aug 1917, AIR 1/2105/207/41/3, 7; Nerney, 'RNAS in Home Waters', AIR 1/677/21/13/1902, 35–37. American Light Cruisers, such as the *Cleveland*, typically led these convoys from New York to Home Waters. Newbolt, *NO*, V: 135n.
62 Spindler, IV: 232.
63 SW Group Patrol Orders, 1 Sep 1917, AIR 1/644/17/122/292.
64 W. L. Anderson Logbooks, FAAM. Between July 17 and the end of the war, Anderson flew only nine escorts while flying Large Americas operationally from the Scillies. Returns from the SW Air (No. 9) Group show that only a small proportion of aeroplane and seaplanes patrols were 'escorts'. *ASR*s, AIR 1/2105/207/41/1–10; *NAOs*, AIR 1/626/17/59/1–7.
65 Development of the Airship Service, 13 Nov 1918, AIR 1/2314/222/1. Through 31 Oct 1918 only.
66 Verry Transcript, IWM/SA/311, 31–3.
67 Fayle, *ST*, III: 473; Historical Section, *Defeat*, 10.
68 Gerrard to Capt(D), 4th Destroyer Flotilla, 12 Jun 1918, ADM 131/64, 98.
69 Briggs to C-in-C Plymouth, nd [*c.* late Sep 18], Doc. No. 271(4) in Roskill, *Documents Relating*, 718–21.
70 Nerney, 'RNAS in Home Waters', AIR 1/677/21/13/1902, 41–42.
71 *NAOs*, AIR 1/626/17/59/1–7.
72 Nerney, 'History of the Anti-Submarine Campaign', AIR 1/675/21/13/1385, III: 2–3.
73 Duff to Bethell, 7 Aug 1917, Bethell Papers. LHCMA.
74 Peyton-Ward, *RAF in Maritime War*, AIR 41/45, I: Appendix I.
75 Air Ministry to Admiralty, 4 Apr 1918, AIR 1/276/15/226/125 Part II.
76 Statement of Work for Air Force, 4 Jan 1918, AIR 1/483/15/312/255.
77 DAD Minute, 8 Sep 1918, AIR 1/288/15/226/138, AD4009.
78 Williams Transcript, IWM/SA/0313, 29–30.
79 CO Luce Bay to Commodore Larne, 20 Aug 1918, AIR 1/651/17/122/450.
80 V-Adm Milford Haven Reports, Escorts and Convoys, Jan–Nov 1918, ADM 137/1509–10. For example, in the 27 Jan report, V-Adm Dare makes a common comment: During OM41, additional patrol vessels joined the escort force, but 'Weather was too rough for airships to make a patrol'. ADM 137/1509, 74.
81 Nerney, 'History of the Anti-Submarine Campaign', AIR 1/675/21/13/1385, III, 2–3; and Admiralty to C-in-C Rosyth and RAECE, 15 Apr 1917, AIR 1/638/17/122/168: here the Admiralty set the stage for cooperation by suggesting that

Howden airships patrol further northward and East Fortune airships further southward, meeting at the Tyne.

82 Beatty to his wife, 13 Oct 1917, Doc. No. 248 in B. McL. Ranft, ed., *The Beatty Papers: Selections from the Private and Official Correspondence of Admiral of the Fleet Earl Beatty, Volume I, 1902–1918* (Aldershot: Scolar Press, 1989), 452.

83 C-in-C Coast of Scotland (Adm F. T. Hamilton) Order No. S 25, 29 Apr 1917, ADM 137/1955, 156–7; CO RN Airship Station Longside to SNO Peterhead, 27 May 1917, AIR 1/660/17/122/618.

84 *ASRs*, AIR 1/2105/207/41/1–10; *NAOs*, AIR 1/626/17/59/1–7.

85 Alterations and Additions No. 7 to Rosyth Secret Memorandum No. 067/19, 15 Feb 1918, AIR 1/291/15/226/140 Parts I and II, AD5623.

86 Ranft, *Beatty Papers*, I: 379.

87 Beatty to C-in-C Coast of Scotland, 1 Jul 1918, ADM 137/1955, 116.

88 Air Division, Appreciation of the Naval Air Effort, Nov 18, ADM 1/8549, 34.

89 East Fortune Convoy Patrols, 10 May 1918 charts, AIR 1/681/21/13/2213, and numerous charts in ADM 137/629, for example.

90 *NAOs*, AIR 1/626/17/59/1–7. About one out of five missions accomplished escorts.

91 Wright Logbook, summer 1918 entries. IWM/DD/85/28/1.

92 RAECE (Nicholson) to C-in-C Grand Fleet, 15 May 1917, ADM 137/1955, 164–65.

93 DAS, Statement Showing Works Carried out by Admiralty for Air Force, 4 Jan 1918, AIR 1/483/15/312/255.

94 Scarlett Memo, AF Officers for Killingholme and VAECE, 28 Mar 1918, AIR 1/275/15/226/125 Part I, AD437; HAW Memoir, Williamson Papers(WLMN4/1b), CCA, 129. According to Williamson, Finch-Noyes was relieved because he had used service vehicles for his personal use.

95 Col H. A. Williamson, Aircraft on Convoy Escort, East Coast Command, 15 Sep 1918, AIR 1/289/15/226/139.

96 Lt Col L. H. Strain, 'Review of Aircraft Anti-Submarine Campaign, 1918', nd, AIR 1/726/137/4, 10. This appears to be a draft version of *TH4* and was probably written in late 1918.

97 *NAOs*, AIR 1/626/17/59/1–7.

98 Convoy Intelligence Officer, Immingham, Report of East Coast Convoys, 20 Dec 1918, ADM 137/2241, 267–319

99 *NAOs*, May–Oct 1918, AIR 1/626/17/59/2–7.

100 Tarrant, *U-Boat Offensive*, 62.

101 Williamson to Stephen Roskill, 18 Jul 1968, Williamson Papers(4/4), CCA; VAECE Monthly report for July 1918, 2 Aug 1918, ADM 137/1553, 97.

102 HAW memoir, Williamson Papers(4/1b), CCA, 134.

103 Report of East Coast Convoys, ADM 137/2241, 267–319.

104 Shirley, *USN Aviation*, 126–31; Van Wyen, *Naval Aviation*, 76–77.

105 Capt Cone's Remarks on Planning Question 12, nd [*c.* Oct 1918], AIR 1/273/15/226/124 Part I, AD98.

106 Admiralty Memo M.011622/17, 12 Sep 1917, ADM 137/1323, 428–36.

107 DAD, Statistics and Notes on Escorts by Aircraft, 25 Jun 1918, Air 1/284/15/226/136 Part I, AD2831.

108 AIR 1/626/17/59/1–7.

109 Statistics and Notes on Escorts by Aircraft, Air 1/284/15/226/136 Part I, AD2831.

110 As inferred by Marder and Barley/Waters. Marder, *FDSF*, V: 91; Historical Section, *Defeat*, 7, 355.

111 Terraine, *Business*, 126.

112 Marder, *FDSF, Volume V*, 92. This statement counters an assertion in the previous

volume (IV:271) that kite balloons 'were used mostly with destroyers for independent submarine hunting'. This inconsistency probably led a recent study to conclude incorrectly that the Admiralty abandoned kite balloon use with convoys. Messimer, *Find and Destroy*, 134.
113 *TH4*, 19.
114 Layman, *Naval Aviation*, 124.
115 Peyton-Ward, *RAF in Maritime War*, AIR 41/45, I: 44; Halpern, *Naval History*, 425.

6 British official assessments

1 Kennett, *First Air War*, 254. The quote continues thus: '. . . and to condemn it for its tendency to enhance the image of the air arm, a tendency that is undeniable.'
2 Technical History Section, *The Technical History and Index, Part 4: Aircraft v. Submarine, Submarine Campaign, 1918*, March 1919, NHB. Other technical histories briefly examine aviation aspects of the anti-submarine war, but *TH4* is the only one solely devoted to this question.
3 *NAOs*, AIR 1/626/17/59/1–7; a draft report entitled 'Review of Aircraft Anti-Submarine Campaign 1918', found in AIR 1/726/137/4, closely matches *TH4* in both organisation and text and appears to have been written by Lt Col L. H. Strain, a high-ranking Air Division staffer.
4 *TH4*, 14–17.
5 Ibid., 12, 19.
6 Ibid., 4–5.
7 Holger Herwig, 'Innovation Ignored: The Submarine Problem', in *Military Innovation in the Interwar Period*, edited by Williamson Murray and Allan Millet (Cambridge: Cambridge University Press, 1996), 249.
8 'Erskine Childers', *The Dictionary of National Biography {DNB}*, CD ROM Version 1.1, Oxford University Press, 1997. Contributed by B. Williams in 1937; Erskine Childers Diary, 29 Apr 1918, Childers Papers, IWM/DD/PP/ MCR/C28: microfilm reel 1; *The Navy List* (London: HMSO, Various); *The Air Force List* (London: HMSO, Various). Raleigh, *WIA*, I: 405.
9 Childers and Morris, *Report of the Aircraft Bombing Committee of Effects of Bombing in Belgium and Enemy Defensive Measures* [hereafter ABC Report], 12 March 1919, AIR 1/2115/207/56/1, 68.
10 ABC Report, 70–75.
11 *Navy List; AF List*. Altham commanded HMS Attentive during its voyage and subsequent service at Murmansk during the summer of 1918. Henry Newbolt, *NO*, V: 319. Bone was a former submariner (1909–13) who like Williamson subsequently earned a pilot certificate at his own expense and transferred to the RNAS in 1913. See Reginald John Bone, 'A Record of Good Luck', *Cross and Cockade Journal* [GB] 9, No. 1 (Spring 1978): 1–7.
12 DAD to Air Ministry (PO2), 14 Nov 1918 and Admiralty to War Office and Air Ministry, 16 Nov 1918, AIR 1/292/15/226/140 Pt. III, AD5903; Gunnery Division, *Report of Committee Appointed to Examine the German Defences on the Belgian Coast, 1919* [CB1524] [hereafter Belgian Coast Report], July 1920, AIR 1/673/17/141/1A, 6.
13 Belgian Coast Report, AIR 1/673/17/141/1A, 16–17, 92–100.
14 H. A. Jones, Some Notes on the Air Historical Branch, Air Ministry, nd, AIR 5/ 495/Pt.IV.
15 Jay Luvaas, 'The First British Official Histories', in *Official Histories: Essays and Bibliographies from Around the World*, edited by Robin Higham (Manhattan, KS: Kansas State University Library, 1970), 488.

16 Franklyn A. Johnson, *Defence by Committee* (London: Oxford University Press, 1960), 168.

17 E. Y. Daniel (Secretary), Memorandum on the Work of the Historical Section of the CID [hereafter HS/CID]. 22 July 1918. Attached as an Appendix to the Minutes of the Official History Sub-Committee of the CID for 24 July 1918, CAB 102/601, 43–51; regarding the popular interest, Daniel also wrote that the official air history was 'not of the nature of a professional or technical history but is intended rather to be an authoritative account on general and popular lines written for the benefit of the intelligent reader'. HS/CID to Air Ministry, 13 Feb 1919, AIR 5/495 Pt V.

18 Marder, *FDSF*, V: 346.

19 Julian S. Corbett and Henry Newbolt, *Naval Operations*, Vol. I–V (London: Longmans, Green and Co., 1920–31); Raleigh and Jones, *WIA*, I–VI; C. Ernest Fayle, *Seaborne Trade*, Vol. I–III (London: John Murray, 1920–24); Archibald Hurd, *The Merchant Navy*, Vol. I–III (London: John Murray, 1921–29).

20 Daniel, HS/CID Report, 21 Nov 1924, CAB 102/600.

21 Jones, *WIA*, IV: 65.

22 Gröner, *German Warships*, 2: 30; Paul Kemp, *U-Boats Destroyed: German Submarine Losses in the World Wars* (Annapolis: Naval Institute Press, 1997), 30; Grant, *U-Boats Destroyed*, 54.

23 Daniel, HS/CID Memo, 5 Feb 1918. Attached as an Appendix to the Minutes of the OH Sub-Committee of the CID for 7 Feb 1918, CAB 102/600, 7. These lines of responsibility were approved in order to avoid overlap in the histories.

24 Julian S. Corbett, *Some Principles of Maritime Strategy*, with an introduction by Eric J. Grove (London: Brassey's, 1988), xiv, xli–xliv.

25 HS/CID Report, 21 Nov 1924, CAB 102/600. The OH Sub-Committee was established in Sep 1923. In a letter to his wife, Newbolt says he was appointed on 14 June 1923. See Margaret Newbolt, ed., *The Later Life and Letters of Sir Henry Newbolt* (London: Faber and Faber, 1942), 302.

26 Layman, *Naval Aviation*, 11.

27 HS/CID Memo, 22 July 1918, CAB 102/601, 48. Slade was the director of the Royal Naval College in 1902 when Corbett began lecturing there.

28 Newbolt, *NO*, IV: 326, 380.

29 Newbolt, *NO*, V: 130, 425–29. Page 35, for example: 'The air patrols of the coastal routes were now recognised to be an exceedingly important item in our system of defence.'

30 The Air Ministry also produced an historical text for RAF cadet use, which presented a balanced narrative of British air power in World War I and included large sections on the RNAS. Little analysis, other than lauding the accomplishments of the airmen, is included in the 300-page work. Air Historical Branch, Air Ministry, *A Short History of the Royal Air Force*, FS Publication 136, Jun 1920, AIR 10/164.

31 H. McAnally, Air Council Précis 149 (A.C. 35/VIII): 'Official History of the Air Services during the War', 17 April 1918, AIR 6/17.

32 H. A. Jones, *Sir Walter Raleigh and the Air History: A Personal Recollection* (London: E. Arnold, 1922), 8, 18–23; 'Preparation of the Official History of the Services of the R.A.F. during the War', AIR 5/495 Pt V.

33 Raleigh, *WIA*, I: 263, 208–10.

34 Capt C. Fairbairn, Air History: Fifth Monthly Report, 24 Dec 1918, AIR 5/495 Pt V. Also, Raleigh, *WIA*, I: Chapter 7, contains extensive passages of Samson's typescript reminiscences found in AIR 1/724/76/5. Draft of 'Chapter VII: The RNAS in 1914' in the Samson Papers, IWM/DD/72/113/3: Here Samson deleted an entire page and a half of text describing squabbling between the RFC and RNAS over aircraft replacements (pages 16–17 of the typescript draft).

35 Raleigh to Trenchard, 20 Jan 1922, and Raleigh to Lady Trenchard, 14 October 1921. Trenchard Papers(MFC 76/1/261), RAFM(H). Generous comments regarding Trenchard's career are found in Raleigh, *WIA*, I: 418–20.

36 Minute by H. A. Jones, 25 Oct 1921, AIR 2/356, 10A, 2; 'Question of Obtaining Air Council Approval for the First Volume of the Air History, 1921', AIR 2/356/139162/21. This file includes War Office to HS/CID, 20 Jan 1922, where the War Office stated that they did not agree with the need for an independent air force, but 'do not wish to delay publication on that account'.

37 Robin Higham, *The Military Intellectuals in Britain: 1918–1939* (New Brunswick, NJ: Rutgers University Press, 1966), 177; Meilinger, *AIRWAR*, 45–46.

38 Raleigh, *WIA*, I: 11, 267.

39 Higham, *Military Intellectuals*, 120n; Robin Higham, ed., *Official Histories: Essays and Bibliographies from Around the World* (Manhattan, KS: Kansas State University Library, 1970), 508; Cooper, *Birth*, xviii; Andrew Boyle, *Trenchard* (London: Collins, 1962), 514–17. Boyle offers the most detail, but uses the negotiations with Lawrence to expand the story of Trenchard's relationship with him.

40 *DNB*, 1997, F. G. Kenyon, pub 1937. Hogarth died from ill health, 'suddenly in his sleep', in 1927.

41 Jones, *WIA*, II: v.

42 HS/CID Report, 21 Nov 1924, CAB 102/600; Hogarth to Trenchard, 12 Feb 1924, Trenchard Papers(MFC 76/1/213), RAFM(H).

43 Air Ministry Interdepartmental Minutes, 24 Mar–18 Dec 1924, AIR 5/495 Pt I. For details of P. R. C. Groves's career and later work as a zealot for an independent RAF, see Robin Higham, *Military Intellectuals*, 170–76.

44 H. A. Jones, *Over the Balkans and South Russia: Being the History of No. 47 Squadron, Royal Air Force* (London: Edward Arnold, 1923), 160. In September 1918 Jones was awarded the Military Cross for the action in which he was wounded. C. Fairbairn, Air History: Fourth Monthly Report, 23 Nov 1918, AIR 5/495 Pt V.

45 Meilinger, *AIRWAR*, 76–77; C. G. Grey, *A History of the Air Ministry* (London: Allen and Unwin, 1940), 184–91.

46 HS/CID Report, 21 Nov 1924, CAB 102/600, 17–18.

47 For example, it is obvious from the content that Jones's chapter on 'Unrestricted U-Boat Warfare' in Volume IV (Jones, *WIA*, IV: 45–77) was largely based on Nerney's narrative entitled, 'History of [the] Anti-Submarine Campaign', located in AIR 1/675/21/13/1385.

48 See, for example, the very positive reviews in *The Times Literary Supplement* (22 June 1923, 403) and *The New Statesman* (Vol. 19: 1 July 1922, 364). Further reviews in 'Raleigh, *War in the Air*', *War in the Air* Files(LB4775), OUP.

49 HS/CID Report, 21 Nov 1924, CAB 102/600, 18.

50 Jones, Some Notes, AIR 5/495 Pt. IV; Minutes of the Official History Sub-Committee of the CID for 24 July 1918, CAB 102/601, 45, contains further comments regarding the scattered nature of RAF and predecessor records.

51 In terms of pages of text, approximately 43 per cent of the volume addresses RNAS operations and policy. See Jones, *WIA*, II: Chapters 1, 6, and 7.

52 Jones to K. Sisam [of Clarendon Press], 25 Feb 1928, *War in the Air* Files(LB6042), OUP.

53 Air Ministry Staff Minute, 6 Apr 1927, Longmore Minute, 30 Mar 1927, and Trenchard Minute, 22 Apr 1927, AIR 2/356/701911/26.

54 Jones, Some Notes, AIR 5/495 Pt IV. This was written while he was still director of the Air Historical Branch.

55 Control of Official Histories Annual Report, 19 Mar 1934, CAB 16/52, 396. An example of muted criticism is found in Volume IV, where Jones attacks the anti-air 'attitude of mind' of Vice-Admiral Sir Lewis Bayly, C-in-C Coast of Ireland, without specifically naming him. Jones, *WIA*, IV: 46–47.

56 H. A. Jones, 'Review of Air Power and War Rights, by J. M. Spaight', *Journal of Public Administration {London}* 3, No. 2 (1925): 185.

57 Review of *The War in the Air*, Volume II, *Punch* 175, 22 Aug 1928, 222–23; Review of Vol. III, *Punch* 180, 1 Jul 1931, 722–23; Review of Vol. IV, *The Times Literary Supplement*, 12 Apr 1934, 252; Review of Vol. V, *TLS*, 9 Nov 1935, 707; Review of Vol. VI, *TLS*, 24 Jul 1937, 535. Reviewers not mentioned by name in any of these.

58 Jones, *WIA*, IV: 107–08; and VI: 392–93.

59 Jones, *WIA*, IV: Chapter 1: 'Aircraft with the Fleet', Chapter 2: 'Unrestricted U-Boat Warfare', and Chapter 3: 'Dunkirk Naval Air Operations'; Control of Official Histories Annual Report, 22 Feb 1933, CAB 16/52, 373–377.

60 Jones, *WIA*, IV: 47, 50, 60.

61 Jones, *WIA*, VI: 330–40, 344–45.

62 Jones, *WIA*, IV: 54–73; and VI: 346–48; Newbolt, *NO*, V: 424–29; *TH4*, 13–14; Grant, *U-Boats Destroyed*; Finnis, *History*, 31–40.

63 Other than brief, yet positive reviews in *The Times Literary Supplement*, it is difficult to locate contemporary opinion. The *RUSI Journal* received the books but did not review them. Air Ministry records, which are readily available for the first three volumes, leave little evidence of the last three. The papers of contemporary Chiefs of the Air Staff (J. M. Salmond and E. L. Ellington) at the RAF Museum make no mention of H. A. Jones or the official histories.

64 HS/CID Report, 25 Apr 1939, CAB 16/53, 276–77.

65 Meilinger, *AIRWAR*, Chapter 6.

66 The nine strictly maritime chapters are: Volume I: Chapter 7, 'RNAS in 1914'; Vol. II: Ch. 1, 'Dardanelles Campaign,' Ch. 6, 'RNAS in Home Waters (1915)', and Ch. 7 'RNAS in Home Waters (1916)'; Vol. IV: Ch. 1, 'Aircraft with the Fleet, 1917–March 1918', Ch 2., 'Unrestricted U-Boat Warfare', and Ch. 3, 'Naval Air Operations from Dunkirk, 1917–March 1918'; Vol. V: Ch. 7, 'Naval Air Operations in the Mediterranean and Near East'; and Vol. VI: Ch. 10, 'Naval Air Developments and Operations, 1918, Home Waters'.

67 By March 1918, the RFC had 144,078 personnel (including 18,286 officers), which outnumbered the 55,066 total (including 5,378 officers) of the RNAS. Peter G. Cooksley, *The RFC/RNAS Handbook, 1914–1918* (Stroud: Sutton, 2000), 199; Capt Hargreaves, Memo of RNAS personnel figures, 22 Nov 1918, AIR 1/626/17/60.

68 Historical Section, *Defeat*, Editor's Introduction, ix–x; Training and Staff Duties Division, *Naval Staff Monograph No. 35 (Historical) Volume XIX, Home Waters Part IX, 1 May 1917 to 31 July 1917*, August 1939, NHB.

69 Historical Section, *Defeat*, Editor's Introduction, x–xi.

70 Captain Alfred Dewar, 'The Necessity for the Compilation of a Naval Staff History', *JRUSI* 66, No. 463 (August 1921): 369–84; Newbolt, *NO*, V: xi.

71 *NSM No. 35*, 84–85, xi–xii, 58–62, and 207–8.

72 John Buckley, *The RAF and Trade Defence, 1919–1945: Constant Endeavour* (Keele: Keele University Press, 1995), 89–90.

73 K. G. B. Dewar, *The Navy from Within* (London: Victor Gollancz, 1939), 218–21; K. G. B. Dewar, 'War on Shipping (1914–1918)', *The Naval Review* 47, No. 1 (January 1959): 3–13; Rear-Admiral R. M. Bellairs, 'Historical Survey of Trade Defence Since 1914', *JRUSI* 99, No. 595 (August 1954): 359–77; Historical Section, *Defeat*, Chapter 1.

74 Historical Section, *Defeat*, Editor's Introduction, ix.

75 Historical Section, Admiralty Papers(P1010), NHB. Other Historical Section documents containing similar arguments include 'Barley on Mining', nd, Barley and Waters Papers (PT135); 'Anti-Submarine Measures in World War I', 30 Nov 1960, Searches (Vol. 29: S.5659); and 'A "New Look" at "Offence" and

"Defence": The Anti-U-Boat Campaign, 1939–1945, A Brief Statement of Facts', 15 Oct 1955, Barley Waters Papers (DWW24, PT134); all NHB.
76 Historical Section, *Defeat*, Editor's Introduction, xii–xiii. Barley, on the other hand, was a mine warfare officer.
77 Marder, *FDSF*, V: vii, 85–88, 93, 98–102; Terraine, *Business*, 126, 148.
78 Historical Section, *Defeat*, 6–10.
79 Peyton-Ward, *RAF in Maritime War*, AIR 41/45, I: Foreword and Chapters 1–2. Peyton-Ward's references to Volume II of this series, written beforehand in 1954, and the fact that Volume VII was written in 1962, leads to the assumption of Volume I's publication in the late 1950s. Details of Peyton-Ward's career from the *Navy List*.
80 Peyton-Ward, *RAF in Maritime War*, AIR 41/45, I: 43–45, Appendices I and III.
81 Ibid., I: 43–45.
82 A recent study uses *TH4* to describe the effects of anti-submarine bombs: Messimer, *Find and Destroy*, Chapter 15. One of the only studies to quote from Childers's report is Wise, *CAFWW*, I: 212.
83 For a few examples, see Wise, *CAFWW*, I; Marder, *FDSF*, IV: 6, 271; Marder, *FDSF, Volume V*, 92, 95; Layman, *Naval Aviation*, Chapter 8; Hugh Popham, *Into Wind: A History of British Naval Flying* (London: Hamish Hamilton, 1969), Chapters 7 and 8; and Hezlet, *Aircraft and Sea Power*, Chapter 4.
84 Meilinger, *AIRWAR*, 80–81.
85 Sqn Ldr C. H. K. Edmonds, 'Aerial Cooperation with the Navy', *JRUSI* 66, No. 462 (May 1921): 244–45.
86 Historical Section, *Defeat*, Editor's Introduction, xiii–xiv.

7 The German assessment

1 R. H. Gibson and Maurice Prendergast, *The German Submarine War, 1914–1918* (London: Constable, 1931), 333, 351. The number of U-boats lost includes 14 that were scuttled in the Adriatic and Flanders during the closing months of the campaign.
2 Messimer, *Find and Destroy*, 130–31, 138–39.
3 Arno Spindler, *Der Handelskrieg mit U-Booten*, Vol. 1–5 (Berlin/Frankfurt: E. S. Mittler, 1932–66); Walther Gladisch, *Der Krieg in der Nordsee*, Vol. 6–7 (Berlin/Frankfurt: E. S. Mittler, 1937–65).
4 Belgian Coast Report, 104; Corum, *Luftwaffe*, 44–45.
5 ABC Report, 72–73.
6 Belgian Coast Report, 100. The NAOs from the period do not mention any losses to night interceptors and neither does a listing of Handley Page O/100 aircraft histories. Sturtivant and Page, *Serials and Units*, 76–78, 85–87.
7 Belgian Coast Report, 99.
8 Mark D. Karau, 'Lost Opportunities: The *Marinekorps Flandern* and the German War Effort, 1914–1918', Ph.D. Diss. (Florida State University, 2000), 524–26.
9 NAO, June 1918, 4, and Aug 1918, 2, AIR 1/626/17/59/3 and 5; Gladisch, *Nordsee*, VII: 327.
10 Gladisch, *Nordsee*, VII: 328; Karau, '*Marinekorps Flandern*', 530.
11 ABC Report, 72.
12 Belgian Coast Report, 96.
13 Karau, '*Marinekorps Flandern*', 527–28.
14 Belgian Coast Report, 108, 115.
15 Gladisch, *Nordsee*, VII: 328.
16 Belgian Coast Report, 109, 113; Edward B. Westermann, 'Sword in the Heavens: German Ground Based Air Defenses, 1914–1945', Ph.D. Diss. (University of North Carolina, 2000), 37–38. It is extremely difficult to determine the impact

of flak on British aircraft. Only a few Handley Pages were shot down outright, but many crash landed on the return trip from missions. Some undetermined number of these accidents must have been as a result of flak damage. See Sturtivant and Page, *Serials and Units*, 76–78, 85–87.

17 ABC Report, 24; *FdU Flandern KTB*, 24 Mar 1918, 17 May 1918, and Monthly Summary for May, dated 19 June 1918, PG62061, National Archives Microfilm Publication T1022, Roll 153. Sheltering U-boats that were damaged included *UB30* on 24 March 1918 and both *UB10* and *UB12* on 16 May 1918.

18 Karau, '*Marinekorps Flandern*', 330; Gladisch, *Nordsee*, VI: 296.

19 *FdU Flandern KTB*, 9 Mar 1917 and 15 June 1917, T1022/153/PG62061.

20 *FdU Flandern KTB*, 16 May 1917, T1022/153/PG62061; *BdU KTB*, 22 Dec 1917, T1022/94–95/PG62020; Belgian Coast Report, 26; CO No. 1 Wing RNAS to SO RNAS, Dover, 8 Mar 1916, ADM 137/2269: Here Groves reported to Lambe that a captured German seaplane observer confessed to the use of seaplanes to escort submarines in early 1916.

21 *TH4*, 15; Historical Section, *Defeat*, 9; Marder, *FDSF*, V: 95.

22 Naval Intelligence Division, *German Navy (Submarines)* [CB1182S], April 1918, Admiralty Papers, NHB, 52–53.

23 Gröner, *German Warships, II*; Rössler, *U-Boat*.

24 Andreas Michelsen, *Der U-Bootskrieg, 1914–1918* (Leipzig: Koehler, 1925), 78; Max Valentiner, *Der Schrecken der Meere: Meine U-Boot-Abenteuer* (Leipzig: Amalthea-Verlag, 1931), 216.

25 Gröner, *German Warships*, 2: 39–40, 332.

26 Werner Fürbringer, *FIPS: Legendary U-Boat Commander, 1915–1918*, translated by Geoffrey Brooks (Annapolis: Naval Institute Press, 1999), 114.

27 NID, CB1182S, NHB, 47.

28 Capt J. E. Barrs, Airship Patrol Report, 7 Dec 1917, AIR 1/720/42/1/1; Nerney, 'History of Anti-Submarine Campaign', AIR 1/675/21/13/1385, IV: 6; Mowthorpe, *Battlebags*, 56.

29 *BdU, KTB*, 22 July 1917, T1022/94–95/PG62020.

30 NID, CB1182S, NHB, 90.

31 Fletcher, *Lecture on . . . Airships*, 27–8, NMM(CL).

32 As demonstrated in the air attack reports on U-boats in the *ASR*s and *NAO*s.

33 Historical Section, *Defeat*, 9; Marder, *FDSF*, V: 94–95.

34 *FdU Flandern KTB*, 15 June 1917 and 15 January 1918, T1022/153/PG62061.

35 *BdU KTB*, 11 July 1917, and 'General Policy for the Guidance of the U-Boat War', Michelsen, 4 Dec 1917, T1022/94–95/PG62020.

36 *FdU Flandern KTB*, 8 Apr, 30 Apr, and 31 May 1918, T1022/153/PG62061.

37 Marder, *FDSF*, V: 96.

38 Peyton-Ward Convoy Statistics, nd, AIR 1/2420/305/17.

39 NID Translation, *Ruthless Submarine Orders*, CB01360, Oct 1917, 10, NHB. This is a translation of Bauer's orders to U-boat captains dated 17 January 1917.

40 Air Department Memo: 'Use of Aircraft for the Protection of Shipping', 30 Mar 1918, AIR 1/279/15/226/133. D. V. Peyton Ward's AHB narrative offers the following overall percentages of night attacks: May–Jul 1917: 17.8 per cent; Aug–Oct 1917: 28.5 per cent; Nov 1917–Jan 1918: 54.2 per cent; Feb–Apr 1918: 41.9 per cent; then down to 31.5 per cent in May–Jul 1918 and 37.5 per cent in Aug–Oct 1918. *RAF in Maritime War*, AIR 41/45, I: 40. Night attacks were thus hardly 'the predominant form of attack in 1918' that Marder claims in *FDSF*, V: 94.

41 'German Records: Home Waters, Atlantic, and Mediterranean', D. V. Peyton-Ward, nd, AIR 1/2420/305/17.

42 See Chapter 5 above.

43 Based on data found in Grant, *U-Boats Destroyed*; Kemp, *U-Boats Destroyed*; and

Messimer, *Verschollen*. Only 57 of 178 lost U-boats (not including the scuttling during October 1918) yielded survivors. The Germans recovered their own survivors on only five occasions during 1917–18: *U76* (Jan 1917), *U59* (May 1917), *U75* (Dec 1917), *UB61* (Nov 1917), and *UC24* (May 1917). Above information based on all theatres of operations.

44 The entire collection of printed Naval Intelligence Department/Division CBs covering interrogations are located in ADM 137/3060 and 4126. These are also found individually, along with other typescript intelligence reports, in ADM 137/3841–3903 and ADM 186/38.

45 The 57 prisoners from the Mediterranean, operating from bases in the Adriatic and captured between December 1917 and August 1918, all agreed that bombing raids on Pola and Cattaro were largely unsuccessful and that patrol aircraft were only a threat if the U-boat was surprised on the surface. NID CB01415, CB01464, and CB01483, ADM 137/4126.

46 'Interrogation of Survivors of *UC26*', NID12572, 13 May 1917, ADM 137/3897, 7.

47 'Examination of the crew of *UC61*', NID198, 17 Aug 1917, ADM 137/3898, 21.

48 CB01414, Feb 1918, ADM 137/4126, 14.

49 DNI, 'Air Raids', 30 Jul 1918, ADM 137/3900; NID Interrogation Reports, CB01468 (*UB110*, Aug 1918) and CB01478 (*UB109*, Sep 1918), ADM 137/4126.

50 See Chapter 3 above.

51 According to Vice-Admiral Dare, *Oberleutnant* Alfred Arnold of *UC33* was evasive and appeared to have been untruthful. VADM Milford Haven, 'Report of Conversation Held with *Ober Leutnant* Alfred Arnold', 28 Sep 1917, ADM 137/3897.

52 'Translation of Diary Kept by *Leutnant d. Reserve* Heinrich Petersen', NID12572, 13 May 1917, ADM 137/3897; Messimer, *Verschollen*, 262–63.

53 'Examination of the Crew of *UC61*', NID198, 17 Aug 1917, ADM 137/3898.

54 'Report of Conversation Held with *Ober Leutnant* Alfred Arnold', ADM 137/3897. According to Spindler, Arnold was actually attacked on 9 Aug 1917. See Spindler, *Handelskrieg*, IV: 232. The attack was carried out by Airship *C-2* from Mullion, 15 miles south-east of the Lizard. *ASR*, Aug 1917, AIR 1/2105/207/41/3, 7. The submarine was not damaged and continued its mission.

55 NID CB01468, Aug 1918, ADM 137/4126.

56 *NAO*, May 1918, AIR 1/626/17/59/2, 13, recounts this attack by a Scillies Large America and the subsequent results of the crew interrogation. CB01444, June 1918, ADM 137/4126, provides further detail.

57 CB01378, Nov 1917, ADM 137/4126, 3.

58 CB01438, May 1918, ADM 137/4126, 13.

59 Since it was declared a classified publication in Germany, Spindler's fourth volume was not issued publicly until after World War II. The semi-official history by the former commander of High Seas Fleet *U-Flotilla III* will not be examined here because of its scope. See Albert Gayer, *Die Deutschen U-Boote in Ihrer Kriegführung, 1914–1918*, Vol. 1–4 (Berlin: E. S. Mittler, 1920–1930). Gayer never completed a planned fifth volume of this series, which would have covered Feb 1917 until the end of the war, and only mentions aircraft three times in Volume 4 (May 1916–February 1917): Two occasions of UC boats having to dive to avoid airship patrols and one incident where *UC11* shot down a British aircraft on 28 Nov 1916, capturing the crew (IV: 69–71). During an Admiralty lecture, Gayer nonetheless assessed Allied aircraft as 'an ever increasing source of trouble to our submarines' after 1916. Albert Gayer, 'Summary of German Submarine Operations in the Various Theaters of War from 1914 to 1918', translated by Commander W. P. Beehler, *USNIP* 52, No. 4 (April 1926): 637.

60 Spindler, *Handelskrieg*, V: vi.

61 Cdr M. G. Saunders, 'Some Notes of Admiral Spindler and the German Official History of U-Boat Warfare, 1914–18', FDS 206/60, 2 June 1960, NHB Miscellaneous MSS.

62 NID Index of German Naval Officers (Part I: Flag Officers), NID01326/45, NHB Miscellaneous MSS, NHB, 155.

63 Philip Lundeberg, of the Smithsonian Institution's Naval History Division, wrote that Spindler's failure to address 'British antisubmarine order-of-battle or indeed an evaluation of Allied weapons development' was a 'major deficiency' of his work. Philip K. Lundeberg, 'The German Naval Critique of the U-Boat Campaign, 1915–1918', Military Affairs 27 (Fall 1963): 113.

64 Spindler, Handelskrieg, IV: 294–96.

65 Saunders generally agreed that Spindler was 'not a profound analyst of these operations or of the constantly changing political policy which governed them'. 'Some Notes on Admiral Spindler . . .,' 1, NHB.

66 Spindler, Handelskrieg, IV: 296–304 Events and comments paraphrased from the German text.

67 Ibid., IV: 415–16.

68 Spindler, Handelskrieg, V: 279.

69 Gladisch, Nordsee, VI: 294–97, 324–27.

70 Gladisch, Nordsee, VII: 319.

71 Gladisch, Nordsee, VI: 294.

72 Admiral R. Scheer, Germany's High Sea Fleet in the World War (London: Cassell and Co., 1920); Alfred von Tirpitz, My Memoirs, Volume II (London: Hurst and Blackett, nd.).

73 Hermann Bauer, Als Führer der U-Boote Im Weltkrieg (Leipzig: Koehler and Amelang, 1943).

74 S. W. Roskill, The Strategy of Sea Power (London: Collins, 1962), 136; Cooper, Birth, xvi. Cooper asserts that air power on the whole had not evolved into a viable 'strategic' weapon by the end of the war.

75 Newbolt, NO, IV, 52–63. Michelsen personally led the German destroyer raid against Dover Patrol forces in late October 1916.

76 Michelsen, Der U-Bootskrieg, 76–78; Sims, Victory at Sea.

77 Spindler, Handelskrieg, V: 310.

78 Michelsen, Der U-Bootskrieg, 121–23; Spindler, Handelskrieg, IV: 280–81. This episode is also mentioned in both Michelsen's and Bartenbach's war diaries (28 Sep 1917 entry).

79 Lieutenant Commander Freiherr von Spiegel, U.Boat 202: The War Diary of a German Submarine, translated by Captain Barry Domville (London: A. Melrose, 1919). This account, originally published in 1917, is based on other U-boat commander diaries in addition to the author's own (see page vi). Memoirs exclusively dealing with the early years or the theatres of operations outside of British Waters are not included in the survey below. Such works include: Hans Fechter, Alarmkoje von U35 (Berlin: Ullstein, 1918); Paul Schulz, Im U-Boot Durch die Weltmeere (Leipzig: Velhagen and Klasing, 1931); and Otto Hersing, U21 Rettet die Dardanellen (Zürich: Amalthea, 1932).

80 Karl Dönitz, Memoirs: Ten Years and Twenty Days, translated by R. H. Stephens (London: Weidenfeld and Nicolson, 1959), 2.

81 Peter Padfield, Dönitz: The Last Führer (London: Victor Gollancz, 1984), 76–77, 80.

82 Fürbringer, FIPS, 87, 114–15. The interrogation account of this incident was mentioned earlier in this chapter.

83 Valentiner, Schrecken, 216.

84 Ernst Hashagen, The Log of a U-Boat Commander {or U-Boats Westward–1914–1918}, translated by R. C. V. Ross (London: Putnam, 1931), 222.

85 Martin Niemöller, *From U-Boat to Pulpit*, translated by Cdr D. Hastie Smith (London: William Hodge, 1936), 58–59, 106–08.

86 Johannes Spiess, *Sechs Jahre U-Bootsfahrten* (Berlin: Reimar Hobbing, 1925), 113. In German, the airships were referred to as '*unangenehme Neuerung*'.

87 Karl Neureuther and Claus Bergen, *U-Boat Stories: Narratives of German U-Boat Sailors*, translated by Eric Sutton (London: Constable, 1931), 130–42, 188–89.

88 Lowell Thomas, *Raiders of the Deep* (Garden City, NY: Doubleday, Doran & Co., 1929), 232–35; Spindler, *Handelskrieg*, IV: 297. Spindler disagrees and claims that *UB20* probably hit a mine on 28 July 1917.

89 Raleigh, *WIA*, I: 267; note 53 above.

90 Translation of 'The Aircraft as an Enemy Anti-U-boat Weapon', Flag Officer Commanding U-Boats, 10 Feb 1945, 2, Coastal Command Papers, AHB.

8 Conclusion

1 Clay Blair, *Hitler's U-Boat War, Volume II: The Hunted, 1942–1945* (New York: Random House, Inc., 1998), Appendix 2 and 666.

2 Kemp, *U-Boats Destroyed*, Glossary and 234.

3 Blair, *HUB*, II: 707.

4 Ibid., 43, 445–52, 518, 583.

5 'Précis of Attack by Warwick Aircraft "K" of 179 Squadron', 21 May 1945, Assessment Committee Serial No. 12 (AUD.379/45), *Proceedings of U-Boat Assessment Committee, April–Nov 1945*, Vol. 18, NHB; Blair, *HUB*, II: 666; Kemp, *U-Boats Destroyed*, 234.

6 H. Saunders, *The Royal Air Force, 1939–1945*, Vol. III (London: HMSO, 1954), 46.

7 Cdr H. W. Fawcett, RN, Memo: Possibilities of the Coming U-Boat Offensive, 1 Dec 1944, AIR 15/469. Fawcett, an ASW specialist and RN liaison to Coastal Command, said that the snorkel 'has reduced the attacking power of aircraft to about a tenth of its former value' and hoped for further improvements in radar and airborne magnetic detection systems to offset the newfound stealth of German submarines.

8 John Terraine, *The Right of the Line: The Royal Air Force in the European War, 1939–1945* (London: Hodder and Stoughton, 1985), 406.

9 Historical Section, *Defeat*, 22–23.

10 Saunders, *RAF*, III: 408. The allocation of Liberators, on the other hand, was a difficult debate between Bomber Command and Coastal Command/Admiralty, and is covered throughout the literature.

11 Oliver Swann, 'Naval Air Requirements', *Naval Review* VII, No. 3 (August 1919): 305–13.

12 C. H. K. Edmonds, 'Aerial Cooperation with the Navy', *JRUSI* 66, No. 462 (May 1921): 237–57.

13 George Franklin, *Britain's Anti-Submarine Capability, 1919–1939* (London: Frank Cass, 2003), 10–21; Friedman, *Seapower*, 156.

14 Joseph A. Maiolo, 'Deception and Intelligence Failure: Anglo-German Preparations for U-Boat Warfare in the 1930s', *The Journal of Strategic Studies* 22, No. 4 (December 1999): 56–60; Goulter, *Forgotten Offensive*, 39.

15 Goulter, *Forgotten Offensive*, 35–38.

16 Ibid., 43.

17 Peyton-Ward, *RAF in Maritime War*, AIR 41/45, I: Appendix IV.

18 Neville Jones, *The Beginnings of Strategic Air Power: A History of the British Bomber Force, 1923–1939* (London: Frank Cass, 1987), 28.

19 Peyton-Ward, *RAF in Maritime War*, AIR 41/45, I: Appendix IV.

20 Again, interwar, interservice squabbling is thoroughly covered in Till, *Air Power*,

Chapters 2–5; Goulter, *Forgotten Offensive*, Chapters 2–3; and Meilinger, *AIR-WAR*, Chapter 4.

21 Meilinger, *AIRWAR*, 39; Jones, *Beginnings*, Chapter 2.

22 Franklin, *Anti-Submarine*, 101–02; Goulter, *Forgotten Offensive*, 76–77.

23 For example, Peyton-Ward criticises Air Ministry and Admiralty unpreparedness in the face of clear lessons from the Great War air anti-submarine experience. *RAF in Maritime War*, AIR 41/45, I: 121–123. See also John Buckley, 'Atlantic Airpower Co-Operation, 1941–1943', in *Air Power: Theory and Practice*, edited by John Gooch (London: Frank Cass, 1999), 132; John Buckley, 'Failing to Learn from the Past: Air Power and Trade Defence, 1917–1943', *War Studies Journal* 2, No. 1 (Autumn 1996): 1–16; David MacGregor, 'The Use, Misuse, and Non-Use of History: The Royal Navy and the Operational Lessons of the First War', *Journal of Military History* 56, No. 4 (October 1992): 603–06; Herwig, 'Innovation Ignored', 241–52.

24 Tactical Division, *Progress in Tactics, 1930*, Jul 1931, NHB, 97–101. These exercises were 1927: KG, KH, and NO; 1928: NX; 1929: OC; 1930: AU.

25 Goulter, *Forgotten Offensive*, 46.

26 Franklin, *Anti-Submarine*, 106.

27 Tactical Division, *Progress in Tactics, 1938*, July 1938, 60–68, and *1939*, June 1939, 57–61, NHB; Report of C-in-C Mediterranean Station, *Short Tactical Exercises, 6–7 December 1938*, 21 Mar 1939, AIR 15/38.

28 Terraine, *Business*, 184; Stephen Bungay, *The Most Dangerous Enemy* (London: Aurum Press, 2000), 179; S. W. Roskill, *The Navy at War, 1939–1945* (Ware, Herts: Wordsworth Editions, 1998), 148–50, 205–07.

29 Franklin, *Anti-Submarine*, 129; Admiralty Letters to Commanders-in-Chief, 31 Aug 1937 and 23 Feb 1939, AIR 15/38; Tactical Division, Memo: Anti-Submarine Striking Forces, Jun 1938, Appendix B, AIR 15/38.

30 Plans Division, *The Protection of Shipping at Sea* [CB01957], Sept 1936, 12–13, 19–24.

31 Goulter, *Forgotten Offensive*, 72, 90–93.

32 Tarrant, *U-Boat Offensive*, 81, 88–89.

33 Terraine, *Right of the Line*, 237; Tarrant, *U-Boat Offensive*, 169–76.

34 Historical Section, *Defeat*, 44.

35 Friedman, *Seapower*, 160.

36 Tarrant, *U-Boat Offensive*, 163–69;Terraine, *Right of the Line*, 236; Historical Section, *Defeat*, Plans 1 & 7.

37 Blair, *HUB*, II: xi–xii.

38 Ibid., 709.

39 Terraine, *Right of the Line*, 233, 456.

40 Historical Section, *Defeat*, Editor's Revised Appendix C, xliv.

41 Terraine, *Right of the Line*, 700.

42 Blair, *HUB*, II: 710–11.

43 Terraine, *Right of the Line*, 245–46.

44 Historical Section, *Defeat*, 69.

45 Saunders, *RAF*, III: 40–41, 51–55, 64–65.

46 Sir Charles Webster and Noble Frankland, *The Strategic Air Offensive Against Germany, 1939–1945* (London: HMSO, 1961), I: 302–306.

47 Historical Section, *Defeat*, 171.

48 HQ USAF Center for Aerospace Doctrine Research and Education, *The United States Strategic Bombing Surveys* (Maxwell AFB, Alabama: Air University Press, 1987), 14; Saunders, *RAF*, III: 47.

49 CADRE, *USSBS*, 29.

50 Historical Section, *Defeat*, 153–54.

51 Blair, *HUB*, II: 804–08 (Appendix 13).

52 Historical Section, *Defeat*, 172–74.
53 Blair, *HUB*, II: 710–11.
54 Franklin, *Anti-Submarine*, 108.
55 Ibid., 710–11.
56 Peyton-Ward, *RAF in Maritime War*, AIR 41/79, VIII: Table 26. Italian submarines are not included nor are German submarines lost outside of the Atlantic and Arctic Oceans, and the Baltic and North Seas.
57 S. W. Roskill, *Admiral of the Fleet Earl Beatty: The Last Naval Hero, an Intimate Biography* (London: Collins, 1980), 266–67.

Bibliography

I. PRIMARY SOURCES

A. Unpublished Primary Sources

Note: Where codes are available for a given collection, they are listed in parentheses.

1. Air Historical Branch, RAF Bentley Priory, Stanmore

Squadron Histories, Nos. 206–248 Squadron (AHB5 Series)
RNAS Papers (AHB8)
RAF Coastal Command Papers (AHB29)
Air Board Minutes Binders

2. Caird Library, National Maritime Museum, Greenwich

Papers of:
K. G. B. Dewar (DEW)
A. L. Duff (DFF)
W. W. Fisher (FHR)
F. T. Hamilton (HTN)

Admiralty Publications:
Airship Department, Admiralty. *Handbook on SS Type Airships: 1917*. January 1917.
——— . *State of Development of the Airship Service on 1st January 1918* [CB819]. January 1918.
——— . *Handbook on the 'Coastal' and 'C. STAR' Airships*. May 1918.
Fletcher, Wing Commander J. N. *Lecture on Maintenance, Flying and Operations of Airships*. Cranwell, 1918.

3. Churchill Archives Centre, Churchill College, Cambridge

Papers of:
T. W. Elmhirst (ELMT)
S. W. Roskill (ROSK)
H. A. Williamson (WLMN)

4. Department of Research and Information Services, Royal Air Force Museum, Hendon

Papers of:
E. L. Ellington (AC 71/12, 17)
J. M. Salmond
H. M. Trenchard (MFC 76/1)
T. B. Williams (DB14)

Logbooks of the following veterans:
J. H. Bentham (B1898)
E. W. Keesey (B294)
W. A. Thompson (B1063)
T. B. Williams (B459)

Printed material and miscellaneous papers:
Polegate *Reminiscences* (002367)
Felixstowe RN Air Station. Report on Experimental Flying Boat Hulls, 1915–1916. (B433)
Service Experiences of Flt Lt S.D. Culley, DSO. RAF Staff College. Andover, May 1930. (B998)
Transcript of a recorded interview with Sqn Ldr Hubert C. G. Allen, *c.* 1960. (B2359)

5. Fleet Air Arm Museum, RNAS Yeovilton

Logbooks and Notebooks of the following veterans:
W. L. Anderson
L. Chivers
J. C. Grant
F. Gurton
J. Havers
R. Jelliffe
C. E. S. Lusk
C. S. Mossop
J. Wooders

Miscellaneous Printed Material:
Air Department, Admiralty. *RNAS Hydrogen Manual*, January 1916.
Airship Department, Admiralty. *Handbook on the SS 'Zero' Type Airship*, March 1918.

6. Imperial War Museum – Department of Documents, London

Papers of:
R. Erskine Childers (microfilm-PP/MCR/C28)
R. M. Groves (P322)
C. R. Samson (72/113/3)
F. D. Silwood (microfilm-PP/MCR/4)
E. C. B. Wright (85/28/1)

7. Imperial War Museum – Sound Archive, London

Interview recordings and transcripts of the following veterans:
C. N. H. Bilney (002)
F. D. H. Bremner (004)
C. P. Bristow (13718)
C. C. Burne (006)
G. Donald (018)
T. W. Elmhirst (998)
R. V. Goddard (303)
W. V. Hawkins (019)
G. F. Hyams (10409)
L. H. Kemp (026)
D. Kidd (15714)
H. deV. Leigh (037)
F. D. Silwood (317)
H. R. Stubbington (298)
T. B. Thomson (309)
F. Verry (311)
W. E. D. Wardrop (029)
T. B. Williams (313)

8. Liddell Hart Centre for Military Archives, King's College London

Papers of:
A. E. Bethell
R. Brooke-Popham
J. S. Corbett
P. W. Cunliffe
J. W. E. Douglas-Scott-Montagu
J. M. Mason

9. National Archives (Public Record Office), Kew

Admiralty Papers
ADM 1   Admiralty, and Ministry of Defence, Navy Department: Correspondence and Papers
ADM 101 Medical Journals
ADM 116 Admiralty Record Office: Cases
ADM 131 Plymouth Station: Correspondence
ADM 137 Historical Section: Records used for Official History, First World War
ADM 151 Nore Station Correspondence
ADM 167 Board of Admiralty: Minutes and Memoranda
ADM 186 Admiralty Publications
ADM 189 Admiralty Torpedo School Reports
ADM 196 Admiralty Officer Service Records (Microfilm)
ADM 239 Confidential Reference Books (CB Series)
ADM 293 BIR Minutes and Reports

Air Ministry Papers

Note: For a complete description of these records, see Simon Fowler, Peter Elliot, Roy
 Conyers Nesbit, and Christina Goulter, *RAF Records in the PRO* (London: PRO
 Publications, 1994).

AIR 1   Air Historical Branch: Papers (Series I)
AIR 2   Air Ministry and Ministry of Defence: Registered Files
AIR 5   Air Historical Branch: Papers (Series II)
AIR 6   Air Board, Air Council, and Air Ministry: Minutes and Memoranda
AIR 8   Chief of the Air Staff: Registered Files
AIR 10   Ministry of Defence and Predecessors: Air Publications and Reports
AIR 11   Admiralty and Air Ministry: Naval Aircraft Works, Later Royal Airship
           Works, Cardington: Correspondence and Papers
AIR 15   Coastal Command: Registered Files
AIR 27   Squadron Operations Record Books, 1911–1977
AIR 41   Air Historical Branch: Narratives and Monographs
AIR 76   Officer Service Records

Cabinet Papers

CAB 16   Committee of Imperial Defence, Subcommittees, 1905–39
CAB 17   Committee of Imperial Defence, Misc. Correspondence, 1902–19
CAB 24   War Cabinet and Cabinet Memoranda
CAB 45   Committee of Imperial Defence, Historical Section, 1904–57
CAB 102   Cabinet Office, Historical Section Papers, 1941–72
CAB 103   Cabinet Office, Historical Section Registered Files, 1906–82

Ministry of Munitions Papers

MUN 2   Weekly Reports, 1915–21
MUN 4   Central Registry Records, 1909–37
MUN 5   Munitions Council Papers, 1901–43
MUN 8   Files Transferred from the Air Ministry, 1916–23

War Office Papers

WO 32   Registered Files, 1845–1985
WO 153   Maps and Plans, 1914–18

10. National Archives of the United States

Records of the German Naval Archives microfilmed by the US Navy (Office of Naval
 Intelligence) at the Admiralty, London; NA Microfilm Publication T1022:

PG62017–PG62022, War Diary of High Sea Fleet U-Boat Forces, Rolls 94–95
PG62061–PG62065, War Diaries of Flanders U-Boat Forces, Roll 153

11. Naval Historical Branch and Admiralty Library, Whitehall

Admiralty Papers and Publications

Air Department, Admiralty. *RNAS Memoranda, General and Temporary Issue, 1916*. 1
 March 1917.
—— . *Naval Air Service Training Manual. November 1914*. 1915.

Director of Statistics, Admiralty. Statistical Review of the War Against Merchant Shipping,. 23 December 1918.

Historical Section, Admiralty. *Historical Research Memorandum No. 1: Surface and Air Anti-Submarine Escort of Shipping in Convoy, and Anti-Submarine Transit Area Patrols in Two World Wars.* May 1953.

——— . *Notes on the Convoy System of Naval Warfare, Thirteenth to Twentieth Centuries. Part 2: First World War, 1914–18.* March 1960.

Naval Intelligence Division, Admiralty. *Index of German Naval Officers, Part I: Flag Officers* [NID01326/45], nd.

——— . *German Naval Warfare, 1914–1919* [CB0693]. nd.

——— . *German Navy (Submarines)* [CB1182S.]. April 1918.

——— . *German Orders for Ruthless Submarine Warfare* [CB01360]. October 1917.

Tactical Division, Admiralty. *Progress in Tactics, 1930.* July 1931.

——— . *Progress in Tactics, 1938.* July 1938.

Technical History Section, *The Technical History and Index, Part 4: Aircraft v. Submarine. Submarine Campaign, 1918* [CB01515(4)]. March 1919.

——— . *The Technical History and Index, Part 7: The Anti-Submarine Division of the Naval Staff, December 1916–November 1918* [CB01515(7)]. July 1919.

——— . *The Technical History and Index, Part 8: Scandinavian and East Coast Convoy Systems, 1917–1918* [CB01515(8)]. July 1919.

——— . *The Technical History and Index, Part 37: Inception and Development of the Northern Base* [CB01515(37)]. February 1920.

——— . *The Technical History and Index, Part 39: Miscellaneous Convoys* [CB01515(39)]. June 1920.

——— . *The Technical History and Index, Part 40: Anti-Submarine Development and Experiments Prior to December 1916* [CB01515(40)]. September 1920.

Training and Staff Duties Division, Admiralty. *History of British Minesweeping in the War.* December 1920.

——— . *Naval Staff Monograph No. 29 (Historical), Volume XIII: Home Waters, Part IV, From February to July 1915.* October 1925.

——— . *Naval Staff Monograph No. 35 (Historical), Volume XIX: Home Waters, Part IX, 1 May 1917 to 31 July 1917.* August 1939.

——— . *Progress in Tactics, 1939.* June 1939.

U-Boat Assessment Committee. Assessment Committee Serial No. 12 [AUD.379/45]. *Proceedings of U-Boat Assessment Committee, April–November 1945, Volume 18.*

Papers of D. W. Waters and F. Barley

Waters: 'Historical Survey of U-Boat and A/S Inshore Campaigns 1918 & 1945', nd. (PT133)

Marshal of the RAF Sir J. C. Slessor Comments on *Defeat of the Enemy Attack On Shipping* and replies. (PT134)

Barley and Waters: 'A "New Look" at "Offence" and "Defence": The Anti-U-Boat Campaign, 1939–1945, A Brief Statement of Facts', 15 Oct 1955 (DWW24).

Barley, 'Mine Warfare', nd. (PT135)

Miscellaneous Papers

Cdr M. G. Saunders, Foreign Documents Section, 'Some Notes on Admiral Spindler and the German Official History of U-Boat Warfare, 1914–18', 2 June 1960, FDS206/60.

Cdr F. Barley, Anti-Submarine Measures in World War I', 30 November 1960, S.5659, Historical Section Information Room Searches, Vol. 29: July to December 1960.

Plans Division, Admiralty. *Mercantile Convoy Instructions* [CB01921]. 1934.

——. *The Protection of Shipping at Sea* [CB01957], September 1936.

12. Oxford University Press Archives, Oxford

Papers relating to the publication of Raleigh and Jones's *The War in the Air*:
HMSO, *The War in the Air* (L363)
Raleigh, *The War in the Air* (LB4775)
The War in the Air, Volume II (LB6042)

B. Memoirs, Published Papers and Other Published Primary Sources

The Air Force List. London: Her Majesty's Stationery Office, Various.

Bacon, Admiral Sir Reginald. *The Dover Patrol 1915–1917, Volume II*. London: Hutchinson, 1919.

——. *From 1900 Onward*. London: Hutchinson, 1940.

Bartlett, C. P. O. *In the Teeth of the Wind*. Edited by Nick Bartlett. Annapolis: Naval Institute Press, 1994.

Bauer, Hermann. *Als Führer der U-Boote Im Weltkrieg*. Leipzig: Koehler and Amelang, 1943.

Bayly, Admiral Sir Lewis. *Pull Together! The Memoirs of Admiral Sir Lewis Bayly*. London: George Harrap, 1939.

Beaverbrook, 1st Baron. *Men and Power, 1917–1918*. London: Hutchinson, 1956.

Benn, Wedgwood. *In the Sideshows*. London: Hodder and Stoughton, 1919.

Bewsher, Paul. *The Bombing of Bruges*. London: Hodder and Stoughton, 1918.

——. *'Green Balls': The Adventures of a Night-Bomber*. London: W. Blackwood and Sons, 1919.

Center for Aerospace Doctrine Research and Education, HQ USAF. *The United States Strategic Bombing Surveys*. Maxwell AFB, Alabama: Air University Press, 1987.

Chalmers, Rear-Admiral W. S. *The Life and Letters of David, Earl Beatty, Admiral of the Fleet, Viscount Borodale of Wexford, Baron Beatty of the North Sea and of Brooksby*. London: Hodder and Stoughton, 1951.

Churchill, The Rt. Hon. Winston S. *The World Crisis, 1911–1918. Volume II*. London: Odhams Press, 1923.

Davies, Vice-Admiral Richard Bell. *Sailor in the Air*. London: Peter Davies, 1967.

Dewar, K. G. B. *The Navy from Within*. London: Victor Gollancz, 1939.

Dönitz, Karl. *Memoirs: Ten Years and Twenty Days*. Translated by R. H. Stephens. London: Weidenfeld and Nicolson, 1959.

Draper, Christopher. *The Mad Major*. Letchworth: Air Review Ltd, 1962.

'Etienne', pseud. *The Diary of a U-Boat Commander*. London: Hutchinson, 1920.

Fechter, Hans. *Alarmkoje von U35*. Berlin: Ullstein, 1918.

Frost, Wesley. *German Submarine Warfare: A Study of Its Methods and Spirit*. New York: D. Appleton, 1918.

Fürbringer, Werner. *FIPS: Legendary U-Boat Commander, 1915–1918*. Translated by Geoffrey Brooks. Annapolis: Naval Institute Press, 1999.

Gordon, Thomas Crouther. *Early Flying in Orkney: Seaplanes in World War One.* Kirkwall: BBC Radio Orkney, 1985.

Groves, Brigadier-General P. R. C. *Behind the Smokescreen.* London: Faber and Faber, 1934.

Hallam, Squadron Leader T. D. *The Spider Web: The Romance of a Flying-Boat Flight in the First World War.* London: Arms and Armour Press, 1979.

Halpern, Paul G., ed. *The Keyes Papers: Selections from the Private and Official Correspondence of Admiral of the Fleet Baron Keyes of Zeebrugge, Volume I: 1914–1918.* London: Naval Records Society, 1972.

—— , ed. *The Royal Navy in the Mediterranean, 1915–1918.* Aldershot: Temple Smith for the Naval Records Society, 1987.

Hankey, Lord. *The Supreme Command, 1914–1918, Volume I.* London: George Allen and Unwin, 1961.

Hashagen, Ernst. *The Log of a U-Boat Commander {or U-Boats Westward – 1914–1918}.* Translated by R. C. V. Ross. London: Putnam, 1931.

Hattendorf, John B. *et al. British Naval Documents, 1204–1960.* Aldershot: Scolar Press, 1993.

Headquarters US Air Force. *Air Force Manual 1–1, Volume 1: Basic Aerospace Doctrine of the United States Air Force.* Washington, DC: US Government Printing Office, 1992.

Hersing, Otto. *U21 Rettet die Dardanellen.* Zürich: Amalthea, 1932.

Historical Section, Admiralty. *The Defeat of the Enemy Attack on Shipping, 1939–1945.* Edited by Eric Grove. Aldershot: Aldgate, 1997.

Insall, A. J. *Observer: Memoir of the R.F.C., 1915–1918.* London: Kimber, 1970.

Jellicoe, J. R. *The Grand Fleet, 1914–1916: Its Creation, Development and Work.* London: Cassell, 1919.

—— . *The Crisis of the Naval War.* London: Cassell, 1920.

—— . *The Submarine Peril: The Admiralty Policy in 1917.* London: Cassell, 1934.

Jones, H. A. *Sir Walter Raleigh and the Air History: A Personal Recollection.* London: E. Arnold, 1922.

Joubert de la Ferté, Air Chief Marshal Sir Philip. *The Third Service: The Story Behind the Royal Air Force.* London: Thames and Hudson, 1955.

Kellaway [no first name]. 'Some Developments in Industry During the War'. *Ministry of Munitions Journal,* No. 25 (December 1918): 369–72.

Kerr, Mark. *Land, Sea, and Air: Reminiscences of Mark Kerr.* London: Longmans, Green and Co., 1927.

Keyes, Admiral of the Fleet Sir Roger. *The Naval Memoirs of Admiral of the Fleet Sir Roger Keyes.* London: Thornton Butterworth, 1935.

Lambert, Andrew, ed. *Letters and Papers of Professor Sir John Knox Laughton, 1830–1915.* Aldershot: Ashgate, 2002.

Lambert, Nicholas, ed. *The Submarine Service, 1900–1918.* Aldershot: Ashgate, 2001.

Leighton, John L. *SIMSADUS, London: The American Navy in Europe.* New York: Henry Holt, 1920.

Livock, Group Captain G. E. *To the Ends of the Air.* London: Her Majesty's Stationery Office, 1973.

Lloyd George, David. *War Memoirs of David Lloyd George, Volumes III–VI.* London: Ivor Nicholson & Watson, 1934–36.

Longmore, Air Chief Marshal Sir Arthur. *From Sea to Sky, 1910–1945.* London: Geoffrey Bles, 1946.

Mahony, J. W. *The Destruction of Great Britain and Collapse of the British Empire, Unless–*. Birmingham: J. W. Mahony, 1910.

Marder, Arthur J., ed. *Fear God and Dread Nought: The Correspondence of Admiral of the Fleet Lord Fisher of Kilverstone, Volume III: Restoration, Abdication, and Last Years, 1914–1920*. London: Jonathan Cape, 1959.

Meager, Captain George. *My Airship Flights, 1915–1930*. London: Kimber, 1970.

Michelsen, Andreas. *Der U-Bootskrieg, 1914–1918*. Leipzig: Koehler, 1925.

Directorate of Air Staff, Ministry of Defence. *AP 3000: British Air Power Doctrine*. 3rd ed., 1999.

Moore, Major W. Geoffrey. *Early Bird*. London: Putnam, 1963.

The Navy List. London: Her Majesty's Stationery Office, Various.

Neureuther, Karl, and Claus Bergen. *U-Boat Stories: Narratives of German U-Boat Sailors*. Translated by Eric Sutton. London: Constable, 1931.

Newbolt, Henry. *My World as in My Time: Memoirs of Sir Henry Newbolt, 1862–1932*. London: Faber and Faber, 1932.

Newbolt, Margaret, ed. *The Later Life and Letters of Sir Henry Newbolt*. London: Faber and Faber, 1942.

Niemöller, Martin. *From U-Boat to Pulpit*. Translated by Cdr D. Hastie Smith. London: William Hodge, 1936.

Patterson, A. Temple, ed. *The Jellicoe Papers, Volume II, 1916–1935*. London: Naval Records Society, 1968.

Ranft, B. McL., ed. *The Beatty Papers: Selections from the Private and Official Correspondence of Admiral of the Fleet Earl Beatty, Volume I, 1902–1918*. Aldershot: Scolar Press, 1989.

Rosher, Harold. *In the Royal Naval Air Service: The War Letters of the Late Harold Rosher to His Family*. London: Chatto and Windus, 1916.

Roskill, S. W., ed. *Documents Relating to the Naval Air Service: Volume 1, 1908–1918*. London: Naval Records Society, 1969.

Samson, Air Commodore Charles Rumney. *Fights and Flights*. London: Ernest Benn, 1930.

Scheer, Admiral R. *Germany's High Sea Fleet in the World War*. London: Cassell and Co., 1920.

Schulz, Paul. *Im U-Boot Durch die Weltmeere*. Leipzig: Velhagen and Klasing, 1931.

Simpson, Michael, ed. *Anglo-American Naval Relations, 1917–1919*. Aldershot: Scolar Press, 1991.

Sims, William S. *The Victory at Sea*. Annapolis: Naval Institute Press, 1984.

Spiegel, Lieutenant Commander Freiherr von. *U.Boat 202: The War Diary of a German Submarine*. Translated by Captain Barry Domville. London: A. Melrose, 1919.

Spiess, Johannes. *Sechs Jahre U-Bootsfarten*. Berlin: Reimar Hobbing, 1925.

Sueter, Rear-Admiral Murray F. *Airmen or Noahs: Fair Play for Our Airmen*. London: Sir Isaac Pitman and Sons, 1928.

Sykes, Major General The Right Hon. Sir Frederick. *From Many Angles: An Autobiography*. London: George Harrap, 1942.

Valentiner, Max. *Der Schrecken der Meere: Meine U-Boot-Abenteuer*. Leipzig: Amalthea-Verlag, 1931.

von Tirpitz, Alfred. *My Memoirs, Volume II*. London: Hurst and Blackett, n.d.

Wemyss, Lady Wester. *The Life and Letters of Lord Wester Wemyss*. London: Eyre and Spottiswode, 1935.

Williams, T. B. *Airship Pilot No. 28*. London: Kimber, 1974.

II. LATER WORKS

A. Books

Abbott, Patrick. *The British Airship at War, 1914–1918.* Lavenham: Terence Dalton, 1989.

Abbott, Willis J. *Aircraft and Submarines.* London: Putnam, 1918.

Ash, Eric. *Sir Frederick Sykes and the Air Revolution, 1912–1918.* London: Frank Cass, 1999.

Barker, Ralph. *A Brief History of the Royal Flying Corps in World War I.* London: Robinson, 2002.

Beckett, Ian F. W. *The First World War: The Essential Guide to Sources in the UK National Archives.* Kew: Public Record Office, 2002.

Beesly, Patrick. *Room 40: British Naval Intelligence, 1914–1918.* London: Hamish Hamilton, 1982.

Beiriger, Eugene Edward. *Churchill, Munitions and Mechanical Warfare.* New York: Peter Lang, 1997.

Blair, Clay. *Hitler's U-Boat War, Volume I: The Hunters, 1939–1942.* New York: Random House, Inc., 1996.

———. *Hitler's U-Boat War, Volume II: The Hunted, 1942–1945.* New York: Random House, Inc., 1998.

Bond, Brian. *The Unquiet Western Front: Britain's Role in Literature and History.* Cambridge: Cambridge University Press, 2002.

Boyle, Andrew. *Trenchard.* London: Collins, 1962.

Brodie, Bernard. *Sea Power in the Machine Age.* New York: Greenwood Press, 1969.

Bruce, J. M. *British Aeroplanes, 1914–18.* London: Putnam, 1957.

———. *Felixstowe F.2A: Windsock Datafile 82.* Berkhamsted: Albatros Productions, Ltd, 2000.

Buckley, John. *The RAF and Trade Defence, 1919–1945: Constant Endeavour.* Keele: Keele University Press, 1995.

———. 'Atlantic Airpower Co-Operation, 1941–1943'. In *Air Power: Theory and Practice*, edited by John Gooch, 175–97. London: Cass, 1999.

Bungay, Stephen. *The Most Dangerous Enemy.* London: Aurum Press, 2000.

Casey, Louis S., and John Batchelor. *Naval Aircraft.* London: Hamlyn, 1977.

———. *The Illustrated History of Seaplanes and Flying Boats.* London: Hamlyn, 1980.

The Chicago Manual of Style. 14th ed. Chicago: University of Chicago Press, 1993.

Compton-Hall, Richard. *Submarines and the War at Sea, 1914–1918.* London: Macmillan, 1991.

Cooksley, Peter G. *The RFC/RNAS Handbook, 1914–1918.* Stroud: Sutton, 2000.

Cooper, Malcolm. *The Birth of Independent Air Power: British Air Policy in the First World War.* London: Allen and Unwin, 1986.

Corbett, Julian S. *Some Principles of Maritime Strategy.* With an introduction by Eric J. Grove. London: Brassey's, 1988.

Corbett, Julian S., and Henry Newbolt. *Naval Operations.* Vol. I–V. London: Longmans, Green and Co., 1920–31.

Corum, James S. *The Luftwaffe: Creating the Operational Air War, 1918–1940.* Lawrence: University of Kansas Press, 1997.

Cronin, Dick. *Royal Navy Shipboard Aircraft Developments.* Tonbridge: Air Britain, 1990.

Dean, Maurice. *The Royal Air Force and Two World Wars.* London: Cassell, 1979.

Edgerton, David. *England and the Aeroplane: An Essay on a Militant and Technological Nation*. London: Macmillan, 1991.

Enser, A. G. S. *A Subject Bibliography of the First World War: Books in English 1914–1987*. Aldershot: Gower, 1990.

Fayle, C. Ernest. *Seaborne Trade*. Vol. I–III. London: John Murray, 1920–24.

Finnis, Bill. *The History of the Fleet Air Arm: From Kites to Carriers*. Shrewsbury: Airlife, 2000.

Fischer, William Edward, Jr. *The Development of Military Night Aviation to 1919*. Maxwell AFB, Alabama: Air University Press, 1998.

Fowler, Simon, Peter Elliot, Roy Conyers Nesbit, and Christina Goulter. *RAF Records in the PRO*. PRO Reader's Guide No. 8. London: PRO Publications, 1994.

Friedman, Norman. *Submarine Design and Development*. London: Conway, 1984.

———. *Seapower as Strategy: Navies and National Interests*. Annapolis: Naval Institute Press, 2001.

Gamble, C. F. Snowden. *The Story of a North Sea Air Station*. London: Oxford University Press, 1928.

Gayer, Albert. *Die Deutschen U-Boote in Ihrer Kriegführung, 1914–1918*. Berlin: E. S. Mittler, 1920–31.

Gibbs-Smith, Charles H. *Aviation: An Historical Survey from Its Origins to the End of World War II*. London: Her Majesty's Stationery Office, 1970.

Gibson, R. H., and Maurice Prendergast. *The German Submarine War, 1914–1918*. London: Constable, 1931.

Gladisch, Walther. *Der Krieg in der Nordsee*, Vol. VI–VII. Berlin/Frankfurt: E. S. Mittler, 1937–65.

Goulter, Christina J. M. *A Forgotten Offensive: Royal Air Force Coastal Command's Anti-Shipping Campaign, 1940–1945*. London: Frank Cass, 1995.

Grant, Robert M. *U-Boats Destroyed: The Effect of Anti-Submarine Warfare, 1914–1918*. London: Putnam, 1964.

———. *U-Boat Intelligence, 1914–1918*. Hamden, CT: Archon Books, 1969.

Gray, Colin S. *The Leverage of Sea Power: The Strategic Advantage of Navies in War*. New York: Free Press, 1992.

Gray, Edwyn A. *The Killing Time: The U-Boat War, 1914–1918*. London: Seeley, Service and Co., Ltd, 1972.

Gretton, Peter. 'The U-Boat Campaign on Two World Wars'. In *Naval Warfare in the Twentieth Century 1900–1945*, edited by Gerald Jordan. London: Croom Helm, 1977.

Grey, C. G. *A History of the Air Ministry*. London: Allen and Unwin, 1940.

———. *Sea Flyers*. London: Faber & Faber, 1942.

Grossnick, Roy A. *United States Naval Aviation 1910–1995*. Washington: Naval Historical Center, 1997.

Gröner, Erich. *German Warships, 1815–1945. Volume 2: U-Boats and Mine Warfare Vessels*. Revised by Dieter Jung and Martin Maass, translated by Keith Thomas and Rachel Magowan. London: Conway, 1991.

Gusewelle, Jack K. 'Science and the Admiralty During World War I: The Case of the BIR'. In *Naval Warfare in the Twentieth Century 1900–1945*, edited by Gerald Jordan. London: Croom Helm, 1977.

Hackmann, Willem. *Seek & Strike: Sonar, Anti-Submarine Warfare and the Royal Navy 1914–54*. London: Her Majesty's Stationery Office, 1984.

Halpern, Paul G. *A Naval History of World War I*. Annapolis: Naval Institute Press, 1995.

Hamer, David. *Bombers Versus Battleships: The Struggle Between Ships and Aircraft for the Control of the Surface of the Sea*. Annapolis: Naval Institute Press, 1998.

Hartcup, Guy. *The Achievement of the Airship: A History of the Development of Rigid, Semi-Rigid, and Non-Rigid Airships*. London: David & Charles, 1974.

——. *The War of Invention: Scientific Developments, 1914–1918*. London: Brassey's Defence Publishers, 1988.

Herwig, Holger H. *The German Naval Officer Corps: A Social and Political History, 1890–1918*. Oxford: Clarendon, 1973.

——. *'Luxury' Fleet: The Imperial German Navy, 1988–1918*. London: Allen and Unwin, 1980.

——. 'Innovation Ignored: The Submarine Problem'. In *Military Innovation in the Interwar Period*, edited by Williamson Murray and Allan Millet, 227–64. Cambridge: Cambridge University Press, 1996.

——. *The First World War: Germany and Austria-Hungary, 1914–1918*. London: Arnold, 1997.

Hezlet, Vice-Admiral Sir Arthur. *The Submarine and Sea Power*. London: Peter Davies, 1967.

——. *Aircraft and Sea Power*. London: Peter Davies, 1970.

——. *The Electron and Sea Power*. London: Peter Davies, 1975.

Higham, Robin, ed. *Official Histories: Essays and Bibliographies from Around the World*. Manhattan, KS: Kansas State University Library, 1970.

——. *The British Rigid Airship, 1908–1931: A Study in Weapons Policy*. London: G. T. Foulis, 1961.

——. *The Military Intellectuals in Britain: 1918–1939*. New Brunswick, NJ: Rutgers University Press, 1966.

——. 'The Peripheral Weapon in Wartime: A Case Study'. In *Naval Warfare in the Twentieth Century 1900–1945*, edited by Gerald Jordan. London: Croom Helm, 1977.

——. 'Airpower in World War I, 1914–1918'. In *The War in the Air, 1914–1994*, edited by Alan Stephens, 1–28. Maxwell AFB, Alabama: Air University Press, 2001.

Holley, I. B., Jr. *Ideas and Weapons*. Washington, DC: US Government Printing Office, 1997.

Hough, Richard. *The Great War at Sea, 1914–1918*. Oxford: Oxford University Press, 1983.

Howard, Michael. *The Lessons of History*. New Haven: Yale University Press, 1991.

Hurd, Archibald. *The Merchant Navy*. Vol. I–III. London: John Murray, 1921–29.

Jackson, A. J. *Blackburn Aircraft Since 1909*. London: Putnam, 1968.

Jackson, Robert. *Strike from the Sea*. London: Arthur Baker Ltd, 1970.

James, Admiral Sir William. *The Eyes of the Navy: A Biographical Study of Admiral Sir Reginald Hall*. London: Methuen, 1955.

Jameson, William. *The Most Formidable Thing: The Story of the Submarine from Its Earliest Days to the End of World War I*. London: Rupert Hart-Davis, 1965.

Jefford, C. G. *Observers and Navigators and Other Non-Pilot Aircrew in the RFC, RNAS and RAF*. Shrewsbury: Airlife, 2001.

Jenkins, Roy. *Churchill*. London: Pan Macmillan, 2001.

Johnson, Franklyn A. *Defence by Committee: The British Committee of Imperial Defence, 1885–1959*. London: Oxford University Press, 1960.

Jones, H. A. *Over the Balkans and South Russia: Being the History of No. 47 Squadron, Royal Air Force*. London: Edward Arnold, 1923.

——. *The War in the Air*. Vol. II. Oxford: Clarendon, 1928.

——. *The War in the Air*. Vol. III. Oxford: Clarendon, 1931.

——. *The War in the Air*. Vol. IV. Oxford: Clarendon, 1934.

——. *The War in the Air*. Vol. V. Oxford: Clarendon, 1935.

——. *The War in the Air*. Vol. VI. Oxford: Clarendon, 1937.

——. *The War in the Air*. Appendices. Oxford: Clarendon, 1937.

Jones, Jerry W. *U.S. Battleship Operations in World War I*. Annapolis: Naval Institute Press, 1998.

Jones, Neville. *The Origins of Strategic Bombing: A Study of the Development of British Air Strategic Thought and Practice up to 1918*. London: Kimber, 1973.

——. *The Beginnings of Strategic Air Power: A History of the British Bomber Force, 1923–1939*. London: Frank Cass, 1987.

Keegan, John. *The Price of Admiralty: The Evolution of Naval Warfare*. New York: Viking, 1988.

Kemp, Paul. *Convoy Protection: The Defence of Seaborne Trade*. London: Arms and Armour Press, 1993.

——. *U-Boats Destroyed: German Submarine Losses in the World Wars*. Annapolis: Naval Institute Press, 1997.

Kemp, P. K. *Fleet Air Arm*. London: Herbert Jenkins, 1954.

Kennedy, Paul. *The Rise and Fall of British Naval Mastery*. 3rd ed. London: Fontana Press, 1991.

Kennett, Lee. *The First Air War, 1914–1918*. New York: Free Press, 1991.

Killen, John. *A History of Marine Aviation*. London: Frederick Muller, 1969.

King, Brad. *Royal Naval Air Service, 1912–1918*. Aldershot: Hikoki Publications, 1997.

Kinsey, Gordon. *Seaplanes – Felixstowe: The Story of the Air Station, 1913–1963*. Lavenham: Terrence Dalton, 1978.

——. *Pulham Pigs: The History of an Airship Station*. Lavenham: Terrence Dalton, 1988.

Knott, Captain Richard C. *The American Flying Boat: An Illustrated History*. Annapolis: Naval Institute Press, 1979.

Knox, Macgregor, and Williamson Murray, eds. *The Dynamics of Military Revolution, 1300–2050*. Cambridge: Cambridge University Press, 2001.

Lambert, Nicholas. *Sir John Fisher's Naval Revolution*. Columbia: University of South Carolina Press, 1999.

Layman, R.D. 'Naval Warfare in a New Dimension, 1914–1918'. In *Warship 1989*, edited by Robert Gardiner, 56–73. London: Conway, 1989.

——. *Naval Aviation in the First World War: Its Impact and Influence*. Annapolis: Naval Institute Press, 1996.

Lewis, Peter. *Squadron Histories: RFC, RNAS and RAF, 1912–1959*. London: Putnam, 1959.

Liddell Hart, B. H. *History of the First World War*. London: Book Club Associates, 1973.

London, Peter. *U-Boat Hunters: Cornwall's Air War, 1916–1919*. Truro: Dyllansow Truran, 1999.

Luvaas, Jay. 'The First British Official Histories'. In *Official Histories: Essays and Bibliographies from Around the World*, edited by Robin Higham, 488–505. Manhattan, KS: Kansas State University Library, 1970.

Macintyre, Captain Donald. *Wings of Neptune: The Story of Naval Aviation*. London: Peter Davies, 1963.

Mackay, Ruddock F. *Balfour: Intellectual Statesman*. Oxford: Oxford University Press, 1985.

Maloney, Elbert S. *Dutton's Navigation & Piloting*. 14th ed. Annapolis: Naval Institute Press, 1985.

Marder, Arthur J. *1917: The Year of Crisis*. Vol. IV of *From Dreadnought to Scapa Flow: The Royal Navy in the Fisher Era, 1904–1919*. London: Oxford University Press, 1969.

——. *Victory and Aftermath (January 1918 – June 1919)*. Vol. V of *From Dreadnought to Scapa Flow: The Royal Navy in the Fisher Era, 1904–1919*. London: Oxford University Press, 1970.

——. *From the Dardanelles to Oran: Studies of the Royal Navy in War and Peace, 1915–1940*. London: Oxford University Press, 1974.

Mason, Group Captain R. A. 'The British Dimension'. In *Air Power and Warfare: Proceedings of the Eighth Military History Symposium, USAF Academy, 1978*, edited by Alfred F. Hurley and Robert C. Ehrhart, 22–35. Washington: US Government Printing Office, 1979.

Meilinger, Phillip S. 'The Development of Air Power Theory'. In *Air Power Leadership: Theory and Practice*, edited by Peter W. Gray and Sebastian Cox, 90–106. London: The Stationery Office, 2002.

——. *AIRWAR: Theory and Practice*. London: Frank Cass, 2003.

Messimer, Dwight R. *Find and Destroy: Antisubmarine Warfare in World War I*. Annapolis: Naval Institute Press, 2001.

——. *Verschollen: World War I U-Boat Losses*. Annapolis: Naval Institute Press, 2003.

Ministry of Munitions. *History of the Ministry of Munitions, Volume XII: The Supply of Munitions, Part I: Aircraft*, 1921.

Moore, John. *Jane's Fighting Ships of World War I*. New York: Military Press, 1990.

Morrow, John H., Jr. *German Air Power in World War I*. Lincoln: University of Nebraska Press, 1982.

——. *The Great War in the Air: Military Aviation from 1909 to 1921*. Washington: Smithsonian Institution Press, 1993.

Mowthorpe, Ces. *Battlebags: British Airships of the First World War*. Stroud: Wrens Park, 1998.

——. *Sky Sailors: The Story of the World's Airshipmen*. Stroud: Sutton, 1999.

Murfett, Malcolm H., ed. *The First Sea Lords: From Fisher to Mountbatten*. Westport: Praeger, 1995.

National Archives and Records Service. *Guides to the Microfilmed Records of the German Navy, 1850–1945: No. 1, U-Boats and T-Boats 1914–1918*. Washington: US General Services Administration, 1984.

The Naval Who's Who, 1917. Polstead: J. B. Hayward, 1981.

Newbolt, Henry. *Submarine and Anti-Submarine*. London: Longmans, Green and Co., 1918.

——. *A Naval History of the War*. London: Hodder and Stoughton, 1920.

——. *Naval Operations*. Vol. IV. London: Longmans, Green and Co., 1928.

——. *Naval Operations*. Vol. V. London: Longmans, Green and Co., 1931.

Padfield, Peter. *Dönitz: The Last Führer*. London: Victor Gollancz, 1984.

Popham, Hugh. *Into Wind: A History of British Naval Flying*. London: Hamish Hamilton, 1969.

Price, Alfred. *Aircraft Versus Submarines: The Evolution of the Anti-Submarine Aircraft 1912–1972*. London: Kimber, 1973.

Prior, Robin. *Churchill's 'World Crisis' as History*. London: Croom Helm, 1983.

Raleigh, Walter. *The War in the Air*. Vol. I. Oxford: Clarendon, 1922.

Raleigh, Sir Walter and H. A. Jones. *The War in the Air: Being the Story of the Part Played in the Great War by the Royal Air Force*. Vol. I–VI. Oxford: Clarendon, 1922–37.

Richards, D. and H. Saunders. *The Royal Air Force, 1939–1945*. Vol. I–III. London: HMSO, 1953–54.

Roskill, S. W. *The Strategy of Sea Power*. London: Collins, 1962.

——. *Churchill and the Admirals*. London: Collins, 1977.

——. *Admiral of the Fleet Earl Beatty: The Last Naval Hero, an Intimate Biography*. London: Collins, 1980.

——. *The Navy at War, 1939–1945*. Ware, Herts: Wordsworth Editions, 1998.

Rössler, Eberhard. *The U-Boat: The Evolution and Technical History of German Submarines*. Translated by Harold Erenberg. London: Arms and Armour Press, 1981.

Schurman, Donald M. *Julian S. Corbett, 1854–1922: Historian of British Maritime Policy from Drake to Jellicoe*. London: Royal Historical Society, 1981.

Shirley, Noel. *United States Naval Aviation, 1910–1918*. Atglen, PA: Schiffer, 2000.

Spector, Ronald. *At War at Sea: Sailors and Naval Warfare in the Twentieth Century*. London: Penguin, 2001.

Spindler, Rear-Admiral Arno. *Der Handelskrieg mit U-Booten*. Vol. 1–5. Berlin/Frankfurt: E. S. Mittler, 1932–66.

Steel, Nigel, and Peter Hart. *Tumult in the Clouds: The British Experience of the War in the Air 1914–1918*. London: Hodder and Stoughton, 1997.

Stern, Robert C. *Battle Beneath the Waves: The U-Boat War*. London: Arms and Armour Press, 1999.

Sturtivant, Ray, and Gordon Page. *Royal Navy Aircraft Serials and Units, 1911 to 1919*. Tonbridge: Air-Britain Ltd, 1992.

Sweetman, Jack, ed. *The Great Admirals: Command at Sea, 1587–1945*. Annapolis: Naval Institute Press, 1997.

Tarrant, V. E. *The U-Boat Offensive, 1914–1945*. London: Arms and Armour Press, 1989.

Taylor, John W. R. *C. F. S.: Birthplace of Air Power*. London: Putnam, 1958.

——. *Jane's Fighting Aircraft of World War I*. London: Random House Group, 2001.

Terraine, John. *The Right of the Line: The Royal Air Force in the European War, 1939–1945*. London: Hodder and Stoughton, 1985.

——. *Business in Great Waters: The U-Boat Wars, 1916–1945*. London: Leo Cooper, 1989.

Thetford, Owen. *British Naval Aircraft Since 1912*. 6th ed. Annapolis: Naval Institute Press, 1991.

Thomas, Lowell. *Raiders of the Deep*. Garden City, NY: Doubleday, Doran & Co., 1929.

Till, Geoffrey. *Air Power and the Royal Navy, 1914–1945: A Historical Survey*. London: Jane's, 1979.

——— . 'Passchendaele: The Maritime Dimension'. In *Passchendaele in Perspective: The Third Battle of Ypres*, edited by Peter H. Liddle, 73–87. London: Leo Cooper, 1997.

Trask, David F. *Captains & Cabinets: Anglo-American Naval Relations, 1917–1918*. Columbia, MO: University of Missouri Press, 1972.

——— . 'William Sowden Sims: The Victory Ashore'. In *Quarterdeck and Bridge: Two Centuries of American Naval Leaders*, edited by James C. Bradford, 275–90. Annapolis: Naval Institute Press, 1997.

Travers, Tim. *How the War Was Won: Command and Technology in the British Army on the Western Front, 1917–1918*. London: Routledge, 1992.

Treadwell, Terry C. *The First Naval Air War*. Stroud: Tempus Publishing, 2002.

Turnbull, Archibald D., and Clifford L. Lord. *History of United States Naval Aviation*. New Haven: Yale University Press, 1949.

Van Wyen, Adrian O. *Naval Aviation in World War I*. Washington: Chief of Naval Operations, US Navy, 1969.

Warnock, A. Timothy. *Air Power Versus U-Boats: Confronting Hitler's Submarine Menace in the European Theater*. Washington, DC: Air Force History and Museums Programme, 1999.

Webster, Sir Charles, and Noble Frankland. *The Strategic Air Offensive Against Germany, 1939–1945, Volume I: Preparation*. London: Her Majesty's Stationery Office, 1961.

Weir, Gary E. *Building the Kaiser's Navy: The Imperial Naval Office and German Industry in the von Tirpitz Era, 1890–1919*. Annapolis: Naval Institute Press, 1992.

Wiest, Andrew A. *Passchendaele and the Royal Navy*. Westport: Greenwood Press, 1995.

Williams, Geoffrey. *Wings Over Westgate: The Story of a Front Line Naval Air Station During World War I*. Malling, Kent: Kent County Library, 1985.

Williams, George K. *Biplanes and Bombsights: British Bombing in World War I*. Maxwell AFB, Alabama: Air University Press, 1999.

Winton, John. *Jellicoe*. London: Michael Joseph, 1981.

——— . *Convoy: The Defence of Sea Trade 1890–1990*. London: Michael Joseph, 1983.

Wise, S. F. *Canadian Airmen and the First World War: The Official History of the Royal Canadian Air Force, Volume I*. Toronto: University of Toronto Press, 1980.

Wragg, David. *Boats of the Air: An Illustrated History of Flying Boats, Seaplanes and Amphibians*. London: Robert Hale, 1984.

Young, Desmond. *Member for Mexico: A Biography of Weetman Pearson, First Viscount Cowdray*. London: Cassell, 1966.

B. Articles

Bailey, Jonathan. 'The First World War and the Birth of the Modern Style of Warfare'. Occasional Paper No. 22. Camberly: Strategic and Combat Studies Institute, 1996.

Bellairs, Rear-Admiral R. M. 'Historical Survey of Trade Defence Since 1914'. *Journal of the Royal United Services Institute* 99, No. 595 (August 1954): 359–77.

Bone, Reginald John. 'A Record of Good Luck'. *Cross and Cockade Journal* [GB] 9, No. 1 (Spring 1978): 1–7.

Buckley, John. 'Failing to Learn from the Past: Air Power and Trade Defence, 1917–1943'. *War Studies Journal* 2, No. 1 (Autumn 1996): 1–16.

Burney, Lt C. D. 'Air Power'. *The Naval Review* 1, No. 2 (May 1913): 105–35.

Dewar, Captain Alfred. 'The Necessity for the Compilation of a Naval Staff History'. *The Journal of the Royal United Services Institute* 66, No. 463 (August 1921): 369–84.

Dewar, K. G. B. 'War on Shipping (1914–1918)'. *The Naval Review* 47, No. 1 (January 1959): 3–13.

Doughty, Lt Commander Leonard. 'The Effect of Depth Charges on Submarines'. *United States Naval Institute Proceedings* 61, No. 3 (March 1935): 353–57.

Dye, Peter. 'Biffy Borton's Bomber'. *Cross and Cockade International Journal* [GB] 34, No. 2 (Summer 2003): 71–78.

Edmonds, Sqn Ldr C. H. K. 'Aerial Cooperation with the Navy'. *The Journal of the Royal United Services Institute* 66, No. 462 (May 1921): 237–57.

Edwards, W. Atlee. 'The U.S. Naval Air Force in Action, 1917–1918'. *United States Naval Institute Proceedings* 48, No. 11 (November 1922): 1863–82.

Gayer, Albert. 'Summary of German Submarine Operations in the Various Theaters of War from 1914 to 1918'. Translated by Commander W. P. Beehler. *United States Naval Institute Proceedings* 52, No. 4 (April 1926): 621–59.

Grant, Robert M. 'Known Sunk – German Submarine Losses, 1914–1918'. *United States Naval Institute Proceedings* 64, No. 1 (January 1938): 66–77.

——— . 'Aircraft Against U-Boats'. *United States Naval Institute Proceedings* 65, No. 6 (June 1939): 824–28.

Johnson, Captain A. W. 'Aviation in Coast Defense'. *United States Naval Institute Proceedings* 51, No. 9 (September 1925): 1652–66.

Jones, H. A. 'Review of *Air Power and War Rights*, by J. M. Spaight.' *Journal of Public Administration* [London] 3, No. 2 (1925): 184–86.

Karau, Mark D. 'Twisting the Dragon's Tail: The Zeebrugge and Ostend Raids of 1918'. *Journal of Military History* 67, No. 2 (April 2003): 455–81.

Kemp, P. K. 'War Studies in the Royal Navy'. *Journal of the Royal United Services Institute* 111, No. 642 (May 1966): 151–55.

Layman, R. D. 'Letter to the Editor'. *The Journal of Military History* 61, No. 1 (January 1997): 215–18.

Layman, R. D., Peter K. Simpson, and E. J. Halpern. 'Allied Aircraft Vs. German Submarines, 1916–1918'. *Cross and Cockade Journal* [US] 11, No. 4 (1970): 289–304.

Lindsey, Lt Col Scott. 'Comment and Discussion'. *United States Naval Institute Proceedings* 129, No. 2 (February 2003): 29.

Lundeberg, Philip K. 'The German Naval Critique of the U-Boat Campaign, 1915–1918'. *Military Affairs* 27 (Fall 1963): 105–18.

MacGregor, David. 'The Use, Misuse, and Non-Use of History: The Royal Navy and the Operational Lessons of the First War'. *Journal of Military History* 56, No. 4 (October 1992): 603–15.

Maiolo, Joseph A. 'Deception and Intelligence Failure: Anglo-German Preparations for U-Boat Warfare in the 1930s'. *The Journal of Strategic Studies* 22, No. 4 (December 1999): 55–76.

Miller, Thomas G., Jr, and Douglas H. Robinson. 'Nonrigid Airships in World War I'. *Cross and Cockade Journal* [US] 5, No. 2 (1964): 97–114.

The New Statesman (Various).

Punch (Various).

'RHN', pseud. 'The Defence of Trade, 1914–1918'. *The Naval Review* 54, No. 2 (April 1966): 136–43.

Rogers, Leslie A. 'RNAS Casualties: 1916–1918'. *Cross and Cockade International Journal* [GB] 15, No. 4 (Winter 1984): 174–81.

Roskill, S. W. 'The U-Boat Campaign of 1917 and Third Ypres'. *Journal of the Royal United Services Institute* 104, No. 616 (November 1959): 440–42.

Schieffelin, John H. 'Boat Pilot'. *Cross and Cockade Journal* [US] 11, No. 1 (1970): 44–57.

Spindler, Rear-Admiral Arno. 'The Value of the Submarine in Naval Warfare'. Translated by Commander W. P. Beehler. *United States Naval Institute Proceedings* 52, No. 5 (May 1926): 835–54.

Strain, L. H. 'Aircraft v. Submarines'. *Journal of the Royal Aeronautical Society* 25, No. 124 (April 1921): 193–204.

Sumida, Jon Tetsuro. 'A Matter of Timing: The Royal Navy and the Tactics of Decisive Battle, 1912–1916'. *Journal of Military History* 67, No. 1 (January 2003): 85–136.

Swann, Oliver. 'Naval Air Requirements'. *The Naval Review* 7, No. 3 (August 1919): 305–13.

The Times and *The Times Literary Supplement* (Various).

Van Swearingen, Lieutenant (j.g.) E. K. 'Vulnerability of Airships to Airplane Attack'. *United States Naval Institute Proceedings* 62, No. 9 (September 1936): 1244–51.

Wicks, Lieutenant Z. W. 'Destruction of the Flanders Triangle'. *United States Naval Institute Proceedings* 45, No. 7 (July 1919): 1093–116.

Wright, Peter. 'Submarine Scout Pusher Pilots: Captain George E Bungay and Lt John E Hoskins RNAS'. *Cross and Cockade International Journal* [GB] 15, No. 4 (Winter 1984): 169–73.

——. 'Dunkerque Days and Nights'. *Cross and Cockade International Journal* [GB] 23, No. 3 (Autumn 1992): 131–44.

C. Theses

Abbatiello, John J. 'British Naval Aviation and the Anti-Submarine Campaign, 1917–1918'. Ph.D. Diss. King's College London, 2004.

Blond, A. J. L. 'Technology and Tradition: Wireless Telegraphy and the Royal Navy, 1895–1920'. Ph.D. Diss. University of Lancaster, 1993.

Bradley, J. K. 'The History and Development of Aircraft Instruments, 1909 to 1919'. Ph.D. Diss. Imperial College of Science and Technology London, 1994.

Easterling, Verlin R. 'Great Britain's Peril and the Convoy Controversy: A Study of the Intended Effects of Unrestricted U-Boat Warfare and the Convoy System as a Countermeasure, World War I'. Ph.D. Diss. University of Colorado-Boulder, 1951.

Karau, Mark D. 'Lost Opportunities: The Marinekorps Flandern and the German War Effort, 1914–1918'. Ph.D. Diss. Florida State University, 2000.

Levitt, Martin L. 'The U.S. Navy and Lighter-Than-Air Aviation'. Ph.D. Diss. Temple University, 1991.

Llewellyn-Jones, Malcolm. 'The Royal Navy on the Threshold of Modern Anti-Submarine Warfare, 1944–1949'. Ph.D. Diss. King's College London, 2004.

Macgregor, David. 'Innovation in Naval Warfare in Britain and the United States Between the First and Second World Wars'. Ph.D. Diss. University of Rochester, 1990.

Pulsipher, Lewis E. 'Aircraft and the Royal Navy, 1908–1918'. Ph.D. Diss. Duke University, 1981.

Stackhouse, Glenn A. 'The Anglo-American Convoy System in World War I, 1917–1918'. Ph.D. Diss. University of South Carolina, 1993.

Westermann, Edward B. 'Sword in the Heavens: German Ground Based Air Defenses, 1914–1945'. Ph.D. Diss. University of North Carolina, 2000.

Wignall, Michael Brown. 'Scientists and the Admiralty: Conflict and Collaboration in Anti-Submarine Warfare, 1914–1921'. Ph.D. Diss. King's College London, 1987.

D. Electronic Sources

The Dictionary of National Biography. CD ROM Version 1.1. Oxford University Press, 1997.

Altavista Babel Fish Website. http://babelfish.altavista.com/babelfish/. Accessed throughout 2003–2004.

Index

Dunkirk RNAS base 59–60, 61, 62;
American operations 125; bomber
force increased 64; criticism of 65–6;
Lambe 64, 65; new squadrons 74;
proximity to targets 62;
reorganisation 73–4; targets 64, 68;
triple campaign 80–1

East Anglian coast : convoy escort 116–17
East Coast: convoy escort 121–5
Eastchurch naval air base 39, 62;
aeroplane training 40; naval observer
training 42
engines *see* aircraft engines
English Channel: convoy escort 117–18;
patrols reorganised 88

Felixstowe naval air base 62; seaplane
training 42; Spider Web patrol
scheme 90–2
Fifth Sea Lord: establishment of position
8, 53
Finch-Noyes, Wing Commander C. R.
123
Fisher, Sir John 6
fixed-wing aircraft 11, 12, 13–18
Flanders ports 60, 61
Flanders U-boat bases: air attacks on
59–81, *see also* bombing Flanders
U-boat bases; German defence of
147–9; German history of defence of
157; losses inflicted on Allied
shipping 61
Fleet Air Arm 167
flight training: advanced 42; basic 42;
pre-war 40; reorganisation 40, 42;
standardisation 43–4
float seaplanes: characteristics 16–17; *see
also* seaplanes
flying boat production 54–5, 56
flying boats 1, 4, 13, 14–15;
characteristics 17, 24; difficulties 17;
hull maintenance 23–4; hydrophone
trials 35; minefield patrol 115,
116–17; performance 15; Spider Web
117; total sorties flown 1917–18
174–5
flying conditions: cloud 26; night flying
26 *see also* night flying; over water
25–6; weather 24–5; *see also*
navigation
flying days by aircraft type 25
France, American airship bases 125; coal
ship convoy escorts 117, 120

Geddes, Sir Eric 73
German aerodromes: raids on: 60, 64,
65, 68, 69, 70, 71, 73, 76
German Army Air Force 69
German defensive measures 62, 65,
147–52; air pursuit 147; altiscope
149; artillery 148, 149–50; night
raids 151, 152; raids on unescorted
ships 150–1; Second World War 168;
tactics 149, 150; vessel shelters 148–9
German naval memoirs 146, 157–9
German Navy: night raids 67; officer
ranks 176; order for *UB* submarines
61
German official histories 146, 155–7
German rearmament under Hitler 165
German submarine capabilities 36–8
German view of anti-submarine
campaign: captured U-boat crews
152–5; contemporary reaction to raids
147–52; memoirs 157–9; official
histories 155–7
Germany: Unrestricted Submarine
Campaign *see* U-boats, Unrestricted
Submarine Campaign
Gerrard, Wing Commander E. L. 89;
convoy escort and 119–20
Gladisch, Walther 155, 157
Gosport Special School of Flying 45–6
Gotha bomber: raids on London and
South-East 69–70
Grand Fleet: air escort 109, 115, 122,
123
Groves, Colonel R. M. 8, 55, 78

Haig, Field Marshal Douglas 66, 70, 71,
74, 75
Haldane Committee 5–6
Hamilton, Admiral Sir F. T. 122
Handelskrieg mit U-Booten, Der 155–7
Handley Page bomber 69, 70
heavier-than-air technology 13–18;
limitations 16
Heligoland Bight minefields 116
Hendon naval air base 62
High Seas Fleet 67; plans to raid at
moorings 79
historiography of air anti-submarine
warfare: British 129–45; German
155–7
Hitler, Adolf 165, 166
HMS *Daedalus* 42, 44
HMS *Empress* 62
HMS *Hermes* 63